CIMA

PRACTICE & REVISION KIT

Stage 4 Paper 16

Management Accounting Control Systems

BPP Publishing
January 2000

First edition 1995
Sixth edition January 2000

ISBN 0 7517 3860 3 (previous edition 0 7517 3879 4)

British Library Cataloguing-in-Publication Data
A catalogue record for this book
is available from the British Library

Published by

BPP Publishing Limited
Aldine House, Aldine Place
London W12 8AW

www.bpp.com

Printed and bound in Great Britain by
Ashford Colour Press Ltd, Gosport, Hampshire

We are grateful to the Chartered Institute of Management Accountants for permission to reproduce past examination questions. The answers to past examination questions have been prepared by BPP Publishing Limited.

CONTENTS

Question and answer checklist/index

The headings indicate the main topics of questions, but questions often cover several different topics.

Tutorial questions, listed in italics, are followed by advice on how to **approach the question,** thus easing the transition from study to examination practice.

A date alone (11/96, say) or 'specimen paper' after the question title refers to a current syllabus paper.

After current syllabus questions, we also indicate whether the question was compulsory.

Questions preceded by * are **key questions** which we think you must attempt in order to pass the exam. Tick them off on this list as you complete them.

REVISION

This is a very important time as you approach the exam. You must remember three things.

Use time sensibly
Set realistic goals
Believe in yourself

Use time sensibly

1 **How much study time do you have?** Remember that you must EAT, SLEEP, and of course, RELAX.

2 **How will you split that available time between each subject?** What are your weaker subjects? They need more time.

3 **What is your learning style?** AM/PM? Little and often/long sessions? Evenings/ weekends?

4 **Are you taking regular breaks?** Most people absorb more if they do not attempt to study for long uninterrupted periods of time. A five minute break every hour (to make coffee, watch the news headlines) can make all the difference.

5 **Do you have quality study time?** Unplug the phone. Let everybody know that you're studying and shouldn't be disturbed.

Set realistic goals

1 Have you set a **clearly defined objective** for each study period?

2 Is the objective **achievable**?

3 Will you **stick to your plan**? Will you make up for any **lost time**?

4 Are you **rewarding yourself** for your hard work?

5 Are you leading a **healthy lifestyle**?

Believe in yourself

Are you cultivating the right attitude of mind? There is absolutely no reason why you should not pass this exam if you adopt the correct approach.

- **Be confident** - you've passed exams before, you can pass them again
- **Be calm** - plenty of adrenaline but no panicking
- **Be focused** - commit yourself to passing the exam

QUESTION PRACTICE

There is little point in simply opening this Kit and, beginning with question 1, attempting all of the questions. You need to ask yourself three questions.

Am I ready to answer questions?
Do I know which questions to do first?
How should I use this Kit?

Am I ready to answer questions?

1 Try to fill in the blanks on the **Do you know? checklist** for a particular syllabus area. Compare your answers with the corresponding **Did you know? checklist**.

2 If you are happy with what you have written, you can go ahead and start answering questions. **Do not attempt questions if you could not fill in any of the blanks**. Go back to your BPP Study Text and revise first.

Do I know which questions to do first?

1 **Start with tutorial questions**. They warm you up for key and difficult areas of the syllabus. Try to produce at least a plan for these questions, using the guidance notes following the question to ensure your answer is structured so as to gain a good pass mark.

2 Don't worry about the time it takes to answer these questions. Concentrate on producing good answers. There are 10 tutorial questions in this Kit.

How should I use this Kit?

1 Once you are confident with the Do you know? checklists and the tutorial questions, you should try as many as possible of the exam-standard questions; at the very least you should attempt the **key questions,** which are highlighted in the **question and answer checklist/index** at the front of the Kit.

2 Try to **produce full answers under timed conditions**; you are practising exam technique as much as knowledge recall here. Don't look at the answer, your BPP Study Text or your notes for any help at all.

3 **Mark your answers to the non-tutorial questions as if you were the examiner**. Only give yourself marks for what you have written, not for what you meant to put down, or would have put down if you had had more time. If you did badly, try another question.

4 Read the **Pass marks** in the answers very carefully and take note of the advice given and any **comments by the examiner**. Don't worry if you found something difficult; **Prizewinners' points** indicate parts of questions that only a prizewinner might get right in an exam.

5 When you have practised the whole syllabus, go back to the areas you had problems with and **practise further questions**.

6 Finally, when you think you really understand the entire subject, **attempt the mock exam** at the end of the Kit. Sit the paper under strict exam conditions, so that you gain experience of selecting and sequencing your questions, and managing your time, as well as of writing answers.

EXAM TECHNIQUE

Passing professional examinations is half about having the knowledge, and half about doing yourself full justice in the examination. You must have the right approach to two things.

The day of the exam
Your time in the exam hall

The day of the exam

1. Set at least one **alarm** (or get an alarm call) for a morning exam.
2. Have **something to eat** but beware of eating too much; you may feel sleepy if your system is digesting a large meal.
3. Allow plenty of **time to get to the exam hall**; have your route worked out in advance and listen to news bulletins to check for potential travel problems.
4. **Don't forget** pens, pencils, rulers, erasers.
5. Put **new batteries** into your calculator and take a spare set (or a spare calculator).
6. **Avoid discussion** about the exam with other candidates outside the exam hall.

Your time in the exam hall

1. ***Read the instructions (the 'rubric') on the front of the exam paper carefully***

   Check that the exam format hasn't changed. It is surprising how often examiners' reports remark on the number of students who attempt too few - or too many - questions, or who attempt the wrong number of questions from different parts of the paper. Make sure that you are planning to answer the **right number of questions**.

2. ***Select questions carefully***

   Read through the paper once, then quickly jot down key points against each question in a second read through. Select those questions where you could latch on to 'what the question is about' - but remember to check carefully that you have got the right end of the stick before putting pen to paper.

3. ***Plan your attack carefully***

   Consider the **order** in which you are going to tackle questions. It is a good idea to start with your best question to boost your morale and get some easy marks 'in the bag'.

4. ***Check the time allocation for each question***

   Each mark carries with it a **time allocation** of 1.8 minutes (including time for selecting and reading questions). A 20 mark question therefore should be completed in 36 minutes. When time is up, you *must* go on to the next question or part. Going even one minute over the time allowed brings you a lot closer to failure.

5. ***Read the question carefully and plan your answer***

   Read through the question again very carefully when you come to answer it. Plan your answer to ensure that you **keep to the point**. Two minutes of planning plus eight minutes of writing is virtually certain to earn you more marks than ten minutes of writing.

6 ***Produce relevant answers***

Particularly with written answers, make sure you **answer the question set**, and not the question you would have preferred to have been set.

7 ***Gain the easy marks***

Include the obvious if it answers the question and don't try to produce the perfect answer.

Don't get bogged down in small parts of questions. If you find a part of a question difficult, get on with the rest of the question. If you are having problems with something, the chances are that everyone else is too.

8 ***Produce an answer in the correct format***

The examiner will **state in the requirements** the format in which the question should be answered, for example in a report or memorandum.

9 ***Follow the examiner's instructions***

You will annoy the examiner if you ignore him or her. The **examiner will state** whether he or she wishes you to 'discuss', 'comment', 'evaluate' or 'recommend' (see the section on examiners' instructions on page (xxiv).

10 ***Lay out your numerical computations and use workings correctly***

Make sure the layout fits the **type of question** and is in a style the examiner likes.

Show all your **workings** clearly and explain what they mean. Cross reference them to your solution. This will help the examiner to follow your method (this is of particular importance where there may be several possible answers).

11 ***Present a tidy paper***

You are a professional, and it should show in the **presentation of your work**. Students are penalised for poor presentation and so you should make sure that you write legibly, label diagrams clearly and lay out your work neatly. Markers of scripts each have hundreds of papers to mark; a badly written scrawl is unlikely to receive the same attention as a neat and well laid out paper.

12 ***Stay until the end of the exam***

Use any spare time **checking and rechecking** your script.

13 ***Don't worry if you feel you have performed badly in the exam***

It is more than likely that the other candidates will have found the exam difficult too. Don't forget that there is a competitive element in these exams. As soon as you get up to leave the exam hall, ***forget*** **that exam** and think about the next - or, if it is the last one, celebrate!

14 ***Don't discuss an exam with other candidates***

This is particularly the case if you **still have other exams to sit**. Even if you have finished, you should put it out of your mind until the day of the results. Forget about exams and relax!

THE EXAM PAPER

Format of the Year 2000 exams

		Number of marks
Section A	two compulsory questions	60
Section B	two questions from four	40
		100

Time allowed : 3 hours

> Recent pass rates
>
> The pass rate (home and overseas candidates combined) for the May 1999 exam was 41.0%, roughly the average pass rate of the four Stage 4 papers. The pass rate for the November 1998 exam was only 36.9%, however, the lowest of the Stage 4 Papers.

Analysis of past papers 1995-1999

The analysis below shows the topics which have been examined in the ten sittings of the syllabus and the CIMA Specimen paper for *Management Accounting Control Systems.*

November 1999

Section A

1 The apportionment of central costs and the impact on managerial remuneration and the organisation
2 Control systems and control problems in a public sector body

Section B

3 Sales and debtors audit
4 Risk assessment
5 Changes to control systems in bank branches
6 Internal auditor's commentary on simplification of manufacturing accounting system

This paper forms the mock exam at the end of the Kit, so only an outline of its contents is shown here.

May 1999

		Question number in this Kit
Section A		
1	Analysis of information using both a management accounting approach and analytical review; discussion on the process of analytical review; outline of internal audit concerns resulting from analytical review of information provided	58
2	Explanation of common features of bonus schemes and their potential effects; discussion on how to motivate non-executive directors	33
Section B		
3	Review of control and performance measurement in multinationals	45
4	Detection of fraud by internal audit; ethics and local practices	57
5	Discussion of problem of determining, gathering and reporting environmental and social information	12
6	Explanations of what can be done to minimise budget slack and the extent to which it should be pursued	19

Examiner's comments

The examiner noted the following.

- The analysis in question 1(a) was reasonably good but a disturbing proportion of candidates made very poor attempts at question 1(b), which involved analytical review. 'A significant minority appeared not to know what was meant by analytical review in the context of internal audit. As the technique is specifically mentioned in the syllabus this suggests very limited preparation for the examination.'
- Some optional questions, particularly question 3, were well answered.
- Some candidates appear to hope to pass the exam by concentrating on that part of the paper dealing with management accounting, ignoring syllabus section (d). As this comprises 25% of the syllabus and each paper is carefully balanced to ensure that this weighting is approximately achieved, this is a poor examination preparation strategy.
- There were *recurring* problems with basic exam technique.
  - Poor answer planning, particularly for questions 2, 4 and 6
  - Providing answers which could be best described as 'all I know about x'
  - Too detailed answer planning
  - Repeating the question detail in the answer
  - Failing to provide sufficiently substantial answers
  - Demonstrating rote-learned knowledge
- Time management was not a major problem with this paper.

November 1998

Section A		*Question number in this Kit*
1	Explanation of economic value added approach to company performance appraisal; discussion of where value is being destroyed; explanation of use of ROI for performance appraisal	27
2	Explanation of controls in information processing and database systems	67
Section B		
3	Explanation and discussion of contingency theory; explanation of impact of senior management recruitment/selection procedures on control systems	8
4	Explanation of aspects of payroll auditing	64
5	Preparation of a report on changes to system of budget preparation	18
6	Explanation of various aspects of activity-based techniques; explanation of non-value-adding activities	22

Examiner's comments

The examiner made the following general comments

- The answers to some of the optional questions were well below the standard expected.
- Opportunities to demonstrate relevant practical experience (in questions 2, 4 and 5) were not taken to any significant extent.
- Time management (spending the appropriate amount of time on a question, given the number of marks available) was poor.
- Answer plans were often too long (at least as long as the answer) and so led to time problems.
- Question detail was often repeated in solutions (especially in question 5).
- Candidates chose optional questions to which they couldn't answer all parts.
- Answers were sometimes insufficiently substantial. A part of a question worth ten marks is likely to require more than a side of average handwriting.
- Answers to questions 4(a) and (b) could often be described as 'all I know about...'.
- Candidates demonstrated rote learned knowledge in any question remotely linked to the topic learned.

Candidates should bear in mind that 'for many questions there is a range of acceptable answers, provided that the answer addresses the question asked. There is sympathy for genuine misunderstandings, provided that it is clear what the candidate is trying to do.'

May 1998

		Question number in this Kit
Section A		
1	Analysis and interpretation of statistical data for comparing the performance of two charities; explanation of appropriate cost management techniques; internal audit planning	44
2	The role of non-executive directors and audit committees; formal arrangements for dealing with complaints	62
Section B		
3	Discussion of internal and external benchmarking	41
4	Critical discussion of budgeting; explanation of possible improvements to the budgeting process	17
5	Discussion of the effectiveness of management control, monthly reporting and forecasting and of ethical issues	42
6	Discussion of aims and role of internal audit department and explanation of how to evaluate internal audit department performance	49

Examiner's comments

The examiner noted that:

- successful candidates were able to apply their knowledge and skills to the questions asked;
- although the quality of a candidate's script is not determined by the amount written, some candidates wrote too little to have any realistic chance of success;
- question 1(a) followed the precedent of the November 1997 exam and demanded analysis of and commentary on information and did not require significant calculations, but calculators, graph paper and mathematical tables may still be required in the future;
- the number of candidates who failed mainly because of their time management skills was noticeable. In particular, not enough time was left for the fourth question, question 1 was left until last and then part or all of the question was attempted without the scenario having been read, and time allocation to parts of questions failed to reflect marks available;
- candidates often tried to demonstrate rote-learned knowledge in any question remotely linked to the topic learned;
- optional questions should be chosen on the basis of ability to answer all the question, not just the first part;
- there is scope for improving skills in planning and structuring answers;
- there are no marks available for substantially rewriting the question as a start to the answer;
- displaying rote-learned knowledge of internal control or internal audit using mnemonics does not demonstrate understanding or an ability to make use of the knowledge.

November 1997		*Question number in this Kit*
Section A		
1	Analysis and interpretation of statistical data for performance measurement in the public sector	43
2	Code for conduct	11
Section B		
3	Development of a computerised system	68
4	Features of the management control cycle	54
5	Variance investigation decisions	23
6	Short-term planning, and control reporting, group planning	16

Examiner's comments

The examiner remarked on;

- the inability of some candidates to cope with problems which had no simple and obvious solution;
- the failure of weaker candidates to apply their knowledge and skills;
- candidates seeking to demonstrate rote learning in any question remotely linked to the topic they have learned;
- the disproportionate time allocations over the paper as a whole and over parts of questions according to the marks available;
- those candidates who did not attempt parts of the optional questions they had chosen, perhaps because they had not read all of the question before starting to answer it;
- the failure of some candidates to allow sufficient time for adequate understanding of the scenario data in question 1;
- the number of candidates who produced answers where almost half of the written answer merely rewrote the question detail;
- the display of rote learning of internal control and internal audit using mnemonics, which does not prove understanding or ability to make use of knowledge, and which will not earn marks at Stage 4;
- the relatively small minority of candidates who appeared to suffer from time pressure.

May 1997	*Question number in this Kit*
Section A	
1 ROI, RI and managerial performance	40
2 Internal audit of a newly-acquired subsidiary	55
Section B	
3 Strategic planning, management control and operational control; organisational changes and control	3
4 Corporate governance; remuneration and motivation	32
5 Participation in budgeting	15
6 Internal audit of financial accounts; audit of a new computerised accounting system	70

Examiner's comments

Overall performance was slightly better than in recent sittings of the examination. There were a number of encouraging features.

- The majority of candidates attempting the numerical parts of question 1 produced reasonable answers. Time could have been saved by adopting better working methods, however, which could then have been spent on writing better commentaries.
- A high proportion of candidates displayed a wide range of knowledge.

There were, however, the usual problems.

- Weaker candidates avoid numerical questions, and make token attempts at them at the end of the exam.
- The little knowledge that many candidates demonstrate of internal audit is learned by rote and not understood.
- In answers to questions 2 and 4(b) there was scope for much improvement in analysing case studies and even simple scenarios.

These problems suggest that candidates would benefit from more practice on answering questions.

The basic exam technique of many candidates was poor.

- Inappropriate time allocation was evident.
- Many answers were of an insufficient depth given the number of marks available.
- Answer plans were muddled.

November 1996		*Question number in this Kit*
Section A		
1	Audit sampling	60
2	Controllability and performance measurement	31
Section B		
3	Strategy and its effects on structure, culture and control systems	7
4	Business process re-engineering	6
5	Outsourced services	39
6	Total quality management and quality costing	46

Examiner's comments

There were fewer poor scripts in this sitting of the exam and 'better scripts were displaying a very wide range of reading, good judgement, and an ability to demonstrate application through well-structured and balanced answers, and the use of relevant examples from current practice in management and management accounting'. High levels of knowledge of new cost management techniques were displayed and even candidates who did to obtain good marks showed evidence of wider reading.

Many candidates seem to have forgotten what they learned at Stages 1-3, however, and have little grasp of internal auditing techniques.

The majority of marginal candidates demonstrated the following poor examination techniques.

- Failing to read the question or failing to read beyond a key word.
- Tackling each part of the question independently rather than approaching the question as a whole (which leads to repetitive answers).
- Spending too much time planning. There is only time for a brief answer plan in note form. Points included in the plan but omitted from the answer cannot be marked if crossed out.
- Poor time management.

The presentation of numerical material was often appalling and far below the required standard, making it difficult for markers to award marks. 'Numerical working should be legible, set out with headings and with an explanation of the intermediate steps taken. The final answer should be clearly identified.'

May 1996		*Question number in this Kit*
Section A		
1	Product costing and overheads; apportionment methods and behaviour; purchasing department performance	14
2	Short-termism	30
Section B		
3	Fraud in purchasing; corporate codes of conduct	52
4	Corporate governance	61
5	Segregation of duties	53
6	Contingency theory; Foucault, Giddens and Marx	-

Examiner's comments

Trends and problems identified previously still apply. The very poor answers to the numerical part of question 1 were most disappointing.

The overall standard of other questions was reasonable. Levels of knowledge, particularly of cost management and internal control and audit were generally satisfactory. However problems arose when candidates had to exercise professional judgement.

Various approaches were possible to a number of questions. However the question set had to be answered. For example, answers to question 3(a) would have recognised the limitations of internal control systems, and general awareness and knowledge of organisational systems.

Weaker scripts often tended to lack substance. A further common failing was answers demonstrating no more than rote learning of the internal control auditing guidelines.

When answering numerical questions, candidates should be able to choose an appropriate technique and use it to assess the information and put forward commentary and recommendations. Too many candidates had not practised questions sufficiently, and hence produced poor workings or ignored the numerical parts of questions.

November 1995	Question number in this Kit
Section A	
1 Performance assessment. Internal audit of bad debts provision	38
2 Ethics	10
Section B	
3 Internal audit: real-time transactions processing and CAATs	71
4 Budgetary control of former local government computer services MBO	51
5 JIT and changes in controls	21
6 Control of R&D	37

Examiner's comments

Too many scripts demonstrated lack of preparation and exam technique. Question 2 was particularly badly answered. Candidates failed to analyse the case study and demonstrated little knowledge of basic commercial practice. It is important that candidates read widely about current practice and on different businesses and industries.

Analysis of numbers was, as often before, generally poor. Some candidates did list in their workings all the possible techniques before choosing one. Most candidates need more question practice, however.

As usual, many candidates failed to answer the question set. Question 2 did not require the CIMA Ethical Guidelines to be set out in full; Question 5 did not require a complete description of JIT. Answers to 1(c) 3, 4 or 6 which gave details of the Auditing Practice Committee Guideline on Internal Control failed to address the question. It will not be possible to answer completely any question in Paper 16 merely by quoting the Guideline.

Markers make some allowance for handwriting. However, where bad handwriting is combined with unclear presentation and poor writing style, markers may be unable to mark the script as a pass.

May 1995	Question number in this Kit
Section A	
1 Purchasing and marketing strategy and risk; financial modelling	13
2 Pros and cons of divisionalised structures	2
Section B	
3 ROI and performance measures	36
4 Computer system controls and internal audit	66
5 Assessing the effectiveness of internal audit	48
6 Shareholder value and divisional performance	-

Examiner's comments

This was the first examination under the new syllabus, but one which did not explore the full range of the new syllabus, as part of the transitional arrangements, for the first year, for those who had not taken the new Stage 3 examinations.

The paper was generally one in which candidates had to use a range of knowledge and skills to answer precise questions which were not covered in the text books in the exact way the questions were asked. The necessary knowledge is generally available in most texts, other than the requirement for question 6, which has been well covered in articles in Management Accounting. But candidates needed to read questions very carefully and to plan structured answers.

The overall impression of the scripts was that the written questions, with the exception of question 6, were reasonably, and sometimes well answered. Many answers displayed substantial effort in studying for the new syllabus.

This was reinforced by the significantly lower number of very poor scripts from candidates who had clearly put little effort into preparing for the examination.

Within the written questions, the answers to questions 2 and 3 often displayed a good knowledge of the subject areas and a good insight into the practical problems. Answers to questions 4 and 5, whilst sometimes good, often displayed a limited understanding. An impression was gained of much rote learning in the syllabus area of internal audit. This causes concern for future examinations, since this part of the syllabus requires the application of knowledge to practical problems (ability level 4).

Answers to question 6 were weak and displayed limited effort in following new developments in Management Accounting.

However, the most important impression was that problems experienced under the old syllabus in terms of weak answers to numerical questions had not been resolved. Stage 4 requires the knowledge and understanding of some new techniques, but the main emphasis is on the application of known techniques to unknown and unpredictable problems The difficulty for candidates arises from the lack of guidance as to which techniques might or might not be useful, and from the need to interpret the results where the recommendations required are not obvious.

The main recommendation for study has to be more practice on numerical questions. Some of this ought to be with difficult questions of a Stage 4 standard. However, very many candidates would benefit significantly from revising basic techniques, which were studied at Stages 2 and 3. This would ensure dependable competence in deriving correct answers to the questions asked, in producing legible and understandable workings and in avoiding too many basic arithmetical errors.

Specimen paper	*Question number in this Kit*
Section A	
1 Reports on staff expansion proposals	35
2 Investment appraisal, DCF and bonuses	29
Section B	
3 Contingency theory; organisational culture	5
4 Audit committees and corporate codes of conduct	56
5 Auditing computer systems	-
6 ABC in service organisations; control of privatised monopolies	20

How the syllabus has been examined - an overview

	11/99	*5/99*	*11/98*	*5/98*	*11/97*	*5/97*	*11/96*	*5/96*	*11/95*	*5/95*	*Specimen*
(a) Control and the organisation											
Control theory	✓	✓	✓	✓			✓	✓		✓	✓
Organisational culture			✓		✓		✓	✓			✓
Ethics		✓		✓	✓	✓		✓	✓		✓
(b) Planning and control systems											
Budgeting		✓	✓	✓		✓			✓		✓
Developments in cost management	✓		✓					✓	✓		✓
Dynamic environment			✓		✓	✓				✓	
Investigation of variances					✓						
(c) Performance and management control											
Divisionalisation	✓		✓	✓		✓				✓	
Performance measurement	✓	✓	✓	✓				✓	✓		✓
Managerial performance	✓	✓		✓		✓		✓			✓
Separately managed units and different sectors	✓	✓		✓	✓	✓	✓	✓	✓		
(d) Quality assurance of systems											
Role of internal audit		✓	✓	✓	✓	✓	✓		✓	✓	
Internal controls			✓	✓	✓			✓	✓		
Risk assessment	✓										
Analytical review		✓									
Systems auditing techniques	✓		✓			✓				✓	✓
Sampling							✓				
Corporate governance	✓			✓	✓			✓	✓		✓

(The full syllabus is on pages (xxv) to (xxvii).)

CURRENT ISSUES

Turnbull committee

The final version of *Internal Control Guidance for Directors on the Combined Code* (the Turnbull report) was published in September 1999. The final report was not significantly different to the draft report (covered in Chapter 24 of the 1999 edition of the *BPP Management Accounting Control Systems* text).

Summary of recent articles

The content of any relevant articles published before July 1999 are reflected in the BPP Study Text for *Management Accounting Control Systems*. A list of those articles published since then has been noted briefly below.

I am their leader, I must follow them!, Keith Reynolds, Management Accounting, December 1999, pages 70 - 71

Focus on quality, David Lynch, Management Accounting, September 1999, pages 30-31

Quality and new order, David Lynch, Management Accounting, October 1999, pages 46-48

Recognising quality in finance, David Lynch, Management Accounting, November 1999, pages 32-33

Never mind the quality, feel the width, Ian Herbert, Management Accounting, November 1999, pages 68-69

Budgeting in the 21st century, John Fanning, Management Accounting, November 1999, pages 24-25

Unlocking overhead value, Nick Develin, Management Accounting, December 1999, pages 22 - 24

Value based management at British Aerospace, Margaret May and Tony Bryan, Management Accounting, December 1999, pages 36 - 37

Outsourcing - a strategy for increased profitability or catastrophe?, Richard Smith, Management Accounting, October 1999, pages 72 -74

The interface between finance and new product development: encouraging a climate of innovation, Pauline Gleadle, July/August 1999, pages 24-25

Avoiding pitfalls in investment appraisal, Rupert Booth, Management Accounting, November 1999, pages 22-23

Quo vadis internal auditing, Andrew Chambers, Management Accounting, October 1999, pages 32-33

> A recent article by the examiner is reproduced on the following pages. You are strongly advised to study it in detail.

Green and social issues and the management accountant

by J.G. Williams

There are broadly two alternative ways of looking at environmental and social issues.

The first is the 'progressive' view that imperfections can be rectified, things that were wrong in the past or present can be changed and improved, and that the world can be made a better place.

The alternative is that resources are finite and demands insatiable. Every action represents a choice of use of scarce resources.

Examinations

The Examiner is not interested in the candidate's view of any particular environmental or social issue. It will be a variation on one of the two above arguments, and fundamentally philosophical or political, in the broadest sense of the term. The candidate is entitled to his or her own view, can express it without penalty—but with no gain.

The Examiner is interested in the candidate's understanding of the way these arguments in society as a whole affect organisations, how organisations need to respond, and the role of the management accountant in helping to formulate the response. This assumes some limited broad knowledge of the arguments—but no more than can be assumed from reading quality newspapers.

Strategy

This set of concerns with environmental and social issues used to be regarded as a matter for the strategic planning process, and of little immediate concern, other than a possible need to comply with specific requirements from legislation. The strategic planning issues are of great importance, and generally well understood. Limited coverage of these strategic issues is given in this article, as they are well covered in the November 1998 issue of *Management Accounting* (Bennett, M. and James, P.: 'The green bottom line').

Changing views on, for instance, socially acceptable treatment of employees or permissible pollution levels, can in the extreme be a significant threat to the continued existence of the organisation unless radical restructuring is undertaken. The obvious example is moving operations to a cheaper and more permissive environment in another country.

Short of this, the usual effect is an increase in the operating costs of the organisation, which may or may not be recoverable from repricing. There are cases where environmental and ethical concerns can provide a significant niche marketing opportunity, as frequently illustrated by the well known examples of the Co-operative Bank and The Body Shop. There are also cases where environmentally friendly waste minimisation programmes can show a net benefit. But the presumption has to be that anything an organisation needs to be pushed into doing will have costs exceeding benefits. If this were not the case, the action would already have been undertaken willingly.

The impact on the organisation

The greatest problems in assessing the potential impact of changing social and environmental requirements on an organisation are:

- the range of activities that could be criticised;
- the range of issues involved;
- the range of possible critics (would-be enforcers of potential new rights).

The range of activities

The range of business activities which can be, and frequently are criticised notably extends beyond the legal boundaries of the organisation. Firms are criticised for the activities of their suppliers and sub-contractors, even if the practices of these companies are not fully known.

Examples of this include the criticism of retailers of footballs which were made by child labour in poor countries, and the criticism of hamburger restaurants because the beef is bought from countries clearing rainforests and displacing tribal people to provide further grazing land. Firms are criticised for providing packaging, especially plastic, which causes environmental problems on disposal or creates pollution when being manufactured.

Anything broadly in the 'value chain' could be criticised and be regarded by activists as the responsibility of the company selling the product.

It is no defence for the firm concerned to point out that senior managers were totally unaware of the perceived problems, and had not knowingly taken any action which would affect the problem.

Issues

The range of issues is very wide and continually expanding. It includes:

- sustainable resources:
  - energy from fossil fuels versus energy from renewable resources, such as hydro electric schemes, windpower, solar energy;
  - sustainable forest management, timber and timber products from managed forests;
- global warming;
- protecting the atmosphere, especially the ozone layer;
- pollution, especially aerial (acid rain) and marine (sewage and industrial water disposal);
- the risks associated with nuclear power, and the storage/disposal of nuclear waste;
- transport, partly as a pollution issue, partly as a use of fossil fuels.

Social issues are primarily employment related—working conditions, union recognition and employee rights to information and consultation on major issues. Interestingly, much of the pressure for improved working conditions in poor countries comes from trade unions in rich countries who perceive cheap labour elsewhere as unfair competition.

Disability issues cover a much wider range than just employment; there is pressure on employers to find ways of employing disabled people, even if it involves significant investment in access facilities and special equipment. Questions of providing disabled customer access can be met relatively easily with new facilities—but can be almost impossible to achieve with old buildings.

Similar issues can affect insurance companies, preventing them discriminating against categories of potential customers they would regard as poor risks, e.g. preventing them from seeking medical tests of potential customers to establish if they are HIV positive.

A separate subset of issues concerns animals:

- animal care, e.g. Compassion in World Farming, Royal Society for the Protection of Animals;
- campaigning, e.g. the anti-hunting lobby; animal rights activists; opponents of the use of animals in experiments; those against breeding animals for fur.

This should not be regarded as a complete list of potential problems (or opportunities). The list will vary between organisations. Unfortunately, most people in most organisations are not very good at identifying potential problems before they become major issues.

The advocates

The case for environmental and social policies is almost always originated by relatively prosperous citizens in rich countries. They can afford to pay more for ethical policies, fair treatment of employees, food produced in environmentally acceptable ways. They can be said to have surplus income, beyond that required for what they regard as an acceptable standard of living, and would prefer the benefit of a better environment to more material benefits.

The problem is that many of the benefits sought, in the form of a better environment, or a more stable society, are only obtainable if everyone is persuaded or coerced into following appropriate policies. Many in both rich and especially poorer countries either cannot afford the extra costs, or regard other uses of income as more important.

The notable feature of the advocacy of these policies is the number of separate 'single issue' campaigns, often quite small numbers of activists very concerned about one specific policy proposal. Fringe groups may move beyond political advocacy to some form of 'direct action', which is usually calculated to obtain maximum free publicity.

It can be very difficult to judge the level of popular support for any issue, as a small group with ample funds can often make a quite disproportionate noise.

Campaigning is often very sophisticated, targeting issues and events which ensure publicity. Examples of direct action to gain publicity include the landing by Greenpeace on the oil rig that Shell proposed to sink, and protests against new road schemes. Publicity campaigns are aimed at large organisations with very important consumer brands to protect, such as Shell petrol and leading retailers and supermarket chains. Political parties can be offered substantial support to encourage them to take up minority causes.

This campaigning can catch the public mood, and can be very successful. An issue which one year appears to be of minor importance can become an issue on which government action is possible, or even in progress, in a very short time.

Campaigning can also start with lawyers, especially now that contingency fees and class action systems make challenging a major organisation easier.

The interesting aspect of these cases is that they address not so much what is wrong now as what was done in the past which would not be done now. One example of this is the pursuit of claims relating to asbestos dust even 30 or 40 years after the event.

Pressures on organisations: direct pressures

The obvious pressures on organisations to respond to calls for environmental or social improvement are those of new legislation or regulation.

The change to note in these direct pressures, compared with even ten years ago, is the range of sources of new regulation, not just formal legislation by the UK government but a wide range of European Union legislation, some treaty obligations (e.g. accepting obligations arising from the Rio 'earth summit') and a very wide range of administrative law and regulation spelling out the practical detail.

There is also a range of pressures that are marginally short of legislation but almost equally effective. The example which accountants will know is the new proposal for regulating accountants, where there is government pressure to produce an acceptable system or face legislation. Similar pressure is developing for better environmental reporting by companies, again under threat of legislation if a solution is not voluntarily found which is acceptable to the government.

Pressures on organisations: indirect pressures

The most important pressure on large organisations is pubic opinion in the form of customer opinion. If the organisation has a consumer brand to protect it will respond to perceived criticism of the brand and accept significant other costs to avoid possible long term effects. Many large organisations are prepared to meet small pressure groups and try to address their concerns at quite early stages in their campaigning.

Pressure is also exerted by such institutions as banks and insurance companies, who deal with a variety of organisations in a range of industries and are in a good position to see how opinion is changing. Banks become reluctant to regard old, possibly polluted, industrial sites as valuable assets, insurance companies start to re-assess public liability and employee liability risks.

New organisations, and some established organisations start selling advice on the new problems, and in so doing increase awareness. A good example of this is the new link up (Financial Times, 7 December 1998) between accountants KPMG and The Body Shop, the cosmetics retailer, to offer advice on social ethical and environmental reporting.

Immediate prospects

Reasonable predictions are that the next few years will see a range of further developments with direct impacts on most organisations:

- more regulation in environmental and social affairs following through from commitments already undertaken:
  - the European social chapter, labour legislation;
  - the Rio 'earth summit', pollution and conservation objectives;
- more regulation in the area in particular of products, safety and health;
- more reporting on ethical, social and environmental issues, leading to pressures for more consistent standardised reporting to allow comparison between organisations.

It is reasonable to look beyond this immediate prospect and see medium-term pressures for organisations to develop formal statements on environmental and social policy broadly in line with the statements already produced in other areas such as mission statements and codes of conduct.

It may not be too far ahead to look at the question of when social, ethical and environmental audits will be required.

The management accountant

There are interesting times ahead: future activities may include developing new information systems to gather and organise a completely new range of information, little of which is captured by current, primarily financial, information systems, but which will have to be related in some way to current operating systems.

There will be a need to develop new systems of control and internal audit to ensure compliance with a much more regulated environment.

But with all these changes, there will still be the need to maintain systems for ensuring profitability, to pay for the better environment.

References

BENNETT, M. and JAMES, P.: 'The green bottom line: management accounting for environmental improvement and business benefit', *Management Accounting*, November 1998.

CAIRNCROSS, F.: *Green Inc* Earthscan Publications, 1995.

EXAMINERS' INSTRUCTIONS

The examinations department of the CIMA has asked the Institute's examiners to be precise when drafting questions. In particular, examiners have been asked to use precise instruction words. It will probably help you to know what instruction words may be used, and what they mean. With the Institute's permission, their list of recommended requirement words, and their meaning, is shown below.

Recommended requirement words

Advise/recommend	Present information, opinions or recommendations to someone to enable that recipient to take action
Amplify	Expand or enlarge upon the meaning of (a statement or quotation)
Analyse	Determine and explain the constituent parts of
Appraise/assess/evaluate	Judge the importance or value of
Assess	See 'appraise'
Clarify	Explain more clearly the meaning of
Comment (critically)	Explain
Compare (with)	Explain similarities and differences between
Contrast	Place in opposition to bring out difference(s)
Criticise	Present the faults in a theory or policy or opinion
Demonstrate	Show by reasoning the truth of
Describe	Present the details and characteristics of
Discuss	Explain the opposing arguments
Distinguish	Specify the differences between
Evaluate	See 'appraise'
Explain/interpret	Set out in detail the meaning of
Illustrate	Use an example - chart, diagram, graph or figure as appropriate - to explain something
Interpret	See 'explain'
Justify	State adequate grounds for
List (and explain)	Itemise (and detail meaning of)
Prove	Show by testing the accuracy of
Recommend	See 'advise'
Reconcile	Make compatible apparently conflicting statements or theories
Relate	Show connections between separate matters
State	Express
Summarise	State briefly the essential points (dispensing with examples and details)
Tabulate	Set out facts or figures in a table

Requirement words which will be avoided

Examiners have been asked to avoid instructions which are imprecise or which may not specifically elicit an answer. The following words will not be used.

Consider	As candidates could do this without writing a word
Define	In the sense of stating exactly what a thing is, as CIMA wishes to avoid requiring evidence of rote learning
Examine	As this is what the examiner is doing, not the examinee
Enumerate	'List' is preferred
Identify	
Justify	When the requirement is not 'to state adequate grounds for' but 'to state the advantage of'
List	On its own, without an additional requirement such as 'list and explain'
Outline	As its meaning is imprecise. The addition of the word 'briefly' to any of the suggested action words is more satisfactory
Review	
Specify	
Trace	

SYLLABUS

The syllabus contains a weighting for each syllabus area, and a ranking of the level of ability required in each topic. The Institute has published the following explanatory notes on these points.

'Study weightings

A percentage weighting is shown against each topic in the syllabus; this is intended as a guide to the amount of study time each topic requires.

All topics in a syllabus must be studied, as a question may examine more than one topic, or carry a higher proportion of marks than the percentage study time suggested.

The weightings do not specify the number of marks which will be allocated to topics in the examination.

Abilities required in the examination

Each examination paper contains a number of topics. Each topic has been given a number to indicate the level of ability required of the candidate.

The numbers range from 1 to 4 and represent the following ability levels:

Appreciation (1)
To understand a knowledge area at an early stage of learning, or outside the core of management accounting, at a level which enables the accountant to communicate and work with other members of the management team.

Knowledge (2)
To have detailed knowledge of such matters as laws, standards, facts and techniques so as to advise at a level appropriate to a management accounting specialist.

Skill (3)
To apply theoretical knowledge, concepts and techniques to the solution of problems where it is clear what technique has to be used and the information needed is clearly indicated.

Application (4)
To apply knowledge and skills where candidates have to determine from a number of techniques which is the most appropriate and select the information required from a fairly wide range of data, some of which might not be relevant; to exercise professional judgement and to communicate and work with members of the management team and other recipients of financial reports.'

Syllabus overview

This syllabus requires the demonstration of understanding of the various systems by which management accounting data is collected, processed and presented to management. Using previously acquired management accounting techniques, the candidate must show competence in the manipulation of data, analysis at an appropriate level and in the persuasive and effective presentation of management control information. Students must be able to evaluate and audit the systems, and to show understanding of the internal control environment in which management accounting systems are performed in an orderly and efficient manner. They must also be able to ensure adherence to management policies, safeguard the assets and secure as far as possible the completeness and accuracy of the records.

Aims

To test the candidates ability to:

- select and utilise control systems which provide management control of the organisation
- provide management with appropriate information for control, assessing and reporting on performance, monitoring efficiency, effectiveness and value for money
- evaluate and audit the relevance of management information systems (including information technology systems)
- assess the quality and reliability of management information systems and control systems
- advise management on the use of these systems, and on issues of personal or corporate conduct

Content and ability required

		Ability required
16(a) Control and the organisation	*(study weighting 15%)*	
(i)	The organisational context in which accounting and other systems are used to achieve control	3
(ii)	Control systems, contingency theory and the design of accounting information systems and management control systems	3
(iii)	The application of control and related theory to management accounting within an organisation	4
(iv)	The interrelationship of management accounting systems and organisational culture and disparate management objectives	4
(v)	Ethics: professional guidelines; organisational guidelines; corporate codes of conduct; audit committee and other controlling influences for achieving ethical conduct throughout the organisation	4
16(b) Planning and control systems	*(study weighting 25%)*	
(i)	Problems of budget centre selection and control	4
(ii)	Management involvement in preparation of budgets and standards. Motivational implications. Inter-relationships within the organisation	4
(iii)	Integration and co-ordination of resource requirements and influence of constraints on budget preparation: relationships of budgets to strategic plans and planned investment	4
(iv)	Changes in planning and control systems required by technological development, and developments in cost management techniques	4
(v)	Use of budgets and standards in dynamic environments	4
(vi)	Investigation of variances; proposals for corrective action	4
(vii)	Preparation and presentation of reports to management	4
(viii)	Management and control of risk	4

		Ability required

16(c) Performance and management control *(study weighting 35%)*

		Ability required
(i)	Analysis and interpretation of external intelligence, eg macro-economic data, agency publications. Comparative analysis, and the effect on management decisions	4
(ii)	Operational performance indicators within the organisation. Internal and external comparisons	4
(iii)	Performance measurement and evaluation; divisional profit centres and other separately managed units; evaluation of support departments: manufacturing service departments, computing services, management accounting as an internal customer service	4
(iv)	Measurement, evaluation and rewarding of managerial performance	4
(v)	Measurement of short-term and long-term performance; evaluation in multinational organisations; not-for-profit organisations	4
(vi)	Performance measures: financial and non-financial; advantages and disadvantages	4
(vii)	Measuring the performance of new technology in manufacturing and service organisations	4

16(d) Quality assurance of systems *(study weighting 25%)*

		Ability required
(i)	Internal control: establishing the whole system of controls, financial and otherwise	4
(ii)	Review of internal control systems	4
(iii)	Role of internal auditor: controlling influences; relationship to external auditor	3
(iv)	Techniques in systems auditing in a computerised environment eg software audit trails, control of systems modifications	3
(v)	Goal analysis. Audit operations. The assessment of audit risk; materiality	3
(vi)	Value for money audit. Management audit	4
(vii)	Analytical review; reasonableness and significance of figures in financial statements	4

CIMA SYLLABUS GUIDANCE NOTES 1999-2000

The following Guidance Notes were published by the CIMA in the August 1999 CIMA Student as an aid to students and lecturers.

'The following guidance notes have been drafted by the Chief Examiner for each of the subjects. They are intended to inform candidates and lecturers about the scope of the syllabus, the emphasis that should be placed on various topics and the approach which the examination papers will adopt.

General guidance note (Stage 4)

As the final test of professional competence in management accountancy, Stage 4 has certain unique characteristics. It is the culmination of the whole experience of practical expertise gained through working blended with knowledge acquired by studying and requires from candidates the highest level of ability.

From Stage 2 onwards, candidates should remember that the syllabus content of subjects at earlier Stages is re-examinable. This does not imply that a Stage 2 question will appear in a Stage 4 question paper. However, it does mean that candidates need the ability to build on knowledge and skills, including numerical skills, learned originally for an earlier stage.

Candidates will be required to integrate new material with that learned earlier, and to use the combined knowledge at a higher level of ability. Revision of earlier material, particularly by those who have been credited with exemptions, must form part of the studying process. The majority of the topics in the four papers are ranked at ability level 4 (Application). This means that candidates must not only be able to select the relevant data and apply the appropriate technique; they must also be able to communicate to others the results obtained.

There is, thus, an emphasis on the practical application of knowledge and skill. To test this, the Examiners rely heavily on case study and scenario-based questions.

A case study is simply a history or description of an organisation, firm or industry facing a particular set of circumstances which could be a problem of some sort, or perhaps an opportunity. There is usually some discussion of how the organisation's current situation developed, and there are often a number of central characters charged with the task of resolving the problem, or exploiting the opportunity.

Such characters are invariably senior members of management, eg the managing director, because it is at this level that policy and strategic decisions are made.

Cases will be between one and three pages long. They may be based around activities of real people and organisations (although candidates do not require any specialist knowledge of any particular organisation), or they may be fictitious.

The essential function of the case study is to test a candidate's ability to resolve relatively complex, unstructured problems. There may be several feasible solutions and candidates should not necessarily expect there to be a single definitive answer. The solution will involve the selection and use of techniques that have been learned, but usually also requires the exercise of judgement and creative thinking. This means that study and examination techniques, which might have been suitable at earlier Stages, need to become more sophisticated and directed when preparing for Stage 4. Preparation for answering case study/scenario-based questions cannot be reliant on reading alone, but must be heavily supplemented by question practice under examination conditions.

It is important to realise that in case study questions marks are earned by the quality of the reasoning and exposition displayed. The ability to structure a coherent report, which leads logically to its conclusion is regarded as essential. Recommendations are often required. Acceptable recommendations may vary, but must be relevant, sensible and fully justified.

As candidates advance through the examination Stages, their career progress can restrict their available study time. Fewer find it possible to obtain contact with a teacher or tutor as part of a class. Yet the nature of the examination makes that contact highly desirable - perhaps more so than at earlier Stages. However, candidates will be gaining a greater breadth of experience in the workplace. This valuable practical experience can be drawn on when answering practical-based questions.

Candidates' chances of success will be significantly enhanced if they are familiar with the current business environment. An easy way to achieve this is to read selectively from the *Financial Times* in the UK which analyses companies' published accounts, comments on marketing and strategy, and publishes a management page on an almost daily basis. There are also other international newspapers outside the UK which carry out the same sort of analysis. It is quite clear that answers are enhanced by examples drawn from press articles and that such answers are given credit by the markers.

Stage 4 involves the integration of all subjects. There is inevitably some overlap between papers as topics are dealt with from the different perspectives of strategy, marketing, information management, control and financial management. The following guidance notes give more information on the syllabuses for the subjects, but candidates should be continually aware of the integrative nature of Stage 4 and, even with credit accumulation, should not view each of the syllabuses in isolation.

Management Accounting Control Systems

This syllabus deals mainly with control processes within organisations, in particular the control processes of management accounting and internal audit. Candidates should be able to advise on the selection of appropriate systems, taking into account the theory of control systems, the organisational behaviour implications, the problems of different organisational circumstances and different management priorities and strategies.

Candidates must understand the problems of installing and operating such systems, and must be able to present data and results to management, and advise on their interpretation and on possible action. They should be able to audit the systems and to assess their economy, efficiency and effectiveness. This syllabus builds on work done in the FNA paper at Stage 2 and the MAA and OMD papers at Stage 3 and emphasises the importance of this work to the control of the organisation. Candidates should note that they are expected to be able to apply their knowledge and skills to the varying situations of large and small companies, in service industries and in the public sector and not-for-profit organisations, as well as in manufacturing.

Most of the syllabus is at ability level 4 - Application. Candidates must be able to demonstrate professional judgement and skill in analysing given information (which may be incomplete), analysing the problem using a chosen technique, and presenting information to management and making recommendations.

Questions will often focus on new developments in control systems. Examples include increased emphasis on ethical issues, developments in organisation theory, new approaches to cost management, innovations in performance evaluation in services and the public sector, and changes in internal control with the increased emphasis on corporate governance. Questions will not be limited to topics covered in textbooks. Candidates must keep up-to-date with new ideas and systems and are assumed to have read reports of new developments in *Management Accounting*. The emphasis in the syllabus on audit and control in a computerised environment, is explained in syllabus section (d).

The examination paper

This will include case study questions, as well as questions requiring the explanation and assessment of particular techniques.

Numerical questions may well be compulsory. They could involve the re-examination of techniques studied for any of the papers on which this one builds. An important test of application skills will often be that candidates are required to select an appropriate analysis technique.

However, a much more critical assessment will be required of the results of the calculations, as well as a higher standard of financial analysis, and an appropriate standard of presentation of findings and recommendations to management. It will rarely be possible to earn the maximum marks on any part of a question by presenting calculations without commentary or interpretation.

A question's requirements may be entirely interpretation, commentary and recommendations.

Ethical issues may be involved in any question asked and may not necessarily feature as a separate question.

It should not be assumed that any question will fall entirely within one syllabus area. Many questions will cover more than one syllabus area.

Any part of the syllabus can be examined in the compulsory section of the question paper.

Control and the organisation

Syllabus reference 16(a)

Study weighting 15%

1 Control theory

Chartered Management Accountants must understand concepts of control and control processes for this section.

They must also understand a wide range of related individual and group behavioural issues for section (b) of the syllabus. It is not appropriate for the aspiring Chartered Management Accountant to study only systems theory, the cybernetic control model and the classical behavioural literature.

Professionals in the field have moved on to a much more extensive range of ideas to help understand organisational control. Equally, given the constraint of all the competing claims on student time, new ideas can only be studied if they are useful.

In the examination, candidates may be required to:

- demonstrate knowledge of systems theory and the cybernetic control model;
- demonstrate knowledge of contingency theory and its uses and limitations, and of why its limitations have led to a search for alternative explanations of organisational structure;
- demonstrate outline knowledge of the existence of a wide range of newer ideas and their relevance to management accounting. Outline knowledge of the main schools of thought, and of major writers such as Foucault is required, but questions will emphasise the application of ideas and the extent of change in thought in this area, not the detail. The range and detail required can be defined by reference to the core reading.

2 Organisational culture

Candidates are expected to understand how people work in groups, how group behaviour can be quite different to individual behaviour, and why companies in similar industries can work in quite different ways.

They should understand the balance between formal and informal systems of control, and the relationship between organisational culture, structure and strategy.

Such knowledge is crucial to understanding how systems do, and do not, work and candidates should be prepared to study practical aspects as well as theoretical constructs.

Questions will emphasise practical aspects, and the relevance of organisational culture to management accounting.

3 Ethics

A knowledge and understanding of the *CIMA Ethical Guidelines* is essential, but not sufficient.

Candidates are expected to be able to apply these guidelines to practical problems arising in organisations. These problems will normally involve an accountant within an organisation, or accounting information. The problems may not be specifically within management accounting.

In the examination, candidates may be required to:

- understand the aims of corporate codes of conduct, their role in ethical guidance and their place in improved corporate governance;
- understand current developments in corporate governance and its ethical impact.

The following item is *not* examinable:

- internal auditors' ethical guidelines and special problems.

Ethical issues arise in SMM as well as in this paper. This overlap is of limited significance as candidates will normally be sitting both papers. MCS will deal, primarily, with internal issues, ethics and control systems, codes of conduct and their enforcement, and the duties of the accountant in an organisation including the responsibilities under the *Ethical Guidelines.* SMM will deal, primarily, with external issues. Case study questions, which may be set in both MCS and SMM, will often involve internal and external issues.

4 Corporate governance

Developments in corporate governance have been mentioned under ethics, and will also be referred to with regard to internal audit in syllabus section (d). Here attention is drawn to the implications of the proposed reforms (and of the continuing public debate on whether further reforms may be needed) for the structure of the organisation, and hence its control. This includes the separation of the roles of chairman and chief executive, the requirement for non-executive directors and the establishment of audit and remuneration committees. Candidates should be aware of the main provisions of the new Combined Code, which consolidates the recommendations of the previous reports on corporate governance, and the subsequent guidance for directors on internal control. Articles written by the examiner and published in *CIMA Student* will explain these.

Planning and control systems

Syllabus reference 16 (b)
Study weighting 25%

In the examination, candidates may be required to:

- understand the problems of adapting systems to particular circumstances and management objectives, and the requirement for new systems for new technologies;
- understand operating systems in all types of activities, not just in manufacturing. This includes knowledge of the application of just-in-time (JIT) and total quality management (TQM) and of their implications for management accounting;
- understand the problems of analysing and interpreting overhead cost, and advising management on its control;
- understand the relationship between budgeting and short-term control systems, strategic planning systems and investment planning and appraisal systems in the overall control of the organisation. Strategic management accounting, studied for SMM, must also be understood as a control problem;
- relate these factors to the overall information systems and their role in providing information for the short and long-term control of the organisation;
- demonstrate a basic knowledge of current motivation theory, including expectancy theory. There are two significant overlaps here with syllabus section (a);
- demonstrate a sound knowledge of variance accounting, and answer questions that require some variance analysis;
- demonstrate knowledge of planning and budgeting under constraints;
- analyse and evaluate risk and recommend policies to minimise or limit risk in particular circumstances.

The following items are *not* examinable:

- a full question on variance analysis;
- simplex calculations.

Performance and management control

Syllabus reference 16 (c)
Study weighting 35%

The requirements of this section include performance evaluation in the following situations:

- in functionally organised as well as divisionalised companies;
- in branches in multi-branch organisations, typically in services such as banking and retail, but also in public sector services;
- in not-for-profit organisations including the public sector;
- in multinational organisations;
- in manufacturing organisations adopting new costing systems and new production management and quality systems.

A wide range of additional reading is suggested in this area. It is *not* expected that candidates will read it all, but that they will read enough to understand the range of practices adopted in response to different problems, and to be able to make and justify appropriate recommendations for specific circumstances.

Much of the additional reading will enable candidates to review studies in the core reading of Berry, Broadbent and Otley in greater depth.

In the examination, candidates may be required to:

- understand the economics of divisionalisation, including transaction cost economics, and the advantages and disadvantages of divisional structures compared with the available alternatives. Questions on divisional performance can involve transfer pricing in that this can affect performance evaluation;
- demonstrate knowledge in considerable depth of most aspects of the problems of performance evaluation, not just those of divisional performance evaluation. This includes knowledge of techniques such as discounted cash flow income, performance indicators, and an outline knowledge of data envelopment analysis;
- understand in particular the problems of segregating managerial performance from the economic performance of the managed unit. The study of the evaluation of management performance will require an understanding of managerial motivation, as required for section (b), and will require a basic understanding of agency theory;
- demonstrate understanding of managerial bonus schemes in the context of performance and motivation. Whilst the general principles of the taxation of these schemes should be understood, no specific taxation knowledge will be assumed;
- answer case study questions which could involve the analysis and interpretation of a wide range of financial and non-financial data for managerial and economic performance appraisal.

Quality assurance of systems

Syllabus reference 16 (d)

Study weighting 25%

This section of the syllabus builds on the CIMA paper, *A Framework for Internal Control*, published for CIMA's Law and Parliamentary Committee in 1992, in the context of a complete system of internal control, and on the work required for the Stage 2 FNA paper, especially in internal control and audit.

This section is not concerned purely with the work done by the internal audit department (if there is such a department).

Syllabus revision, effective from May 1997, emphasises the computerised environment. This is normal in virtually all large organisations. Questions, whether on internal control or internal audit, will assume this environment. However, this does not limit questioning to specialised techniques required for the audit of computer systems, though these will receive increased emphasis.

Candidates are expected to understand and be able to recommend and apply appropriate control techniques, and assess their effectiveness, in the organisation as a whole.

There is a degree of overlap with IFM, and the reading on some control aspects of computerised systems and their development may be duplicated. Knowledge of information strategy and systems is assumed from IFM.

Developments intended to improve corporate governance (the Cadbury, Greenbury and Hampel reports, and the subsequent Combined Code, which simplifies the detail to some extent) are examinable. These include, in particular, the role of non-executive directors and audit committees, and the requirement for directors to report on internal control.

This last very important issue for internal control and internal audit has been reviewed in the recent Guidance for Directors of Listed Companies on Internal control, Consolidation Draft published by the ICAEW (Institute of Chartered Accountants in England and Wales).

Guidance notes

Candidates should make every effort to keep up-to-date in this field, and will be assisted by articles written by the Examiner in *CIMA Student*.

In the examination, candidates may be required to:

- demonstrate skill in the use of conventional internal audit techniques;
- answer case study questions that require the selection of appropriate techniques in the described situation, and an ability to apply the techniques;
- interpret, and comment critically on, systems described in flow charts;
- answer numerical questions on sampling techniques, possibly as part of a case study. In such a question, appropriate formulae would be provided and marking would depend primarily on the candidate's interpretation of the results;
- understand the application of value for money audit and management and operational audit in a public or private sector setting.

MATHEMATICAL TABLES

PRESENT VALUE TABLE

Present value of 1 = $(1+r)^{-n}$ where r = discount rate, n = number of periods until payment

This table shows the present value of £1 per annum, receivable or payable at the end of *n* years.

Periods (n)	Discount rates (r) 1%	2%	3%	4%	5%	6%	7%	8%	9%	10%
1	0.990	0.980	0.971	0.962	0.952	0.943	0.935	0.926	0.917	0.909
2	0.980	0.961	0.943	0.925	0.907	0.890	0.873	0.857	0.842	0.826
3	0.971	0.942	0.915	0.889	0.864	0.840	0.816	0.794	0.772	0.751
4	0.961	0.924	0.888	0.855	0.823	0.792	0.763	0.735	0.708	0.683
5	0.951	0.906	0.863	0.822	0.784	0.747	0.713	0.681	0.650	0.621
6	0.942	0.888	0.837	0.790	0.746	0.705	0.666	0.630	0.596	0.564
7	0.933	0.871	0.813	0.760	0.711	0.665	0.623	0.583	0.547	0.513
8	0.923	0.853	0.789	0.731	0.677	0.627	0.582	0.540	0.502	0.467
9	0.914	0.837	0.766	0.703	0.645	0.592	0.544	0.500	0.460	0.424
10	0.905	0.820	0.744	0.676	0.614	0.558	0.508	0.463	0.422	0.386
11	0.896	0.804	0.722	0.650	0.585	0.527	0.475	0.429	0.388	0.350
12	0.887	0.788	0.701	0.625	0.557	0.497	0.444	0.397	0.356	0.319
13	0.879	0.773	0.681	0.601	0.530	0.469	0.415	0.368	0.326	0.290
14	0.870	0.758	0.661	0.577	0.505	0.442	0.388	0.340	0.299	0.263
15	0.861	0.743	0.642	0.555	0.481	0.417	0.362	0.315	0.275	0.239

Periods (n)	Discount rates (r) 11%	12%	13%	14%	15%	16%	17%	18%	19%	20%
1	0.901	0.893	0.885	0.877	0.870	0.862	0.855	0.847	0.840	0.833
2	0.812	0.797	0.783	0.769	0.756	0.743	0.731	0.718	0.706	0.694
3	0.731	0.712	0.693	0.675	0.658	0.641	0.624	0.609	0.593	0.579
4	0.659	0.636	0.613	0.592	0.572	0.552	0.534	0.516	0.499	0.482
5	0.593	0.567	0.543	0.519	0.497	0.476	0.456	0.437	0.419	0.402
6	0.535	0.507	0.480	0.456	0.432	0.410	0.390	0.370	0.352	0.335
7	0.482	0.452	0.425	0.400	0.376	0.354	0.333	0.314	0.296	0.279
8	0.434	0.404	0.376	0.351	0.327	0.305	0.285	0.266	0.249	0.233
9	0.391	0.361	0.333	0.308	0.284	0.263	0.243	0.225	0.209	0.194
10	0.352	0.322	0.295	0.270	0.247	0.227	0.208	0.191	0.176	0.162
11	0.317	0.287	0.261	0.237	0.215	0.195	0.178	0.162	0.148	0.135
12	0.286	0.257	0.231	0.208	0.187	0.168	0.152	0.137	0.124	0.112
13	0.258	0.229	0.204	0.182	0.163	0.145	0.130	0.116	0.104	0.093
14	0.232	0.205	0.181	0.160	0.141	0.125	0.111	0.099	0.088	0.078
15	0.209	0.183	0.160	0.140	0.123	0.108	0.095	0.084	0.074	0.065

CUMULATIVE PRESENT VALUE TABLE

This table shows the present value of £1 per annum, receivable or payable at the end of each year for *n* years.

Periods (n)	Discount rates (r) 1%	2%	3%	4%	5%	6%	7%	8%	9%	10%
1	0.990	0.980	0.971	0.962	0.952	0.943	0.935	0.926	0.917	0.909
2	1.970	1.942	1.913	1.886	1.859	1.833	1.808	1.783	1.759	1.736
3	2.941	2.884	2.829	2.775	2.723	2.673	2.624	2.577	2.531	2.487
4	3.902	3.808	3.717	3.630	3.546	3.465	3.387	3.312	3.240	3.170
5	4.853	4.713	4.580	4.452	4.329	4.212	4.100	3.993	3.890	3.791
6	5.795	5.601	5.417	5.242	5.076	4.917	4.767	4.623	4.486	4.355
7	6.728	6.472	6.230	6.002	5.786	5.582	5.389	5.206	5.033	4.868
8	7.652	7.325	7.020	6.733	6.463	6.210	5.971	5.747	5.535	5.335
9	8.566	8.162	7.786	7.435	7.108	6.802	6.515	6.247	5.995	5.759
10	9.471	8.983	8.530	8.111	7.722	7.360	7.024	6.710	6.418	6.145
11	10.368	9.787	9.253	8.760	8.306	7.887	7.499	7.139	6.805	6.495
12	11.255	10.575	9.954	9.385	8.863	8.384	7.943	7.536	7.161	6.814
13	12.134	11.348	10.635	9.986	9.394	8.853	8.358	7.904	7.487	7.103
14	13.004	12.106	11.296	10.563	9.899	9.295	8.745	8.244	7.786	7.367
15	13.865	12.849	11.938	11.118	10.380	9.712	9.108	8.559	8.061	7.606

Periods (n)	Discount rates (r) 11%	12%	13%	14%	15%	16%	17%	18%	19%	20%
1	0.901	0.893	0.885	0.877	0.870	0.862	0.855	0.847	0.840	0.833
2	1.713	1.690	1.668	1.647	1.626	1.605	1.585	1.566	1.547	1.528
3	2.444	2.402	2.361	2.322	2.283	2.246	2.210	2.174	2.140	2.106
4	3.102	3.037	2.974	2.914	2.855	2.798	2.743	2.690	2.639	2.589
5	3.696	3.605	3.517	3.433	3.352	3.274	3.199	3.127	3.058	2.991
6	4.231	4.111	3.998	3.889	3.784	3.685	3.589	3.498	3.410	3.326
7	4.712	4.564	4.423	4.288	4.160	4.039	3.922	3.812	3.706	3.605
8	5.146	4.968	4.799	4.639	4.487	4.344	4.207	4.078	3.954	3.837
9	5.537	5.328	5.132	4.946	4.772	4.607	4.451	4.303	4.163	4.031
10	5.889	5.650	5.426	5.216	5.019	4.833	4.659	4.494	4.339	4.192
11	6.207	5.938	5.687	5.453	5.234	5.029	4.836	4.656	4.486	4.327
12	6.492	6.194	5.918	5.660	5.421	5.197	4.988	4.793	4.611	4.439
13	6.750	6.424	6.122	5.842	5.583	5.342	5.118	4.910	4.715	4.533
14	6.982	6.628	6.302	6.002	5.724	5.468	5.229	5.008	4.802	4.611
15	7.191	6.811	6.462	6.142	5.847	5.575	5.324	5.092	4.876	4.675

Question bank

DO YOU KNOW? - CONTROL AND THE ORGANISATION

- *Check that you can fill in the blanks in the statements below before you attempt any questions. If in doubt, you should go back to your BPP Study Text and revise first.*
- Be sure that you feel comfortable using the language of control theory and cybernetics: inputs, processes and outputs; feedback and feedforward control; open and closed systems and so on. Make sure you realise that the control process is not as straightforward in practice as the theory suggests. Planning realistically is fraught with difficulties due to .... and ....
  Not all deviations from plan are controllable. Outputs and outcomes are often not easy to measure. The relationship between inputs and outputs may be impossible to determine. Formal controls may be cumbersome and out of touch with reality.
- Emmanuel *et al* describe four necessary conditions for control. A .... decision is one whose outcome can be relied upon to turn out as expected. A .... decision is subject to uncertainty about its outcome.

  TRY QUESTIONS 2, 3 AND 6
- Management accounting systems are used for a variety of purposes and this affects their design (the inputs and processes used and the outputs obtained). .... theorists try to identify the specific features of an organisation's context (environment, structure, culture, technology etc) that impact upon particular features of accounting system design. This approach has a number of limitations. Simons' and Goold and Campbell's works are also important. Newer ideas include symbolic interactionism, ethnomethodology, structuration theory, radical theory and Foucault's ideas.

  TRY QUESTIONS 1, 4, 5, 7 AND 8
- Organisation structure is influenced by factors such as size, task, staff, environment, age, culture and management style. Know about delayering and empowerment, matrix structures and Business Process Re-engineering (BPR). Consider the methods and implications of divisionalisation, particularly the M-form.
- Culture in an organisation is the sum total of the ...., ..., ... and .... to which people are exposed. Handy sums up culture as 'that's the way we do things round here'. For Schein, it is 'the pattern of basic assumptions ... that have worked well enough to be considered valid and, therefore, to be taught to new members as the correct way to perceive, think and feel in relation to problems.' An organisational culture may be negative or unhealthy but it can be changed.
- Handy identifies four basic types of organisational culture: .... (small organisations influenced by a central source); ...... (bureaucracy); .... (project teams and task forces): and .... (individual interests).
- Motivation in an organisational sense refers to attempts to get people to put in more effort by various means such as targets and/or rewards. You should know about several different motivation theories. The most relevant to management accounting control systems research seems to be expectancy theory (the force of someone's motivation equals ....). Other useful theories include Maslow and Herzberg's ....theories.
- Group behaviour and leadership are key factors influencing the effectiveness of organisations. According to Handy, group effectiveness depends upon ...., ... and .... Handy identifies six types of leadership power: ....
- Ethics is the science of accepted rules or standards of behaviour. You should learn the CIMA Ethical Guidelines, especially the fundamental principles: .... Also be aware of the influence of corporate codes and standards and the organisational implications of ethical dilemmas.

  TRY QUESTIONS 9, 10,11 AND 12
- *Possible pitfalls*

  Write down the mistakes you know you should avoid.

DID YOU KNOW? - CONTROL AND THE ORGANISATION

- *Could you can fill in the blanks? The answers are in bold. Use this page for revision purposes as you approach the exam.*
- Be sure that you feel comfortable using the language of control theory and cybernetics: inputs, processes and outputs; feedback and feedforward control; open and closed systems and so on. Make sure you realise that the control process is not as straightforward in practice as the theory suggests. Planning realistically is fraught with difficulties due to **the uncertainties of the environment** and **the unpredictability of people's behaviour**. Not all deviations from plan are controllable. Outputs and outcomes are often not easy to measure. The relationship between inputs and outputs may be impossible to determine. Formal controls may be cumbersome and out of touch with reality.
- Emmanuel et al describe four necessary conditions for control. A **programmed** decision is one whose outcome can be relied upon to turn out as expected. A **non-programmed** decision is subject to uncertainty about its outcome.

  TRY QUESTIONS 2, 3 AND 6
- Management accounting systems are used for a variety of purposes and this affects their design (the inputs and processes used and the outputs obtained). **Contingency** theorists try to identify the specific features of an organisation's context (environment, structure, culture, technology etc) that impact upon particular features of accounting system design. This approach has a number of limitations. Simons' and Goold and Campbell's works are also important. Newer ideas include symbolic interactionism, ethnomethodology, structuration theory, radical theory, and Foucault's ideas.

  TRY QUESTIONS 1, 4, 5, 7 AND 8
- Organisation structure is influenced by factors such as size, task, staff, environment, age, culture and management style. Know about delayering and empowerment, matrix structures and Business Process Re-engineering (BPR). Consider the methods and implications of divisionalisation, particularly the M-form.
- Culture in an organisation is the sum total of the **beliefs, knowledge, attitudes of mind** and **customs** to which people are exposed. Handy sums up culture as 'that's the way we do things round here'. For Schein, it is 'the pattern of basic assumptions ... that have worked well enough to be considered valid and, therefore, to be taught to new members as the correct way to perceive, think and feel in relation to problems.' An organisational culture may be negative or unhealthy but it can be changed.
- Handy identifies four basic types of organisational culture: **power** (small organisations influenced by a central source); **role** (bureaucracy); **task** (project teams and task forces): and **person** (individual interests).
- Motivation in an organisational sense refers to attempts to get people to put in more effort by various means such as targets and/or rewards. You should know about several different motivation theories. The most relevant to management accounting control systems research seems to be expectancy theory (the force of someone's motivation equals **their strength of preference for a certain outcome multiplied by their expectation that that outcome will in fact result from a certain behaviour**). Other useful theories include Maslow and Herzberg's **need** theories.
- Group behaviour and leadership are key factors influencing the effectiveness of organisations. According to Handy, group effectiveness depends upon **the 'givens', the 'intervening factors'** and **the 'outcomes'**. Handy identifies six types of leadership power: **physical, resource, position, expert, personal and negative power.**
- Ethics is the science of accepted rules or standards of behaviour. You should learn the CIMA Ethical Guidelines, especially the fundamental principles: **integrity, objectivity, professional competence and care, confidentiality, professional behaviour, technical standards and freedom from conflicts of interest**. Also be aware of the influence of corporate codes and standards and the organisational implications of ethical dilemmas.

  TRY QUESTIONS 9, 10,11 AND 12
- *Possible pitfall*
  - **Quoting the *CIMA Ethical Guidelines* at length without applying them to situations/ scenarios**

1 TUTORIAL QUESTION: IDEAS ABOUT CONTROL AND ORGANISATIONS

(a) What are the four necessary conditions for control, according to Emmanuel, Otley and Merchant?

(b) What does systems theory contribute to the understanding of how organisations operate?

(c) What is the relevance of radical theory to management accounting control systems?

(d) What are the attributes of multidivisional ('M-form') organisation structures?

(e) List some of the symptoms of group think.

(f) What factors influence organisational culture?

Approaching the question

1 Each of our answers except the answer to (c) includes at least four or five separate points. Try to answer with a sentence or two for each of your points, not just with one word answers or lists (except in the case of (e)).

2 This is a warming-up exercise, designed to get you thinking about *some* of the important issues in Part A of the syllabus. You may find question (c) difficult to answer, but if you have problems with any of the others you need to do more revision before tackling the exam questions that follow.

3 If you find these questions easy, start to think how your knowledge could be used in potential MCS exam question scenarios: the MD asking your advice on changing the organisation's culture (introducing TQM, say), the degree to which Emmanuel *et al*'s conditions apply in different types of business, and so on.

2 DIVISIONALISED STRUCTURES (5/95) *36 mins*

Divisionalised structures are normal in large firms, and occur even when centralised structures would be feasible.

Required

(a) Explain and discuss the arguments for divisionalised structures in large firms. **6 Marks**

(b) Explain the costs and potential inefficiencies of a divisionalised structure. **6 Marks**

(c) Explain how adoption of a divisionalised structure changes the role of top management and their control of subordinates. **8 Marks**

Total Marks = 20

3 MANAGEMENT CONTROL (5/97) *36 mins*

(a) Conventional approaches to the process of management control distinguish between strategic planning, management control, and task control. Formal hierarchical processes are recommended for these, especially management control and task control.

Required

Explain:

(i) the nature of problems and of decisions;
(ii) the systems and information requirements;
(iii) the levels of management involved;

for each of strategic planning, management control, and task (operational) control.

10 Marks

(b) Many organisational changes may make the boundaries of the organisation less precise and clear. These changes include:

(i) the growth of outsourcing of services and activities not regarded as core activities;

(ii) the increasing use of contract, part-time or temporary staff, who may not necessarily work at the organisation's offices;

(iii) the development of long-term relationships with customers and suppliers.

Required

Explain how the changes outlined above, which make the boundaries of the organisation less clear, may affect the management control process.

10 Marks

Total Marks = 20

4 TUTORIAL QUESTION: ACTIVATION, AGENCY, CONTINGENCY

(a) 'The central concept of modern motivation theory is that of activation ...the level of activation can be considered to be roughly determined by the multiplicative effect of three factors ... namely:

Activation = Uncertainty about the outcome of the event × Importance of the outcome of the event × Ability to influence the outcome of the event.'

(Emmanuel et al, *Accounting for Management Control*, 1990)

Required

(i) To what extent do you agree that 'activation' is central to modern motivation theories?

(ii) What is the relevance of activation to the design of management accounting control systems?

(b) What is agency theory and what are its advantages and limitations?

(c) What are the features of studies of management accounting control systems based on contingency theory?

Approaching the question

1 You don't need to know any more than you are told in the question to answer part (a). See if you can find parallels between the elements of activation and the other motivation theories you know about. Then think about how a MAS activates people.

2 The Syllabus Guidance Notes clearly state that agency theory will not form the basis of an entire question. This is your chance to acquire the basic understanding that you might need. If you cannot remember anything about agency theory, copy out the definition from your BPP Study Text and then read it critically, perhaps considering how far it applies to you and your job. Our answer gives you some new information which may help with your revision.

3 Question (c) should be easy if you have revised this area. We include strategy and culture in our answer.

5 CONTINGENCY THEORY, CULTURE AND ATTITUDE CHANGE (SPECIMEN PAPER) *36 mins*

There has been much research into the differences in management control systems between organisations. Much of this research has stressed the contingent factors affecting the organisation-contingency theory. But in recent years, more interest has developed in other approaches, including an interest in organisational culture.

Required

(a) Explain the main criticisms of contingency theory. **6 Marks**

(b) Handy* gives four varieties of organisation culture - Power (or club), Role, Task and Person (or existential). For each of these culture types, explain how the culture (and related contingency factors) is relevant to the design of effective management control systems. **Understanding Organisations* (1981) **7 Marks**

(c) Many organisations have undergone significant changes in aims and objectives. Examples include organisations transferred from the public sector to the private sector (such as telecommunications), or which, whilst remaining in the public sector, are expected to adopt a more commercial approach (such as higher education). Other examples could include changes in healthcare services, and changes in manufacturing companies which adopt Total Quality Management.

Explain how, in this sort of situation, changes in the management accounting system and the management control system can help change attitudes in the planned direction. **7 Marks**

Total Marks = 20

6 BUSINESS PROCESS RE-ENGINEERING (11/96) *36 mins*

Business process re-engineering (BPR) has been promoted as a major management technique, but is also criticised as little more than cost reduction.

Required

(a) Briefly explain business process re-engineering. **4 Marks**

(b) Explain the contribution the management accountant should make to the planning and implementation of a business process re-engineering programme. **8 Marks**

(c) Explain the main advantages and criticisms of business process re-engineering programmes. **8 Marks**

Total Marks = 20

7 STRUCTURE, CULTURE AND CONTROL SYSTEMS (11/96) *36 mins*

The A Group has been a very successful product innovator, and its shares were rated as a growth stock. Recently, with products reaching maturity, earnings have been erratic and the share price has fallen.

The Chairman commissioned a report from strategy consultants which recommended a change from a strategy of market leadership to one of cost leadership.

The Executive Directors, with the exception of the Finance Director, who was formerly the audit partner, have all spent their entire careers with the company. They have similar personal backgrounds, and have risen primarily from success in sales and marketing worldwide. Remuneration is by modest basic salaries, and bonuses on current profits. Share option schemes have been ineffective as the price/earnings ratio has progressively fallen. The Directors are formally responsible for separate product groups, but often have personal responsibility for sales to specific customers or relations with specific suppliers, regardless of product group.

Control has been exercised by informal meetings and discussions between the Directors and other senior long-service executives. Control systems have been simple financial control systems. These have emphasised the profit to be achieved in the current financial year as the key objective. There has been minimal long-term planning. Cash management has not been a problem, with little direct investment, and product development often by the acquisition (using shares) of smaller companies. Manufacture has frequently been contracted out.

Required

As Management Accountant, write a report to the Chairman, explaining what changes will be required in structure, culture, and control systems to implement the recommendations of the consultants' report.

Note: You are NOT required to discuss the merits of the proposed strategy.

20 Marks

8 PROMOTION (11/98)

36 mins

(a) Contingency theory has frequently been used to explain variations in the functioning of organisations. It has also been criticised on a number of grounds, including whether sufficient attention has been paid to people and culture.

Required

Explain and discuss, from a management control perspective, the criticism that contingency theory pays insufficient attention to the people in organisations and to organisational culture. **10 Marks**

(b) Some organisations have long-standing practices of promoting from existing staff, as a consequence of which they rarely recruit outsiders to any senior position. Staff turnover is very low. Other organisations have frequent management and structural changes, and often recruit senior managers from outside the organisation.

Required

Explain the differences in control systems and approaches to management control that could be expected with these alternative practices. **10 Marks**

Total Marks = 20

9 TUTORIAL QUESTION: ETHICS

We *outline* below two possible ethical dilemmas that may be faced by a management accountant.

(a) Cedric is manipulating his subsidiary's sales figures. His bonus is based on market share. He is the brother of your new boss, the Group Financial Director and you are working in Cedric's Division as internal auditor.

(b) The marketing director of your company frequently 'entertains' local government officials since the company tenders - usually successfully - for local government contracts. The expenditure on 'entertainment' is about three times what might be expected and includes substantial payments with no supporting documents. The financial director has asked you, his assistant, to hide a sizeable proportion of the expenditure in costs of sales.

Required

In each case, either by group discussion or on paper:

(i) briefly analyse the facts;

(ii) identify the organisational and ethical problems involved;

(iii) identify the major ethical principle(s) involved;

(iv) specify possible alternative actions;

(v) determine whether there is a single compelling principle; if not assess the major alternatives and their consequences;

(vi) decide what to do and how the action you propose might be implemented.

Approaching the question

1 The requirements ask you to perform an analysis in the way suggested in a *CIMA Student* article on ethics questions (August 1993). Exam questions may be structured like this or they may have different requirements, so be aware that you may have to be flexible in your approach. As you should know by now, you should always answer the question set, not one you prepared earlier.

2 We have been deliberately vague in our scenarios to promote discussion and alternative interpretations and solutions. A range of answers is likely to be acceptable: our answers are not comprehensive.

10 ETHICAL CONSIDERATIONS (11/95) *36 mins*

You were appointed Financial Controller of a firm of builders' merchants almost a year ago, with the prospect of becoming Finance Director if you performed well.

The problem customer

An old-established customer, a contractor, X Ltd, which has expanded to take on a very large contract, is causing problems with delayed payments. X Ltd is a family firm, largely owned by its Managing Director, Y.

Following a discussion at a management meeting, the Sales Director and a member of your staff visited the customer with instructions to 'try and resolve the matter of delayed payments'.

The meeting

At the meeting, the Sales Director took the lead, having known Y for many years. Y provided the last annual acccounts and the latest management accounts and contract accounts. This one large contract that X Ltd had undertaken represents some 70% of its current activity.

If all, or almost all, suppliers allow additional credit for material, and X Ltd uses its very limited remaining bank facilities to pay the workforce, Y thinks the company should be able to complete the next stage of the contract, get the architect to certify the work has been completed, and obtain a progress payment. This would enable X Ltd to pay suppliers, get more materials, and finish the contract. However, Y considers the company will make a significant loss on the contract and will only be able to trade on a much reduced scale thereafter.

The Sales Director suggested, and Y agreed, an arrangement by which Y would make a payment from personal funds, against which your company would release materials to X Ltd. When it receives the progress payment X Ltd will pay your company from its company's funds and reduce the amount owing to well within normal terms. Your company will then repay Y the personal funds he has paid.

It was agreed that this arrangement should be discussed and agreed with your Managing Director in the morning.

After the meeting

On his return, the Sales Director commented that this sort of arrangement was probably the only way of getting any money back - if X Ltd went into liquidation nothing would be recovered.

Later you received a telephone message that Z, the Finance Director of another firm of builders' merchants and whom you know through CIMA branch meetings, has asked you to telephone urgently regarding the credit status of X Ltd.

Required

Write a report to your Managing Director explaining the issues involved and recommending the action to be taken on the account and on the telephone message.

20 Marks

11 LARGE FINANCIAL SERVICES CO (11/97) *36 mins*

The chairman of a large financial services company, after discussion with the non-executive directors and the Audit Committee, has become concerned that the company is taking too many risks in its business operations.

The company has been very successful and has grown rapidly by being more innovative than its competitors in designing and selling new products. These include investment and savings plans and long-term loans to high-income individuals This has been achieved in a decentralised environment by rewarding product managers with substantial bonuses on current profits earned by products they have designed and for which they are responsible. Sales executives have been rewarded by high commissions on sales. The company has been successful in recruiting and retaining very able staff by providing the highest rewards in the industry. Staff have the maximum freedom to maximise their earnings.

Regulation of the industry has increased considerably, and is expected to increase further. There have been no major problems with the regulatory authorities. However, following a series of minor problems, some products have had to be withdrawn or modified and some sales staff have been disciplined. The company has often been criticised by consumer organisations and journalists for its treatment of customers, and its products appear poor value for money in comparative surveys.

The Chairman is proposing to introduce a company code of conduct with the aims of instilling ethical values and helping the company appear in a better light in newspapers and surveys.

Required

As Chief Internal Auditor, prepare a report on this proposal for the Audit Committee. In your report:

(a) explain the extent to which a code of conduct can help to change organisational culture and encourage ethical behaviour;

(b) propose any other changes, including possible control systems, that may be needed to achieve the Chairman's aims.

20 Marks

12 ENVIRONMENTAL AND SOCIAL ISSUES (5/99) *36 mins*

Z plc is a publicly quoted company. Its products are based on raw materials grown in tropical countries and processed either in these countries or in the eventual sales markets. Processing is undertaken partly by Z plc and partly by sub-contractors. The products are branded and sold worldwide, but mainly in the United Kingdom and North America. They are sold to consumers through a very large number of outlets.

The non-executive directors have for some time expressed concern that the company has not developed any systems of environmental or social reporting to shareholders, although many comparable companies already publish such information as part of their Annual Report. A government minister has now stated that legislation will be considered if all companies do not make progress on reporting on social and environmental policies.

The chief executive has always regarded reporting as ideally never exceeding legal requirements.

As management accountant, you have been asked by the finance director to draft a report to the Board on the potential environmental and social issues on which reporting may be required.

Required

Explain the process and the problems involved in preparing this report, dealing specifically with the following.

(a) Determining the range of environmental and social issues to cover in the annual report

(b) Determining the range of business activity to cover in the annual report

(c) Assessing the information requirements at Board level as well as the information to be published

Note. You are not required to discuss the environmental and social policy of Z plc.

20 Marks

DO YOU KNOW? - PLANNING AND CONTROL SYSTEMS

- *Check that you can fill in the blanks in the statements below before you attempt any questions. If in doubt, you should go back to your BPP Study Text and revise first.*
- Budgeting is a multi-purpose activity which has five principal roles: .... These roles may sometimes be in conflict.
- A traditional system of management accounting control has a hierarchy of budget centres, and clearly identified responsibilities for the achievement of budget targets. Types of budget centre include ...., ..., ..., ... and .... The choice depends upon what management wishes to achieve.
- Management involvement in the preparation of budgets and standards revolves around the problem of .... and ways of avoiding it. Managers are people and behave accordingly. Control systems may be subverted by overriding personal aspirations, mistrust, divided loyalties, poor communication, inappropriate management style and so on. Management must therefore be motivated to work towards the goals of the organisation.
- Motivation has two aspects: .... (running rather than walking) and .... (harmony of interests between the organisation and the individual). The writings of Argyris, Hofstede and Hopwood are of key importance, especially their views on the importance of participation.

  TRY QUESTIONS 15 AND 19
- The MCS examination is highly likely to test your practical skills in preparing and presenting reports to management so practise getting into role, laying out calculations (and particularly workings) neatly. Imagine that your report will actually be sent to the important people mentioned in the question and take appropriate account of their information needs.
- You should also think about management accounting reports in general. What information should a monthly report contain? How can the system be set up to produce reports to aid day to day decision making?
- All budgets are prepared under various resource constraints; the aim is to .... Linear programming may be necessary. In the longer term more resources can be obtained, for example by capital investment. Budgeting systems and investment appraisal systems may be difficult to harmonise. Never forget that a budget is a short-term means of controlling progress towards long-term strategic aims.

  TRY QUESTION 16
- Traditional management accounting systems are now widely regarded as inadequate for a modern business environment. You should be aware of the impact of .... (flexibility, production to order, shorter batch production runs and set up times, an emphasis on quality, minimal stocks of raw materials).

  TRY QUESTION 21
- Activity based approaches to management accounting (activity based costing/budgeting/ management and so on) relate costs to .... (the activities that cause or drive them). This requires a fresh look at every aspect of the business to gain a better understanding of the way the organisation operates, and how it could operate differently. In particular, it helps to identify and control .... activities.

  TRY QUESTIONS 14, 20 AND 22
- Budgeting is also affected by environmental influences, especially conditions of change like inflation, growing or declining markets, or new technology. Various methods have been devised for dealing with such situations including ...., ..., ..., ... and ....

  TRY QUESTIONS 13, 17 AND 18
- Variance analysis is a key part of the control process but it must be carried out judiciously. There are four basic types of cost-variance investigation model: ....

  TRY QUESTION 23
- An operational variance compares .... A planning variance compares ....
- *Possible pitfalls*

  Write down the mistakes you know you should avoid.

DID YOU KNOW? - PLANNING AND CONTROL SYSTEMS

- *Could you can fill in the blanks? The answers are in bold. Use this page for revision purposes as you approach the exam.*
- Budgeting is a multi-purpose activity which has five principal roles: **planning, communication; co-ordination; performance measurement; motivation**. These roles may sometimes be in conflict.
- A traditional system of management accounting control has a hierarchy of budget centres, and clearly identified responsibilities for the achievement of budget targets. Types of budget centre include **cost centres, revenue centres, profit centres, investment centres** and **performance centres**. The choice depends upon what management wishes to achieve.
- Management involvement in the preparation of budgets and standards revolves around the problem of **sub-optimality** and ways of avoiding it. Managers are people and behave accordingly. Control systems may be subverted by overriding personal aspirations, mistrust, divided loyalties, poor communication, inappropriate management style and so on. Management must therefore be motivated to work towards the goals of the organisation.
- Motivation has two aspects: **incentive** (running rather than walking) and **goal congruence** (harmony of interests between the organisation and the individual). The writings of Argyris, Hofstede and Hopwood are of key importance, especially their views on the importance of participation.

  TRY QUESTIONS 15 AND 19
- The MCS examination is highly likely to test your practical skills in preparing and presenting reports to management so practise getting into role, laying out calculations (and particularly workings) neatly. Imagine that your report will actually be sent to the important people mentioned in the question and take appropriate account of their information needs.
- You should also think about management accounting reports in general. What information should a monthly report contain? How can the system be set up to produce reports to aid day to day decision making?
- All budgets are prepared under various resource constraints; the aim is to **utilise resources in the optimum way**. Linear programming may be necessary. In the longer term more resources can be obtained, for example by capital investment. Budgeting systems and investment appraisal systems may be difficult to harmonise. Never forget that a budget is a short-term means of controlling progress towards long-term strategic aims.

  TRY QUESTION 16
- Traditional management accounting systems are now widely regarded as inadequate for a modern business environment. You should be aware of the impact of **just-in-time** (flexibility, production to order, shorter batch production runs and set up times, an emphasis on quality, minimal stocks of raw materials).

  TRY QUESTION 21
- Activity based approaches to management accounting (activity based costing/budgeting/ management and so on) relate costs to **cost drivers** (the activities that cause or drive them). This requires a fresh look at every aspect of the business to gain a better understanding of the way the organisation operates, and how it could operate differently. In particular, it helps to identify and control **non-value-added** activities.

  TRY QUESTIONS 14, 20 AND 22
- Budgeting is also affected by environmental influences, especially conditions of change like inflation, growing or declining markets, or new technology. Various methods have been devised for dealing with such situations including **rolling budgets, long-term contracts, sensitivity analysis, probability theory** and **simulation models**.

  TRY QUESTIONS 13, 17 AND 18
- Variance analysis is a key part of the control process but it must be carried out judiciously. There are four basic types of cost-variance investigation model: **a materiality significance model; a statistical model; a control charts model and a cost/benefit decision model**.

  TRY QUESTION 23
- An operational variance compares **actual results with a plan revised in hindsight**. A planning variance compares **the original plan with the revised plan**.
- *Possible pitfalls*
  - **Producing standard essays on and/or lists of modern techniques**
  - **Producing poorly structured reports**

13 DIVISION X (5/95) *72 mins*

As a management accountant in the head office of a large group, you have been asked to make a special study to help Division X in its decision on whether or not to decentralise its basic marketing decisions. This issue could need to be studied in other Divisions at a later stage.

Division X designs and sells special products which are manufactured on its behalf in the Far East. Each year it designs a new product, and plans and predicts sales in two distinct markets. It orders in January the necessary quantity to be delivered in November to achieve forecast sales in December. No additional orders can be placed during the year. Anything unsold after December is scrapped.

For next year, a product has been designed to sell at £200.

Purchasing

There are four potential suppliers who have quoted firm prices for the quantities offered.

Price per unit ordered

	Supplier K	*Supplier L*	*Supplier M*	*Supplier N*
Number ordered	£	£	£	£
1,000	70	90	130	110
2,000	65	80	120	110
3,000	60	70	120	110
4,000	60	70	130	110
5,000	60	70	-	-
6,000	60	70	-	-
7,000	80	-	-	-
8,000	90	-	-	-

The annual cost of working with each chosen supplier is £250,000. This cost relates to operating quality control at their factories, and to storing finished products for sale in December. It is important that suppliers are chosen only if the revenues from sales of products purchased from them exceed the associated fixed costs.

Marketing - centralised

The present structure is centralised. There are fixed costs of £200,000 for designing and planning the basic marketing approach, and £100,000 per market for the marketing and selling in each market.

Sales demand has been forecast.

Probability	*Unit sales*
0.2	14,000
0.2	16,000
0.2	18,000
0.2	20,000
0.2	22,000

Marketing - decentralised

If decision making and marketing were decentralised, the central design and planning cost would be unchanged, the cost of marketing and selling in each market would be £40,000 plus 5% of sales.

However, with decentralisation, higher sales demand is forecast.

Market X1		*Market X2*	
Probability	*Unit sales*	*Probability*	*Unit sales*
0.3	9,000		
0.4	10,000	0.2	10,000
0.3	11,000	0.6	11,000
		0.2	12,000
1.0		1.0	

Required

(a) Make appropriate calculations and recommendations to Division X *based on these calculations.*

(i) For both centralised and decentralised marketing situations, calculate the minimum quantities which should be purchased from each supplier, based on their price quotations.

You should ignore sales demand for this part of the question. **10 Marks**

(ii) Whether to retain the centralised structure, or to adopt a decentralised structure.

For this part of the question you should take into account all the information in the scenario. **15 Marks**

(b) Explain the limitations of the approach taken to the ascertainment of risk and its evaluation and explain the alternative possible approaches. **7 Marks**

(c) A modelling approach has been taken in the use of probabilities in this scenario and its evaluation. There is a wide range of modelling techniques.

Explain how a formal financial modelling approach can assist in performance evaluation in a large group. **8 Marks**

Total Marks = 40

14 X DIVISION (5/96) *72 mins*

Background

X Division assembles and sells specialist electronic equipment. Component parts, which are often sub-assemblies, are sourced worldwide by the purchasing department, from manufacturers able to meet demanding quality standards. Products are then assembled, tested and sold. The assembly cycle time is quite short, days not weeks. Considerable progress has been made towards both total quality management (TQM) and just-in-time (JIT).

An approximate breakdown of product costs, based on the current financial year, is as follows.

Material	72%
Labour	4%
Overhead	24%
	100%

This varies between products. It excludes sales and marketing costs and substantial product development costs.

Alternative ways of making a new product

The cost of a new product is under review, as there are two alternative ways of making the product.

- Method E: entirely using existing components used in other products.

- Method N: using, in addition to some existing components, a new sub-assembly from a new supplier. This new sub-assembly will eliminate the need for two existing components.

The forecast volume for the new product is 300 units per year. Components that are common to both methods E and N are also used in other products; the average total quantity of each component used last year was 12,000 per component.

Summary data for the alternative methods and Division X

	Method E	*Method N*	*Division X last year*
	£ per unit	*£ per unit*	*£ total*
Assembly-related overhead			15,500,000
Material-related overhead			15,500,000
Material cost	653.00	612.00	134,000,000
Labour cost	39.90	35.15	
	Method E	*Method N*	*Division X last year*
	Per unit	*Per unit*	*Total*
Total quantity of components used	88	87	8,880,000
Number of different components	18	17	740
Number of suppliers	7	8	170

Overhead apportionment

There are several methods of apportioning overheads. Last year, direct labour cost was used as the basis for all overhead apportionment, and on that basis manufacturing cost for the two alternatives would be as follows.

Unit cost	*Method E*	*Method N*
	£	£
Material	653.00	612.00
Labour	39.90	35.15
Overhead (600%)	239.40	210.90
	932.30	858.05

It was decided for the current year to adopt a system of overhead apportionment which provides for a separate analysis of assembly and testing overhead (assembly-related) and material procurement and scheduling overhead (material-related).

In this approach, overhead is considered 50% related to the assembly and testing processes; this is charged to products as a percentage on the labour cost. The other 50% relates to the material procurement and scheduling, for which three apportionment bases were considered.

- **Material cost basis**

  The initial basis considered was to charge material-related overhead as a percentage on material cost.

- **Total quantity of components basis**

  An alternative basis considered was a simple one-stage calculation of material-related overhead based on the total quantity of all components used.

- **Transactions basis**

  The transactions basis involves a two-stage calculation

  - The total material-related overhead is divided by the number of different components.
  - This cost per different component is then divided by the quantity of that component to give a unit cost per component.

  The transactions basis was adopted, and is currently used for material-related overhead.

Required

(a) Calculate the manufacturing cost of the proposed new product, made with existing parts (Method E) *and* also with the new sub-assembly (Method N). For the material-related overhead, use the following bases of calculating overheads.

(i) The material basis
(ii) The total quantity of components basis
(iii) The transactions basis (the number of different components used)

Comment on your results and make an appropriate recommendation on whether the new sub-assembly should be used. Also explain precisely what further information you would wish to have to improve the accuracy of your analysis, and whether it would be likely to change your recommendation. **20 Marks**

(b) The financial director of X division made the following statement.

'We chose an apportionment basis - the number of different components. We could have chosen labour; in fact, we used to last year. We could have chosen material value; we could have chosen anything - but our goal is to influence behaviour, not to create a five-decimal accounting number that is very precise and not very accurate.'

Explain, on the basis of the above quotation, how the choice of an overhead apportionment basis can influence behaviour: give examples and discuss the problems which arise from this. **10 Marks**

(c) Explain, in a report to the Finance Director, how you would assess the performance of the purchasing department. Include in your report an explanation of any quantitative measures you would use, the sources of the necessary information, and the extent to which you would rely on these measures. **10 Marks**

Total Marks = 40

15 PARTICIPATION (5/97) *36 mins*

There is an extensive literature on participation by managers in the budgeting process, and wide discussion of the rights of all employees to participate in some way in the management and control of their work.

Some firms have introduced systems of works councils in response to the new environment; some have voluntarily used these systems for some considerable time.

Required

(a) Explain the arguments for, and problems arising from, managers participating in setting their budget targets. **8 Marks**

(b) Explain the arguments for, and problems arising from, employee participation in budgeting and in the determination of company policy. **6 Marks**

(c) Explain the circumstances in which systems of participation (for managers and/or employees) are likely to operate successfully. **6 Marks**

Total Marks = 20

16 EF (11/97) *36 mins*

EF is a division of a large group, and is in the food processing industry. It employs about 1,000 people in a number of plants in isolated rural areas, processing and packing food sold mainly through supermarkets.

There has recently been a considerable body of new regulation, following a series of incidents, some of which were extensively publicised. These have raised significant concern regarding public health.

There have also been sudden major changes in demand, to the extent that it now appears unlikely that demand would exceed 50% of budget. Indeed, it seems that future demand may never again reach these levels. Hence it is clear that major cuts are needed in capacity. The budget for the financial year which started one month ago was prepared on the assumption that demand would be similar to previous demand.

Required

(a) Explain your role, as division management accountant of EF, in helping management within EF to produce and justify to head office a preferred solution to the problems of overcapacity. Recommend how activity should be reported against the original budget and any revised forecast during the remainder of the financial year. **14 Marks**

(b) Explain how a senior management accountant at head office would review the proposed solution to the overcapacity problem, and determine the solution's adequacy and effectiveness. **6 Marks**

Total Marks = 20

17 CUMBERSOME PROCESS (5/98) *36 mins*

Budgeting has been criticised as

- a cumbersome process which occupies considerable management time;
- concentrating unduly on short-term financial control;
- having undesirable effects on the motivation of managers;
- emphasising formal organisation structure.

Required

(a) Explain these criticisms. **8 Marks**

(b) Explain what changes can be made in response to these criticisms to improve the budgeting process. **12 Marks**

Total Marks = 20

18 PROPOSED CHANGES (11/98) *36 mins*

The newly appointed group finance director of a medium-sized quoted company has expressed considerable dissatisfaction with the budget prepared before his appointment. He considered that the comparisons of the budget with the results of the first quarter of the current financial year, which he had recently reviewed, were far from helpful in understanding changes in the business environment. He proposes significant changes in the process of budget preparation for next year.

In the past, budgets have been prepared after the third quarter's results were known and the fourth quarter forecast prepared. This timetable left finance staff very little time to prepare the budgets before the end of the financial year and the start of the new year. The group finance director proposes that the preparation of the budget for the next financial year should be commenced after the half-year results for the current financial year have been completed.

The group finance director wishes to implement the change in the current year, preparing the budget for the next financial year, but there are three problems.

- Division A has no managing director. He resigned after very poor results for the first quarter followed disappointing results for the last financial year. A search is being made for a new managing director, almost certainly an external appointment, but this could take several months. In the meantime, the divisional financial director is acting as managing director as well as carrying out his own duties.
- Division B has launched in the first quarter of this year a new product range aiming at a new group of customers. This is effectively a new marketing strategy.
- Division C is installing new plant which will not be fully operational until the third quarter. There are some doubts whether the plant will produce, without modification, products of acceptable quality, as customer requirements have changed since the plant was ordered.

Required

Prepare a report, on behalf of the group finance director, to the board, explaining the reasons for the proposed changes in budget preparation and planning for next year.

Discuss the three specific problems and any other anticipated difficulties, and advise how they could be dealt with in the new proposed system.

20 Marks

19 BUDGETARY PADDING (5/99) *36 mins*

An article in *Management Accounting* concluded that there will always be some budgetary padding in any organisation.

Required

(a) As management accountant, write a report to your finance director, explaining what steps can be taken by you and by senior management when approving budgets, to minimise budgetary slack **8 Marks**

(b) The finance director, having read the report referred to in part (a), discussed the problem with the managing director and suggested that appropriate action be taken to reduce budgetary slack.

The managing director expressed doubts, stating that in his opinion removing all budget padding could cause considerable problems.

Explain the arguments that can be advanced for accepting some budgetary slack, and the advantages of this to the manager being appraised and to the organisation. Discuss whether the budget review and approval process should permit managers to build in some budgetary slack. **12 Marks**

Total Marks = 20

20 ABC AND SERVICE ORGANISATIONS (SPECIMEN PAPER) *36 mins*

Large service organisations, such as banks and hospitals, used to be noted for their lack of standard costing systems, and their relatively unsophisticated budgeting and control systems compared with large manufacturing organisations. But this is changing and many large service organisations are now revising their use of management accounting techniques.

Required

(a) Explain which features of large-scale service organisations encourage the application of Activity Based approaches to the analysis of cost information.

6 Marks

(b) Explain which features of service organisations may create problems for the application of Activity Based Costing. **4 Marks**

(c) Explain the uses for activity based cost information in service industries. **4 Marks**

(d) Many large service organisations were at one time state-owned, but have been privatised. Examples in some countries include electricity supply and telecommunications. They are often regulated. Similar systems of regulation of prices by an independent authority exist in many countries, and are designed to act as a surrogate for market competition in industries where it is difficult to ensure a genuinely competitive market.

Explain which aspects of cost information and systems in service organisations would particularly interest a regulator, and why these features would be of interest. **6 Marks**

Total Marks = 20

21 JUST-IN-TIME (11/95) *36 mins*

Just-in-time (JIT) systems are coming into increasing use in manufacturing, with varying degrees of success. One result of this can be purchasing and production each period of a large number of different products in small quantities, rather than large quantities of relatively few products.

Required

(a) Explain how the benefits claimed for JIT should affect profits and product costs, and how these benefits should appear in routine control information. **12 Marks**

(b) Explain the possible changes in routine factory accounting and control systems that may become necessary with a transition to JIT. **8 Marks**

Total Marks = 20

22 ABC AND ABB (11/98) *36 mins*

The basic ideas justifying the use of activity based costing (ABC) and activity based budgeting (ABB) are well publicised, and the number of applications has increased. However, there are apparently still significant problems in changing from existing systems.

Required

(a) Explain which characteristics of an organisation, such as its structure, product range, or environment, may make the use of activity based techniques particularly useful. **5 Marks**

(b) Explain the problems that may cause an organisation to decide not to use, or to abandon use of, activity based techniques. **8 Marks**

(c) Some categorisation of cost drivers provide hierarchical models.

- Unit-level activities
- Batch activities
- Product sustaining activities
- Facility sustaining activities

Other analyses focus on 'value adding' and 'non-value adding' activities.

Explain what is meant by 'non-value adding activities', and discuss the usefulness of this form of analysis. **7 Marks**

Total Marks = 20

23 VARIANCE INVESTIGATION (11/97) *36 mins*

Variance investigation decisions are normally explained in textbooks by simple models, which assume the availability of a significant amount of information.

An example of this approach is:

The managers estimate the probability of any variance being due to a controllable, and therefore correctable, cause at 25%. They estimate the cost of investigating a variance at £1,400, and the cost of correcting the cause of a correctable variance at £400. The investigation process is regarded as 100% reliable in that a correctable cause of the variance will be found if it exists.

Managers estimate the loss due to not investigating, and hence not discovering, a correctable cause of the variance, averages 75% of the size of the variance. For example, the loss from the failure to discover a correctable £4,000 variance would be £3,000.

Required

(a) Calculate the minimum size of variance that would justify investigation. **8 Marks**

(b) In addition to the approach described above, alternative approaches exist to decide whether to investigate variances by using criteria related to the absolute size of the variance, and criteria based on the percentage from standard.

(i) Explain why these approaches are taken rather than the approach described in (a) above.

(ii) Comment on the appropriateness of the alternative approaches described above. **12 Marks**

Total Marks = 20

DO YOU KNOW? - PERFORMANCE AND MANAGEMENT CONTROL

- *Check that you can fill in the blanks in the statements below before you attempt any questions. If in doubt, you should go back to your BPP Study Text and revise first.*
- Approaches to performance measurement include the use of critical success factors, the balanced scorecard, ideal income and strategic value analysis. Three possible points of reference of measurement are ...., ... and .... Financial performance measures, operational performance indicators, multiple measures of performance (such as the balanced scorecard approach) and external intelligence (such as schemes of .... and ....) can also be used.
- A distinction should be made between judging the performance of business units and the performance of the managers of those units. Besides accounting measures, organisations use .... and .... to assess managerial performance.
- Agency theory sees the relationship between an organisation's owners and managers as ....
- Any reward can be linked with any performance measure(s): the problem is .... Various incentive schemes exist, but there are problems associated with them.
- Performance-related rewards may encourage managers to run rather than walk towards the organisation's goals but it is difficult to devise a fair scheme and one that does not risk encouraging dysfunctional behaviour.
- Decentralisation frees senior management from routine planning and control activities, allowing them to concentrate on strategic development, co-ordination and control. However there is an increased likelihood that .... decisions will be made.

  TRY QUESTIONS 29, 30, 32 AND 33
- Support departments need to be evaluated to ensure that they are making good use of resources. Problems include defining the boundaries of a service and identifying outputs or benefits .... of activities that are not central to an organisation's purpose is becoming very common.

  TRY QUESTIONS 28, 35, 37 AND 39
- .... is the most commonly-used measure of divisional financial performance. It can be calculated in various ways and concentrates on the short term. ..... tends to encourage better investment decisions.
- Many organisations are discovering the usefulness of non-financial indicators relating to ...., ..., ... and so on. This kind of information is more relevant to its users, quicker to provide and easier to understand.

  TRY QUESTIONS 24, 25, 26, 27, 31, 34, 36 AND 40
- Quality has been elevated into a philosophy that guides every activity within a business. Quality costs can be classified as ...., ..., ... and .... costs.
- Evaluation of the performance of services will focus upon how the service is using up resources, what the resources cost and whether improved efficiency is possible. One problem is that outputs can be difficult to quantify because services are ...., ..., ... and .... Fitzgerald *et al* recommend the use of a range of performance measures covering six 'dimensions'.
- Differences in ...., ... and .... must be taken into account when assessing the performance of multinational organisations.
- There are certain differences between not-for-profit and commercial organisations but there are also, increasingly, similarities between the sectors, as .... is introduced in the public sector and private sector organisations become more and more .... Performance measurement in the not-for-profit organisation has traditionally been seen as highly problematic

  TRY QUESTIONS 38, 41, 42, 43, 44, 45 AND 46
- *Possible pitfalls*

  Write down the mistakes you know you should avoid.

DID YOU KNOW? - PERFORMANCE AND MANAGEMENT CONTROL

- *Could you fill in the blanks? The answers are in bold. Use this page for revision purposes as you approach the exam.*
- Approaches to performance measurement include the use of critical success factors, the balanced scorecard, ideal income and strategic value analysis. Three possible points of reference of measurement are **profitability**, **activity** and **productivity**. Financial performance measures, operational performance indicators, multiple measures of performance (such as the balanced scorecard approach) and external intelligence (such as schemes of **interfirm comparison** and **benchmarking**) can also be used.
- A distinction should be made between judging the performance of business units and the performance of the managers of those units. Besides accounting measures, organisations use **subjective judgement** and **upward appraisal** to assess managerial performance.
- Agency theory sees the relationship between an organisation's owners and managers as **a contract, with both parties trying to maximise their utility**.
- Any reward can be linked with any performance measure(s): the problem is **finding the right reward and finding an effective way of linking it with desired performance**. Various incentive schemes exist, but there are problems associated with them.
- Performance-related rewards may encourage managers to run rather than walk towards the organisation's goals but it is difficult to devise a fair scheme and one that does not risk encouraging dysfunctional behaviour.
- Decentralisation frees senior management from routine planning and control activities, allowing them to concentrate on strategic development, co-ordination and control. However there is an increased likelihood that **dysfunctional** decisions will be made.

  TRY QUESTIONS 29, 30, 32 AND 33
- Support departments need to be evaluated to ensure that they are making good use of resources. Problems include defining the boundaries of a service and identifying outputs or benefits. **Outsourcing** of activities that are not central to an organisation's purpose is becoming very common.

  TRY QUESTIONS 28, 35, 37, AND 39
- **ROI** is the most commonly-used measure of divisional financial performance. It can be calculated in various ways and concentrates on the short term. **RI** tends to encourage better investment decisions.
- Many organisations are discovering the usefulness of non-financial indicators relating to **quality, customer complaints, lead times** and so on. This kind of information is more relevant to its users, quicker to provide and easier to understand.

  TRY QUESTIONS 24, 25, 26, 27, 31, 34, 36 AND 40
- Quality has been elevated into a philosophy that guides every activity within a business. Quality costs can be classified as **prevention**, **appraisal**, **internal failure** and **external failure** costs.
- Evaluation of the performance of services will focus upon how the service is using up resources, what the resources cost and whether improved efficiency is possible. One problem is that outputs can be difficult to quantify because services are **intangible**, **perishable**, **heterogeneous** and **are produced and consumed simultaneously**. Fitzgerald *et al* recommend the use of a range of performance measures covering six 'dimensions'.
- Differences in **national culture, tradition** and **behaviour** must be taken into account when assessing the performance of multinational organisations.
- There are certain differences between not-for-profit and commercial organisations but there are also, increasingly, similarities between the sectors, as **competition** is introduced in the public sector and private sector organisations become more and more **customer focused**. Performance measurement in the not-for-profit organisation has traditionally been seen as highly problematic

  TRY QUESTIONS 38, 41, 42, 43, 44, 45 AND 46
- *Possible pitfalls*
  - **Inability to select an appropriate technique to deal with numerical questions and producing incoherent and often illegible workings and careless arithmetic**
  - **Displaying a lack of knowledge of topics covered at an earlier stage**

24 TUTORIAL QUESTION: COMPUTATION OF PERFORMANCE MEASURES

ABE Ltd and KIM Ltd are two newly established divisions of RAT plc. They operate as independent trading units, though some of their final product markets overlap.

The managing directors each agreed an initial plan based on a 20% per annum charge for capital by RAT plc. The plan showed both divisions to be capable of meeting the 20% target.

During the course of the first year's operations, ABE Ltd secured a contract to supply items to LO plc, a company not within the RAT group and a direct competitor in KIM Ltd's market. KIM Ltd could have purchased the same supplies from ABE Ltd but preferred to buy from a supplier outside the RAT group.

In the first year of operation LO plc secured a 5% increase (in relative terms) in its share of the market at the expense of KIM Ltd, based on the previous market size. A major factor in LO plc's success was considered to be the superiority of ABE Ltd's product over those of its competitors.

KIM Ltd and LO plc were each initially expected to have a 50% share in the final product market, the latter being KIM Ltd's sole market outlet.

The key elements of the budgets agreed at the outset by ABE Ltd and KIM Ltd are:

	ABE Ltd	*KIM Ltd*
Initial investment in plant and equipment (£m)	10	15
Cost of capital charge	20%	20%
Expected net cash flows in £m:		
First year	1.9	3.2
Years 2 - 8, per annum	2.9	4.2

Assume that:

- the operating efficiencies of KIM Ltd and LO plc are broadly the same;
- the 5% increase in the market share made by LO plc results in a pro rata 5% increase in ABE Ltd's net cash flow.

Required

(a) Evaluate the two divisions' expected performances as seen by RAT plc at the time of their establishment.

(b) Evaluate the actual performance of the two divisions in their first year of operation, giving a reasoned interpretation of the outcomes.

Note. Taxation is to be ignored.

Approaching the question

1. 'Evaluate' means more than just 'calculate a few numbers' - it includes an element of judgement so you must comment on the figures you calculate.
2. You are given enough information to measure performance by ROI, RI and NPV, but you will have to make (and state) assumptions about depreciation and the way ROI and RI are to be calculated.
3. Your 'reasoned interpretation' in part (b) should include a numerical comparison of the expected and actual outcomes of each division, and of the two divisions combined, plus comments as appropriate. Begin, though, by explaining why you cannot use the DCF approach for this part of the question.

25 TUTORIAL QUESTION: RESIDUAL INCOME AND ROI

Residual Income and Return on Investment are commonly used measures of performance. However, they are frequently criticised for placing too great an emphasis on the achievement of short-term results, possibly damaging longer-term performance.

Required

Discuss the following.

(a) The issues involved in the long-term:short-term conflict referred to in the above statement

(b) Suggestions which have been made to reconcile this difference

Approaching the question

1 Tackle tutorial question 24 before this one, because the two questions are linked and question 24 will give you ideas for your answer here.

2 Part (a) requires straightforward book knowledge.

3 Part (b) tests your awareness of the issues in greater depth. Consider asset values, the use of DCF, post-audit and non-financial measures.

26 BALANCED SCORECARD (MCA, 11/93) *36 mins*

Recent articles have focused on summary information for running a business and on a 'balanced scorecard' approach, using a number of performance measures.

Required

Explain the following.

(a) The arguments for using the profit measure as the all-encompassing measure of the performance of a business **6 Marks**

(b) The limitations of this profit-measurement approach and of undue dependence on the profit measure **8 Marks**

(c) The problems of using a broad range of non-financial measures for the short- and long-term control of a business **6 Marks**

Total Marks = 20

27 DESTROYING VALUE (11/98) *72 mins*

The most recent published results for V plc are shown below.

	£m
19X7 profit before tax	13.6
Summary consolidated balance sheet at 31 December 19X7	
Fixed assets	35.9
Current assets	137.2
Less: current liabilities	(95.7)
Net current assets	41.5
Total assets less current liabilities	77.4
Borrowings	(15.0)
Deferred tax provisions	(7.6)
Net assets	54.8
Capital and reserves	54.8

An analyst working for a stockbroker has taken these published results, made the adjustments shown below, and has reported his conclusion that 'the management of V plc is destroying value'.

Analyst's adjustments to profit before tax

		£m
Profit before tax		13.6
Adjustments		
Add:	Interest paid (net)	1.6
	R&D (research and development)	2.1
	Advertising	2.3
	Amortisation of goodwill	1.3
Less:	Taxation paid	(4.8)
Adjusted profit		16.1

Analyst's adjustments to summary consolidated balance sheet at 31 December 19X7

		£m	
Capital and reserves		54.8	
Adjustments			
Add:	Borrowings	15.0	
	Deferred tax provisions	7.6	
	R&D	17.4	Last 7 years' expenditure
	Advertising	10.5	Last 5 years' expenditure
	Goodwill	40.7	Written off against reserves on acquisitions in previous years
Adjusted capital employed		146.0	
Required return		17.5	12% cost of capital
Adjusted profit		16.1	
Value destroyed		1.4	

The chairman of V plc has obtained a copy of the analyst's report.

Required

(a) Explain, as management accountant of V plc, in a report to your chairman, the principles of the approach taken by the analyst. Comment on the treatment of the specific adjustments to R&D, advertising, interest and borrowings and goodwill.

12 Marks

(b) Having read your report, the chairman wishes to know which division or divisions are 'destroying value', when the current internal statements show satisfactory returns on investment (ROIs). The following summary statement is available.

Divisional performance, 19X7

	Division A (Retail) £m	*Division B (Manufacturing)* £m	*Division C (Services)* £m	*Head office* £m	*Total* £m
Turnover	81.7	63.2	231.8	-	376.7
Profit before interest and tax	5.7	5.6	5.8	(1.9)	15.2
Total assets *less* current liabilities	27.1	23.9	23.2	3.2	77.4
ROI	21.0%	23.4%	25.0%		

Some of the adjustments made by the analyst can be related to specific divisions:

- Advertising relates entirely to Division A (retail)
- R & D relates entirely to Division B (manufacturing)

- Goodwill write-offs relate to

Division B (Manufacturing)	£10.3m
Division C (Services)	£30.4m

- The deferred tax relates to

Division B (Manufacturing)	£1.4m
Division C (Services)	£6.2m

- Borrowings and interest, per divisional accounts, are as follows.

	Division A (Retail)	*Division B (Manufact-uring)*	*Division C (Services)*	*Head office*	*Total*
	£m	£m	£m	£m	£m
Borrowings	-	6.6	6.9	1.5	15.0
Interest paid/(received)	(0.4)	0.7	0.9	0.4	1.6

Required

Explain, with appropriate comment, in a report to the chairman, where 'value is being destroyed'. Your report should include:

- a statement of divisional performance;
- an explanation of any adjustments you make;
- a statement and explanation of the assumptions made; and
- comment on the limitations of the answers reached.

20 Marks

(c) The use of ROI has often been criticised as emphasising short-term profit, but many companies continue to use the measure. Explain the role of ROI in managing business performance, and how the potential problems of short-termism may be overcome. **8 Marks**

Total Marks = 40

28 TUTORIAL QUESTION: INTERNAL SERVICE DEPARTMENT

In establishing a charge to departments utilising an internal service department, the following issues may be given attention.

- The charge could be determined entirely irrespective of use, variable dependent upon use, or a combination of these two.
- The charge could be based on actual or budgeted costs, with or without a profit mark-up.
- Estimated market rates could be used.

Required

Discuss each of these issues in relation to the following.

(a) The assessment of the performance of the service department.

(b) The action of user departments in the achievement of their own and organisational objectives.

Approaching the question

1 Try not to produce a rambling essay about transfer pricing and goal congruence. You will be able to give some structure to your thoughts and to your answer if you deal separately with each distinct part of the question in the way that we have done in our solution.

2 Think about how costs will be controlled with each method of charging and whether use of the department will be encouraged or discouraged.

29 OWNERS AND MANAGERS (SPECIMEN PAPER) *36 mins*

(a) In a company which depends on regular investment in new model design to generate profits, management must select projects under the following conditions.

- The funds available for investment are a maximum of £2,500,000.
- Fixed costs of £100,000 per annum must be met as well as the cost of capital.
- The cost of capital is 10%.
- Cash flows must show a rising trend over the next three years, and, subject to this condition, the best net present value (NPV) of cash flows over these three years. (This is because the owners wish to sell the company after three years.)

The following projects (which are not divisible) are available.

Project		*A*	*B*	*C*	*D*	*E*	*F*
	Year	£'000	£'000	£'000	£'000	£'000	£'000
Investment	0	500	600	900	1,000	1,000	600
Net cash inflows/	1	400	300	-	(200)	(400)	200
(outflows):	2	400	300	500	600	1,400	900
	3	-	300	1,000	1,700	1,200	400
	4	-	300	800	-	-	-

Required

From the perspective of the owners, select the projects which meet the stated conditions and show the maximum NPV of cash flows over three years.

8 Marks

(b) Managers have in the past received bonuses based on annual accounting profits.

Required

If this system of paying bonuses were to be continued, which projects would managers prefer to select? Managers do not know about the owners' wish to sell the company.

Comment on the differences between the managers' choice of projects and the owners' preferences. Assume, for simplicity, that depreciation is straight-line over the project life. **4 Marks**

(c) It has been suggested that a new performance measurement scheme for business units could be based on discounting future estimated cash flows.

Required

Explain how this could be done, and the advantages and disadvantages of such schemes. **8 Marks**

Total Marks = 20

30 MANAGERIAL MOTIVATION (5/96) *36 mins*

The problems of the short-term bias in accounting measures of performance are explained by many writers on management accounting. There is a range of actions that profit-responsible managers can take that would increase short-term profit, as measured, possibly at the expense of long-term profits.

Many commentators assume that managers should be discouraged from taking short-term approaches.

Required

(a) Explain the circumstances in which a short-term approach by a profit centre manager is appropriate, and should be encouraged. **8 Marks**

(b) Explain the difficulties with each of the following approaches which are designed to encourage the adoption of longer-term views by profit-responsible managers.

(i) Regular review of one or more key performance indicators, other than accounting profit

(ii) Promising rewards for long-term profit centre performance, or for individual managerial performance, however defined

(iii) Reducing the pressure on managers to achieve short-term results **12 Marks**

Total Marks = 20

31 CONTROLLABILITY (11/96) *36 mins*

Controllability is one of the main principles of responsibility accounting. It implies that managers should be substantially in control of all items which contribute to the measurement used to assess their performance.

However, there is some case study evidence that divisional managers are assessed using divisional management accounts which include uncontrollable items.

Required

(a) Explain briefly the arguments for using the controllability principle in divisional management accounts. **6 Marks**

(b) Explain why large diversified firms may not adopt this principle in their divisional management accounts.

Comment on the inclusion of the following in divisional management accounts used for assessing divisional managerial performance.

(i) Interest

(ii) Head office expenses

(iii) Major changes in economic circumstances which have led to a significant change in industry volume **14 Marks**

Total Marks = 20

32 REMUNERATION (5/97) *36 mins*

(a) As a consequence of the Cadbury and Greenbury reports, there is increasing disclosure in the accounts of public companies of the procedures for determining the remuneration of directors, and the actual remuneration.

The following statements are quoted from recent accounts:

'The (two) non-executive directors constitute the Remuneration Committee.'

'No member of the committee has a personal financial interest, other than as a shareholder, in the matters to be decided. There are no conflicts of interest arising from cross directorships....'

'The Chairman has a service contract with a notice period of three years. This was originally drawn up in 1987 and was considered at that time to afford protection for the Group against the loss of the services of a key executive. ....the Board does not intend to seek to vary the terms.'

Required

Explain the significance in corporate governance of each of the above *three* statements. **6 Marks**

(b) Under contractual remuneration arrangements, the Chief Executive of X Group received in 19X6, as disclosed in the annual report and accounts:

	£
Salary	316,000
Bonus	50,000
Employee profit-sharing scheme	8,000
Benefits	21,000

He has a three-year rolling contract. The Group contribution to his pension scheme was £85,000.

The bonus is determined by the Remuneration Committee, and is non-pensionable. It is based on the Committee's assessment of the annual performance of the company and the individual's contribution thereto. The bonus may not exceed 25% of salary. Participation in the employee profit-sharing scheme is limited to £8,000. The benefits relate to the use of a company car and accommodation.

In addition to the above, the contract provides that the Chief Executive can receive, as part of his remuneration package, the following.

(i) A conditional allocation of ordinary shares, which may be approved annually by the Remuneration Committee, based on a percentage of salary not exceeding 50%.

Shares are held by trustees during the measurement period of three years.

Vesting (formal ownership and possession) of the shares is subject to a performance test at the end of the period. The test involves ranking the total shareholder return (TSR) against those of other top 100 companies (FT-SE 100).

(1) An upper quartile ranking will produce 100% vesting, a lower quartile zero.

(2) The calculation of intermediate points is linear.

The shares required are purchased in the market. Conditional allocations are expected to be at 50% of salary (the maximum).

(ii) Share options may be granted, at the market price at the date of grant. The maximum share options granted in a three-year period cannot exceed four times annual salary.

These cannot be exercised for three years, and can be exercised only if the percentage growth of the TSR of the company equals or exceeds that of the average of the FT-SE 100 companies.

Required

Analyse and explain the motivational effect on the Chief Executive of each element of the remuneration package, and of the total package. **14 Marks**

Total Marks = 20

33 BONUS SCHEMES (5/99) *36 mins*

It has been suggested that optimal bonus schemes for profit centre managers promise significant rewards for the achievement of challenging targets in areas they can influence. These schemes balance short-term pressure with incentives to maintain a long-term focus and protect managers from the distorting effects of uncontrollable factors.

It has also been suggested that many bonus schemes have additional features with different motivational effects.

Required

(a) The following are two possible features of bonus schemes.

- Limiting the range of performance within which rewards are linked to results, in particular ignoring losses and limiting maximum payments
- Linking incentive payments wholly or partly to the profit of the organisation as a whole

Explain why bonus schemes might include these features.

Explain the effects of incorporating these features in bonus schemes **14 Marks**

(b) Bonus schemes are normally designed to motivate full-time employees who have no other employment and are wholly dependent upon the organisation for their income. Part-time employees and short-term employees might not be included.

Describe and justify the possible features of bonus schemes which are designed to motivate non-executive directors who are part-time and remunerated by fees under contracts for a fixed term of years. **6 Marks**

Total Marks = 20

34 TUTORIAL QUESTION: DIVISIONALISED ORGANISATION

As a result of entry into new products and markets, a company is adopting a divisionalised organisation structure and is considering its accounting information system (AIS).

Required

(a) Discuss the requirements such a company faces in developing an AIS which provides and communicates information for planning and control at the levels of both top management and divisional management.

(b) Assess the main features to be recognised in the operation of performance measures which seek to ensure the achievement of corporate objectives in this divisionalised organisation.

Approaching the question

1. There are a great many points that you could make in answer to both parts of the question. We suggest that you make a detailed plan rather than trying to write up an answer in long form.
2. For part (a) think in terms of both planning and control. What sort of information is needed, when, and by whom? We make eleven points in our answer.
3. Part (b) asks about performance measures and the achievement of corporate objectives in a divisionalised organisation, suggesting perhaps the need to discuss degree of divisional control, dysfunctional decision-making, the problems of transfer pricing and so on. (We make seven main points in our suggested answer.)

35 SUBCONTRACTING SERVICES (SPECIMEN PAPER) *72 mins*

The company of which you are finance director manufactures and sells branded electronic consumer durables.

It has a large market share in its home market, and good sales in some other markets. However, it is small in terms of the world market.

From small beginnings in 1970 it grew rapidly until 1989, but then suffered badly from competition from much larger multinational companies.

Devaluation, making competitive imports more expensive, has produced a marked increase in domestic sales since 1992, and technical advances made by the company suggest buoyant sales and profits in future.

Staff are under acute pressure coping with the volume of business and have little time to plan and develop the profitable opportunities created by new products and improvements to existing products. Departmental heads are pressing for more staff and facilities to enable them to achieve objectives.

However, both the chairman and the managing director are concerned about the risks involved in recruiting new staff. They are aware that the future is far from certain. Therefore, they do not wish to recruit staff and then, in a few years time, find it necessary to make them redundant, unless there is no alternative strategy. They remember the cutbacks and redundancies of 1989, 1990 and 1991 as very painful.

They have convened a special conference of the board and senior managers to discuss the internal implications of the planned expansion, and have asked you to prepare certain reports for this meeting.

Required

(a) Write a report for this meeting explaining how you would require staff expansion proposals to be justified in the budgeting process.

The present system of budgeting, which was installed some years ago, provides a detailed breakdown of proposed budgets compared with the latest estimates for the current year, but little else.

Explain and justify in your report the extent to which you might change this and what supplementary information you might require from departmental managers, or from other sources, to enable the proposed budgets to be adequately reviewed.

15 Marks

(b) Write a report explaining the case for subcontracting services, rather than providing these services by the use of full-time staff. Deal with the problems to be anticipated and the likely solutions.

As part of this report, deal specifically with the advantages and problems of subcontracting:

(i) *payroll services:* calculations, payment, record maintenance;

(ii) *legal services:* primarily patents, trademarks, and brands;

(iii) *computing:* the main workload is the integrated system which schedules production at the company's own and suppliers' factories, and controls stock and sales.

Explain also, as part of this report, the criteria for selecting which services should or should not be subcontracted. **15 Marks**

(c) Explain the role of internal audit and management audit in the expansion of the business. Include in your report an explanation of their aims, and how the requirements in a period of expansion will differ from those in a stable or declining business. **10 Marks**

Total Marks = 40

36 ROI AND APPROPRIATE MEASURES (5/95) *36 mins*

You have just been appointed financial controller of an old-established family-controlled business which operates a large number of shops. These shops are located in most towns in the country. It also owns a number of factories which manufacture a variety of products, most of which are sold through the shops.

The new managing director, appointed at the same time as you, is very critical of the limited management information available for the various operations, which consists of:

(a) quarterly internal financial accounts;
(b) daily and weekly sales;
(c) statements comparing ratios of gross profit and costs to sales.

He wishes to introduce better ways of measuring performance, as a preliminary step towards assessing the quality of the management of the various operations, and towards starting some rationalisation. His initial view is that both management and the operations are very variable in quality.

His first thoughts on defining this requirement were that it could be useful to produce statements of the return on investment (ROI) for each operation.

Required

Write a report to the managing director which does the following.

(a) Explains the problems in measuring the 'investment' in the ROI and the practical problems this causes in developing and interpreting the ROI measure for the purposes envisaged **12 Marks**

(b) Explains the process of determining which performance measurements are appropriate in a particular business. **8 Marks**

Total Marks = 20

37 CONTROL OF R & D (11/95) *36 mins*

You are employed as a management accountant on the staff of the Finance Director of a diversified Group.

The Group has recently acquired a very successful high technology company from the three directors who founded the company, and who now wish to retire, and the venture capitalists who had backed them for many years. The company will be managed as a division of the Group, which has not been involved in any high technology industry in the past. New managers will be recruited to succeed the founders within the next year.

You have been asked to review the control procedures for R & D, and have discussed the problems with one of the three original directors. This was helpful as he was in a position to explain the present limited systems, having been in charge of R & D since the company had been founded.

He explained that R & D had never been analysed beyond the detail required for financial accounting. Total staff was just over 100, of whom 60% were highly qualified scientists, and the rest support staff. There was a loose matrix structure of some senior staff being responsible for specialisms and others responsible for projects, but lines were often blurred.

There were, he explained, broadly four sorts of output.

(a) Work on major projects, which could last several years, and which may or may not be successful. This he commissioned on the basis of his and his fellow directors' knowledge of trends.

(b) Work on specific minor product modifications requested by customers or by the marketing department. These projects were normally completed in 6 to 12 months.

(c) Technical support to production and engineering departments.

(d) Review of current technological development in areas broadly relevant to the product range.

Projects were not documented, and he allocated resources according to his knowledge of the industry.

At the end of the discussion he commented that he supposed more paperwork was inevitable in large groups, but that he would be surprised if it led to better decision making or performance.

Required

Write a report to the Finance Director explaining what control procedures are required and how they will contribute to better management of the research and development function.

In your report, explain how the control procedures you propose would apply to expenditure on each of the four types of output from R & D

20 Marks

38 BRANCH OPERATIONS (11/95) *72 mins*

A key part of the business of a large multi-branch bank is making personal unsecured loans.

Loan applications processing is carried out in different branches in a variety of ways, using a number of different computer packages and using different grades of staff, whilst the merits of the various processing systems are being evaluated. It is difficult to establish appropriate costs for the staff, but average times are available.

Branch	*Staff hours per transaction*	*Computer minutes per transaction*
01	2	30
02	3	20
03	4	10
04	2	20
05	1	40
06	1.5	35
07	5	10
08	4.5	10
09	0.9	37.5

Required

(a) Analyse this information and determine the relative efficiency of these branches, as far as it is possible to do so with the available data. Explain the assumptions that you are making. Graph paper [may be used]. **15 Marks**

(b) Two of these branches have been studied in greater detail, and the following information is available.

	Branch 03	*Branch 04*
Loan applications approved	59%	42%
Average initial loan	£6,560	£9,468
Average loan outstanding	£3,280	£4,734
Bad debt provision as percentage of loan outstanding	1.9%	1.4%
Margin on lending over bank borrowing rate on loan outstanding	7.3% per annum	6.4% per annum
Loan approval processing, estimated cost per application	£90	£90
Loan repayment processing, estimated cost as percentage of loan outstanding	2.4%	2.2%
Average duration of loan	2.4 years	2.7 years

Required

Analyse and comment on the above data, assessing as far as possible the profitability of the lending performance of each branch. Explain clearly any assumptions made, and comment on the validity of the data as a basis for comparing branch performance. **15 Marks**

(c) Discussion of your findings with management leads to views being expressed on the adequacy of the provision for bad debts.

Required

Explain how the provision for bad debts should be reviewed by internal audit, and how this review may differ in the case of a bank from the situation in a manufacturing company selling to wholesale customers on normal terms of trade.

Note. Knowledge of external auditing standards and guidelines and requirements under legislation regulating banks is not expected or required. **10 Marks**

Total Marks = 40

39 OUTSOURCING (11/96) *36 mins*

As Chief Internal Auditor of a large diversified organisation, you have been asked by the Finance Director to re-assess the control processes required as the organisation increasingly buys in services (outsources). Parts of the business which are not regarded as core activities are also outsourced. He recognises that the business has been simplified, but is concerned that control may now be less effective.

Required

(a) Explain how an internal audit approach to a service which can be supplied internally would differ from an internal audit approach to the same service if this were outsourced. **6 Marks**

(b) Explain whether value-for-money (VFM) techniques can be applied to outsourced services, and discuss other approaches to the performance measurement of these services. **6 Marks**

(c) Explain how control can be exercised over the cost of outsourced services, and how overall budgetary control can be exercised within an organisation which outsources a significant proportion of its activities. **8 Marks**

Total Marks = 20

40 DIVISION X (5/97) *72 mins*

Division X is in a stable market. The first draft of its plan for the next three years is regarded as unacceptable to group management because it shows a slow decline in profit and return on investment.

	Year 1	*Year 2*	*Year 3*
	£m	£m	£m
Profit before interest and tax (PBIT)	3.0	2.7	2.4
Asset base (at beginning of year)	24.0	25.0	26.0

Proposals which may improve the situation in the next three years are being discussed; *only one* can be accepted because of cash limitations. Projects are evaluated with a 10% required return on investment. These proposed projects are shown below.

(a) **Special purpose machine**

Capital expenditure in years 1 and 2, followed by operating cash flow in year 3:

Year 1	*Year 2*	*Year 3*	*NPV*
£m	£m	£m	£m
–0.5	–0.5	2.0	0.634

(b) **R & D project**

Revenue expenditure in years 1 and 2, followed by operating cash flow in year 3:

Year 1	*Year 2*	*Year 3*	*NPV*
£m	£m	£m	£m
–1.0	–1.0	4.0	1.269

(c) **Advertising**

This can be done in each year if required. Each annual campaign costs £1m, but produces additional contributions of £0.4m in the year of the campaign and £1.1m in the subsequent year. A decision has been made to run annual campaigns in years 1 and 2 only. The combined cash flows are:

Year 1	*Year 2*	*Year 3*	*NPV*
£m	£m	£m	£m
–0.6	+0.5	+1.1	0.694

Managers are currently evaluated on return on investment (ROI), and paid bonuses when this reaches or exceeds 10%. At 10% ROI the manager of Division X will receive 25% of his salary of £50,000 pa. For each 1% increase in ROI above 10%, and *pro rata*, he will receive an additional 2.5% of basic salary with an upper bonus limit of 50% of salary for that year.

Thus, for the first draft of the plan, the bonus based on the ROI has been correctly calculated as follows.

	Year 1	*Year 2*	*Year 3*
Bonus	£15,625	£13,500	£ zero

Calculations ignore tax and depreciation. The asset base represents the assets employed in the division at the beginning of each year, and excludes cash balances which are transferred to the group, and is used for the calculation of residual income (RI) and ROI.

Required

(a) Calculate the ROI, and the manager's bonus each year for the three alternative proposals. Comment on the effects of the bonus system on the manager's choice of project. **14 Marks**

(b) A proposal is under consideration to change the bonus scheme to 2% of residual income (RI) with a limit of 50% of salary. A 10% rate of interest would be used in the calculation of RI.

For the plan including the special-purpose machine, the bonus, based on the RI, has been correctly calculated as follows.

	Year 1	*Year 2*	*Year 3*
Bonus	£12,000	£3,000	£25,000

(i) Calculate the RI and bonuses each year, both for the first draft of the plan and for the R&D and Advertising alternatives.

(ii) Comment on whether the proposed revised bonus system would influence the manager's choice of project in a different way from that based on the ROI. **10 Marks**

(c) Explain whether the manager's project choices are beneficial to the company, under the current bonus scheme and under the proposed bonus scheme. If not, what would be the requirements for a bonus scheme which would produce better decision making? **6 Marks**

(d) It has been argued that the debate on the use of ROI and RI is irrelevant, first because Boards, not divisional managers, take the major investment decisions, and secondly because managerial performance should be measured purely on controllable profit.

Discuss this statement **10 Marks**

Total Marks = 40

41 BENCHMARKING (5/98) *36 mins*

(a) Within a diversified group, one division, which operates many similar branches in a service industry, has used internal benchmarking and regards it as very useful.

Group central management is now considering the wider use of benchmarking.

Required

Explain the aims, operation, and limitations of internal benchmarking, and explain how external benchmarking differs in these respects. **10 Marks**

(b) A multinational group wishes to internally benchmark the production of identical components made in several plants in different countries. Investments have been made in some plants in installing new Advanced Manufacturing Technology (AMT) and supporting this with new manufacturing management systems such as Just in Time (JIT) and Total Quality Management (TQM). Preliminary comparisons suggest that the standard cost in plants using new technology is no lower than that in plants using older technology.

Required

Explain possible reasons for the similar standard costs in plants with differing technology. Recommend appropriate benchmarking measures, recognising that total standard costs may not provide the most useful measurement of performance. **10 Marks**

Total Marks = 20

42 THREE DIVISIONS (5/98) *36 mins*

Within a large group, divisional managers are paid a bonus which can represent a large proportion of their annual earnings. The bonus is paid when the budgeted divisional profit for the financial year is achieved or exceeded.

Meetings of divisional boards are held monthly and attended by the senior management of the division, and senior members of group management.

With the end of the financial year approaching, there had been discussions in all divisional board meetings of forecast profit for the year, and whether budgeted profit would be achieved. In three board meetings, for divisions which were having difficulty in achieving budgeted profits, the following divisional actions had been discussed. In each case, the amounts involved would have been material in determining whether the division would achieve its budget.

- Division A had severely cut spending on training, and postponed routine re-painting of premises.
- Division B had re-negotiated a contract for consultancy services. It was in the process of installing Total Quality Management (TQM) systems, and had originally agreed to pay progress payments to the consultants, and had budgeted to make these payments. It had re-negotiated that the consultancy would invoice the division with the total cost only when the work was completed in the next financial year.
- Division C had persuaded some major customers to take early delivery, in the current financial year, of products originally ordered for delivery early in the next financial year. This would ensure virtually nil stock at year end.

Required

Discuss the financial accounting, budgeting, ethical and motivational issues which arise from these divisional actions.

Comment on whether any group management action is necessary. **20 Marks**

43 UNIVERSITIES (11/97) *72 mins*

Universities are self-governing institutions, which gain most of their income from government grants and fees charged to students, many of which are paid by the government. Lesser sums are gained from research contracts, and other income from providing catering and accommodation to students and conferences, and from a wide range of other sources. The universities are self-governing in respect of determining the portfolio of courses to be offered and the means by which these courses are funded.

Comparative statistics are collected, and used centrally by the government as a basis for assessing annual grants to universities, and as a guide to considering any possible changes in the courses to be provided and funded. These statistics are also used by individual universities as a guide to their relative performance.

The key problem for the central authority in using these statistics as a basis for allocating grants is in assessing quality as well as cost efficiency in value for money.

The statistics shown below form part of the annual bid for grants submitted to the central authority by a number of universities which provide broadly similar courses.

The central authority intends to expand the number of students on business and management courses, but considers it better to expand one of the universities substantially, rather than expand all marginally. The final decision will be made on the basis of bids for grants submitted by the universities. They will be invited to tender, offering courses for additional students.

However, an assessment of present relative performance is also regarded as important.

Required

(a) Making use of the data available, recommend to the central authority which of the four universities should be provided with an additional grant to expand the number of students receiving business and management courses on the basis of its current relative performance.

Give the reasons for your recommendation. **20 Marks**

(b) Making use of the data available, comment on the relative performance of West University. Discuss the problems, and recommend possible changes to improve performance. **10 Marks**

(c) Discuss the limitations of the data available in the Performance Indicators table as measures of the quality of the courses provided.

Suggest, with reasons, other ways of measuring the quality of the courses. **10 Marks**

Total Marks = 40

Performance Indicators

(please refer to the definitions given below)

University	*North*	*South*	*East*	*West*
University data:				
University revenue				
Grant as % of total revenue	48	38	43	41
Fees as % of total revenue	19	23	20	22
Net financial surplus/(deficit) as % of total revenue	3.9	(1.7)	1.1	(3.1)
Business & Management Department data:				
Student numbers:				
Undergraduate	1,287	120	660	358
Other	355	175	132	168
Total	1,642	295	792	526
Academic staff numbers	72	18	44	29
SSR (student:staff ratio) calculated on undergraduate courses	23.8	12.8	18.0	14.6
Departmental revenue				
Income generated per staff member from research activities	£4,060	£24,960	£1,610	0
Departmental expenditure				
Total (£'000)	4,213	1,277	2,236	1,531
For each undergraduate student	£2,450	£4,330	£2,200	£2,060
Related to each member of academic staff teaching undergraduates	£55,990	£70,200	£39,300	£37,900
Cost of support staff per member of academic staff	£14,000	£14,600	£6,800	£4,200
Student data				
Average A-level points on entry	22.7	20.7	25.6	18.9
% 1st and 2.1 class degrees	50	52	45	49
% completing course in normal time	81	86	84	80
% graduates unemployed	9	14	6	12

Definitions:

Student and staff numbers are on a full-time equivalent basis ie adjustments have been made for part-time staff and students.

The student: staff ratio (SSR) has been calculated using the staff with teaching duties, excluding research staff.

The student data relate to undergraduate courses.

Undergraduates are typically, but not exclusively, students entering university from school to undertake a course for a first degree.

Other students vary considerably, but will include those who have already acquired one degree and are studying for research degrees or MBA (Master of Business Administration) degrees. These courses require better-qualified staff.

Revenue from research is one indicator of staff being involved in new developments.

The departmental expenditure for business and management includes allocations of central university costs.

A-level points (graded A to E) are calculated counting a grade A as 10, B as 8, C as 6 etc. Most students are accepted for university on the basis of their A-level (or equivalent) results. The average A-level points on entry indicates the level of achievement of students prior to entering university - the higher the score, the greater the level of achievement.

Degree classes indicate the level of achievement. 1st and 2.1 are equivalent to marks above 70% and 60% in CIMA examinations. Lower class and unclassified degrees are also awarded to undergraduates successfully completing their courses. These classes apply only to first degrees.

The percentage completing is the percentage of students who graduate at the normal time, after three or four years of undergraduate study.

The percentage unemployed is the percentage of recent graduates unemployed six months after the end of the course.

44 MUSIC SOCIETIES (5/98) *72 mins*

In a number of cities, music societies, which are charitable organisations, provide classical music concerts by operating concert halls and supporting orchestras employing full-time musicians. Earned income arises mainly from giving concerts, with additional earned income from catering activities, ancillary sales programmes, CDs and cassettes, and souvenirs, and hiring out the concert hall facilities. The earned income is much less than the cost of running the orchestras and concert halls, which are also supported by subsidies in the form of annual grants from local government authorities and the central government, and from business sponsorship, which is a form of corporate public relations expenditure.

The broad aims of the music societies are to provide the best possible standard of live performance of classical music in their home cities (supported by grants from their local government authority) and in other areas of the country (supported by grants from the central government), and to encourage new music and musicians.

As they are charities, music societies do not aim to make a profit. Any surpluses are invested in improvements to the concert halls and spent on additional musicians.

Costs are largely fixed and are broadly 75% orchestral and 25% concert hall and administration (mostly staff). Levels of remuneration, especially for musicians, are low, considering the skills and training required.

The scope for increases in income is very limited. Grants will not increase, and may decrease. The orchestras (allowing for rehearsal time) are fully occupied. Fees for engagements elsewhere in the country and abroad are falling due to the competition from orchestras from other countries.

The chairman of the manufacturing company for which you are a management accountant, has recently become a non-executive director of the local music society (X Music), which owns the concert hall and employs the orchestra. His first impressions are that the music is probably excellent, though he is no expert, but that the data available on operations is very limited.

Some comparisons are available with another music society (Y Music) in a smaller city: these are given below.

Required

(a) On the basis of the available data, prepare a report for the Chairman, comparing the key features of the business and financial performance of X Music with that of Y Music. **22 Marks**

(b) Explain which cost management techniques should be most useful to X Music, where the accounting staff is very small and available data is limited. **8 Marks**

Comparative data

	19X7		*19X2*		*19W7*	
Number of performances	*X*	*Y*	*X*	*Y*	*X*	*Y*
Concerts in home city	74	84	77	91	75	91
Other concerts in home country	63	26	88	38	81	52
Overseas concerts	8	8	15	-	11	-
TV/radio/recording	5	11	9	5	14	9
Total	150	129	189	134	181	152
Income	£'000	£'000	£'000	£'000	£'000	£'000
Concerts in home city	698	1,043	540	717	410	459
Other concerts in home country	916	762	697	361	518	371
Overseas concerts	282	333	154	-	100	-
TV/radio/recording	70	210	72	128	53	118
Other earned income	466	133	76	41	56	22
Business sponsorship	397	607	141	135	56	44
Total earned income	2,829	3,088	1,680	1,382	1,193	1,014
Grant - central government	1,300	1,500	900	1,000	500	900
Grant - local government authority	655	950	150	750	400	500
Total income	4,784	5,538	2,730	3,132	2,093	2,414
Total costs	4,872	5,356	2,703	3,147	2,059	2,402
Surplus/(deficit)	(88)	182	27	(15)	34	12
Cumulative surplus/(deficit)	(686)	311	80	(26)	141	62

(c) The following features of the operations of the concert hall are noted during preliminary discussions of the finances of X Music.

- Takings from catering and ancillary sales are almost entirely in cash.
- Advance bookings of tickets are almost entirely paid by credit card or cheque, only 10% are paid in cash.
- Sales of tickets on the night of the performance (some 15% of the total) are over 50% cash sales.
- The number of permanent staff for the ticket booking office and catering is quire small. They are supplemented by the use of part-time staff, temporary staff and unpaid volunteers to guide the audience to their seats and for sales at performances.

Required

Explain how these features should influence any internal audit planning. **10 Marks**

Total Marks = 40

45 MULTINATIONALS (5/99) *36 mins*

X plc has in recent years been forced to restructure. It has considerably reduced its size, as its former main business in electrical engineering has largely become obsolete because of technological advance. There remains a sound but much smaller business in specialist electronic equipment.

This electronics business, like the former electrical one, is a global business, with manufacturing, service and sales in a large number of countries. Operations in different countries vary in size. Some undertake sales and servicing and may have fewer than ten employees; others manufacture and may employ up to 200 people.

Head office structures, procedures and control systems still reflect a much larger, stable, prosperous past. The detailed systems of planning, budgeting and reporting, with a requirement for Head Office approval for a wide range of actions, reflect a 'financial control' style of management. The current requirement is for a control system to match a smaller, fast-changing business.

Required

Explain and justify the minimum central control system required to ensure that effective control is maintained in the global business. Your explanation should do the following.

- Specify the decisions which will be retained for head office
- Describe the minimum reporting system required for control
- State the criteria for the performance evaluation of individual country operations and their managers
- Discuss the main problems anticipated in evaluating the performance of individual country operations and those of their managers

20 Marks

46 QUALITY COSTS (11/96) *36 mins*

As part of a Total Quality Management (TQM) programme in a large manufacturing company, quality costing has been introduced and is regarded as useful by senior managers. They are now planning to extend the TQM programme, and quality costing, from manufacturing to the whole of the company. You have been asked to devise a TQM programme, including appropriate quality measures and calculations of quality cost in the management accounting section of the Finance Department.

Required

(a) Briefly explain each of the four categories of quality cost (prevention cost, appraisal cost, internal failure cost, and external failure cost). Give examples of each category appropriate to a manufacturing environment, and examples relevant to management accounting. **8 Marks**

(b) Explain how this cost categorisation mentioned in (a) above can be used to help to develop performance measures within management accounting. Explain and justify a set of performance measures that can be used by the Finance Director in assessing the management accounting service. **12 Marks**

Total Marks = 20

DO YOU KNOW? - QUALITY ASSURANCE OF SYSTEMS: INTERNAL CONTROLS, AUDIT TECHNIQUES AND CORPORATE GOVERNANCE

- *Check that you can fill in the blanks in the statements below before you attempt any questions. If in doubt, you should go back to your BPP Study Text and revise first.*
- A definition of *internal control* '... the whole system of controls, established by the management in order to carry on business in an .... and .... manner, ensure adherence to ...., ... the assets and secure the .... and .... of the records'.

  TRY QUESTION 47

- The functions of internal audit include review of the .... and .... systems, examination of internal .... , review of the .... , ... and .... of operations, review of compliance with .... , review of the implementation of .... , identification of .... and .... risks, and special investigations.
- CIPFA suggests that assessment of internal audit should focus on outputs. Measures include the .... and .... of reports and comparison of findings with other information.

  TRY QUESTIONS 48 TO 50

- The main types of internal control are as follows:

  ....

  ....

  ....

  ....

- Audit planning can be divided into three parts, ... , ... and .... planning.
- The APB definition of audit risk is as the product of .... , ... and .... risk. A matter is .... if its non-disclosure, misstatement or omission would make possible a distortion of the view given by the accounts or other financial information.

  TRY QUESTIONS 51 TO 57

- Analytical review can be used at all stages of the audit process. Analytical procedures include .... , ... and ....
- If auditors use audit sampling, sample sizes should depend on .... , and .... and .... errors. Sample selection methods include .... , ... and .... selection.

  TRY QUESTIONS 58 TO 60

- Corporate governance has been addressed recently by the .... , ... and .... reports. Areas these reports cover include non-executive directors, audit committees, directors' remuneration, review of internal controls, and financial and audit reporting.

  TRY QUESTIONS 61 AND 62

- VFM audits are used to measure performance according to the criteria of .... , ... , and .... These criteria are studied by considering .... , ... and ....

  TRY QUESTIONS 63 AND 64

- *Possible pitfalls*

  Write down the mistakes you know you should avoid.

DID YOU KNOW? - QUALITY ASSURANCE OF SYSTEMS: INTERNAL CONTROLS, AUDIT TECHNIQUES AND CORPORATE GOVERNANCE

- *Could you fill in the blanks? The answers are in bold. Use this page for revision purposes as you approach the exam.*
- A definition of *internal control* '... the whole system of controls, established by the management in order to carry on business in an **orderly** and **efficient** manner, ensure adherence to **management policies**, **safeguard** the assets and secure the **completeness** and **accuracy** of the records'.

  TRY QUESTION 47
- The functions of internal audit include review of the **accounting** and **internal control** systems, examination of internal **information**, review of the **economy**, **efficiency** and **effectiveness** of operations, review of compliance with **laws and regulations**, review of the implementation of **corporate objectives**, identification of **business** and **financial** risks, and special investigations.
- CIPFA suggests that assessment of internal audit should focus on outputs. Measures include the **quality** and **timeliness** of reports and comparison of findings with other information.

  TRY QUESTIONS 48 TO 50
- The main types of internal control are as follows:

Segregation of duties	**Supervision**
Organisation	**Personnel**
Arithmetic and accounting	**Authorisation and approval**
Physical	**Management**
- Audit planning can be divided into three parts, **tactical, strategic** and **operational** planning.
- The APB definition of audit risk is the product of **inherent**, **control** and **detection** risk. A matter is **material** if its non-disclosure, misstatement or omission would make possible a distortion of the view given by the accounts or other financial information.

  TRY QUESTIONS 51 TO 57
- Analytical review can be used at all stages of the audit process. Analytical procedures include **ratio analysis, trend analysis** and **reasonableness tests**.
- If auditors use audit sampling, sample sizes should depend on **risk levels**, and **tolerable** and **expected** errors. Sample selection methods include **random**, **systematic** and **haphazard** selection.

  TRY QUESTIONS 58 TO 60
- Corporate governance has been addressed recently by the **Cadbury**, **Greenbury** and **Hampel** reports. Areas these reports cover include non-executive directors, audit committees, directors' remuneration, review of internal controls, and financial and audit reporting.

  TRY QUESTIONS 61 AND 62
- VFM audits are used to measure performance according to the criteria of **economy**, **efficiency**, and **effectiveness.** These criteria are studied by considering **inputs**, **outputs** and **impacts**.

  TRY QUESTIONS 63 AND 64
- *Possible pitfalls*
  - **Failure to make recommendations for action, or making recommendations that were inappropriate for the situation**
  - **Lack of detailed knowledge of the aims and requirements of the corporate governance reports**

47 TUTORIAL QUESTION: INTERNAL AUDIT AND INTERNAL CONTROLS

The old Auditing Practices Committee identified eight means by which internal control can be established for audit purposes. It is suggested that one of these, management, provides control in the following ways:

(a) analysis and review of management accounts;
(b) other special reviews;
(c) provision of internal audit procedures.

Required

(a) Identify the seven other means for obtaining internal control, explaining how each of these achieves its purpose.

(b) Explain how the internal audit function should be managed, giving attention to planning, recording, quality control and staffing considerations.

Approaching the question

1 You should remember the mnemonic for internal controls - SOAPSPAM - to answer this question.

2 Part (b) is straightforward, but you should make sure that you cover all the aspects mentioned in the question.

48 IA EFFECTIVENESS (5/95) *36 mins*

As the newly-appointed finance director of a quoted company, you have just been asked by the chairman to advise him on the effectiveness of the existing internal audit department.

The chairman explained that internal audit has been established in the company for many years. The chief internal auditor, who has held this post for many years, has reported direct to the chairman. He has always had a right of access to the Board, and, since the establishment of an Audit Committee, has worked closely with that committee.

However, there had been increasing friction in recent years between the chief internal auditor and your predecessor as finance director. Internal audit had been regarded by your predecessor as expensive, slow and cumbersome, and ineffective.

Required

Write a report to the chairman explaining how the effectiveness of the internal audit department should be assessed.

Your report should deal specifically with the following issues.

(a) Whether you should carry out the assessment yourself, or, if not, who should do so.

(b) How the detailed work of gathering the appropriate information should be conducted.

(c) The information required, and any specific financial or non-financial measures required.

20 Marks

49 OBJECTIVES OF INTERNAL AUDIT (5/98) *36 mins*

You are the chief internal auditor of a public company in which the process of management control is exercised through a system of annual review of performance against agreed predetermined objectives (Management by Objectives). To prepare for the annual review of the internal audit department, you are expected to report progress on the current objectives, and propose appropriate objectives linked to the aims of the internal audit department, for the forthcoming year.

Required

Explain the broad aims or purposes of the internal audit department, both in its role as an important part of the system of internal control, and in contributing to the overall effectiveness of the organisation.

Propose specific objectives for the internal audit department related to the aims of the department.

Explain how performance of the internal audit department against each of its objectives could be evaluated, and provide for each objective an example of a performance measure that could assist in this. **20 Marks**

50 INDEPENDENCE *36 mins*

'The internal auditor should have the independence in terms of organisational status and personal objectivity which permits the proper performance of his duties.'

(*Guidance for Internal Auditors*, Auditing Practices Committee, 1990)

Required

(a) Explain what is meant by independence in this context, listing and briefly explaining the freedoms and privileges needed for employees of an organisation to be able to act effectively as internal auditors. **6 Marks**

(b) Explain the alternative organisational structures which can help to achieve this independence of internal audit, and the ways in which an Audit Committee can contribute to this. **8 Marks**

(c) In many organisations, bonus payments related to annual profits form a significant part of the total remuneration of all senior managers, not just the top few managers.

Discuss whether it is appropriate for the Chief Internal Auditor to receive a bonus based on the organisation's profit, or whether it could be seen to compromise his independence. **6 Marks**

Total Marks = 20

51 CONTROLS IN NEW COMPANY (11/95) *36 mins*

A large local government authority in the United Kingdom has decided to seek competitive tenders for all its internal computer requirements. The present managers of the authority's Computer Services Department have decided that they wish to tender for the work, and if successful, form a company to acquire the existing assets and carry out work for the local government authority and other customers.

They think that the work that they currently do for their own local government authority is technically far in advance of that done by neighbouring local government authorities. They consider that additional volume would allow them to reward more highly the good staff who are currently employed at low public sector rates of pay.

A group of local businessmen and potential investors has discussed this proposal with the Director of Computing, who would lead the proposed management buy-out (MBO). They are quite impressed with the technical competence of the staff, and the prospects for gaining additional work.

However, they have a number of reservations, as the staff have no experience outside information technology, and no commercial experience. Their experience of budgeting is also limited. The local government authority does not subdivide its budget for the Computer Services Department. It manages this department as a cost centre, and receives reports of expenditure against budget at quarterly intervals.

The investors have asked consultants to advise on certain aspects of the proposals.

Required

Write a report to the investors. This report should:

(a) recommend the form and level of detail of budgetary control required in the new company; **8 Marks**

(b) recommend the structure and formal controls required at Board level in the new company. **12 Marks**

Total Marks = 20

52 PURCHASING AND ENTERTAINMENT (5/96) *36 mins*

(a) Explain how management control system can help to minimise the risk of fraud in purchasing. **10 Marks**

(b) Some codes of conduct appear to have a double standard. One such is quoted below.

Customer and supplier relations

The company does not seek to gain any advantage through the improper use of business courtesies or other inducements. Good judgement and moderation must be exercised to avoid misinterpretation and adverse effect on the reputation of the company and its employees. Offering, giving, soliciting or receiving any form of bribe is prohibited.

Business courtesies

Gifts, favours and entertainment may be given in the following circumstances.

(i) If they are consistent with customary business practices.
(ii) If they are not excessive in value and cannot be construed as a bribe or payoff.
(iii) If they are not in contravention of applicable law or ethical standards.
(iv) If they will not embarrass the company or the employee if publicly disclosed.

Gifts, favours, entertainment or other inducements may not be accepted by employees from any person or organisation that does or seeks business with, or is a competitor of, the company, except as common courtesies usually associated with customary business practices. An espeoially strict standard applies when suppliers are involved. Favours or entertainment, appropriate in our sales programmes may not be appropriate or acceptable from suppliers. It is never acceptable to accept a gift in cash or cash equivalent.

Required

Comment on the acceptability of the above code of conduct. If you consider it appropriate, suggest with reasons any amendments you would wish to see in the code of conduct. **10 Marks**

Total Marks = 20

53 SEGREGATION OF DUTIES (5/96) *36 mins*

The Auditing Practices Committee Guideline on internal control lists eight types of internal control, including organisation and segregation of duties.

Required

(a) Explain briefly what is meant by segregation of duties, why it is important in internal control, and how internal auditors can confirm its effectiveness. **6 Marks**

A small branch has one manager and few managerial staff, which makes segregation of duties within the branch impossible.

Required

(b) Explain how Head Office can maintain internal control of the branch **6 Marks**

A large company has restructured. This has considerably reduced the number of managers and eliminated much of what was deemed to be unnecessary bureaucracy including many controls on stock, purchases and time recording. In a flatter structure, junior managers and supervisors have been provided with authority (empowered) to take a wide range of decisions of immediate concern, and with access to much of the company database. The new structure emphasises team work to implement rapid changes.

Required

(c) Explain how internal control can be maintained in this situation. **8 Marks**

Total Marks = 20

54 MANAGEMENT CONTROL FRAMEWORK (11/97) *36 mins*

(a) A typical description of the framework of the management control cycle is:

(i) defining the objectives;
(ii) planning the activity necessary to achieve the objectives;
(iii) organising resources and directing performance;
(iv) monitoring results;
(v) regulating by reviewing and adjusting plans or directives.

Required

Use the framework of the management control cycle above to explain how a board should ensure that an adequate system of internal control exists. **12 Marks**

(b) The non-executive directors of a multinational have expressed concern regarding their awareness of and control over a range of transactions that:

either have effects beyond the short term;

and/or are not fully disclosed by normal monthly management accounting information or published financial statements.

These include:

(i) long-term purchase contracts
(ii) long-term supply contracts
(iii) the use of derivatives

Required

Describe the application of the framework of the management control cycle, described in part (a), to one area where you consider there may be inadequate disclosures.

Note. You are not restricted to choosing an example quoted in the question. You can choose another specific example or functional area such ad treasury management.

8 Marks

Total Marks = 20

55 NEW SUBSIDIARY (5/97) *36 mins*

You are employed as a senior internal auditor in a very large conglomerate firm. The chief internal auditor has asked you to carry out the initial internal audit of a newly-acquired subsidiary.

The newly-acquired subsidiary imports specialised building products, mainly plumbing and drainage equipment, and sells them through 23 regional warehouses, the majority of which are in the United Kingdom. The head office is small - fewer than 50 people are employed. The regional warehouses employ more people - numbers vary between 20 and 80 at each warehouse, and include salesmen, drivers, storemen, and a small number of office and accounting staff.

Regional warehouse managers have considerable autonomy in buying from approved suppliers, and selling, including negotiating special prices with large customers and allowing credit. They are totally responsible for their local staff. The business has grown rapidly and achieved a significant market share by having good stocks available, and allowing generous credit to small and large builder customers. It has been financed by extended credit from suppliers.

The group is not involved in sales to the same markets as the newly-acquired subsidiary, but similar products are bought and sold to retail customers through stores.

The management team of the subsidiary has remained the same after the acquisition, and will be paid very highly as part of the purchase arrangements if forecast profits are achieved for the first two years after acquisition.

Required

(a) Explain how you would analyse and determine the main potential audit problems.
6 Marks

(b) Explain and justify the aims of, and provide the framework for, your proposed initial audit programme. **14 Marks**

Note. As part of the purchase agreement for the new subsidiary, extensive work was done by an independent firm of auditors on the stocks and account balances at the date of purchase. You are *not* required to duplicate this work.

Total Marks = 20

56 CODES OF CONDUCT (SPECIMEN PAPER) *36 mins*

The Managing Director of a company which makes and sells defence equipment worldwide has had a most unhappy meeting with his Chairman.

They have both just read a newspaper report of a statement made by a disgruntled ex-employee, after a court case for compensation for his dismissal.

In the statement, the ex-employee stated that the company had been selling equipment in breach of a United Nations embargo, and that such sales have been made on a number of occasions.

The Chairman is concerned because:

(a) he did not anticipate such unfortunate public criticism of the company;

(b) he was not aware of such irregular sales;

(c) he thought all possible had been done, by establishing an Audit Committee in line with the Cadbury Report recommendations, to ensure that such problems would never arise;

(d) he thought the Internal Audit department should have detected *all* actions contrary to the Company Code of Conduct and reported them to him immediately.

Required

(a) Explain the case for establishing an audit committee and how it may contribute to the solution of problems such as those outlined above. **8 Marks**

(b) Explain to what extent the Internal Audit department may be involved in ensuring compliance with the Company Code of Conduct, and what other steps may be desirable to ensure that decisions taken within a company are ethical. **12 Marks**

Total Marks = 20

57 FRAUD DETECTION (5/99) *36 mins*

Y plc operates a large number of hotels. The manager of one hotel has been convicted for defrauding the company. The Chairman has expressed concern that the fraud was not detected by internal audit or by operational management. He has asked that internal audit policies and plans are reconsidered and revised to emphasise the detection of fraud.

Required

(a) As Chief Internal Auditor explain, in a report to the chairman, what specific steps could be taken by internal audit to detect fraud. Discuss whether emphasising fraud detection in internal audit policies and plans is desirable, and recommend the appropriate future policy regarding fraud detection. **10 Marks**

The Operations Director has raised concerns that emphasis on the detection of fraud could cause major problems with some of his best hotel managers. He said, 'customs and practice exist in hotels, such as unofficial additional income (perquisites). If these were ended, managers and staff would either become dissatisfied and resign, or require significant salary increases.' **10 marks**

Required

(b) As Chief Internal Auditor, state, explain, and justify your response to the Operations Director.

Total Marks = 20

58 PERFORMANCE REVIEW (5/99) *72 mins*

S plc operates 740 supermarket stores selling food and other household supplies.

There is considerable competition between supermarkets, especially when too many supermarkets attempt to operate in an area in relation to the potential number of customers, or when a local or national price war develops from one operator attempting to gain market share.

Control and performance evaluation within S plc are primarily exercised by:

- review of league tables of profitability;
- review of key ratios and indicators.

Budgets are used, but are relatively less important as predictable change year-on-year is relatively small. Sales growth for comparable stores that are unaffected by changes in the local competitive situation, is at best 3% excluding inflation. Cost control permits only limited local managerial discretion.

In view of the acute competition there is a need to review the systems and criteria used for control and performance evaluation, and the possibility of improving these systems.

As part of the review process, you have been asked to analyse the data shown for stores A, B and C, which are broadly similar stores in the southern region, using your analysis to illustrate your view on possible system improvements.

Summary data for S plc for the year to 31 December 19X8 are given below.

Required

(a) Comment on the performance of stores A, B and C, using the available information. Explain, with reasons, which key ratios you, as Management Accountant of S plc, would recommend be used for operational control and performance valuation of existing stores. **20 Marks**

(b) The internal auditor will also look in detail at the variable information for each store.

(i) Explain the purposes, methods and limitations of analytical review as conducted by the internal auditor. **8 Marks**

(ii) Outline the main internal audit concerns in planning each of the internal audits of stores A, B and C arising from the analytical review of the data for these stores. **12 Marks**

Total Marks = 40

SUMMARY DATA FOR S PLC FOR YOUR TO 31 DECEMBER 19X8

	Store A	*Store B*	*Store C*	*Group (Total of 740 stores)*
Floor area (square metres)	1,200	1,000	1,100	630,000
Number of employees	72	70	67	35,700
	£'000	£'000	£'000	£'000
Sales	7,680	7,200	7,370	3,849,000
Gross profit	1,698	1,744	1,738	862,000
Labour	917	907	886	434,000
Other costs	731	647	692	328,000
Total costs	1,648	1,554	1,578	762,000
Net profit	50	190	160	100,000
Note. Gross profit is calculated after wastage				
Gross profit pre wastage	24.4%	25.6%	25.5%	24.2%
Wastage	2.3%	1.4%	1.9%	1.8%
Gross profit	22.1%	24.2%	23.6%	22.4%

SIMPLIFIED CAPITAL EMPLOYED IN S PLC SUPERMARKETS AT 31 DECEMBER 19X8

	Store A	*Store B*	*Store C*	*Group*
	£'000	£'000	£'000	£'000
Stock	324	329	343	170,000
less: Creditors	(1,241)	(1,164)	(1,191)	(622,000)
fixed assets	720	940	1,122	548,000
Net assets	(197)	105	274	96,000

There are no significant debtors.

YEAR TO 31 DECEMBER 19X7

	Store A	*Store B*	*Store C*	*Group*
	£'000	£'000	£'000	£'000
Sales	8,320	6,963	7,038	3,739,000
Gross profit	1,947	1,693	1,655	841,000
Net profit	317	232	152	114,000

59 ANALYTICAL REVIEW AND SAMPLING *36 mins*

An old-established group of companies whose main business is the sale of building materials and timber through a large number of builders' merchants with virtually complete national coverage, is facing recession and the need to reduce its costs to the minimum.

The internal audit department was established many years ago, to counter persistent minor fraud by yard managers and to reduce external audit charges.

The board is now asking whether the present level of cost of the internal audit department is appropriate for the group, and whether the methods used are up to date and efficient.

You are required to draft a report to the board explaining:

(a) how an analytical review of the activities of the branches could be carried out and how it would enable better planning of the audit programme. You may assume that the monthly management accounts of the group give very full details of every branch; **8 Marks**

(b) the case for sampling rather than inspecting every item, and describing four forms of sampling which could be used, and the circumstances in which they should be used. **12 Marks**

Total Marks = 20

60 DIVISION X (11/96) *72 mins*

Division X, which imports audio equipment from Japan for sale in the United Kingdom, started selling to individual customers by mail order one year ago. In this first year, sales to 13,600 customers have produced £25,160,000 revenue. Unit prices vary from £1,200 to £3,000.

Credit cards (or debit cards) are used by 28% of customers. 11% pay by cheques, which are cleared prior to despatch of products. The remainder take extended credit, being permitted to pay over 6 or 12 months by equal instalments with no interest charged. At present 166 customers are 3 months or more overdue on payments.

Sales administrators answer customers' telephone enquiries, and agree the sale on the telephone, entering customer details for payment and despatch on a Local Area Network (LAN). They receive a significant part of their remuneration as a commission on sales.

It has been suggested that the problem with customers being overdue could be because of failures by the sales administrators to make credit checks prior to agreeing sales on credit with the customers.

Two alternative sampling methods are considered to ascertain whether credit sales are allowed without credit checks being made.

Using *discovery sampling*. To be 95% certain that there are not more than 50 such cases, a sample of 481 without finding one erroneous item is required.

Using *attribute sampling*. To be 95% certain that the error rate is no more than 5%, within ±2½% of the true error rate, the required sample size is 282.

Attribute sampling is chosen.

Required

(a) (i) Explain why the sample size for attribute sampling is materially different in size from that for discovery sampling. **4 Marks**

(ii) Examining this sample, you find five errors (failures to carry out credit checks). You also note that four of these errors are in 42 transactions originated by one sales administrator.

Given the findings from the attribute sampling, outline what audit checks should be made on the sales system. **10 Marks**

(b) Explain the potential advantages of judgement sampling in this case, and in internal auditing generally, and the limitations of using judgement sampling. **6 Marks**

(c) Another division, Y, uses acceptance sampling on raw materials supplied. One of its suppliers, DZ, is expected to deliver a component (CY) with 95% being within a narrow tolerance range. DZ is the only supplier which makes component CY. However, DZ cannot meet the desired specification: experience shows that it can achieve only 91 acceptable components per 100 delivered. In the longer term, it may be possible to get an alternative supplier, but in the meantime, division Y has to use DZ's components.

The costs of the sub-assembly BCY, incorporating this component, are as follows.

	£
Component CY	5.70
Other direct materials	12.30
Direct labour @ £8 per hour	2.00
Overhead 250%	5.00
	25.00

The overhead is the budgeted rate for factory overhead: 100% relates to fixed costs, 150% to variable costs.

There are *three* possible ways of using component CY.

(i) Using without inspection on receipt, and stripping down defective sub-assemblies and fitting a new, uninspected, CY component. The stripping down and re-assembly takes 30 minutes. The defective component is then scrap, and no credit is received.

(ii) Using without inspection on receipt, stripping down defective sub-assemblies, and fitting new pre-inspected component CY.

(iii) Inspecting 100% of CY components on receipt, returning defective units for credit.

Inspection of component CY on receipt takes 5 minutes of direct labour time.

Required

(i) Calculate the costs of each of the three ways of using component CY to produce 100 good sub-assemblies. **7 Marks**

(ii) Calculate the maximum possible price per component CY that could be paid to an alternative supplier for 100% perfect supplies. **3 Marks**

(d) Explain the objectives and limitations of sampling in internal auditing and compare these with the objectives and limitations of sampling in quality control.

10 Marks

Total Marks = 40

61 CORPORATE GOVERNANCE (5/96) *36 mins*

To comply with the Code of Practice in the Cadbury Report, listed companies must include in their annual reports for years beginning on or after 1 January 1995, a statement on internal financial control.

This must include, as well as other minimum requirements,

(a) a description of the key procedures that the directors have established and which are designed to provide effective internal financial control; and

(b) confirmation that the directors (or a board committee) have reviewed the effectiveness of the system of internal financial control

Required

(a) Explain how the directors should satisfy themselves that the system of internal financial control is effective. **6 Marks**

The Greenbury Committee has extended the Cadbury Code requirements for a remuneration committee, and its recommendations have been incorporated in the Stock Exchange Listing rules.

Required

(b) Explain the purpose, constitution, and functioning of a Remuneration Committee, and what information its members will require to assist them. **8 Marks**

(c) Explain the aims of the Cadbury reforms of corporate governance, and the extent to which the changes being made meet these aims. **6 Marks**

Total Marks = 20

62 AUDIT COMMITTEES (5/98) *36 mins*

Attempts to improve corporate governance have depended heavily on the appointment of non-executive directors and committees of non-executive directors, such as audit committees.

Required

(a) (i) Explain the limitations of depending on non-executive directors to improve corporate governance.

(ii) Explain how audit committees might be made more effective. **12 Marks**

(b) Whilst most companies selling fast-moving consumer goods in competitive markets pay considerable attention to customer reactions and problems, this may not always apply with monopolies, regulated industries, and companies entering into long-term financial service contracts with customers. It has been suggested that formal arrangements, with a degree of independence from the management of the company, may be needed to ensure that complaints are heard and fairly dealt with. These arrangements could consist of, for example, systems such as consultative committees, independent ombudsmen, customer charters or regulatory bodies.

Explain briefly what improvements would be needed in control systems if such formal arrangements were introduced, and how the role of the audit committee might change. **8 Marks**

Total Marks = 20

63 VFM AND PERFORMANCE INDICATORS *36 mins*

(a) Give three specific examples of methods of analysis which may be employed in value for money audits. **6 Marks**

(b) Explain the use of performance indicators and the advantages and limitations of using these indicators in a value for money audit in the public sector. Include three examples of performance indicators in your explanation. **14 Marks**

Total Marks = 20

64 VFM AND PAYROLL (11/98) *36 mins*

XY Ltd is a small subsidiary of a large group. Its business is servicing and repairing electronic equipment, mostly on customer sites, but also in its own regional workshops. Some of its skilled engineers are based at these workshops; most work from home, visiting a number of customers.

The equipment being serviced is partly that manufactured and sold by another subsidiary, and partly that of other manufacturers. The work is done under maintenance contracts.

Profits in XY Ltd have never been high, and recent losses have caused the group to undertake a review of its activities. The primary aim is cost reduction. You have been asked to contribute to this as a member of the group internal audit department. The IA department has done very little work in XY Ltd for a considerable time, because of other priorities.

XY Ltd has had its payroll administered by a computer service bureau for many years; the bureau receives advice of employee and pay rate changes, normal and overtime hours from a section in XY Ltd's personnel department. Some other group subsidiaries use other (different) service bureaux; others use their own computer facilities. Group Internal Audit has been asked whether it would be worthwhile to review the payroll arrangements.

Required

(a) Explain, in a report to the cost reduction team leader, what features of the payroll arrangements you would review in a value for money (VFM) audit. Recommend, with reasons, whether undertaking such a VFM audit would be a sensible use of internal audit department resources. **10 Marks**

(b) Explain what audit checks should be carried out on XY Ltd's payroll to ensure that the payments to each category of employee are made in conformity with the company's contractual and legal obligations, and that the risks of fraud are minimised. **10 Marks**

Total Marks = 20

DO YOU KNOW? – QUALITY ASSURANCE OF SYSTEMS: AUDITING IN A COMPUTERISED ENVIRONMENT

- *Check that you can fill in the 20 blanks in the statements below before you attempt any questions. If in doubt, you should go back to your BPP Study Text and revise first.*
- Security is the protection of data from actual or deliberate threats including the following:
  - ....
  - ....
  - ....
  - ....
  - ....
  - ....
  - ....
  - ....
  - ....

  TRY QUESTION 65
- Computer processing can take place by batch processing, or commonly now, in real-time systems. Key controls in real-time systems are .... , ... , ... , ... , ... and ....

  TRY QUESTION 66
- Systems development controls are designed to ensure that any new system does not present any new risk to the environment. They include controls over .... , ... , ... , ... and ....
- As well as considering the specific controls over the development process, internal audit may also consider the wider project management issues such as .... , ... , ... and ....

  TRY QUESTIONS 67 AND 68
- Examples of computer assisted audit techniques which auditors might use include:
  - ....
  - ....
  - ....
  - ....
  - ....
  - ....

  TRY QUESTIONS 69 TO 71
- *Possible pitfalls*

  Write down the mistakes you know you should avoid.

DID YOU KNOW? – QUALITY ASSURANCE OF SYSTEMS: AUDITING IN A COMPUTERISED ENVIRONMENT

- *Could you fill in the blanks? The answers are in bold. Use this page for revision purposes as you approach the exam.*
- Security is the protection of data from actual or deliberate threats including the following:
  - **Human errors, accidents or omissions**
  - **Dishonest employees**
  - **Disgruntled employees**
  - **Hackers**
  - **Environmental damage**
  - **Electrical fluctuations and failures**
  - **Natural disasters and other physical threats**
  - **Civil disruption**
  - **Viruses**

  TRY QUESTION 65
- Computer processing can take place by batch processing, or commonly now, in real-time systems. Key controls in real-time systems are **segregation of duties**, **physical restrictions**, **passwords**, **logging of attempted violations**, **back-ups** and **disaster recovery procedures**.

  TRY QUESTION 66
- Systems development controls are designed to ensure that any new system does not present any new risk to the environment. They include controls over **system testing**, **file conversion**, **user training**, **program amendment** and **review of progress**.
- As well as considering the specific controls over the development process, internal audit may also consider the wider project management issues such as **personnel**, **suppliers used**, **cost-benefit analysis** and **the needs of users**.

  TRY QUESTIONS 67 AND 68
- Examples of computer assisted audit techniques which auditors might use include:
  - **Audit interrogation software**
  - **Test data**
  - **Embedded audit facilities**
  - **Simulation**
  - **Logical path analysis**
  - **Code comparison programs**

  TRY QUESTIONS 69 TO 71
- *Possible pitfalls*
  - **Failure to explain and justify actions required**
  - **Making suggestions that do not reflect the needs of the organisation**

65 TUTORIAL QUESTION: SECURITY FACTORS

(a) Examine the factors which you consider most affect the security of an organisation's computer systems.

(b) Identify ways in which the risk associated with computer security might be successfully managed.

Approaching the question

1 You might start part (a) by thinking about computer security in your own organisation.

2 This is a very broad question, so do not unbalance it by concentrating too much on one aspect, such as physical security or data/system issues

66 COMPUTER PROBLEMS (5/95) *36 mins*

On your first morning as financial controller of a large manufacturing division of a group of companies, you meet, for the first time, some of the key staff reporting to you.

The manager of the divisional computer installation (the computer services manager) announces that he wishes to give one month's notice and resign to take up another post.

Discussions with him produce the following information.

(a) Much of the computer's work is on an integrated system of stock and production control and invoicing.

(b) This system was bought from a large firm of consultants, which installed the system, five years ago.

(c) After the consultants had installed the system there was a disagreement over their fees and the system has since been maintained by the operating staff. The computer services manager had done most of the system modification, and had been helped by one of the shift supervisors. The computer services manager considered that the shift supervisor could continue to make any necessary changes.

(d) The computer services manager had a file of his (handwritten) amendment notes, but did not have an up-to-date set of system operating instructions.

(e) The computer services manager is concerned that there is no back-up system. Until a year ago there had been reciprocal emergency arrangements with a firm in a similar industry, but not a competitor, some twenty miles away. However, it had now closed, and no alternative arrangements had been made.

You are due to meet the key group staff, including the finance director, internal audit manager, and group IT (Information Technology) adviser (who has responsibility for IT policy within the group) tomorrow.

Required

(a) Write a memorandum to your managing director, explaining what action you need to take during the next month. **12 Marks**

(b) Explain what action the Internal Audit Department should have taken in recent years. **8 Marks**

Total Marks = 20

67 INFORMATION PROCESSING (11/98) *36 mins*

A government department is responsible for awarding grants to a large number of applicants. The award of grants is based on detailed information supplied by the applicant. There is some cross-checking of the accuracy of the information supplied.

The old system

The work was done by local offices. Forms were completed by applicants and sent to their local office, which would process claim forms and, where necessary, interview applicants to clarify information supplied, and inspect forms and other documents. The application would be either approved or rejected, the applicant informed, and payment made if the application was successful.

The new system

A very large central processing department, using a new computer system, has been established, which has taken over the work of all the local offices, which have now closed. The new system has moved completely from a largely paper form-based system to a unified database system. In this system, all claims and details are received by post or telephone and entered on to the database.

During the changeover period there was no review by internal audit, but one is now planned.

Required

(a) Explain what general control procedures management should be reviewing to ensure an acceptable level of accuracy and service in any large information processing department, whether using paper-based forms or a computer database. **8 Marks**

(b) Explain what systems of internal control and internal check can be applied to database systems with real-time processing. **12 Marks**

Total Marks = 20

68 INTEGRATED COMPUTER SYSTEM DEVELOPMENT (11/97) *36 mins*

KL Group has developed rapidly from a wholesaler supplying specialist stores in one region of the country into a much larger organisation with a significant share of the national market. This has been achieved by:

(a) acquiring other regional wholesalers;
(b) acquiring local groups of retail shops;
(c) making long-term agreements with stores to act as exclusive suppliers.

The group is in the process of consolidating its position, and plans to introduce as quickly as possible an integrated computer system for the whole business, to replace all the current mixture of systems. The main justification for this is to enable central purchasing to use the combined volumes to obtain the best prices and minimise stockholdings. It is envisaged that the integrated system will enable the number of warehouses to be rationalised and reduced.

The finance director has expressed his concern to you, as chief internal auditor, regarding he progress of the project. he fully agrees the need for speed, and the general direction of the project, but does not consider he is adequately informed of the progress made, or of the steps taken to ensure that accounting (and audit) problems will not arise on implementation of the integrated system.

Required

(a) Explain what steps should be taken in the management of a major project, such as the project described above, to ensure that all senior managers are fully aware of the progress made, and any problems arising. **6 Marks**

(b) Explain briefly the potential accounting and audit problems arising from the implementation of the new integrated system, and recommend the actions required to deal with these problems. **14 Marks**

Note. You are not required to discuss the design of the new integrated systems.

Total Marks = 20

69 TUTORIAL QUESTION: COMPUTER SYSTEM AUDIT

(a) In the context of the development of a new accounting information system, you are required:

(i) to explain the purpose and function of a preliminary analysis;

(ii) to describe the studies it would be necessary to carry out in order to perform such an analysis.

(b) An internal audit is to be carried out on certain newly installed computer-based accounting systems. Amongst them, for example, are sales and purchase order processing systems.

You are required to discuss alternative approaches which an auditor may use to assess the operational efficiency of such computer-based systems.

Approaching the question

1 You should take your time over this question to make sure you get all the relevant points down.

2 You need to consider *all* aspects of the system, who will be affected by it and what it will be used for.

70 NEW SYSTEM (5/97) *36 mins*

The chief internal auditor of a large group has become aware of a problem in a major division of the group, regarding the accounts of that division. The division concerned manufactures automobile components on several sites, selling to manufacturers and to a range of wholesalers who resell spares. Components can be made on more than one site, and can be transferred part-finished between sites.

The division has recently installed the financial accounting part of the group's new computerised accounting system.

The group finance director has stated that the interim results for that division are very far below expectations based on their management accounts. No-one in his department or the division seems to know why. He needs to know urgently what the true position is because the six-month interim statement for the group is due to be published next week. The scale of the problem in the division is material in the group accounts. The interim accounts are not audited, but are full accounts and include a balance sheet and profit and loss account: they are the basis of the decision on the interim dividend.

The divisional managing director considered that the attempt to implement the new computer system for the divisional accounts was mistaken, bearing in mind that the divisional finance staff were relatively inexperienced. He said that he would welcome an internal audit recommendation to scrap the system, and start again when the group system being installed has been modified for the division's requirements.

The divisional finance director wanted temporary help. Ideally, he would like the secondment for several months of some experienced staff from internal audit. This would enable him to implement the management accounting part of the group accounting package, as the division had implemented only the financial accounting part. This would eliminate problems of reconciliation.

The internal auditor at present working on the division's accounts, looking primarily at stock control systems, has complained that he is making little progress as all key staff are preoccupied with other matters and unable to discuss weaknesses in stock control with him.

Required

(a) As group finance director, prepare clear and detailed guidance to your staff on how the financial accounts should be investigated to establish their accuracy. **10 Marks**

(b) As chief internal auditor, prepare detailed guidance for the internal auditor working at the division on how he should undertake a preliminary review of the computer system.

Explain, with reasons, which potential problems with a new system should be examined. **10 Marks**

Note. Make and explain any necessary assumptions regarding the systems employed in the group and in the division.

Total Marks = 20

71 REAL TIME TRANSACTION PROCESSING (11/95) *36 mins*

Real-time transaction processing systems are now far from unusual, although few reach the scale and complexity of the systems used for the sale of airline tickets.

However, they have common features such as network operation and the ability of remote terminal operators to access and change the centrally-held data.

Required

(a) Explain what additional problems real-time transactions processing systems cause the internal auditor compared with a batch processing environment. **6 Marks**

(b) Explain what steps the internal auditor needs to take to solve the problems explained in the answer to (a). **8 Marks**

(c) Explain with reasons which computer-assisted audit techniques (CAATS) could be used in this real-time environment. **6 Marks**

Total Marks = 20

Answer bank

1 TUTORIAL QUESTION: IDEAS ABOUT CONTROL AND ORGANISATIONS

(a) **Emmanuel *et al*'s concept of control** embraces the formulation of objectives as well as monitoring their attainment by way of feedback. The **four conditions** they describe are as follows.

(i) **Objectives** for the process being controlled **must exist,** for without an aim or purpose control has no meaning.

(ii) The **output** of the process **must be measurable** in terms of the dimensions defined by the objectives.

(iii) A **predictive model** of the process being controlled is required so that causes for the non-attainment of objectives can be determined and proposed corrective actions evaluated.

(iv) There must be a **capability of taking action** so that deviations of attainment from objectives can be reduced.

(b) **Systems theory** may help as follows.

(i) It draws attention to the **dynamic aspects of organisation,** and the factors influencing the growth and development of all its sub-systems.

(ii) It creates an **awareness of sub-systems,** each with potentially conflicting goals which must be integrated. Sub-optimisation (where sub-systems pursue their own goals to the detriment of the system as a whole) is a feature of organisational behaviour.

(iii) It focuses **attention on interrelationships** between aspects of the organisation, and between it and its environment, that is, on the needs of the system as a whole: management should not get so bogged down in detail and small political arenas that they lose sight of the overall objectives and processes.

(iv) It teaches managers to **reject the deterministic idea** that A will always cause B to happen. 'Linear causality' may occur, but only rarely, because of the unpredictability and uncontrollability of many inputs.

(v) The importance of the **environment** on a system is acknowledged.

(c) The **radical view** argues that it is in the **owner's interests to maximise the value extracted from the employee** and this leads inevitably to the **employee's being exploited**. The management accounting system is controlled and operated by the owners and therefore cannot be for the mutual benefit of all parties. The main radical approach to management accounting is concerned with **labour process theory** which argues that labour has become an ever more formalised process rather than the satisfying activity it ought to be. Movements such as **Taylor's scientific management** aim to deskill workers and concentrate control in the hands of management. Accounting is seen as 'a system to reinforce the power of owners over their employees by permitting control over every aspect of their work through the minutiae of cost analysis' (Puxty).

(d) (i) Each division has **quasi-autonomous status.**

(ii) **Strategic decisions** are taken by **senior managers,** while **operational decisions** are made by **divisional managers.**

(iii) An **incentive mechanism** exists and is used to encourage divisional managers to share the interests of senior managers.

(iv) An **internal audit system** is in place, with performance measures to evaluate the success or otherwise, both of managers and of divisions.

(v) There is a **system of allocating resources** whereby senior managers distinguish the most profitable alternatives from amongst *all* divisions.

(e) Symptoms include:

(i) a sense of **invulnerability** - blindness to the risk involved in 'pet' strategies;
(ii) **rationalisations for inconsistent facts;**
(iii) **moral blindness** - 'might is right';
(iv) a tendency to **stereotype** 'outsiders' and 'enemies';
(v) strong **group pressure** to quell dissent;
(vi) **self-censorship** by members - not 'rocking the boat';
(vii) perception of **unanimity** - filtering out divergent views;
(viii) mutual support and **solidarity** to 'guard' the decision.

(f) Many **factors influence the organisational culture,** including the following.

(i) **Economic conditions and strategy**

In prosperous times organisations will either be complacent or adventurous, full of new ideas and initiatives. In recession they may be depressed, or challenged. The struggle against a main competitor may take on 'heroic' dimensions.

(ii) **The nature of the business and its tasks**

The types of technology used in different forms of business create the pace and priorities associated with different forms of work, for example the hustle and frantic conditions for people dealing in the international money market compared with the studious life of a research officer. Task also influences work environment to an extent, and this is an important visual cultural indicator.

(iii) **Leadership style**

The approach used in exercising authority will determine the extent to which subordinates feel alienated and uninterested or involved and important. Leaders are also the creators and 'sellers' of organisational culture: it is up to them to put across the vision.

(iv) **Policies and practices**

The level of trust and understanding which exists between members of an organisation can often be seen in the way policies and objectives are achieved, for example the extent to which they are imposed by tight written rules and procedures or implied through custom and understanding.

(v) **Structure**

The way in which work is organised, authority exercised and people rewarded will reflect an emphasis on freedom or formal control, flexibility or rigidity.

(vi) **Characteristics of the work force**

Organisation culture will be affected by the demographic nature of the workforce, for example its typical manual/clerical division, age, sex and personality.

2 DIVISIONALISED STRUCTURES

> **Pass marks**. Parts (a) and (b) can be answered from book knowledge, and this would have been perfectly acceptable. Part (c), however, looks at the question from a slightly different angle, which requires some thought. You will almost always find that questions in the MCS exam do this. Many candidates will leave out these parts of questions, so any sensible comments you can find to make will impress the examiner and make your paper stand out from the others. In part (c) it is very helpful to think of control as 'making sure that the right things get done by subordinates'.
>
> *Other points.* Instead of repeating book knowledge, an alternative approach to part (a) might adopt Williamson's ideas about transaction cost economics. We have included both approaches. Matters that you may legitimately have mentioned in part (c) but which are not included in our answer are organisational culture and leadership style.
>
> **Examiner's comment**. Common errors were: misreading part (a) and setting out the arguments for *and against* divisionalisation; writing about the *measurement* of divisional performance (marks were not available for expositions of ROI and RI); writing far too much in answer to parts (a) and (b). Marks were allowed if candidates answered part (c) from the perspective of top *divisional* management, although the question was intended to be about top *group* management.

(a) **Arguments for divisionalised structures in large firms**

(i) **Decision makers at divisional level** have **more awareness** of their markets and products and of local problems. They are closer to, and so have a better understanding of, day-to-day operational problems.

(ii) There is **greater speed of decision making** and response to changing events since there is no need to refer decisions upwards. This is valued by customers and is particularly important in a modern, rapidly changing environment.

(iii) Divisionalisation allows more **senior management** to **concentrate on strategic problems** affecting the organisation as a whole. They need not be burdened by large amounts of information that is not relevant to their role.

(iv) Divisionalisation helps more **junior managers** to **develop** in roles of responsibility. Divisional managers can be more adventurous and are better motivated.

An alternative approach to the question might adopt Williamson's ideas about **transaction cost economics**. This sees all work as a series of transactions that can either be carried out through a market or take place within an organisational hierarchy.

As the **complexity of the transactions** required for a business to operate **increases, transaction costs can be reduced by adopting some kind of hierarchy**. For example, a firm that only needs legal advice on very rare occasions will engage a firm of solicitors from outside (from the market). If, as that firm grows, it needs legal advice more and more it will eventually be cheaper to set up a full time legal department within the organisation (in an hierarchical structure).

As the **level of complexity increases** still further and we get into the realm of the 'large firms' envisaged in the question, the **cost savings are counterbalanced by the increasing costs of keeping control**. These costs arise because managers are prevented by the hierarchical division of responsibilities from taking the best decisions in their limited area of control, and because information tends to be lost or distorted as it passes through the hierarchy.

This **leads to** the development of the **multi-divisional** or **M-form organisation** which, by mixing the features of both markets and hierarchies, has the following **advantages.**

(i) Each division has **quasi-autonomous** status: it is a separate business unit.

(ii) **Strategic decisions** are taken by **senior managers** (the hierarchy), while **operational decisions** are made by **divisional managers** (the market).

(iii) An **incentive mechanism** exists and is used to encourage divisional managers to share the interests of senior managers.

(iv) An **internal audit system** is in place, with performance measures to evaluate the success or otherwise of both managers and of divisions.

(v) There is a system of **allocating resources** whereby senior managers distinguish the most profitable alternatives from amongst all divisions.

(b) **The costs and potential inefficiencies of a divisionalised structure**

(i) **Duplication of functions and facilities**. It is perhaps wasteful for each division to have, say, its own management accounting department or production equipment.

(ii) In spite of Williamson's ideals, there will inevitably be some **loss of information** *needed* by the senior managers to take strategic decisions. At the extreme, for example, a divisional manager may be able to hide the truth about a division's poor performance from the top management, who would close down the division or change its manager if they were aware of the full story.

(iii) Competition between divisions *may* be healthy and encourage all divisions to do better. If divisions are dependent upon each other for input, processing or output, however, competition may cause them to take **decisions that are not in the interests of the organisation as a whole.**

(iv) **Senior management** may find that it is spending much of its **time resolving disputes between divisions** about, say, unfair transfer prices or biased allocation of capital investment, rather than concentrating on strategic issues.

As Christopher Lorenz has pointed out, as business conditions alter, the balance of power must be able to *shift* between the central authority and the divisions if the organisation as a whole is to be capable consistently of striking the optimum balance between integration and autonomy.

(c) **The role of top management and their control of subordinates**

In a centralised structure **senior managers** are responsible for both the strategic management of the organisation as a whole and for the day-to-day operations of the functions they represent. With a **divisionalised structure** these managers hand over the management of functions to their subordinates. Their role **becomes one more like that of an investor looking for a return on an investment.**

(i) They need to learn to **manage with 'hands off'**, on the basis of summary data, without getting involved in the day -to-day detail. The control system needs to develop appropriate **performance measures** that facilitate this approach. An **internal audit department** reporting directly to top management may be needed for reassurance that day to day operations are being properly managed.

(ii) Rather than fighting their own function's corner in matters such as transfer pricing and capital investment they need to be able to look at these issues from the **point of view of group interests** and **proper co-ordination** of the activities of the organisation as a whole.

(iii) They may need to develop **reward systems** for subordinates **that ensure goal congruence.**

(iv) They will manage from the point of view of the changing environment in which the business as a whole operates, but their perspective of the environment and their subordinates' perspective may be different. **Mutual sharing of environmental data** will become essential.

A useful exposition of the problems of control in large diversified companies is provided by **Goold and Campbell** who identify three different styles of central management.

(i) **Strategic planning,** which entails the centre participating in and influencing the strategies of the core businesses.

(ii) **Financial control,** which focuses on annual profit targets rather than getting involved in the detail of how these are achieved.

(iii) **Strategic control,** where the top management is concerned with the plans of its business units but believes in autonomy for business unit managers. Control is maintained through financial targets and strategic objectives, but top management do not advocate strategies or interfere in major decisions.

3 MANAGEMENT CONTROL

Pass marks. For our answer to (a) we use the three dimensions in the question (problems, systems etc) as the *overall* framework, rather than the textbook strategic/management/operational framework that you have learned. It may seem perverse to make things more difficult for yourself in this way, but think of it as an exam technique that will help you to focus your mind on the question asked, and avoid the very strong temptation to write all you know, relevant or not, about a topic.

In part (b), you may have difficulty distinguishing between outsourcing and a long-term relationship with a supplier (this probably accounts for the problems reported by the examiner: see below). They amount to much the same thing in our opinion, although they may initially come about in very different ways. We therefore focus mainly on long-term relationships with customers.

Other points. Our answer to part (b)(ii) is very much a Theory X answer, and other answers may be equally valid. Arguably, if the right contractors/part-timers are engaged in the first place, there is no reason why they should not perform perfectly satisfactorily. In fact the insecure nature of their employment may make them perform more diligently than their full-time counterparts. If this is so, control is exercised at the *selection* stage.

Examiner's comment. Part (a) was generally well answered, although many candidates failed to earn all of the available marks because of: ineffective explanations and meaningless statements; unbalanced explanations of the three levels (for example too much detail on strategic planning, too little on task control); detailed plans but less detailed answers; and failing to refer to the dimensions in the question (problems, systems, levels etc). Answers to part (b) were poor, apparently because too much time was spent on part (a) and/or because candidates failed to read the question. Pre-prepared essays of only partial relevance were produced on outsourcing while the other two examples (especially long-term relationships) were barely mentioned. Where long-term relationships were addressed, answers tended to be pre-prepared ones about TQM or JIT, with no mention of management control.

(a) (i) **Problems and decisions**

(1) Probably the chief **strategic planning** problem is **uncertainty** because at this level management are concerned with factors that are difficult or impossible to control: what happens in the **external environment (PEST factors)** and what happens in the **future.**

Other problems that are common at this level are **investment-related issues** (what projects to proceed with and what resources to devote to them), and **organisation-wide people issues** (how to promote a particular culture).

Strategic planning **decisions** relate to the **overall mission and objectives of the organisation**, to the **resources used** to attain those objectives and to the **policies that govern** the acquisition, use and disposition of **these resources**, for instance how the organisation should be structured.

(2) **Management control problems** centre around **obtaining adequate resources** and **using them efficiently and effectively**. The difficulty of devising and maintaining systems to monitor whether resources are available and whether they are being used efficiently and effectively will vary according to the type of work and type of resource. For instance ensuring the economical use of raw materials presents different control problems to ensuring that the behaviour of employees is goal-congruent, or that cash is available to pay debts as they fall due.

Decisions are taken **within the framework of strategic plans and objectives**. They typically involve **recruiting staff** or **selecting suppliers**, switching resources between projects, determining what control actions are necessary in response to routine (eg monthly) reports.

(3) **Task control problems** relate to **individual tasks and day-to-day difficulties**, such as re-scheduling sales visits if a sales rep is ill, dealing with a breakdown on the production line, refusing further credit to a customer who is over their credit limit, or deciding on *ad hoc* action to appease a dissatisfied customer.

Decisions are taken **within the strict guidelines of strategic planning and management control**. Many operational control decisions can be **automated or programmed on the basis of organisational rules and past experience.**

(ii) **Systems and information requirements**

(1) At the **strategic level** systems need to be set up to **provide highly summarised information**, concerned with the **organisation as a whole,** and derived from both **internal and external sources**. Information will be relevant to the **long-term** (the future) and will incorporate **forecasts**: **systems** should therefore be capable of presenting **different scenarios** and taking account of **risk and uncertainty**. Systems also need to be **flexible** enough to provide information as and when required rather than at fixed intervals.

(2) For **management control, information** requirements include **performance measurements, budgetary control** information and variance analysis, cash flow forecasts, manning levels, departmental profit reports, labour turnover statistics and so on. Information is primarily derived from **internal sources** and is relevant to the **short and medium term.**

The primary **systems** are likely to be the **financial accounting** system and the **budgetary control** system, providing **routine reports at regular intervals.**

(3) For **task control, information** is **short-term,** almost entirely derived from **internal sources** and may often be **non-financial**. The **systems** used are those that **support the accounting system,** such as time

recording systems, stock control systems, quality control reports. **Reporting** may be on a **daily** basis or even more frequent.

(iii) **Levels of management**

Traditionally these three types of management control are associated with the management hierarchy.

(1) **Strategic planning** is done at a **senior** level, for instance by directors.

(2) **Management control** is the responsibility of **middle managers**, such as departmental heads

(3) **Task control** is the responsibility of more **junior, front-line managers,** such as supervisors, foremen, chief cashier and so on.

Modern trends have tended to **undermine this distinction**. For instance many large organisations have responded to a more quickly-changing and competitive environment by setting up a **strategic planning department**. Meanwhile the influence of information technology and the re-engineering of processes has led to the **removal of many middle managers** and the **empowerment** of more junior staff, with appropriate responsibility for control matters.

The distinction between different *types* of control remains valid, but the traditional association with particular *levels* of management is less so in many organisations.

(b) (i) **Outsourcing**

The initial decision to outsource non-core activities may be made at board level, but thereafter ongoing responsibilities will probably be a **management control task**. The process will be very different from management control of internal resources.

(1) **Systems** will need to be set up to **assess potential contractors** according to defined criteria such as cost, quality, financial stability and so on. The organisation may also **benchmark** against its own facilities for providing the outsourced service or activity, although it will increasingly lose touch with developments.

(2) **Formal contracts** should be entered into. The contract may need board authorisation before it is finally signed. Besides practical, operational issues, contracts may need to include terms about continued availability of information needed to manage the business and confidentiality.

(3) **Control** should be maintained throughout the period of the contract to ensure that its terms are being adhered to. This would include regular **monitoring** of the quality and timeliness of supplies and of the amount charged for them, and of all of the matters considered before entering into the contract. Deviations from the contract should be drawn to the attention of the contractors and any penalties on failure to comply with the terms should be exacted. The organisation itself should also have control procedures to ensure that it fulfils its part of the bargain.

However, outsourcing **should remove the need for any sort of task control**: this will be exercised by the contractors themselves.

(ii) **Contract, part-time or temporary staff**

Staff who are not employed by the organisation on a permanent basis will be **more difficult to control** than full-time employees.

By the very nature of their work they will be **less committed to the organisation's long term future.**

(1) This needs to be recognised in terms of **reward systems** (job security and career progression are not on offer, and extra remuneration may be needed in compensation).

(2) It also needs to be recognised in terms of **quality control,** which may need to be stricter, given that individuals have no reason to maintain the standards of the organisation if these do not happen to coincide with their own self-interest.

Because of their limited time with the company it will be difficult or **impossible to instil aspects of corporate culture** (clan control: shared values and assumptions such as a belief in quality), **depriving managers of an important control mechanism.** Instead it may be necessary to set out required **procedures for working in a more formal and clearly defined way,** leaving little room for self-interested interpretation.

For staff who **work off premises** there may need to be **more rigorous monitoring procedures** to ensure that work is proceeding according to plan and to the required quality.

(iii) **Long-term relationships**

Management control of a long-term relationship with a **supplier** is very much **like control of an outsourcing arrangement** (as discussed in (b)(i)), once the arrangement has been entered into, so this answer concentrates mainly on **customers.**

The differences in management control processes in this case include the following.

(1) There will be **less need to manage cash inflows and outflows** in respect of the customer or supplier, since these are likely to be contractually agreed and certain.

(2) **Performance measures may be set by the customer** rather than internally, and there may be a need to **supply the customer with management information.**

(3) **Quality** is likely to be **assured** as part of the relationship, and the **cost of any failure** to meet the required standard will be **met by the supplier.** This will mean that the onus is on the supplier to set up systems capable of ensuring quality.

(4) **Production processes** may need to be **flexible** enough to cope with unexpected orders, and this may entail closer monitoring of WIP and the ability to deploy flexible resources where they are most needed.

4 TUTORIAL QUESTION: ACTIVATION, AGENCY, CONTINGENCY

(a) (i) The quotation from Emmanuel *et al* is a little misleading. The idea of 'activation' is extracted from a book nearly 20 years old on managerial *stress*, not motivation. However, with a little interpretation the **idea does contain the essential elements** of many of the theories put forward at various times. Two examples may be given.

(1) **Expectancy theory** is the closest parallel: force of motivation is equivalent to the strength of preference for a certain outcome (its

importance) multiplied by the expectation that doing x will result in y (a combination of *uncertainty* and *ability to influence*).

(2) **Goal theory** suggests that people will be more highly motivated by *specific* (not *uncertain*), difficult (*important*) goals, so long as they have accepted them and are kept informed of progress (*ability to influence*/not *uncertain*).

(ii) The idea of activation suggests that in order to motivate people a MAS needs to incorporate features such as the following.

(1) A **reliable, credible forecasting system** and **fast accurate feedback to reduce uncertainty** whenever possible.

(2) Some means of **drawing attention to important outcomes** and of **making them important to the people who are trying to achieve them.** In a MAS this might mean distinguishing between significant and insignificant variances, offering bonuses for achieving targets, penalising poor quality and so on.

(3) A system of **responsibility accounting** whereby individuals are only held responsible for operations that they can control.

(b) As its name suggests, agency theory **regards the relationship between owners and managers of organisations as one between principal and agent**: the principal hires the agent to perform a task in an uncertain environment. The theory makes certain **assumptions about individuals as agents,** listed in Wilson and Chan, *Managerial Accounting: Method and Meaning* (1993) as follows:

(i) they behave rationally in seeking to maximise their own utility;

(ii) they seek financial and non-financial rewards;

(iii) they tend to be risk-averse and, hence, reluctant to innovate;

(iv) their individual interests will not always coincide with those of their principals;

(v) they prefer leisure to hard work;

(vi) they have greater knowledge about their operating performance and actions than is available to their principals.

Key issues in agency theory are **attitudes to risk and the observability of effort.**

(i) Conventional management accounting assumes that principals protect agents from risk - it only makes managers responsible for things they can control. Agency theory suggests that if principals are risk averse then they should *share* the risk with agents and this can increase the utility of both parties. Making a large part of an executive's potential reward subject to some profit target is a simple example of such a contract.

(ii) The principal may find it difficult to *observe* the agent's effort (for example in a decentralised organisation) encouraging the agent to shirk. Alternatively the principal may not be able to *evaluate* the effort because he does not know the information on which the decision to expend that much effort was based.

It is argued that agency theory **provides a formal framework for behavioural issues** compared with the less precise frameworks of other theories, and it may provide the **basis for a more coherent theory of management accounting.** At the very least it is a **fresh way of communicating and disseminating valuable ideas** that may appeal to those who are used to viewing problems in the language of economics.

Many of the **assumptions** of agency theory are **open to question,** however. Wilson and Chan describe the **limitations** of agency theory as follows.

> 'Firstly, it is essentially a **two-person analysis** and, although it may be possible to extend it to a whole hierarchical organization, this has yet to be done. Secondly, it is a **single period model** which neglects the potential impact of a continuing employment relationship. Finally, the **descriptive validity of the utility maximizing assumptions is open to question**.'

(c) Studies of **management accounting systems** based on **contingency theory** look at the **impact on their design of factors such as** the following.

(i) **The environment**. For example:

(1) its degree of predictability;
(2) the degree of competition faced;
(3) the number of different product markets faced;
(4) the degree of hostility exhibited by competing organisations.

(ii) **Organisational structure**. For example:

(1) size;
(2) interdependence of parts;
(3) degree of decentralisation;
(4) availability of resources.

(iii) **Technology**. For example:

(1) the nature of the production process;
(2) the routineness/complexity of the production process;
(3) how well the relationship between ends and means is understood;
(4) the amount of variety in each task that has to be performed.

(iv) **Strategy**. For example resources may be deployed (and so controlled) differently in periods of rapid organisational growth than they are when earnings maximisation is the aim, and measurement systems will have different emphases depending upon objectives.

(v) **Culture**. For example:

(1) control systems may conflict with value systems;
(2) controls may threaten existing power relationships;
(3) culture can be a form of control in itself.

5 CONTINGENCY THEORY, CULTURE AND ATTITUDE CHANGE

Pass marks. The most recent edition of Handy's *Understanding Organisations* was published in 1993. His ideas are explored in greater depth in his book *Gods of Management*.

Our answer is longer than you could have managed in the time available.

Examiner's comment. This question is on topics within section 16a of the syllabus - control and the organisation. Part (a) requires commentary on contingency theory which is dealt with extensively in *Accounting for Management Control* by Emmanuel, Otley & Merchant, which is on the reading list. Parts (b) and (c) are both on organisational culture. Part (b) requires a clear explanation of the effect on the choice of management accounting systems of differing cultures. Part (c) seeks explanation of the ways in which management accounting systems and management control systems can be used to influence culture. It does not suggest that these are the only ways of influencing culture, or that the process is unproblematic.

(a) Although Otley says 'contingency theory ... appears to afford a potential explanation for the bewildering variety of management accounting systems actually observed in practice', it is subject to a number of criticisms.

(i) The nature of appropriate **contingent variables** is **by no means clear** and, though many have been suggested, there is little agreement.

(ii) Explicit consideration of **organisational effectiveness** has been **neglected** by contingency theorists.

(iii) The interconnected nature of the components that make up a control package suggests that the **management accounting information system cannot be studied in isolation** from its wider context.

(iv) It is **not clear how** the various **contingent variables** proposed **affect the management accounting system**. Often, for example, it seems that it is the organisation structure that adapts to its environment and the management accounting system simply reflects the organisation structure.

(v) Contingency theory **plays down the importance of power** of the strategically-placed managers and the power of the organisation itself. For example, a management accountant who is regarded as having considerable expert power may be able to obtain acceptance of a MAS which is far more scientifically based than his or her organisation would otherwise be willing to use.

(vi) For financial accounting purposes accountants are expected to accept the idea of 'best practice' and to follow the rules and regulations of accounting standards and company law. Although **financial accounting** does not go quite so far as to insist upon one best way, it **does not allow many alternatives** for external reporting purposes. This is quite at odds with the contingency approach.

(vii) Most, if not all, of the **writing on contingency theory** and management accounting is written in a highly abstruse style and **aimed at fellow academics** rather than practising accountants. A good contrast is provided by the way in which Activity Based Costing has been popularised by the writings of management consultants.

(b) Handy's discussion recognises that an organisation may have within it elements of different cultures. However, we shall assume for simplicity that organisations as a whole can be said to have a single prevailing culture.

(i) The **power culture** exists mainly in smaller organisations, where power and influence stem from a central source, through whom all communication, decisions and control are channelled. Political competition for a share of power is rife, and emotional behaviour is encouraged by the 'personality' cult surrounding the leader.

The **management control system** in such an organisation will be one that ensures that **all information flows to and from the central figure**. In fact the system, such as it is, will probably be **operated by and for the benefit of the leader,** who will communicate plans directly to those responsible for implementing them and make personal checks on their progress. In this instance there are no **related contingent factors.**

(ii) The **role culture** or **bureaucracy** is one in which everything and everybody are in their proper place. There is a **formal structure** and the **organisation operates by well-established rules and procedures.**

In this case the **management control system** will closely **reflect the formal structure of the organisation**, and the parts and their interaction will be controlled by **written rules and procedures** governing roles, communications and settlement of disputes. The climate is ideal for a **responsibility accounting system**. The textbook 'budget manual' and 'budget committee' approach to management control will be adopted, there are likely to be standard costs, and proforma management reports will be produced on a regular basis. The **system**, like the organisation as a whole, will **find it difficult to adapt to new conditions.**

(iii) The **task culture** is reflected in a **matrix organisation**, in project teams and task forces. The principal concern in a task culture is to get the job done and such organisations are **flexible** and **constantly changing** as tasks are accomplished and new needs arise. **Innovation** and **creativity** are highly prized. There is a great deal of **individual participation**, and **strong communication** and **group identity**.

Because of the **pace of change** it may be **difficult to establish a 'system' of control** in such an organisation. Handy describes the ideal situation as one in which senior managers are content to **exercise control merely by allocating resources and letting people get on with it.** Modern organisations are finding that the task culture can nevertheless be *reinforced* by a system of performance measurement designed to support and reward behaviour that is in keeping with it, however.

(iv) The **person culture** prevails in an organisation whose **purpose is to serve the interests of individuals within it**. Handy gives the examples of 'barristers' chambers, architects' partnerships, hippy communes, social groups, families, [and] some small consultancy firms'.

Control in such an organisation is, by its definition, **exercised by the individual** over his or her own activities. To the extent that there is a need to draw on common resources, there may very well be a highly formalised set of controls, akin to those existing in the role culture, because the individuals concerned will have agreed that certain practices are fair. But because each individual is merely using the organisation to fulfil his or her own personal objectives, there are **no organisational objectives** as such and there is **little that a system of management control can contribute.**

(Accountants and universities are probably not examples of person-culture organisations, as the CIMA model answer would have you believe: these seem to us to be archetypal *role* cultures.)

(c) Organisations that have transferred from the public sector to the private sector have been forced to **recognise** that their overriding aim or **objective is to make a profit.** Others that have remained in public ownership have been forced to recognise that **what they do has a cost**. The adoption of total quality management forces companies to realise that **mistakes should not occur.**

In each of these situations the **management accounting system and the management control system have a great deal to contribute.**

(i) The organisation can adopt **normal commercial accounting practices** and make sure that the financial **information** that is needed **to make decisions** is **available** to (and **understandable** by) the people who make those decisions.

(ii) The **reporting structure** of the new system should closely **reflect changes in the structure** of the organisation, reallocations of responsibilities and so on.

(iii) Accounting **targets** or **budgets** and periodic reports on actual performance can **emphasise the new aims and objectives**: cost and profit can be highlighted, as can the costs of poor quality and measurable improvements in performance over time.

(iv) **Managers** will be used to having targets and limits imposed upon them from above. In the new culture they can be **encouraged to take part in setting their own goals.**

(v) The **reward system** can be used to encourage and reinforce new attitudes and behaviour, while those who do not commit themselves to the change miss out or are punished, or pressured to 'buy in or get out'.

(vi) Emblems of the **culture** - for example the physical design of reports and the language used ('excellent' performance, 'right first time', or whatever) - can be used to reflect the new 'style'.

6 BUSINESS PROCESS RE-ENGINEERING

Pass marks. You should have encountered BPR in your Stage 3 MAA studies and SMM, MCS and especially IFM at Stage 4. As is often the case with MCS examination questions, one or more parts merely ask you to describe a process or technique (part (a) in this instance), whereas other parts of the question ask you to apply what you know about that process or technique to a particular set of circumstances (part (b)). The examiner's comment (below) about mixing up issues in part (b) seems rather unfair: the question should have been better worded to elicit the sort of answers expected.

Examiner's comment. Part (a) was generally well-answered. Failure to earn marks was generally due to answers that were too short for four marks, or to lack of understanding of BPR. Part (b) was often answered poorly: some answers lacked structure and mixed issues of planning and implementation; others assumed that BPR could be implemented wholly by the management accountant , rather than by a team. Answers to part (c) were mixed: errors included not discussing criticisms at all; identifying a feature of BPR without explaining whether or not it was an *advantage*; discussing TQM, ABC, ABM, JIT etc and anything else relatively fashionable and assuming that BPR incorporates all; and providing only short notes.

(a) **Business process re-engineering**

Business process re-engineering (BPR), also known as process innovation and core process re-design, is the **introduction of radical changes in business processes to achieve breakthrough results in terms of major gains in levels of performance plus reductions in costs.**

The main writing on the subject is Hammer and Champy's *Reengineering the Corporation* (1993), from which the following definition is taken.

> Reengineering is 'the **fundamental** rethinking and **radical** redesign of business **processes** to achieve **dramatic** improvements in critical contemporary measures of performance, such as cost, quality, service and speed'.

The key words in the definition, identified as Hammer and Champy, are 'fundamental', 'radical', 'dramatic' and 'process'.

(i) The first two indicate that BPR is somewhat **akin to zero base budgeting**; it starts by asking basic questions such as 'why do we do what we do?', without making any assumptions or looking back to what has always been done in the past.

(ii) 'Dramatic' means that BPR **should achieve 'quantum leaps in performance'**, not just marginal, incremental improvements.

(iii) The most **important word is 'process'**, by which Hammer and Champy mean 'a collection of activities that takes one or more kinds of input and creates an output that is of value to the customer'.

For example, order fulfilment is a process that takes an order as its input and results in the delivery of the ordered goods. Part of this process is the manufacture of the goods, but under BPR the aim of manufacturing is not merely to *make* the goods. Manufacturing should aim to *deliver* the goods that were *ordered*, and any aspect of the manufacturing process that hinders this aim should be re-engineered. The first question to ask might be 'Do they need to be manufactured at all?'.

The difference between traditional approaches to efficiency improvement and BPR is that BPR more typically **breaks away from** conventional wisdom and the **constraints of organisational or departmental/functional boundaries**. BPR is more concerned, too, with exploiting the **power of information technology - not to automate existing processes, but to facilitate new ones.**

(b) **Contribution of the management accountant to the planning of a BPR programme**

Having overall responsibility for the organisation's information systems, the management accountant will be the **main provider of the information** required by the BPR programme. Because BPR involves the introduction of significant changes to business processes, the organisation's information requirements are likely to change. Users will require alternative types of information in alternative formats.

At the outset there will be no way of knowing for sure the precise information requirements of the organisation, however, because the chief tool of BPR is a clean sheet of paper. It is only once the programme commences that precise information requirements will become clear.

At the planning stage of a BPR programme the management accountant will therefore need to **liaise with all others on the team** and consider the changes that will be necessary to the **organisation's information systems** as a result of different ways of organising work.

Benchmarking exercises, comparing processes with those used in other organisations may need to be set up, and the management accountant is likely to be heavily involved in devising ways of collecting and analysing data from such exercises.

A **modelling approach** will help to assess the validity and consequences of alternative ways of re-engineering processes.

Costing systems may need to be reappraised: for example it might be useful to set up activity based costing systems, but the consequent changes to information collection and analysis and to accounting software need to be thought through fully.

For reporting purposes, **alternative performance measures will need to be devised,** since information will no longer be required on a departmental/ functional basis but on a process basis.

Contribution of the management accountant to the implementation of a BPR programme

When the BPR programme is being implemented, the management accountant will need to **ensure that managers within the organisation are provided with the information they require.** It is likely that the management accounting function will need to provide a broader range of information than previously, but the emphasis must be on user friendliness and sharing. This is likely to mean the introduction of

new software and telecommunications links, capable of handling different flows of information.

As one example, sales processes may be re-engineered so that they are geared to types of customer rather than to types of product: information will need to cut across a variety of product categories or brands. As another, re-engineered work may be devolved to lower levels in the organisation hierarchy, and the managers at these levels may have quite different information requirements to those that were catered for previously.

An important aspect of implementation will be **monitoring of progress**: are the expected benefits of BPR being realised, and if not what action is required? Indicators of success might include reduced costs, faster delivery, more satisfied customers and so on, but systems need to be in operation to measure such things.

The **management accounting function itself is likely to need to change**, as part of the BPR programme, so that it can provide the information required.

(c) **Advantages of BPR**

(i) It offers a **strategic as opposed to operational approach to seeking improvements** in performance, as major rather than marginal changes to processes are encouraged.

(ii) As a method of **cost reduction**, BPR 'is very good at getting rid of the rodents of inefficiency and the pests of waste' (Bentley).

(iii) Because it encourages cost reduction, it can offer an organisation **competitive advantage.**

(iv) The improvements to business processes should result in **improved levels of customer service.**

(v) Because of the concentration on processes rather than the traditional department/functional boundaries, it provides a **different approach to strategy formulation.**

(vi) This concentration on processes (which straddle the entire organisational operation) rather than on departments/functions also provides new links between the different functions of the organisation, and this may encourage further **new ideas.**

(vii) It goes some way to **decreasing organisational complexity** because it concentrates on core processes and attempts to eradicate any activity which is not economic or necessary.

Criticisms of BPR

BPR received a great deal of attention in the early 1990s and, perhaps because it coincided with a worldwide recession, it **became misunderstood.** BPR became allied in managers minds with narrow targets such as reductions in staff numbers and cost-cutting measures, whereas if BPR concentrates on better ways of achieving an end (satisfying customers), a re-engineered solution could equally involve more staff and higher investment.

Managers are not used to thinking in systems terms so, instead of looking at the whole picture (which might affect their own jobs), they tend to **seize on individual aspects of the organisation,** for instance re-engineering the sales process alone, rather than looking at the organisation-wide task of getting products to customers.

It tends to be an **all-or-nothing proposition,** often with an uncertain result. It is therefore a high risk undertaking and perhaps not worth attempting unless there is a pressing need to rethink what the organisation is doing overall in a major area.

Many organisations trying BPR do not achieve good results because they fail to think it through, do not engage hearts and minds sufficiently, act on bad advice or cannot override established departmental/functional power groups which have a vested interest in the *status quo*, or in incremental change rather than radical revolution.

7 STRUCTURE, CULTURE AND CONTROL SYSTEMS

> **Pass marks**. The issues you could have covered in this question range right across MCS syllabus sections A, B and C. Your report is unlikely to be the same as ours since the scope of the question was so broad.
>
> *Other points*. You could have discussed the issues in terms of writers such as Goold and Campbell or Simons, not mentioned in our answer.
>
> **Examiner's comment**. A range of answers would have been acceptable if they were well argued and explained. The main problem with the weaker answers was the initial analysis, noting the key features of the scenario: there were no marks available for any description of the scenario which did not add anything to the detail already provided. Another common failing was to ignore the note that there was no requirement to discuss the merits of the proposed strategy. There were no marks available for discussion of product life cycles or Porter's generic strategies or of corporate governance.

REPORT

To: Chairman
From: Management Accountant — Date: XX.XX.XX
Subject: Changes required to implement proposed change in strategy

This report explains the changes that will be required in the structure, culture and control systems of our organisation if the recommendations of the strategy consultants are to be implemented.

Introduction

In the past we have been successful product innovators, having followed a **strategy of market leadership**. It has been proposed, however, that our future prosperity depends upon **switching to a strategy of cost leadership**. Such a strategy entails attempting to achieve the position of lowest-cost producer in the industry as a whole, focuses on competition on prices in order to obtain the highest market share and demands stringent cost control, high volumes of sale and excellent product quality.

Given the current structure, culture and control systems of the organisation, such a radical change will not be easy and will require significant efforts on the part of everybody in the organisation if it is to be successful.

Changes required to organisational structure

The organisation's current structure is informally based upon and centred around groups of products and individual customers. A strategy of cost leadership will require that **Directors** are **responsible for particular functional areas rather than product groups,** however, to ensure that the entire value chain is controlled in the most effective and efficient way possible.

It may be necessary to **establish a customer services/marketing department** which will be responsible for maintaining contact with customers, currently the responsibility of the Directors.

Although the marketing function will still have a significant role within the organisation, the change in strategy and the reduction in importance of product innovation will **move the spotlight onto the manufacturing function**. Instead of being contracted out, manufacturing should be **brought in-house** in order to maintain control over cost and quality and to produce economies of scale.

Specialists may need to be employed for various functions, given the move to in-house manufacturing and the change to a functional organisational structure, so as to **provide the necessary technical expertise** to support Directors who are principally experienced in sales and marketing.

Overall, the **Directors** should be encouraged to **delegate** more of their responsibilities than at present and to adopt a more **hands-off approach** to management, although they will need to provide strong communication links between the customer services/marketing function and the manufacturing function.

Changes required to organisational culture

Given the fact that the **Executive Directors,** with the exception of the Finance Director, have spent their entire careers with the company, they must have been **instrumental in implementing and maintaining the current strategy** and are likely to find it very **difficult to switch to an alternative,** especially if the alternative clashes with their personal views.

Their personal views have become part of the organisational culture and so the cultural changes necessary if the **new strategy** is to be implemented will have to be **conveyed by the directors** themselves to the entire organisation.

These **cultural changes** will centre around more **rigorous supervision** (to ensure that costs are being controlled), a switch from being proactive within the market to **reacting to changes in the market, a focus on quality rather than innovation.** Achievements will be measured in terms of **maintaining customers** because of the high quality and affordability of our products and innovation in production processes.

Changes required to control systems

The changes to the organisation's control systems will need to reflect the changes necessary to the structure and culture of the organisation.

(a) The control systems will need to become far **more formalised** to ensure tight cost control, especially over manufacturing costs.

(b) To become the cost leader we will need to gather **external intelligence** on our competitors. **Competitor benchmarking** would be one source of such information.

(c) The switch to in-house manufacturing is likely to require significant **investment in manufacturing capacity,** with the result that cash management may become more problematic, given the fairly long payback period on the type of investment we will require. **Long-term planning and cash management** must therefore be given a higher priority.

(d) The **range of performance indicators used needs to be increased.** They will need to cover both the financial aspects of the organisation's operations (labour costs, raw material prices, market share and so on) as well as qualitative issues such as number of customer complaints, number of on-time deliveries and so on. The **balanced scorecard approach** to performance measurement would ensure that all aspects of the organisation's activities were being considered.

(e) The **reward system** may need to be revised since it can be used to convey the necessary changes in organisational culture to the organisation's workforce.

   (i) Given the falling price/earnings ratio, the share option scheme has been ineffective. The anticipated improvements in profit levels from the change in strategy may eventually have a favourable effect on the price/earnings ratio, however, and so the share option scheme may prove useful as a motivating reward.

(ii) For those employees not part of the share option scheme, bonuses could be tied to vital performance measures such as levels of customer complaints and direct labour productivity.

I hope this information has been of use to you. If you would like to discuss any of the issues covered in this report further, please do not hesitate to contact me.

Signed: Management Accountant

8 PROMOTION

> **Pass marks.** You may have been able to incorporate facets of your own organisation's control system into your answer to part (b).
>
> **Examiner's comment.** Many answers to part (a) could be described as 'write all you know about contingency theory and organisational culture'. The main problem in answering part (b) was failure to focus on control systems.

(a) **Contingency theory** suggests that there is **no universally appropriate accounting system** applicable to all organisations because each organisation's **individual circumstances will have an impact** on the most appropriate accounting system design.

Despite the obvious appeal of the theory, a number of reservations have been raised. One **objection** is that its **perception of the contingent variables** (the environment, organisational structure and technology - the specific features of an organisation's context that impact on accounting system design identified by contingent theorists) is **too straightforward, narrow and simplistic**. The theory appears to suggest that once the appropriate easy-to-measure aspects of the contingent variables have been identified for a particular organisation (such as the number of different product markets faced, the degree of decentralisation, the variety in each task that has to be performed), the design of an accounting control system follows easily.

So how is it that organisations can be in the same industry and can be operating within what appear to be very similar conditions but yet have developed quite different approaches to management control?

The answer to this question lies in the fact that the **theory tends to ignore the influence of aspects of an organisation's context which are more difficult to quantify**. It fails to recognise the impact of the **people** within an organisation, of **management structure, managerial style** and, particularly, organisational **culture** - those factors that make an organisation unique. Control systems which are inconsistent with an organisation's culture and value system are likely to **create resistance,** however, and could motivate managers and employees to work against the purposes of the control system. Consider what Handy describes as role culture or bureaucracy; a system of formal controls would probably be effective. Such a system would be less effective with task culture, where more informal controls would be appropriate.

The introduction of a new control system that alters existing **power relationships** could be thwarted by those who consider their position to be threatened by the new system. Or, despite the technical sophistication of a new computerised accounting and control system which has been carefully designed to take account of the organisation's environment, structure and technology, its introduction might be unsuccessful if the design has paid insufficient attention to the people in the organisation and to organisational culture.

Control processes will therefore be most effective if they operate by generating a corporate culture that is supportive of organisational aims, objectives and methods of working, and which is consistent with the demands of the environment in which the organisation operates.

(b) A major influence on an organisation's success is the calibre of its employees and the strength of its management team. It is therefore vital that the **careful selection and recruitment of suitable staff at all levels**, but particularly at the senior management level, is an **organisational priority**.

The control systems and approach to management control necessary to ensure that the appropriate personnel are employed will depend on the manner in which the selection and recruitment processes are carried out. For example, there are basically two alternative approaches to recruiting senior staff; existing staff may be promoted or senior managers might be recruited from outside the organisation.

Internal promotion

When an existing member of staff is promoted, there will be **less need for controls** over the recruitment process because the person will already be known to the management team. He or she will already have **proven** himself or herself capable of working within the organisation's culture, will have shown himself or herself to be in tune with the organisation's mission and ethical values and will have demonstrated the necessary technical competence and skills. Moreover, the costs associated with external selection and recruitment (advertising, use of an agency, interview time and so on) will be **saved.**

External recruitment

Although external recruitment is **more risky** because the appointee is unknown, it does offer the opportunity for the introduction into the organisation of **fresh ideas,** new ways of doing things, an **alternative viewpoint** and, possibly, a wealth of **experience**. It also **avoids** the risk of any **favouritism** connected with an internal promotion, which could cause motivational problems in other members of staff.

Internal promotion and controls

Given that managers who are promoted internally should be in tune with the organisation's culture, controls can be more informal than those necessary for external recruitment. That is not to say that a control system will not be required, however.

(i) Controls will be required to ensure not only that there is **no possibility of favouritism** influencing a promotion, but that promotions are made purely on merit.

(ii) The control system will also be required to ensure that promoted managers are provided with the **training** (in management skills and/or in technical competencies as appropriate) necessary to enable them to carry out their new duties.

(iii) To stop mangers accepting posts in other organisations it is vital that there are controls in place to provide for **career development opportunities.**

(iv) It is most important that the senior management team has a **wide age range** so the managers do not leave the organisation at the same time (due to retirement, obvious career progression and so on).

External recruitment and controls

External recruitment requires a more **formal** control system than that acceptable for internal promotion.

(i) There must be no possibility that appointments are made simply on the basis of friendships or personal contacts. The control system will need to ensure that a **comprehensive selection and recruitment process** is carried out in order that the most suitable candidate for the post is employed.

(ii) The new recruit must be provided with adequate **training** to ensure that he or she is made aware of the organisation's cultural and value system, its mission and objectives. He or she must also be given the necessary technical and/or management skills training.

(iii) The new manager's personal work **objectives** must be decided on appointment and regular **appraisals** must be carried out to ensure that these objectives are being met.

9 TUTORIAL QUESTION: ETHICS

> **Pass marks**. As stated in the Guidance Notes, these answers should not be regarded as prescriptive or all-inclusive. There is room for different interpretations of the information and different actions depending on the interpretation.

(a) (i) A senior manager in a subsidiary is **falsifying figures in order to gain a larger bonus.**

(ii) **Organisational and ethical problems** arising are that the accounts will not give a true and fair view, overstated sales may lead to unachievable targets next year, stakeholders will be misled, controls preventing manipulation of figures are absent, the blood relationship between the group FD and the senior manager invites bias, and the management accountant also has conflicts of interest since his/her position is vulnerable.

(iii) The **major ethical principal** involved is **integrity.** Cedric's action is dishonest.

(iv) **Possible alternatives for action** for the management accountant are:

(1) doing nothing;
(2) asking Cedric to revise the figures;
(3) reporting the matter to the group FD;
(4) reporting the matter to the group board.

(v) **Action must clearly be taken but it is not clear what the best course is.** Merely asking for the figures to be changed does not guarantee that they will be changed. Even if they are changed there is still a case for bringing Cedric's intentions to the attention of more senior management. Reporting to the group FD (Cedric's brother) may have no effect and may damage the management accountant's position.

(vi) Reporting to the group board would therefore seem to be the **best course of action**. The report should address the control problems that allow the figures to be manipulated and suggest alternative bonus schemes that do not encourage manipulation of figures.

(b) (i) The company is **possibly guilty of bribing government officials and the accountant is being asked to disguise this.**

(ii) **Organisational and ethical problems** arising are that the organisation would be seriously damaged if there were to be legal proceedings connected with this matter; the corruption possibly pervades the entire organisation, since the board (or at least the finance director) condones it and wants it covered up; disclosure of its practices could jeopardise the survival of the organisation and the well-being of its employees.

(iii) The **ethical principles** involved are integrity and technical standards. There are also conflicts of interest: behaving according to ethical standards will damage the organisation and the accountant personally.

(iv) **Possible alternatives for action** are as follows.

(1) Comply with the request.

(2) Refuse to comply.

(3) Conduct further investigations to determine whether the suspicion of corruption is true.

(4) Report the matter to the financial director's superior (the board/ managing director).

(v) Option (1) is untenable. **What of the other courses of action?** Option (3) may place the accountant in a stronger position than simply refusing. If the suspicions prove to be true the only possible action is to report the matter to the board. If the board do nothing the accountant must resign and take legal advice regarding disclosure to third parties.

Even if the suspicions are unfounded or the evidence is inconclusive the accountant must still refuse to comply with the request. If the records are then falsified by someone else the matter should be drawn to the attention of the board. Depending on their attitude, resignation may again be the only option.

(vi) Having made sure that his understanding of the situation is correct the accountant should **refuse to comply with the request and explain why**. If (as seems likely) he is immediately marched off the premises he should take legal advice concerning further action.

10 ETHICAL CONSIDERATIONS

Pass marks. The CIMA model answer opens with a very useful trick – it refers to 'a management meeting' in which we are to assume that the details given in the question have already been discussed with the MD. This avoids any need or temptation to repeat large chunks of the question so we have used a similar device at the opening of our report, leaving us free to comment on the issues, which is what the question asks for.

Examiner's comment. The examiner found the standard of answers to this question notably worse than the average standard of answers and far worse than expected. Candidates were expected to realise that this was not a question where a particular set of recommendations was required. However the examiner commented that impractical or unreasonable recommendations, such as advising debt factoring, the use of a cheque guarantee card, borrowing from the pension fund or giving misleading replies to the telephone enquiry, did not attract marks.

REPORT

To: The Managing Director
From: The Financial Controller Date: XX.XX.XX
Subject: Issues arising from the meeting with X Ltd regarding payment of their debt

This report **assumes that you have read the enclosed documents** prepared by the Sales Director concerning her recent meeting with Y, the Managing Director of X Ltd. **In brief,** we are being asked to supply further materials on credit to X Ltd on the understanding that this offers our best chance of being paid both for long-outstanding existing debts and the further debts that will arise.

Firstly I need to point out that our **Sales Director** feels that we should accept what has been informally agreed but she has **openly admitted that she has difficulty in taking an objective view of the situation,** having done business with Y for many years.

However, the agreement that is being proposed leaves me with **grave doubts,** both on ethical grounds and from the point of view of the business.

Our options are:

- to accept the agreement as proposed;
- to refuse the payment from Y but supply further materials in any case;
- to sue for payment or simply write off the debt.

Accepting the agreement

This option puts us in a position where we are owed (and are at risk of losing) not only our existing debt of £A but also a further amount (say £B, based on past trading experience).

I am not sure what the **role of the personal payment** is meant to be. It is not a bribe, although it has that taste about it, since the intention is that it would be repaid. Presumably it is a sign of good faith, but why not inject the funds directly into the company and pay off some debts now? If Y is not willing to risk loaning the funds to his company, why should we be any more willing to take the risk of supplying further goods?

In any case, recovery of our debt depends not only on our support but also that of all or almost all of **X Ltd's other suppliers.** We have no guarantee that this support will be forthcoming. (Indeed, I have just received a telephone message from another supplier indicating that they too are worried about X Ltd's position, and asking for our view (see below).)

If the company is forced into liquidation by other creditors (or if X Ltd cannot complete the next stage of the work) what are we expected to do about the personal payment? I am not sure how it would be viewed by the law. It would put us in a more advantageous position than other creditors, but unfairly so.

There are other matters that cause me to have doubts.

- Why can X Ltd not obtain an advance from their bank against the promise of the next progress payment? Has this option been attempted? If not, are the bank fully aware of the difficulties of X Ltd?

- Are X Ltd already '*trading wrongfully*', which is illegal? To knowingly enter into an agreement that allows this to continue calls our own integrity into question.

Refuse the payment but supply the materials

This is a better option because it leaves us with a clear conscience **regarding the payment, and does not compromise Y in any way**. The **other problems remain,** however.

We need to be assured:

- that X Ltd really can complete the next stage of the contract; and
- that X Ltd can secure the support of its other creditors.

If we are satisfied on point (a), we could encourage X Ltd to enter into negotiations with all of its suppliers. We can let it be known that we will be willing to help if others are: this will put X Ltd in a stronger position.

If X Ltd is able to get the level of support needed, this option is the one that I recommend.

If both you and Y agree to this I may have an immediate opportunity to help out, since (as I mentioned) I have already had an enquiry from an acquaintance working for another supplier who will also, I think, be keen to salvage something from the situation if at all possible.

Confidentiality is an issue at present, so for the time being I have sent a fax explaining that we are currently negotiating with X Ltd and that I will be in touch once I know the outcome of our talks. (You will realise that my own professional integrity could be compromised if I supply information that could be considered misleading. I cannot simply ignore the enquiry or be cagey about it since this could itself be construed as a 'bad' reference.)

Suing for payment or writing off the debt

Since we are unlikely to recover our debt this option will simply increase our loss because we will have to pay legal costs. X Ltd may be counting on the fact that we know this.

One possible virtue of this option is that the threat of liquidation, or liquidation itself, may force Y to come to an arrangement with all creditors if we are unable to persuade him to try this by other means.

Writing off the debt now has the virtue that we do not risk losing a further amount by supplying more materials. On the down side, it could make us look 'soft' to other customers, and it is possibly unduly harsh not to give X Ltd a chance to recover the situation. It is not in our long-term interests for our customers to go out of business.

I cannot recommend either of these options except in the very last resort.

Wider issues

We need to consider whether this situation has arisen due to problems with credit control on our part. It could perhaps be argued that we should have worked more closely with X Ltd to prevent the problem arising in the first place. We should have been aware that X Ltd was taking on a much larger contract than it has previously been used to dealing with and we should have anticipated problems.

Over the next few days I shall be looking into ways in which our credit control systems can be adapted to ensure that external matters such as this are taken into account.

Signed: Financial Controller

11 LARGE FINANCIAL SERVICES CO

Pass marks. It would have been helpful if you were able to draw on your Paper 14 knowledge, as well as Paper 16 knowledge, in your answer to this question. Answers taking a more critical approach – that is, not assuming that a code of conduct is all that is necessary – are likely to have scored higher marks. It is not clear how many marks were allocated to each part of the question, presumably allowing scope for a variety of different approaches to the question. For instance some of the points made in the first part of our answer appear in the second part of the official CIMA solution and *vice versa*.

Our solution is longer than could have been produced in an exam because it aims to cover a variety of different possible answers, and to provide extra material to help with your revision.

Prizewinners' points and other points. In his report the examiner agreed that 'only exceptional answers would cover all topics in reasonable depth:

- discuss top management responsibility; managerial control
- top management attitudes and communication
- company mission and beliefs system
- existence and enforcement of code of conduct
- organisational culture, and the problems of changing culture
- recruitment and assessment of staff
- the reward system and possible changes
- formal product approval, and separation of this approval from product sales
- trade-offs/balanced conclusions
- the limits of an incremental approach to change, and the risks in rapid change of preventing innovation and losing competitive advantage.

The question does not mention the mis-selling of pensions, but it could be related to this problem which has been discussed extensively in the financial press. It could also be related to the commission-driven approaches of insurance and fund sales staff which have been a problem for many years.'

Examiner's comment. Weaker and average candidates failed to grasp the scale of change required and the possible timescales for effective implementation. There were three frequently-recurring errors.

- Wasting time and space repeating the detail of the scenario without adding much additional commentary or interpretation
- Writing too little, no more than a side (excluding repetition of the scenario) being insufficient
- Providing rote-learnt definitions of codes of conduct, ethical guidelines and organisational culture without making use of these to discuss the case

Discussion of quality control, the enforcement of the code of conduct, corporate governance and corporate image were not relevant.

REPORT

To: The Audit Committee
From: Chief Internal Auditor — Date: XX.XX.XX
Subject: Ethical values and public relations

Situation analysis

In recent years we have seen the financial services industry come under **increasing scrutiny**, both in terms of formal regulation and in terms of public awareness. This trend is expected to continue. The industry is also **increasingly competitive,** and others appear to have been more successful than this company at responding to the needs of the market.

Corporate **culture** here is based around a **risk-taking strategy** which is **not appropriate** in the current climate. It has therefore been suggested that a **formal code of conduct** be introduced to help **change organisational culture** and **encourage more ethical behaviour** on the part of staff.

Company code of conduct

A corporate code typically contains a series of statements setting out the company's values and explaining how it sees its responsibilities towards stakeholders.

Typical statements in a corporate code	Comment
The company conducts all of its business on **ethical principles** and **expects** staff to do likewise.	At present this company conducts its business with a view to maximising **sales and growth**, and encourages staff to promote this aim by giving them maximum freedom to maximise their own sales-related earnings
Employees are seen as the most important component of the company and are expected to work on a basis of trust, respect, honesty, fairness, decency and equality. The company will only employ people who follow its ethical ideals.	Employees are likely to be highly competitive and self-interested. They are attracted to the company because they are offered the chance of earning high rewards.
Customers should be treated courteously and politely at all times, and the company should always respond promptly to customer needs by listening, understanding and then performing to the customer requirements.	The company has been criticised for its treatment of customers. Products do not meet customer requirements in the sense that they appear to be poor value for money.
The company is dedicated to complying with **legal or regulatory standards** of the industry, and employees are expected to do likewise.	There have been no major problems yet, but this may just be a matter of time, since small problems have already forced the withdrawal or modification of products and disciplinary action against staff.

Pass mark. Codes may also contain statements about matters such as above-board dealings with suppliers and competitors, respect for company assets, health and safety, ecological commitments and responsibility to the community. No information is available in the scenario about these aspects.

The impact of a code of conduct on this company

A code of conduct can **set out the company's expectations,** and in principle a code such as that outlined above will **address many of the problems** that the organisation is experiencing.

However, merely **issuing a code is not enough.**

- The **commitment of senior management** to the code needs to be real, and it needs to be very clearly communicated to all staff. The prevailing, sales-maximising culture is clearly very strong, and staff need to be persuaded that expectations really have changed.
- Measures need to be taken to **discourage previous behaviours** that conflict with the code.
- **Staff** need to understand that it is in the organisation's best interests to change behaviour, and become **committed to the same ideals.**

Some employees – including very able ones - may find it very difficult to buy into a code that they perceive may limit their own earnings and/or restrict their freedom to do their job.

There is a very real danger that the **spirit of innovation** upon which the success of the company is founded **may be harmed**.

Other changes necessary

At senior management level, **new reporting systems** need to be set up, emphasising matters that are now perceived to be important such as level of customer complaints. It may be necessary to **restrict staff freedom** in developing new products, at least by requiring **more formal authorisation procedures** at senior level. If current products really do offer poor value then they also need to be changed.

In addition to the general statement of ethical conduct envisaged above, **more detailed statements** (codes of practice) will be needed to set out formal procedures that must now be followed. For instance there should be formal procedures designed to ensure compliance with any new regulation: this should not be left up to individuals.

The increase in regulation is likely to require regular **training** or briefing sessions for all staff whose actions could result in regulations being breached.

Many larger organisations have set up an **ethics office**, to monitor instances of non-compliance with ethical principles. Some have a 'hot-line' that staff might use, for instance, to 'whistle blow' if they are being asked to engage in unethical behaviour by their seniors.

Many companies have also set up a range of **other ethical support measures** such as ethical review committees, ethical audits, and ethics counsellors or ombudsmen.

Reward systems in the company need to be thoroughly **overhauled**. Bonuses and commissions (which encourage self-interest) need to be de-emphasised in favour of **rewards based on excellence of customer service**. A similar **change of emphasis** may be necessary in **recruitment** and **personnel policies**: it may be necessary to redefine what is meant by 'very able' staff and find ways other than high rewards to attract and retain staff of the required calibre.

Public perceptions of the company need to be monitored more formally, and it may be possible to enter into closer, more active relationships with consumer bodies.

Finally, it may be possible to conduct **benchmarking exercises** to see if the company is following best industry practice in its operations.

Signed: Chief Internal Auditor

12 ENVIRONMENTAL AND SOCIAL ISSUES

> **Pass marks.** This topic was the subject of a number of articles in *Management Accounting* prior to the exam. If you had read them you would have found this question easier, though still quite daunting. You may have thought 'How can I write on this topic for 35 minutes?' – a reaction not uncommon in the MCS exam.
>
> Taking a moment to visualize a real company similar to the one in the scenario helps. Nike is an example. Try to find a suitable theoretical model around which to structure your answer. With the question asking you to 'determine the range of business activity', Porter's Value Chain is a great starting point, providing a comprehensive range of possible activities to discuss. We have used the Input, Process, Output model borrowed from IFM when considering the environmental issues.
>
> Make sure you avoid the temptation to drift off into what you consider to be the rights and wrongs of issues such as child labour – you have been asked not to and won't be kindly treated by a marker if you do so.
>
> **Examiner's comment.** Weaker answers deteriorated into lists and short notes which, even if relevant, were too brief to earn significant marks.

REPORT

To: The Board
From: Management accountant **Date:** XX.XX.XX
Subject: Environmental and social reporting

Reasons for the inclusion of environmental and social issues in the Annual Report

As the Chief Executive has observed, our Annual Report contains all the disclosures currently required. Any additional disclosure may be to the benefit of our competitors and could draw attention to any perceived weaknesses in our performance in this sensitive area. Despite such arguments, we cannot ignore the increasing pressure on us to include environmental and social issues within our Annual Report.

As the non-executive directors have observed, many **comparable companies already do include such issues** in their Annual Report and we may attract adverse publicity if we do not follow this trend. Tesco and Manchester United are but two examples of organisations which have suffered from bad press, having been deemed to have made insufficient progress on environmental and social issues.

There may be **positive benefits** to reporting such issues too. For example, an increasing amount of attention is being devoted to environmental and social issues. **'Green' and 'ethical' fund mangers** have increasing funds available for investment and we may be able to demonstrate that we are suitable for such investment, thereby increasing our share price. Moreover, the Board should be constantly **scanning the environment** in which the organisation operates, including social and environmental areas, in order to assess the impact of any changes on the future of the business.

There have also been recent comments by a government minister that 'if all companies do not make progress', legislation on environmental and social issues will be introduced. If we were to include such issues in our Annual Report we **avoid being forced into providing damaging disclosures required by a more stringent regime.**

(a) **The range of environmental and social issues to cover**

A first step should be to **obtain copies of Annual Reports of companies who do positively report** on such issues in order to familiarise ourselves with current best practice, thereby identifying **benchmarks** against which we might be measured. We also need to be **aware of current high-profile pressure groups**, and a regular review of the press should highlight these 'popular' concerns.

The greatest focus from an environmental point of view is likely to be on our **consumption of raw materials from tropical areas**. We may wish to consider the concept of '**sustainability**' – are we replanting at a rate equal to or greater than that at which we are harvesting. If so, we are likely to be viewed favourably.

The **costs of processing** should also be considered, in particular the percentage of **energy** coming from renewable and non-renewable sources and the steps we have taken to increase the efficiency with which we use energy.

Packaging is of increasing concern to many consumers. The proportion of both our products and their packaging made from recycled material should be measured, as should the ease with which they can be recycled after use.

Social issues to cover include minimum rates of pay, the minimum age of child labour, working conditions and living conditions, such as the availability of health care and education. The public's interest in our consumer markets tends to focus on the **discrepancies between 'living standards' in their affluent market compared to those in less developed countries**. In setting standards we need to gather data about these issues in the source countries. Rates of pay expressed in relation to UK earnings may seem derisory but when expressed in relation to the local average they may seem much more acceptable. Using children aged just 14 as part of the labour force may seem less offensive if local schooling is provided up to the age of 12 and the company provides additional education as part of its benefits package.

How well our actual performance compares with what we consider to be acceptable standards will determine the nature and extent of any reporting on these issues. If we believe our performance is above average we may well make extensive disclosures in order to gain maximum benefit. The poorer our performance, the less we may choose to disclose. If there are any single issues that, were they disclosed would lead to adverse publicity, we may choose to make no disclosures until these issues are resolved to an acceptable level.

The appointment of one or more **non-executive directors** with experience in areas of our operations which might be deemed particularly sensitive could also be considered.

It should be noted, however, that the **popularity** or otherwise of environmental and social issues moves constantly with **changes in public opinion and government policy**. We should endeavor to **anticipate the demands of our stakeholders**, however, rather than appear to be simply reacting to the current 'popular' issues.

(b) **Determining the range of business activity**

There are a number of factors to consider when determining the range of business activity to cover in the Annual Report.

A first step could be to **identify the value chain** within the organisation, thereby allowing for all activities (from the sourcing of raw materials through to the selling activity) to be **assessed for their current and future impact on social and environmental issues**. High-risk areas are those that are likely to have a significant impact on profitability if appropriate contingency plans are not in place.

We also need to consider **whether to report on the activities of Z plc alone or on those of all of our business partners**, including those from whom we source our raw materials and the sub-contractors we employ during production.

It could be **argued that we cannot control our sub-contractors**, and therefore should not include their activities within our report. For example, it could be deemed unfair if we were held responsible for contractors employing young children without our knowledge.

It is **unlikely that 'we didn't know' would be accepted as a defense were damaging information made public**, however. Once the range of performance benchmarks is established, we should therefore provide it to all of our sub-contractors and advise them that we expect them to conform to such standards. These could be included as a requirement in the supplier tendering process.

Problems are likely to centre on **identifying those issues that will be of concern in the future to stakeholders and hence how those issues will affect our activities**, and of **balancing the demands of shareholders for maintaining a profitable activity with the concerns of pressure groups over the activity in question.**

(c) **Assessing the information requirements at Board level**

The **additional information** to be supplied at board level will **depend on the company's ongoing attitude to environmental and social issues.**

The company may take the view that environmental and social issues are **of no concern.** The company should therefore only be interested in **ensuring that current legal requirements are met and that the costs of adverse publicity are avoided.** If this is the case, I would recommend that an **individual becomes responsible for monitoring social and environmental developments** and advises the Board if or when the company is required to take additional steps. Disclosure would be kept to a minimum, and would concentrate on practices that are of benefit to the community at large, rather than those that may be of interest to competitors.

Given that there is substantial interest amongst consumers and investment fund managers in doing business with companies who are environmentally and socially responsible, we may intend to **report on environmental and social issues as part of our competitive strategy**. The information requirements at board level would then increase significantly. A **study** would need to be conducted into establishing what is considered to be **best practice**. This would identify the **investment requirements of the ethical investment funds** and the **current thinking on environmental and social issues by the various pressure groups**, such as Amnesty International and Greenpeace.

The company should then establish a **formal code of challenging targets** (such as 95% of packaging used should be made from recycled materials) to be achieved on these environmental and social issues and a **report on how these targets are being met should be included as part of the normal reporting package**. Areas in which we are particularly successful and which are not commercially damaging (such as a change in product design) could then be included in the Annual Report

Conclusion

I believe that the impact of social and environmental issues will grow in importance and I would be happy to provide any help the Board may require in developing our environmental and social reporting systems.

Signed: Management Accountant

13 DIVISION X

> **Pass marks**. Parts (b) and (c) of this question were far more straightforward than part (a).
>
> *Prizewinners' points.* Part (a) of this question is very difficult, not because it involves difficult maths or techniques that you have not encountered before, but simply because there is no clear indication of what technique you need to use. This is a deliberate policy on the part of the examiner and you can expect more questions like this in the future. Take heart from the examiner's initial comments (see below) if you were confused but still had a decent attempt at the question.
>
> The other problem with part (a) is that even if you do work out what to do and how to do it, there is still a great deal of work to get through in the time that would be left after allowing for reading, understanding and thinking time. Well done if your answer looks anything like the one shown below. Our answer shows a pragmatic approach, but one that would require you to be very clear-headed about the problem, not something that many people find easy in an exam. Parts (b) and (c) should have been much more straightforward.
>
> **Examiner's comment**. Candidates are permitted to gain marks if they use an incorrect approach, but logical technique which leads to some useful conclusions. However, they must make it clear what they are attempting to do in their answer, and state assumptions. Marking allows for genuine misunderstandings and follows through the logic of what the candidate is attempting to do.
>
> However, in this case 'the standard of the numerical workings was dreadful. Figures were illegible and frequently unlabelled. Workings were often omitted ... Trivial and silly arithmetical errors were far too frequent ... Failing to comment on the numbers and make a clear recommendation based upon the calculations was a very common fault'.
>
> Common errors in part (b) were devoting insufficient time to the question, not explaining the alternative approaches suggested and failure to recognise that this was a one year decision, not an investment decision. In part (c) candidates often explained computer techniques of modelling at length without referring to the use of the techniques, or not their use in performance measurement, and particularly failing to recognise that budgets are the most obvious example of models used for performance evaluation.

(a) (i) The **costs and revenues relevant to the minimum quantity to be purchased** from each supplier are as follows.

(1) The revenue with centralised marketing as opposed to decentralised marketing (it is reduced by 5% with decentralised marketing).

(2) The cost per unit at each level.

(3) The annual cost of working with a supplier at each level (for example the annual cost is an average of £250 per unit if only 1,000 units are purchased from a supplier, but only £31.25 if 8,000 units are purchased).

The design and planning costs and the fixed marketing and selling costs must be covered, but they do not affect the decision about purchases from different suppliers. (They are relevant to the decision in (a)(ii), however.)

Supplier K

				REVENUES FROM SALES		NET CONTRIBUTION	
Qty	*Price per unit*	*Total price*	*Cost including annual cost*	*Centralised*	*Decentralised*	*Centralised*	*Decentralised*
		£	£	£	£	£	£
1,000	70	70,000	320,000	200,000	190,000	(120,000)	(130,000)
2,000	65	130,000	380,000	400,000	380,000	**20,000**	0
3,000	60	180,000	430,000	600,000	570,000	170,000	**140,000**
4,000	60	240,000	490,000	800,000	760,000	310,000	270,000
5,000	60	300,000	550,000	1,000,000	950,000	450,000	400,000
6,000	60	360,000	610,000	1,200,000	1,140,000	590,000	530,000
7,000	80	560,000	810,000	1,400,000	1,330,000	590,000	520,000
8,000	90	720,000	970,000	1,600,000	1,520,000	630,000	550,000

Supplier L

Qty	Price per unit	Total price	Cost including annual cost	REVENUES FROM SALES Centralised	Decentralised	NET CONTRIBUTION Centralised	Decentralised
		£	£	£	£	£	£
1,000	90	90,000	340,000	200,000	190,000	(140,000)	(150,000)
2,000	80	160,000	410,000	400,000	380,000	(10,000)	(30,000)
3,000	70	210,000	460,000	600,000	570,000	**140,000**	**110,000**
4,000	70	280,000	530,000	800,000	760,000	270,000	230,000
5,000	70	350,000	600,000	1,000,000	950,000	400,000	350,000
6,000	70	420,000	670,000	1,200,000	1,140,000	530,000	470,000

Supplier M

Qty	Price per unit	Total price	Cost including annual cost	REVENUES FROM SALES Centralised	Decentralised	NET CONTRIBUTION Centralised	Decentralised
		£	£	£	£	£	£
1,000	130	130,000	380,000	200,000	190,000	(180,000)	(190,000)
2,000	120	240,000	490,000	400,000	380,000	(90,000)	(110,000)
3,000	120	360,000	610,000	600,000	570,000	(10,000)	(40,000)
4,000	130	520,000	770,000	800,000	760,000	**30,000**	(10,000)

Supplier N

Qty	Price per unit	Total price	Cost including annual cost	REVENUES FROM SALES Centralised	Decentralised	NET CONTRIBUTION Centralised	Decentralised
		£	£	£	£	£	£
1,000	110	110,000	360,000	200,000	190,000	(160,000)	(170,000)
2,000	110	220,000	470,000	400,000	380,000	(70,000)	(90,000)
3,000	110	330,000	580,000	600,000	570,000	**20,000**	(10,000)
4,000	110	440,000	690,000	800,000	760,000	110,000	**70,000**

Figures in **bold** represent the **lowest level of purchases at which revenues exceed associated fixed costs.** This may be **summarised** as follows.

	K	*L*	*M*	*N*
Centralised	2,000	3,000	4,000	3,000
Decentralised	3,000	3,000	–	4,000

The figures show, for example, that with centralised marketing if the Division had a demand for 19,000 units it would only actually be worth selling 18,000 (8,000 + 6,000 + 4,000), since a *negative* contribution would be made on the extra thousand.

(ii) **Centralised marketing**

Ignoring the probabilities and assuming the best possible level of demand (22,000) for the *centralised* option the contribution (from part (a)) and profit will be as follows.

Supplier	*Units*	£'000
K	8,000	630
L	6,000	530
M	4,000	30
N	4,000	110
Contribution		1,300
Design and planning		200
Marketing and selling	(2 × 100)	200
Profit		900

However, it can only be said *with certainty* under this option that 14,000 units will be sold, giving a profit of only £(630 + 530 – 400) = £760,000.

Expected sales if 22,000 units are purchased are:

0.2 × 14,000	2,800
0.2 × 16,000	3,200
0.2 × 18,000	3,600
0.2 × 20,000	4,000
0.2 × 22,000	4,400
	18,000

In other words the probabilities suggest that in the event, 4,000 units will remain unsold, reducing profit by 4,000 × £200 to only £100,000.

Other possibilities give higher levels of profit but not above the £760,000 obtained from buying and selling 14,000 units (W1).

Decentralised marketing

For the *decentralised* option, ignoring the probabilities, it is never worth buying from Supplier M, and so these 4,000 units must be ignored. Only 18,000 units would be purchased.

Supplier	*Units*	£'000
K	8,000	550
L	6,000	470
N	4,000	70
Contribution		1,090
Design and planning		200
Marketing and selling	(2 × 40)	80
Profit		810

Under the decentralised option demand is 100% *certain* to be at least 19,000 units (exceeding worthwhile purchases), and so a profit of £810,000 is also certain. This is better than the £760,000 obtained with centralised marketing.

Decentralised marketing should therefore be introduced if the information provided in the question holds true.

Workings

1 This can be proved as follows.

Bought	*Sold* (W2)	*Unsold*	*Contribution* (W3)	*Unsold* (W4)	*Net contribution*	*Profit* (W5)
'000	'000	'000	£'000	£'000	£'000	£'000
16	15.6	-0.4	1,090	-80	1,010	610
18	16.8	-1.2	1,270	-240	1,030	630
20	17.6	-2.4	1,180	-480	700	300

2 Expected sales are calculated as follows.

	Buy 16,000			*Buy 18,000*			*Buy 20,000*	
0.2	14,000	2,800	0.2	14,000	2,800	0.2	14,000	2,800
0.8	16,000	12,800	0.2	16,000	3,200	0.2	16,000	3,200
		15,600	0.6	18,000	10,800	0.2	18,000	3,600
					16,800	0.4	20,000	8,000
								17,600

3 Contribution is derived from the tables in part (a)(i). For example one way of making up 16,000 units is to buy 8,000 from K, 6,000 from L and 2,000 from N. The contribution earned in each case is added to find the total. (See also W6)

	K	*L*	*M*	*N*	*Total*
Units ('000)	£'000	£'000	£'000	£'000	£'000
16	630	530		-70	1,090
18	630	530		110	1,270
20	630	530	-90	110	1,180

4 This is the unsold stock in units (column 2) multiplied by the lost revenue per unit (£200).

5 This is the net contribution after allowing for unsold stock less the marketing costs of £400,000.

6 **If you were very clever** you may have realised that slightly better profits can be earned at the 16,000 and 20,000 unit levels by careful choice of supplier. The best options are found by calculating the contribution per unit at each level. For example the contribution per unit from supplier K at 6,000 units is £98.33 (590,000/6,000) as opposed to £78.75 at the 8,000 level. It is better to buy the missing units from supplier N. The best options are as follows.

Supplier	*Level*	*Contribution*	*Contribution per unit*
K	6,000	590,000	98.33
L	6,000	530,000	88.33
N	4,000	110,000	27.50
M	4,000	30,000	7.50

The revised figures are then as follows.

Bought	*Sold*	*Unsold*	*Contribution* (see below)	*Unsold*	*Net contribution*	*Profit*
'000	'000	'000	£'000	£'000	£'000	£'000
16	15.6	-0.4	1,230	-80	1,150	750
18	16.8	-1.2	1,270	-240	1,030	630
20	17.6	-2.4	1,260	-480	780	380

	K	*L*	*M*	*N*	*Total*
Units ('000)	£'000	£'000	£'000	£'000	£'000
16	590	530		110	1,230
18	630	530		110	1,270
20	590	530	30	110	1,260

This does not change the overall decision. **Full marks would have been gained for the calculations shown in workings 1 to 5.**

(b) Probability and expected values are most useful when they refer to outcomes which will occur many times over. This is not the case with this decision. Probabilities can be calculated by reference to past experience, but in this instance **past experience cannot be considered a reliable guide** to what will happen in the future. Presumably the **probabilities given in the question** are the product of the **subjective judgement** of managers, and there is no reason to suppose that they are accurate. (In any case, the manager who has assigned equal probability to any level of sales between 14,000 units and 22,000 units is clearly reluctant to stick his or her neck out and make a serious guess.)

The existing approach might be **improved** if it gave an indication of a **range of possible outcomes** rather than a single point estimate: worst possible, most likely and best possible scenarios could be built up. **Attitude to risk** such as risk aversion could be **taken into account** by, say, assuming that costs will be higher or income lower.

Another option would be to **try Monte Carlo (random numbers) simulation,** which would entail building a computer model of the problem and trying out all the different possibilities. This is a 'non-optimising' technique – it does not provide a single result that clearly indicates the best course of action – but it will give the analyst a very clear **idea of the possible spread of outcomes.**

(c) **Financial modelling might assist in performance evaluation** in the following ways.

(i) **Identifying the variables involved in performing tasks and the relationships between them.** This is necessary so that the model can be built in the first place. Model building therefore shows what should be measured, helps to explain how a particular level of performance can be achieved, and identifies factors in performance that the organisation cannot expect to control.

(ii) **Setting targets for future performance.** The most obvious example of this is a budgetary control system, which is a means of planning and co-ordinating future performance levels, and a way of communicating expectations of future performance.

(iii) **Monitoring actual performance.** Again a budget is a good example of a financial model that is used in this way. Flexible budgets adjust the original plan to reflect actual conditions and measure actual performance against what should have been achieved.

(iv) **Co-ordinating long-term strategic plans with short term operational actions.** Modelling can reflect the dynamic nature of the real world and evaluate how likely it is that short-term actions will achieve the longer-term plan, given new conditions.

14 X DIVISION

Pass marks. In part (a) you had to determine the manufacturing cost using the three bases for apportioning the overheads. The assembly-related overhead remains the same each time but the material-related overhead changes. Once you had worked out that this is what you had to do, the calculations required in part (a) were actually quite straightforward. But to gain the full 20 marks you also had to provide a commentary and discuss the further information required. Don't skimp on these written sections.

Examiner's comment. The examiner provided a very in-depth report on candidates' performance on this question. Common errors in part (a) included failing to devote sufficient time to a serious attempt at the numerical analysis, incomprehensible workings and providing figures without a narrative explanation. The examiner explained that it was not expected that the approach and answer to part (a) would be obvious after a two-minute reading, that time was allowed for careful consideration and that maximum marks could not be obtained by arriving at the correct answers without an explanation of what they meant.

According to the examiner, answers to part (b) could vary in the extent to which they referred back to the problem in (a) and the extent to which they discussed the general issues of the effects of overhead apportionment systems on behaviour without reference to (a).

Good answers to part (c) apparently discussed all aspects of performance measurement; weaker ones concentrated on efficiency rather than effectiveness.

(a) (i) **Manufacturing cost using material cost basis for apportioning overheads**

	Method E	*Method N*
	£ per unit	£ per unit
Material	653.00	612.00
Labour	39.90	35.15
Assembly-related overhead (W1)	119.70	105.45
Material-related overhead (W2)	75.53	70.79
Manufacturing cost	888.13	823.39

Workings

1 50% of unit overhead = £119.70

(Method E) 50% × £239.40 = £119.70

(Method N) 50% × £210.90 = £105.45

2 Total material-related overheads are $\frac{15{,}500{,}000}{134{,}000{,}000} \times 100\%$

= 11.567% of total material cost

∴ Material-related overhead per unit =

(Method E) 11.567% × £653.00 = £75.53

(Method N) 11.567% × £612.00 = £70.79

(ii) **Manufacturing cost using total quantity of components basis for apportioning overheads**

	Method E	*Method N*
	£ per unit	£ per unit
Material	653.00	612.00
Labour	39.90	35.15
Assembly-related overhead (W1)	119.70	105.45
Material-related overhead (W2)	153.56	151.82
Manufacturing cost	966.16	904.42

Workings

1 As for (i) above

2 Material-related overheads are $\frac{£15{,}500{,}000}{8{,}880{,}000}$ per component = £1.745 approx

∴ Material-related overhead per unit =

(Method E) 88 × £1.745 = £153.56

(Method N) 87 × £1.745 = £151.82

(iii) **Manufacturing cost using transactions basis for apportioning overheads**

	Method E	*Method N*
	£ per unit	£ per unit
Material	653.00	612.00
Labour	39.90	35.15
Assembly-related overhead (W1)	119.70	105.45
Material-related overhead (W2)	154.00	220.32
Manufacturing cost	966.60	972.92

Workings

1 As for (i) above

2 Stage 1: Begin with total material-related overhead ÷ number of different components = $\frac{£15{,}500{,}000}{740}$

= £20,946 per different component

Stage 2: Cost per different component ÷ quantity of that component = unit cost per component =

(for existing components)	£20,946 ÷ 12,000* = £1.75
(for new sub-assembly)	£20,946 ÷ 300* = £69.82

* quantity of each component used last year
** forecast volume for new product

∴ Material-related overhead cost per product =

			£
(Method E)	88	(existing) components × £1.75 = £154	
(Method N)	86	(existing) components × £1.75 =	150.50
	1	(new sub-assembly) component × £69.82 =	69.82
	87		220.32

Commentary on the above results

The unit manufacturing costs vary according to the basis used to apportion material-related overheads. Management should not forget, however, that the total overhead incurred for a certain level of production will be the same whatever the method chosen to apportion it to individual products. The 'book' manufacturing cost of the product may be cheaper using the material cost basis rather than the total quantity of components basis to apportion overheads but the **'true' cost of producing the product will be the same, whatever apportionment method is used.** Management should therefore be **wary of making decisions on the basis of these unit cost calculations.**

The first two methods of apportioning overheads show that method N produces the lower manufacturing cost. The transactions basis (the current method), on the other hand, shows Method N to be more expensive. A decision as to **which method is better** should therefore not be made on the basis of the various manufacturing costs. A more appropriate approach is to **consider material and labour costs.** Using Method E the unit material and labour cost is £692.90 whereas using Method N it is £647.15. If 300 units per year are to be sold, Method N produces a saving of £45.75 × 300 = £13,725. In the light of the cost information about Division X with which we have been provided, however, the saving is insignificant.

The choice between Methods E and N should also **take into account the impact of introducing a new supplier if Method N is adopted**. Given that Division X is moving towards just-in-time, the introduction of yet another supplier when attempts should be being made to strengthen relationships with a few key suppliers **must be questioned.** There is, of course, no guarantee that the new supplier would be able to fit in with the division's JIT and TQM ethos. Could the new supplier deliver just-in-time? Would the component be of an acceptable quality?

A **reduction in the product complexity,** possible by adopting Method N (which saves one component), may well **reduce overhead costs** associated with material procurement and scheduling.

Recommendations

Despite the possible reduction in overhead cost associated with material procurement and scheduling if Method N were to be adopted in preference to Method E, given the problems of working with a new supplier in a JIT/TQM environment, and the small sales volumes anticipated, it seems **unwise to adopt Method N.**

Further information required

Additional analysis of overhead costs should be carried out before a final decision is made. By breaking down the total into separate components and choosing **cost drivers** for each component, more logical links between products and costs can be established. Such an analysis may allow those costs which might increase if a new supplier were to be introduced or a new component used to be ascertained. This could allow management to determine whether Method N was worthwhile.

Information about **product development costs** could also be brought into the analysis. It is quite likely that significant costs are associated with the introduction of a new component and it would be valuable to know whether any further costs of this type are yet to be incurred. If significant levels of such costs are still to be incurred, Method N may prove unacceptable. However the existence of a detailed product cost suggests that all development work has been done and that development costs are irrelevant to any decision making.

(b) **The way in which the choice of an overhead apportionment basis can influence behaviour**

Especially in the modern business environment, overheads make up an increasingly large proportion of an organisation's total costs. Although many organisations use marginal costing, many others use absorption costing or activity based costing and hence include overheads in product costs. The basis on which overheads are apportioned to the various products and services of such organisations is therefore bound to have an impact on the behaviour of those organisations.

For example, **pricing and marketing decisions** (what price to charge, what product mix to offer, what markets to sell in, which customers to supply) are often based on a product's unit cost. The amount of overhead apportioned to a product will therefore influence such decisions. Incorrect overhead apportionment could lead to the promotion of apparently low-cost products at the expense of apparently unprofitable (but, in reality, profitable) products.

Decisions about whether to **subcontract or supply a service in-house** can similarly be affected by the way in which overheads are apportioned to services.

The basis on which overheads are apportioned can also influence the **design of a product**. Final unit costs of products are often determined at the product design stage. If it is decided to apportion overheads to products on a labour cost basis, efforts to use a less highly skilled, and hence cheaper, grade of labour may be made in an attempt to lower the level of both the overhead apportioned to the product and the final unit cost. This may, of course, have an impact on the quality of the final product, the level of material wastage, the time taken to produce the product, the attitude of the more highly-skilled workers who were anticipating working on the product and so on.

The problems which can arise from the choice of an inappropriate basis of apportionment

In the most general sense, if overheads are significant, and an unrealistic basis which fails to reflect the relationship between overheads and products is chosen to apportion them to products, **product costs** are likely to be **inaccurate**. Some products will be charged with too much overhead and hence will be over-costed while others will be charged with too little overhead and will be under-costed. To use such information as the basis for managerial decision making is, as we have seen, dangerous.

Moreover, by choosing the wrong basis of apportionment, management are likely to **focus on the wrong areas for cost control**. If machine cost is to be the apportionment basis, management may attempt to control machine costs, possibly at the expense of product quality, when overheads are driven by labour costs and it is labour costs which should be controlled. They may also attempt to replace machine working with labour working in an attempt to reduce costs but, by doing so, will actually increase costs.

The implications for X Division

The choice of the number of different components as the apportionment basis by X Division was so as to be able to influence the choice of design of the proposed new product and to be able to determine the cost of the product at the design stage. The labour basis used in the past may have led to the replacement of labour costs with machine or technology costs. There is a danger, however, whatever method is used, that **managers will be mislead into thinking that sophisticated methods of overhead apportionment will lead to more accurate product costs which will provide the basis for improved decision making**. Calculating rates to five decimal places may well lull managers into a false sense of security: they may think that if the rate is provided to such an accurate degree then the product cost they are using for the basis of their decision making must be as accurate. This is simply not the case.

(c) REPORT

To: Finance Director
From: Chartered Management Accountant Date: XX.XX.XX
Subject: Assessing the performance of the purchasing department

As a result of our recent meeting, I have been considering the ways in which the performance of the purchasing department could be assessed. Set out below are details of the various approaches we could adopt and, as per our discussion, an explanation of the quantitative measures we could use, the sources of the necessary information and the extent to which we would be able to rely on these measures.

One possible way of assessing the department's performance is to consider its economy, its efficiency and its effectiveness.

Economy

A conventional budgetary control system, in which actual costs are compared with budgeted costs, would enable management to assess the extent to which they were managing to control costs (in other words, it might give some guidance as to the department's economy) but it would do little to allow any measurement of efficiency or effectiveness to be carried out. A more appropriate **comparison might be between the costs of X Division's purchasing department and those of similar purchasing departments of either other divisions within the group or other organisations operating under similar conditions.**

Efficiency

The department's efficiency, which is the **relationship between what the department achieves (its outputs) and what it costs (its inputs) to achieve those outputs,** could be assessed in a number of ways. If valid internal or external benchmarks can be obtained, **benchmarking** would allow us to determine whether the purchasing department is producing an efficient enough service given the resources it is using. Current performance levels could also be compared with those in the past, although technology will no doubt have had a favourable impact on the efficiency of the department.

Effectiveness

We should perhaps be most concerned with the level of effectiveness within the department, in other words the **degree to which the department is meeting its objectives.**

Before we can measure this, however, we need to **ensure that formal objectives have been defined** for the department as a whole and for each of its main sections. As well as procuring products of the highest quality (which accords with the division's philosophy of TQM) at a competitive price, other possible objectives might include establishing relationships with suppliers who are able to guarantee delivery of components on a just-in-time basis and providing a quality service to other departments within the division.

It is **difficult to assess whether such objectives have been met**, however, for a number of reasons.

(i) They are difficult to quantify in monetary terms.

(ii) Given the recent shift towards TQM/JIT, it is difficult to use information about past performance for comparison purposes.

(iii) It may also be difficult to obtain external data to assess the validity of results.

(iv) It is not just the purchasing department which might be responsible for the achievement or failure to achieve such objectives. Senior management might have the responsibility of selecting suppliers, for example.

Performance measures

Despite these problems, there are a number of measures that could be used to assess performance.

(i) The number of **items received on time**

(ii) The number of **items failing to meet quality specifications**

(iii) The number of **complaints** by departments using the items about quality/late delivery of items

(iv) The **frequency of visits** to key suppliers

(v) The percentage of **items supplied under a quality assurance scheme**

(vi) The number of **returns**

(vii) The number of **stockouts**

(viii) The proportion of **prices** fluctuating above or below x% (JIT purchasing should involve negotiating long-term contracts with suppliers, which hold prices constant until they are re-negotiated)

(ix) The proportion of **stock lines** on which inventory levels have reduced

Targets will obviously have to be set as part of the establishment of the department's objectives. Targets **based on the results of similar organisations** operating in the same industry are preferable and are probably best established from a review of published accounts of companies, from information provided by trade associations or from government statistics. A competitive price target could be difficult to establish and hence it may prove difficult to establish whether a competitive price has been paid. Perhaps the best approach is to compare actual material costs against turnover with the same measure for other organisations in the industry. It would be dangerous to establish targets on the basis of past performance, given the changes in technology and volumes which have occurred, however, but the comparison of targets and actual results for the above measures will allow an assessment of the department's effectiveness in achieving its objectives.

As with any comparison, there is always the **possibility that like is not being compared with like**, especially when information about targets is sourced from published accounts, for example. Particular care must also be taken when using purchase price indices of basic raw materials over the period.

I hope the above information has proved useful. If I can provide any further assistance please do not hesitate to contact me.

Signed: Chartered Management Accountant

15 PARTICIPATION

Pass marks. A solution to a question like this is likely to benefit from the use of an essay plan. The same points were often relevant to all three sections of the question but marks would only have been gained in each part if the points were tailored to the specific question. Marks could also be boosted by the use of practical illustrations.

Examiner's comment. In part (a) good answers dealt with a range of issues beyond the motivation of the manager and possible defensive behaviour. Common errors were dealing with the advantages of participation only, making too few separate points and repetition of the same point. In part (b) the points made in part (a) were often repeated, with no attempt to distinguish the two parts of the question. In part (c) one aspect was often discussed at length when discussion of a variety of factors was needed to gain an adequate mark.

(a) **Arguments for manager participation**

Managers have **experience of the day-to-day running** of the business. Their knowledge can help ensure that budget targets are, on the one hand, realistic and, on the other hand, a reflection of the full capabilities of the business.

Through manager participation the budgeting process can also become an **opportunity for senior management to communicate** organisational strategy, policies and expectations. This should encourage subordinate managers to concentrate on corporate goals rather than their own personal goals and will therefore help to achieve **goal congruence**.

Participation tends to **increase motivation** since managers feel they are valued. In addition, input to target setting encourages **greater commitment** to budgets as the budgets are then perceived to be fair. This again leads to improved goal congruence.

A final advantage can be the **grooming of managers for top posts**. The consultation processes involved can be used to assess manager potential and help provide training in the skills needed for higher-level management.

Problems arising from manager participation

Since managers are required to implement budgets, they may attempt to **set easily-achievable targets**, over-estimating resource requirements for instance. This can be a particular problem if bonuses depend on achieving such targets. Occasionally the **reverse problem** can arise: managers might be **over optimistic**, thinking an ambitious target will improve their status.

Managers may have **differing degrees of skill** in determining an appropriate level of difficulty for budget targets, particularly in a changing business environment. **Lack of confidence** may also make a manager reluctant to participate

Although participation is usually perceived to improve motivation, if managers' ideas are rejected they may feel **slighted** and have less motivation and commitment to the budget than if it had been imposed from above.

(b) **Arguments for employee participation**

Employees have a detailed **knowledge of day-to-day working practices and problems**. This knowledge and managers' overview can be used to produce a detailed and workable budget. Moreover, those involved in the process are often best placed to suggest **innovations**.

Just as the participation of managers provides a means of communication, the budgeting process can be used to **communicate important ideas** such as the cost to the company of various working practices and the success and direction of the company. As well as focusing employee attention on cost control and corporate objectives, the employee may feel a **greater sense of belonging** to the organisation, which fosters **loyalty**, and a sense of **purpose** and **motivation**. Wage negotiations may be easier as employees have a better understanding of the organisation and its business environment.

As well as communication, participation itself can **motivate** employees; they feel their job is more important, which fosters self esteem. They may also be **less resistant to change** since they have had a hand in the decision-making process.

Problems arising from employee participation

Some employees **prefer an authoritarian-style management**. They may not wish or feel able to take much responsibility. Indeed, in situations where order and control are paramount (such as in the army), an authoritarian approach provides better results. In general, the less skilled the workers the more direction they need.

If an 'us and them' culture is very entrenched, attempts to involve employees in decision making may **be perceived as merely an attempt to cut costs or achieve greater productivity**. This is a particular problem if individuals feel they have little influence over their working environment. Even if employees can be persuaded to participate, they will rarely take a long-term view.

There are a number of other problems.

(i) Participation may lead to a **clash of personal goals**. Management may be dynamic and ambitious but employees may want a stable, stress-free working environment.

(ii) Budgets sometimes have **little direct relevance to employees**; employee performance measures may be non-financial which, although important, may be difficult to link to budget targets.

(iii) Sometimes standards need to be set by management, for instance when benchmarking productivity against competitors or industry averages. Employee-set targets are likely to **incorporate current inefficiencies**, however.

(iv) Participation tends to **slow down decision making**, which may be inappropriate in a high speed environment.

(c) **Circumstances in which participation is likely to be successful**

Decentralised organisations lend themselves to participation in budgeting since responsibility for some decision making has already been delegated down the corporate ladder. Areas of responsibility, limits of authority and objectives must be clearly defined, however. Whether decentralised or not, participation is most likely to succeed where managers or employees **feel they have some control over the factors affecting their performance**.

If budgets are imposed in situations where initiative or innovation are required (for instance with sales or research), a 'budget-constrained approach' may be fostered, so participation is likely to be beneficial. Moreover if urgent problems require difficult and potentially unpopular solutions, **consultation can help diffuse some of the hostility**.

If a participative approach is to be adopted, **good communication skills** are needed by all, but particularly by management. Corporate objectives need to be explained fully to managers and employees. Managers and employees must feel they have genuinely been consulted and, if their ideas are not used, they must understand why.

All management must be **genuinely committed to participation**. If they impose their own ideas regardless, the process becomes a sham, leaving lower management and employees with no incentive to make a well-researched and thought out contribution. Employees must also want to participate and it helps if their attitudes are similar to management.

A **stable business environment** is best, as managers and employees are more likely to have the knowledge necessary to set good targets, and slower decision-making is not a problem. Even under these conditions, however, some **training** of managers and employees will help.

Finally, it is vital that participation is **introduced slowly** or it may be seen merely as a management ploy.

16 EF

> **Pass marks**. Solutions to the question should be mainly based on common sense. An essay plan is a good idea because it will help to determine in which part of the question particular points should be included. A range of detailed points needs to be made to earn adequate marks.
>
> **Examiner's comment**. The examiner was surprised that this was not a more popular question. The main problem with part (a) was a failure to read the question and plan an answer before rushing into a partial answer. Most answers to part (b) were poor.

(a) **The role of the divisional manager**

It is in the interests of EF's management that they produce a **plan that is acceptable to head office but that also safeguards their interests and those of the division** as far as possible. EF division is a cost centre. The **divisional management accountant (DMA)** will have had the responsibility of accounting for divisional costs to head office. His understanding of the division's cost structure will be important to EF's management in the formulation of their plan. He will be able to make recommendations and analyse the feasibility of any proposals.

Overcapacity appears to be at least 50%. This can be dealt with by either a severe **cost reduction programme** or by putting the **spare capacity to alternative uses** (or a mixture of both).

(i) Cost reduction could involve closing some plant completely or reducing capacity in all plants. The DMA would obtain information abut the costs and savings of the alternatives and the qualitative factors such as effect on staff morale.

(ii) If plans were made to use spare capacity, the DMA would estimate marginal costs as a guide for setting fees for subcontracting. He would also estimate the fixed costs which need to be covered in the long term.

The DMA would calculate short-term cash flow forecasts and longer-term NPV calculations to assist EF's management in choosing a preferred option to put forward to head office and would present to head office the calculations to justify the chosen proposal.

Recommendations for reporting

Regular budgetary control reports should be designed to inform divisional management and head office as to whether the division is on target or if there is a problem.

The original budget is no longer considered achievable. If actual figures were compared against it, the change in the market would be highlighted but the comparison would not bring to light any factor controllable by the division. Actual figures should therefore be compared to a **revised budget**.

The differences between the original budget and the revised forecast should be reported as **planning variances**. This will assist any future planning reviews.

Either a cost reduction programme or sub-contracting would result in **exceptional costs** or a **change in gross margins**. These need to be **separated out** from ordinary operating costs for control purposes.

In the short term, the revised budget needs **to take account of future closures or rationalisation**. This might be difficult as such factors would have to be estimated.

(b) **Head office review**

The **senior management accountant (SMA)** would **review** any proposals made by the division. The proposals should be accompanied by detailed figures. He should **check the basis of the calculations** and as far as possible **verify their completeness and accuracy**. He would also review the burden of head office costs currently carried by EF.

If the proposal is to **maintain capacity**, the SMA must consider whether this is **commercially realistic** in both the short and long term. The SMA would determine whether EF is placing **reliance on one type of sub-contracting** or whether they have the necessary **fall-back plans** if initial plans to maintain capacity fail.

If the recommendation is to **reduce capacity**, the SMA will consider the **implications of this for the group**. Closures will lead to redundancies which would affect morale not only in the division but in the group. It may also lead to bad publicity and loss of confidence by investors. This could cause the SMA to consider the option of selling off the division as a going concern.

17 CUMBERSOME PROCESS

Pass marks. This question highlights the importance of reading relevant article in *Management Accounting* as it reflects a number published recently on budgeting and its associated problems.

Examiner's comment. According to the examiner, the question in part (a) was often restated using much the same phrases, at no greater length and it was difficult to award marks to candidates who did this. Answers to part (b) were very limited. The marks and time available should have allowed scope for candidates to make and fully explain a number of suggestions. Many proposals appeared odd and possibly counter productive.

(a) **Cumbersome and time-consuming process**

Even with the arrival of spreadsheets on PCs in the 1980s, producing the budget in all but the smallest organisation is a time-consuming and laborious task. **Forecasts** have to be made, **data gathered** from a multitude of sources and a **budget drawn up** that is both achievable and appropriate to the position the manager in question perceives he has in the organisation. It is not unusual for **line mangers and their staff to spend weeks preparing budget submissions.**

Once a spreadsheet is actually set up to produce a budget, it is still quite a task to flex the figures and/or change the assumptions upon which the model is based. So **budget officers and management accountants** might then spend at least as long **coordinating** and **revising** the individual budgets, **consolidating** them into, and finally distributing, the master budget.

A benchmarking exercise by Price Waterhouse in 1995 found that budgeting costs a median of $63,000 for every $100m of base revenue within finance departments alone and that budget preparation takes an average of 110 days from start to finish.

Short-term financial control

Budgets are an expression of an organisation's plans and objectives in financial terms. Achieving these financial results can therefore take on an **overriding importance** if the management accounting control system gives signals to the effect that doing so is the only way of achieving the plans and objectives. **Longer-term aims and objectives** (increasing market share, improving levels of customer satisfaction) are often **forgotten** in the rush to hit budgeted profit. **Short-term profit levels can be manipulated,** however (and often are if managerial bonuses are based on budgeted profit), usually to the detriment of those factors which provide for the long-term success of the organisation (such as product quality, customer satisfaction and employee motivation).

Motivation of managers

Targets for bonuses tend to be **based on the figures contained in the budget** and so the budget can be seen as a **commitment** and a **constraint.** It might encourage **rigidity** and **discourage flexibility** in operational decision making since managers are likely to concern themselves simply with achieving the budgeted results. The budgeting and associated reward system might motivate employees to **manipulate results for short-term gain** (perhaps by cutting discretionary expenditure) rather than motivate them to think of ways of improving departmental efficiency, say, as a means of reducing expenditure.

The **degree of difficulty of the budget target** can also have **undesirable effects on the motivation** of managers. If the target is too difficult employees will become demotivated as they cannot achieve it. If it is too easy there will be no sense of achievement in attaining the required standard and hence no motivating force.

Formal organisation structure

Budgets tend to be **based on a system of responsibility centres organised on a departmental or functional basis.** Such organisational structures tend to be **bureaucratic, communication is often slow** and **responsibilities overlap.** Achieving, say, departmental targets becomes of paramount importance, regardless of the effect this might have on overall company performance. Functional hierarchies encourage functional excellence but functional departments do not work well together in meeting customers' requirements; they incur excess cost, are too slow and create quality problems.

'Traditional budgeting....strengthens the vertical chain of command and control rather than empowering the front-line. It **constrains** rather than increases flexibility and responsiveness. It **reinforces departmental barriers** rather than encouraging knowledge-sharing across the organisation. It makes people feel undervalued - as "costs to be minimised" rather than as assets to be developed. And it is **bureaucratic, internally focused** and **time-consuming.** In short, its time is up.' (Hope and Fraser, *Management Accounting*, December 1997)

(b) **Cumbersome and time consuming process**

There are a number of steps that can be taken to reduce the bureaucracy and time associated with budgeting.

- The **time allowed to build the budget should be reduced.** Employees are likely to use up as much time as they are given and will continue to 'fine tune' figures until the last possible moment.
- The **number of versions made of the budget should also be reduced**; the precision gained with each cycle rarely justifies the extra effort.
- The **budget period should be reduced.** A system of rolling budgets will be more accurate than a conventional budget that looks 15 or 18 months into the future.

Alternatively, managers could be given **board-approved targets** which they could aim to achieve in their own way. There would be no need to submit detailed plans for approval, just planning assumptions and overall targets.

Short-term financial control

Extensive surveys conducted by the leading accounting firms indicate that 99% of all companies in Europe still operate with formal budgeting systems. Peter Bunce and Robin Fraser reported in *Management Accounting* (February 1997) of a number of Scandinavian organisations which are adopting alternative and, they hope, more effective methods of financial planning and performance measurement. IKEA, the world's largest furniture manufacturer and retailer, abandoned budgeting in 1992. Business managers now simply have to **keep costs within certain revenue ratios.**

ABB is implementing its own version of the **balanced scorecard.** This method of performance analysis considers not just financial performance but also customer knowledge, internal business processes and learning and growth. It emphasises non-financial as well as financial information, looks at the medium and long term objectives as well as short-term targets and takes into account external as well as internal information.

Volvo's new planning process focuses on **objectives** and employs **key performance indicators.**

Instead of using the budget as a means of concentrating on short-term profitability and maximising return to shareholders, other organisations are concentrating on **finding and profitably satisfying customers.** This involves adopting a programme of total quality management and establishing employee, customer and shareholder loyalty and, in the long term, maximising value creation for all of the organisation's stakeholders.

Motivation of managers

Rather than appraising managerial performance in terms of targets based on an internally-generated budget, it should be **based on external intelligence** derived from benchmarking exercises and customer feedback. **Targets** should not simply be short term and financially orientated but **cover a wide range of measures** as advocated by the balanced scorecard approach. Mangers will thus be motivated to work towards the organisation's goals and objectives rather than concentrating on departmental or personal ones.

Formal organisation structure

To cope with the demands of today's rapidly-changing and competitive business environment, organisations need to be **decentralised** to allow greater speed of decision making and response to changing events. ABB, for example, is highly decentralised, each unit managing its own finances as if it were an independent company. **Processes** and **teams** are of paramount importance. Processes offer managers a clearer view of which work should be done and, when new technology is applied, how such work can be done faster and more effectively. Svenska Handelsbanken, for example, abandoned traditional budgeting in 1979 and operates each branch like an independent business.

It is therefore evident that although the budgeting process can be criticised, many organisations are evolving ways of overcoming the problems.

18 PROPOSED CHANGES

> **Pass marks.** You may have been able to incorporate you own experiences into your solution to this question. Remember that you are preparing the report on behalf of the group finance director who suggested the change to the budget timetable and so you should aim to promote the idea and suggest how problems can be overcome rather than to dismiss it.
>
> **Examiner's comment.** This question could have been answered in a variety of ways and provided scope for candidates to demonstrate experience. Most solutions to this question were poor, candidates spending too much time repeating the scenario detail.

REPORT

To: Members of the board
From: Management accountant Date: XX.XX.XX
Subject: Proposed changes to the budget preparation timetable

This report has been **prepared on behalf of the group finance director** and explains the reasons for the proposed changes in budget preparation and planning for next year and considers how specific problems and anticipated difficulties could be dealt with.

Reasons for the proposed changes

Our **current budget preparation timetable** requires that budgets are prepared after the third quarter's results are known and the fourth quarter forecast is prepared. The budgets are therefore based on information which is as **up-to-date** and accurate as possible, which is particularly important for the managerial **performance evaluation, resource allocation** and **control** functions of the budget: targets must be realistic if they are to motivate; budgets must accurate if they are to be used as the basis for optimal plans when resources are scarce; control will be useless if actual results are not compared with achievable expected results.

But despite the fact that leaving budget preparation as late as possible means that the budgets are based on up-to-date information, there are **disadvantages** to such an approach. We have found that there is often **insufficient time** between the beginning of the preparation process and the new budget period for:

(a) an evaluation of the current position of the organisation in terms of both its internal resources and the external environment;

(b) planning by senior management;

(c) gathering of data;

(d) lower-level managers to be involved in the budgeting process;

(e) discussions on resource allocation issues to take place;

(f) the budget negotiation process to be carried out;

(g) the final agreement of budgets.

There is a very real danger that operational managers in particular conclude that our budget preparation process as a whole is too rushed, that it is really nothing more than a planning exercise for senior management. **Negative attitudes** towards the budget can form and its **positive motivational impact fall.**

The **advantage of the group finance director's suggestion** of a budget preparation timetable that begins after the half-year results for the current financial year is therefore the time it gives management, at both the senior level and operational level, **to research, discuss and prepare** the budgets. Operational-level managers will be able to **participate** in the process, improving motivation and morale and increasing acceptance of and commitment to the organisation's goals and objectives.

Specific problems

(a) **Division A**

Because the appointment of a new managing director could take several months, it is likely that the divisional finance director, acting as managing director, will be in charge of the budget preparation process if the timetable changes are adopted. There are thus two potential problems: the **new managing director** will inherit and have to **implement a budget over which he has had no input** and with which he might disagree strongly; there may be a **conflict of interest** as the finance director/acting managing director has no one to whom he should report.

Given this, it might be advisable to leave budget preparation until as late as possible, at least until a new managing director is appointed. But it is possible to work to the suggested revised timetable, however. The division's **budget** for next year could be **based on this year's budget plus long-term divisional plans,** ignoring the poor performance in the first quarter. A contingency plan would need to be drawn up, however, to cover the possibility of poor performance during the remainder of the year. Regular reviews would need to be made of divisional results to assess whether the contingency plan needed to be implemented.

If the **new managing director** is not appointed until after the final agreement of the budget, he should **not be held accountable** for any failure to achieve targets.

(b) **Division B**

As the division's **new product range** was only launched in the first three months of this year, its **success can not yet be gauged.** In order that the proposed budget timetable can be adopted in the division, however, divisional management's knowledge and experience needs to be used to incorporate the anticipated results into the division's budget if the results are likely to have a significant impact on divisional and/or group profits. **Budgets based on worst possible/most likely/best possible outcomes** could be drawn up, for example, or a **budget based on the probabilities of outcomes** could be used.

Even if management's estimates of the success or otherwise of the range are inaccurate, the budget will still be effective: the budget results can be **flexed** to reflect the actual level of activity for control purposes; a system of **planning and operational variances** can be used and the difference between the original standard activity level and the revised standard activity level set later this year be classified as a planning variance.

(c) **Division C**

It is currently anticipated that the **new plant** will be operational in the third quarter but given the doubts over the likely quality of the output, it **could be the fourth quarter** or even next year before production can begin.

The expected **materiality** of the impact of the new machine in terms of the division's and the group's results affects the course of action which the division should adopt towards budget preparation. If the impact is expected to be significant, the preparation of a realistic and accurate budget after the half-year results have been completed will be difficult. Following discussions with group management, the division's management could adopt the approach suggested for division B and prepare **optimistic/pessimistic/most likely budgets** or a **budget based on probabilities.**

Other anticipated difficulties

There are a number of other difficulties with the proposed change to the budget timetable.

(a) The change implies that **operational managers** will have to **devote more time and effort** to the budget preparation process. This, coupled with the fact that they might feel that the current approach is perfectly acceptable, may mean that they have to be **convinced of its shortcomings and the benefits of the proposal.**

(b) Many managers' **bonuses** are based on their success in achieving budget targets and they may consider targets based on what could be out-of-date information to be far more difficult to achieve than the more realistic ones drawn up under the current system. This problem could be overcome by introducing a broader range of performance measures, perhaps incorporating **some non-financial indicators** such as reject rates, on-time deliveries and so on, which do not rely on the budget.

I hope this information is of use. If you have any questions please do not hesitate to contact me.

Signed: Management accountant

19 BUDGETARY PADDING

Pass marks. The key to earning marks is to take a structured approach to addressing all of the question's requirements. In part (a) you must therefore provide your answer in a report format, state what both 'you' (the management accountant) and senior managers can do when approving budgets.

Similarly part (b) has a number of requirements – explaining arguments, stating advantages for both the manager and the organisation and discussing the inclusion of some level of slack. Remember that a discussion should have points both in favour and against the issue you have been asked to cover.

Examiner's comment. In part (a), many candidates appeared to regard authoritarian systems, imposed budgets and arbitrary percentage cuts in budgets as acceptable and reasonable. A common fault was failure to respond to the clear prompt in the question requiring explanation of separate actions by the management accountant and by senior management.

(a) REPORT

To: Finance Director
From: Management Accountant Date: XX.XX.XX
Subject: Minimising Budgetary Slack

Following our recent meeting and subsequent telephone discussion, I set out below the various **steps** that can be taken in the processes of preparing and approving budgets that will **minimise budgetary slack.**

Action by myself as Management Accountant

Budget holders have far greater knowledge of the area of operations that is their responsibility and are likely to use this knowledge in demands for additional resources in their area or for easier targets. In order that I can deal equitably with such demands it is therefore **vital that I become fully aware of the workings and business of the area of operations of each budget holder.**

Budgetary slack could also be controlled if, **prior to budgets being prepared,** I establish the following.

- A requirement for a **detailed analysis of and justification for any movements in provisions and any cost categories where it is felt that budget padding could be concealed**
- The adoption of a **'Kaizen' approach,** whereby managers would be required to achieve a reduction on previous years' costs
- **Demanding sales growth targets**
- **Standard forecasts** for any values that managers might otherwise have to estimate (such as inflation, market growth and so on)

During the **budget preparation process** I would undertake **regular reviews of budgets.** The **main focus** of these reviews would be as follows.

- Discussing with budget holders **about how they intend to develop their business unit's performance**
- Requiring managers to **justify expenditure** - both timing and amounts - on **discretionary expense** areas such as marketing, training and so on
- **Reviewing past trends** to assess the reasonableness of budget requests (taking into consideration changes in activity levels, inflation, efficiency levels and working practices)
- Reviewing **current year's spending to ensure it offers value for money** rather than being incurred to justify budgeted amounts
- **Comparing budgets** on a business unit/departmental/divisional basis so as to judge the reasonableness of the individual budgets
- Performing a **detailed review of the complete draft budget** to ensure its reasonableness
- **Comparing draft budgets with any available external data** such as competitors' published results, information from trade associations, quotations from external suppliers (for comparison with internal service departments)

Action by Senior Management during the budget approval process

The steps described above should minimise the opportunities that budget holders have for padding their budgets and should ensure that the budgets presented to senior managers are reasonable.

During the **approval process** senior managers can further attempt to prevent any slack by taking the following action.

- Impressing upon budget holders the **importance of accurate budgets**
- Suggesting that **future appraisals and rewards will include an assessment of the accuracy of the budget**
- Reminding managers that they will be **appraised on a number of non-financial performance indicators** as well as on their ability to achieve budget targets
- **Reducing pressure on the budget holder** (such as the requirement to improve quality levels without an associated increase in costs)

I trust that the information set out above will prove useful. If you have any questions or require further detail, please do not hesitate to contact me.

Signed: Management Accountant

(b) A number of **general arguments** can be advanced for **accepting some level of budgetary slack.**

- Few, if any, budgets can be one hundred percent accurate and attempts to achieve this level of accuracy are unlikely to be cost-effective. If mangers feel that actual results must be exactly the same as budget figures, they may begin to **act dysfunctionally during the year to minimise reasonable variances.**
- **Forecasting errors** are always likely and the inclusion of some slack should take account of the repercussions of such errors so that budget targets are still achievable.
- If quoted companies do not achieve profit forecasts, **share prices may fall.**
- A certain level of padding should provide **public sector organisations with sufficient resources** at the beginning of the budget period to provide a reasonable level of service throughout the period.

Considering specifically the **managers being appraised,** if some level of budgetary slack is accepted, the **budget will be perceived as being more achievable.** Achieving budget is highly motivating and managers will want to become more **involved** in the budget-setting process. By **removing the pressure on managers** to exactly attain budget figures, they may concentrate less on the numbers, worry less about cost items which they may have forgotten to include within the budget and **give more thought to the specific action needed to achieve better results.** During the year, by removing the impression that adherence to budget is the only thing that matters, managers may be encouraged to be **more creative in their efforts at running the business.** For instance, if spending which would be to the benefit of the organisation cannot be met by available funds in the budget category in question, cost savings in other categories could be utilised.

The **organisation** should benefit from having **managers who are concentrating on managing business performance** rather than attempting to adherence strictly to budgets. There will be more **flexibility** to allow for both reaction to changes in the market and for managers to take innovative action for long-term benefit, even if in the short-term costs increase. If major additional expenditure is required in one area of the organisation's operations, **slack from other areas can be taken up to ensure that customer needs and interests are satisfied.** Directors should be confident that any forecasts or briefings given will be achievable given the slack that exists, thereby **avoiding damage to the organisation's share price in the event of failure**

to meet forecasts; budgets that are 'guaranteed to be achieved' should keep shareholders and funding bodies happy

Actively permitting slack goes one step further than accepting it is there.

If **managers** are permitted to incorporate some slack, they may feel **empowered** and should be **motivated** to achieve 'their budget'. The slack available will give them much more **opportunity to react to any unexpected opportunities** that arise during the period, increasing their job satisfaction.

The organisation and its managers may become more dynamic, seizing new opportunities as they arise. By reducing the time spent on the budget review and approval process, senior mangers should have **more time to review the new opportunities generated by and available to the organisation.**

There are possible **disadvantages** in permitting budgetary slack, however. Managers may feel that there is **no point in preparing an accurate budget** if variances from it are acceptable. They may also become **less conscious of the importance of controlling costs,** since any overspends can simply be absorbed into the slack.

By losing the tight control afforded by establishing and attempting to attain extremely accurate budgets, **the organisation may begin to lose direction** as managers deviate from the agreed budget in a more 'laissez-faire' environment. There may be a **failure to reach critical financial targets** such as positive cash flow requirements for organisations with liquidity problems.

Whether to permit budgetary slack will depend largely on the nature of the business. It is a suitable policy where the company is in a **highly dynamic market** and **needs flexibility** to react to changes, or in organisations that **rely heavily on the skills, actions and reactions of individual managers.**

20 ABC AND SERVICE ORGANISATIONS

> **Pass marks**. This question concerns the use of new activity based cost information in a service industry. Candidates should be aware of the problems of service industries and the possible uses of activity based information from a variety of CIMA publications and articles in *Management Accounting*. Even if they had not read the articles and publications dealing with the use of ABC in services, they should be able to apply their knowledge of the principles of ABC to the known features of large service organisations. Part (d) requires a basic understanding of the problem of external price control. This has been much discussed in the UK in the context of the regulation of privatised monopolies; similar problems of price control have occurred in many countries, as have the similar problems of price control in 'cost plus' defence procurement. It should be possible for a candidate to deduce the probable requirements, in outline at least, from basic principles without specific experience of the situation.

(a) A large-scale **service organisation** is likely to have **characteristics** very similar to those **required for the successful application of ABC** in manufacturing industry.

(i) A highly competitive market.

(ii) Diversity of products, processes and customers.

(iii) Significant overhead costs not easily assigned to individual products.

(iv) Demands on overhead resources placed by individual products and customers, not proportional to volume.

Moreover, given the fact that, as the question says, such organisations have historically had relatively unsophisticated budgeting and control systems, they have an advantage over manufacturing organisations in that the **introduction** of ABC is likely to be **less disruptive to existing systems** and **more easily accepted** by **managers**, to whom the whole concept of costing is new.

(b) (i) **Heterogeneity**. All service performances are unique, and the inputs will never be precisely the same. For example, BR might run a train service at the same time each day, but the level of the activity of selling tickets for that service will vary considerably from day to day

(ii) **Intangibility**. It is very difficult to define the boundaries of a service. What activities, for example, constitute the provision of a bank account

(iii) Even with ABC, there are some unresolved problems **about overhead allocation.**

'Activity based costing does not solve the problem of allocating general manufacturing overheads where the decisions and processes which cause these overheads are unknown or are past, where those overheads reflect past decisions and where the cost causing activities cannot be identified because of the commonality of costs. More general problems of overhead allocation remain unresolved. Should, for instance, set-up costs in switching from one product to another and back be allocated to both products equally?'

(Bromwich and Bhimani, *Management accounting: evolution not revolution*)

Innes and Mitchell, Activity based costing: a review with case studies (CIMA, 1990) identify other procedural problems.

(i) **Some measure of (arbitrary) cost apportionment may still be required** at the cost pooling stage for items like rent, rates and building depreciation. If an ABC system has many cost pools the amount of apportionment needed may be greater than ever.

(ii) The ability of a **single cost driver to fully explain the cost behaviour** of all items in its associated pool is **questionable**.

(iii) To have a useable cost driver a cost must be caused by an activity that is measurable in quantitative terms and which can be related to production output. Some costs might be attributed to customers or market segments rather than to products, but not all costs can be treated in this way. For example, what **drives corporate as opposed to product-based advertising** (British Airways adverts, for instance) or the cost of the annual external audit?

(c) (i) In a more competitive environment, companies must be able to assess the profitability of the services that they provide realistically. To do this, they must have a good understanding of what drives overhead costs. **ABC** gives a meaningful analysis of costs which can provide a suitable basis for **service performance measurement.**

Just as it can for products, ABC can give valuable insights into service design, service mix, service delivery methods, administration and pricing. To paraphrase Kaplan, because a company is able to **see clearly where the majority of its indirect expenses are going, it can make changes to its processes so that these expenses can be minimised**. ... Pricing decisions, mix decisions, design decisions and service delivery decisions can all be much better understood when the background analysis and modelling from ABC is available. Companies may be selling services at a loss, subsidising their customers, because they do not understand the true cost of a service owing to the distortion of the costing system. The ABC approach gives them a better way of making that kind of assessment.

(ii) ABC recognises that the complexity of an organisation's activities has increased and there are multiple cost drivers, many of them transaction-based rather than volume-based.

(d) **Pass mark.** Our answer includes some real life examples to enhance your understanding of this area.

Regulators of privatised industries act as a kind of **watchdog** to ensure that the newly created monopolies **do not charge unfair prices or earn excessive returns.**

For example, **Ofwat**, the UK water industry regulator, recently announced its plans to set new **'K factors' - the rate above inflation at which prices may rise** - in July 1994.

> 'The tussle between the industry and Ofwat will turn on the complex detail of the calculations. Companies have made it clear that they disagree with the regulator over some of its assumptions.
>
> In particular they have clashed on the method of valuing companies' assets, and on the rate of return companies should be allowed to earn on that capital.'
>
> (*Financial Times*, May 1994)

Again, in May 1994, **Ofgas**, the UK gas industry regulator, released a document setting out its vision of how the **present monopoly of British Gas will be ended.** In the market there are fears that wide price variations will emerge.

> 'Consumer groups had warned that under present arrangements consumers of small amounts of gas are in effect subsidised by households which are large users. They feared that the removal of such "cross-subsidies" would lead to price variations which would tend to penalise the less well-off.'
>
> 'The document notes that British Gas's costing systems are not set up in a way which would allow the "cross-subsidies to be readily identified". But it says most of these subsidies appear to be in the transport side of the business.' (*Financial Times*, May 1994)

To carry out their task, then, **regulators will be interested in information** of the following kind.

(i) **The allocation of costs.** Problem areas may include depreciation, where typically massive investments in fixed assets and infrastructure are made, research and development, maintenance and distribution and administration costs shared across several different types of service.

(ii) **The costing basis.** Government bodies have lagged far behind private industry in the sophistication of costing systems and may attempt to take advantage of the confusion caused by bringing methods up to date, for example by disguising dubiously incurred expenditure by means of new methods like activity based costing.

(iii) **The validity and treatment of costs supposedly incurred** because of the need to comply with EU regulations such as EU environmental regulations, a frequent cause of complaint amongst privatised industries.

(iv) **The consistency of the methods used,** from year to year and with standard industry practice.

Pass mark. The CIMA model solution also mentions the need to identify international and selling expenses (as 'discretionary costs'?) and charitable donations, all of which it claims the regulator would want to disallow.

21 JUST-IN-TIME

> **Pass marks**. In our answer to part (a) we show you how even at Stage 4 you can use the CIMA *Official Terminology* to your advantage. Rather than just churning out the official definition, here we use it to provide pegs on which to hang an answer. The CIMA answer is loosely structured around the various aspects of JIT summarised by E J Hay in *Management Accounting* (see the BPP Study Text). Part (b) overlaps with part (a), and it is quite difficult to know what to save up for this part. Indications are that the examiner recognised this problem and allowed for it in marking.
>
> *Other points*. At the end of the CIMA answer the examiner suggests that 'It would have been equally logical to go through areas of cost and revenue and discuss profit impact, the visibility of this in product costs and control systems, and the factory accounting and system changes.' See if you can write an answer along these lines, too, if your answer looks like ours.
>
> **Examiner's comment**. The examiner reported that this question produced some very good answers and a very respectable number of solid answers which displayed a good knowledge of JIT. Common errors in part (a) included discussing AMT, CIM, ABC and many other fairly new techniques as well as JIT and producing answers to a different question to that asked (for example, 'Write all you know about JIT').
>
> Answers to part (b) were significantly weaker than those to part (a). A common error was to use initials without even brief explanations of their meaning and significance.

(a) The first part of the question may be answered in outline by reference to the CIMA definition of JIT.

(i) It is a technique should increase sales and profits because it allows 'rapid, high quality, flexible production': it allows the manufacturing firm to deliver more quickly than competitors, to charge a premium for quality, and meet customer needs more precisely.

(ii) It does this 'whilst minimising waste and stock levels', and so reducing costs.

This can be expanded by dealing in turn with the two aspects of JIT identified in the *Official Terminology*: JIT production and JIT purchasing.

JIT production

This is associated with **cellular manufacturing**, involving less time wasted on set-ups, better pacing of the production process (so that there is less time spent idle waiting for the previous stage to be completed or else working too quickly and making costly mistakes), and more cost-effective use of machines and machine operators. **Operators are multi-skilled**, again reducing idle time and improving motivation and so quality and productivity.

JIT often involves the use of a **Kanban**, or signal, to ensure that **products or components are only produced when needed** (as soon as it is demanded by a customer but only then.) Nothing is produced in anticipation of need and then remains in stock consuming resources, but customers are still satisfied because the system can produce goods quickly enough for the customer not to experience a delay.

JIT purchasing

This involves **matching the receipt of material closely with usage** so that **raw material stocks are reduced to near zero**. Supplies are delivered on a long-term contract basis as soon as they are needed, but in small quantities. Therefore the costs of space for holding stock, and costs such as damage or deterioration in store, stores administration and security are minimal. In particular the interest cost and opportunity costs of tying up working capital in large inventories are avoided.

JIT usually entails some sort of **quality assurance scheme**: the quality of materials delivered is guaranteed by suppliers, and the effect of this is to reduce the costs of wastage, returns, and reworking.

Against this, setting up a JIT system may involve negotiation of **long-term contracts with suppliers, the costs of operating and monitoring a quality assurance scheme, extra delivery costs and probably a premium in the price of materials,** all of which will have a negative impact on profitability. **Stockouts** should not occur in theory, but if they do in practice there may be quite significant knock-on costs through idle production facilities, loss of customer goodwill, and rushing work when stock becomes available again.

Routine control information will obviously reflect the above in higher reported sales and lower costs overall. For control purposes **information** should be made available on a routine basis about **set-up times, production lead times, levels of stock held, levels of wastage and reworking, levels of quality achieved, delivery times (both deliveries *from* suppliers and *to* customers), materials prices (these should be constant unless the contract is renegotiated).** Hi tech machine tools may produce highly detailed information about usage that can be used for control purposes. Of a regular, but less routine nature may be information about more **qualitative issues** such as customer satisfaction and levels of employee skills and motivation.

(b) Assuming that the transition is from traditional systems of cost and financial accounting and budgetary control to the new system, **changes** might include the following.

(i) Perhaps the **abandonment of records and procedures needed for stock valuation purposes.** The extent to which this can be achieved will depend on the products: if they can be produced and despatched within a day there will be practically no stock held at the end of each day. If production takes longer than this there will always be some work-in-progress, but very little raw materials stock or finished goods stock.

(ii) Likewise the **abandonment of traditional administrative systems for stock control** involving delivery notes, GRNs, inspection notes, and stock counts.

(iii) **Enhanced controls over purchasing,** especially monitoring of delivery times and delays due to late deliveries or internal failures in the purchasing system.

(iv) **Standard costs** will need to be **recalculated** incorporating the extra costs of JIT delivery and quality assurance schemes, but excluding elements such as scrap allowances or idle time allowances.

(v) Materials needs will change, both over time and as new products are introduced, and new JIT contracts will need to be put in place from time to time. **Purchasing habits need to be closely monitored** to identify unusual orders and changing requirements.

(vi) **Labour** costs will be largely fixed, and with multi-skilled and 'empowered' employees it may **not be necessary or cost-effective to record labour time in detail,** except for work study purposes or training. In a highly automated environment, labour costs may become relatively insignificant overheads in any case.

(vii) The system needs to be able to **identify and rectify any reasons for hold-ups** in the flow of work, and any associated costs (as suggested in (a)).

Some years ago management accounting literature gave some attention to a system known as **backflush costing.** This is a simplified standard costing system for allocating costs between stocks and cost of goods sold, and which attempts to eliminate detailed accounting transactions. Backflush accounting works backwards from the outputs and there is no separate accounting for work in progress.

There appears to be little empirical evidence to suggest that backflush costing is used or even understood in many organisations at present.

22 ABC AND ABB

> **Pass marks.** We have assumed in part (c) that 'this form of analysis' refers to the value-adding/non-value-adding analysis and not the hierarchical model.
>
> **Examiner's comment.** This question was reasonably well answered, especially by candidates who focused on the exact requirements of each section of the question.
>
> Common weaknesses in part (b) included producing little more than an answer plan, repetition of the same point (albeit in different words) and making comments which appeared to contradict statements made in part (a).

(a) The usefulness of activity-based techniques will depend on the characteristics of an organisation, in particular its cost structure, product range and environment.

Cost structure

Activity-based techniques are particularly useful in organisations where **overheads account for a significant proportion of total costs.** The allocation of material costs and direct labour costs to cost objects is fairly straightforward but the traditional methods used to apportion and absorb overheads can often produce misleading product cost information. The higher the level of overheads, the less accurate the product costs are likely to be.

If an organisation has **introduced new technology** (leading to a large reduction in direct labour and a significant increase in overheads) or **business process re-engineering,** for example, an investigation is required into whether or not the existing cost system still provides a reasonable estimate of product or service costs as its cost structure is likely to be affected. Activity-based techniques can be used to review the cost allocation process.

Product range and diversity

If an organisation produces only a small number of products, product mix decisions for example can be made on a relevant cost basis. If a **vast number of products** are produced, however, the number of individual products and the number of combinations of products would make relevant cost analysis impossible. A general-purpose activity-based system is required that reports long-run product costs. The product costs reported are not designed to be used directly for decision making; instead they should provide attention-directing information and highlight problem areas that need more detailed analysis and the attention of management.

With the current focus on satisfying the customer, many organisations produce a **huge range of diverse products.** ABC is useful if increased product diversity means that an organisation produces **both high-volume standard products and low-volume variant products.** A more sophisticated costing system is required because, as the level of diversity increases, so does the level of distortion reported by absorption costing systems (which tend to allocate too high a proportion of overheads to high-volume products and too low a proportion of overheads to low-volume products).

Likewise, if an organisation's **customer base is wide,** ABC can provide information for customer profitability analysis. Costs such as those associated with travelling to call on a customer, after-sales service and special delivery methods are revealed, thereby assisting with the identification of profit-making/loss-making customers.

Environment

Increased **competition** may occur if other organisations recognise a particular product or service's profit potential, if the product or service has become feasible in terms of cost to make or perform, or if an industry has been deregulated. Organisations operating in a more competitive environment have a greater need for the more accurate cost information produced by activity-based techniques, since competitors are more likely to take advantage of any errors arising from the use of distorted cost information.

(b) Despite the many advantages claimed by researchers and writers, there are a number of reasons why an organisation might decide not to use, or even to abandon the use of, activity-based techniques.

(i) The implementation of activity-based techniques is a **time-consuming** and **expensive** process. Activities and cost drivers have to be identified, involving data collection, interviews and observation. Management may feel that the possible benefits are outweighed by the associated costs.

(ii) The introduction of any new technique will be met with **resistance from those employees** who feel threatened by a change to the status quo or who feel that the current system is more than adequate. Such resistance can be reduced if employees are kept fully informed of the reasons for, and the process of, the techniques' introduction, however.

(iii) Any change to the established way of doing things is unlikely to succeed unless the change has a **powerful champion** within the organisation. The champion of any activity-based techniques is likely to be the finance director. If the finance director is not supportive of their introduction or he/she is replaced by another director who is not supportive, their introduction and implementation is likely to fail.

(iv) Even if overheads make up a significant proportion of an organisation's costs, if those **overheads cannot be traced easily to products and services** because cost driver identification is difficult (perhaps if the majority of them are administration costs), the introduction of activity-based techniques might not increase the accuracy of product cost information and hence will not be welcomed by management.

(v) If the techniques appear to be part of a **policy of overhead cost reduction,** employees may worry about possible redundancies and **resist** their introduction. It is therefore vital that a detailed explanation of the reasoning behind any decision to introduce ABC, ABB, ABM and so on is given to affected members of the workforce.

(vi) An organisation may decide not to used activity-based techniques if it becomes clear that they will not **provide additional information** for management planning and control decisions. If managers are not going to use the techniques to control non-value-added activities, for example, it would be much easier to stick with a simpler absorption costing system.

(c) An activity may **increase the worth of a product or service to the customer**; in this case the customer will be willing to pay for that activity and so it will be considered to be a **value-adding activity**. Actual production activities such as assembly, machining and so on are value-adding activities. Getting luggage on the proper flights is a value-adding activity for airlines.

Some activities, however, simply increase the time spent on a product or service but **do not increase its worth to the customer**; these are **non-value-adding activities.** Such activities can be eliminated without the customer perceiving a deterioration in the performance, function or other quality of a product. The additional time spent on the activity simply creates **additional costs** that are unnecessary. If non-value-adding activities were eliminated, costs would decrease without affecting the market value or quality of the product or service. Such activities therefore include setting-up production runs, moving products from one part of the factory to another, repairing faulty items, inspection and so on.

Because they invariably involve handling work in progress and because handling often leads to damage, non-value-adding activities often **degrade, but never improve, quality**. Because they are not done instantaneously, they **decrease levels of customer service** by increasing lead times and by increasing the amount of time it takes to discover mistakes, thereby increasing the number of mistakes that are made. Non-value-adding activities usually **reflect an organisation's limitations and constraints** and therefore they often **reduce**, but never increase, **flexibility**. Because they are never cost less, they increase costs.

This form of analysis is particularly **useful for highlighting areas for cost reduction measures**; if organisations could remove non-value-adding activities such as reworking or setting-up, costs would be reduced. But the activities cannot simply be eliminated; the underlying process that makes the non-value-adding activities necessary must be changed so that they are no longer required. For example, if the rework activity is simply eliminated faulty items will be sold to customers. It is the production process itself that needs changing so that rework is not necessary.

Many support activities, such as administration, may be classified as non-value-adding. The analysis facilitates an assessment of their cost effectiveness and **provides a basis for outsourcing decisions**, for example. Outsourcing the activities which are not sources of competitive advantages provide management with the opportunity to focus on the essential core activities that are valued by customers.

While it is theoretically correct to view inspection as a non-value adding activity, it is important to realise that **very few organisations can completely eliminate all quality control functions**. But understanding the non-value-adding nature of such activities should help managers strive to minimise them as far as possible.

Some **activities are difficult to classify**, however. For example the law may require that a factory should not pollute the environment and so pollution abatement activities might be classified as value adding. If the process could be redesigned so that pollution was not created, however, the cost of the pollution abatement activities could be avoided. Moreover, the analysis and subsequent cost reduction measures may meet with resistance if employees perceive them as nothing more than a sophisticated cost-cutting exercise with redundancies as the end result.

23 VARIANCE INVESTIGATION

> **Pass marks**. Part (a) should be an easy eight marks but, particularly if you find such calculations difficult, make sure your workings are easy to follow with plenty of explanation. In part (b) the 12 marks will only be gained for a *detailed* analysis of the problems and benefits of the approaches.
>
> *Other points*. You could have used a decision tree in part (a).
>
> **Examiner's comment**. A few candidates clearly welcomed this question, and scored well, including maximum marks for part (a). The remainder who attempted it clearly chose it as the least unappealing optional question as their fourth question. Many made no attempt at part (a), while others made a weak attempt without really understanding how to approach the question, although they made reasonable attempts at (b).
>
> Generous marks were available in part (a) for logical working, even if this did not produce the correct answer.

(a) **To justify investigation:**

probable benefit of investigation must be greater than probable cost of investigation and correction

ie $\mathbf{p \times B > I + (p \times C)}$

where p = probability the variance is due to a correctable cause

B = benefit if a correctable problem is corrected

I = cost of investigation

C = cost of correction

$\therefore$ To justify investigation, $0.25 \times (0.75 \times \text{variance}) > £1{,}400 + (0.25 \times £400)$

$0.1875 \times \text{variance} > £1{,}500$

$\text{variance} > £1{,}500 \div 0.1875$

$\text{variance} > £8{,}000$

$\therefore$ The minimum size of variance that would justify investigation is £8,000.

(b) (i) There are a number of reasons why these approaches are taken rather the approach described in (a) above.

(1) The calculation above is **based on expected values,** for example the probable cost of correction is p × C which, in the example, is 0.25 × £400 = £100. It is the **average cost** of correction per investigation if a series of investigations are carried out. For a single investigation the cost is £400 (if there is a correctable problem) or £0 (if the problem is not correctable).

(2) The calculation is **only valid if the decision is always repeated under the same conditions.** It also **relies on all the information being known and accurate.** There can be problems with each element of the model, however.

(3) The probability of a variance being correctable may be estimated from past data but there is **no guarantee this pattern will continue.** Working conditions may change – for example, lower quality materials might increase the incidence of variances that cannot be corrected.

(4) **Costs of investigation** and correction are likely to be calculated as the cost of man hours used plus lost production while investigation/correction occurs. The real cost to the company may be more **difficult to determine** and may vary. If the investigation is undertaken by someone on a fixed salary there is no marginal cost to the

company. This would change if the investigation had to be undertaken in overtime, however. The cost of lost production will only be a real cost in times of full production, or where stocks are insufficient to supply demand during the down time.

(5) The **potential cost of not correcting a correctable problem** is also **difficult to predict**. This may also change with changes in working conditions.

(ii) **The appropriateness of the alternative approaches**

The **model described in (a) is quite complex**, requires detailed analysis of past data and the probabilities, relevant costs and benefits are difficult to estimate accurately.

The **investigation approach based on absolute size of variance** or percentage from standard is, on the other hand, **straightforward and easy to follow**. The criteria for investigation are also easy to understand and therefore easier to justify to managers.

Past data does need to be considered in order to set the limit. Either an estimate can be made of normal fluctuation or, more precisely, the standard deviation of variances can be calculated and an investigation limit of 2 to 3 standard deviations set. It is assumed that variances within the limit represent normal random variation. Up to the limit no action is taken. Above the limit all variances are investigated.

The **problem with this approach** is that, unlike the previous model, there is **no attempt at cost benefit analysis**. In addition, any **current inefficiencies** may well be **built into the limit** and therefore be perpetuated. It implicitly **assumes all variances** within the limit are **uncontrollable** or of immaterial cost. More thorough variance investigation fosters a move towards total quality processes.

24 TUTORIAL QUESTION: COMPUTATION OF PERFORMANCE MEASURES

(a) The expected performance of the two divisions will be measured by:

(i) ROI;
(ii) residual income; and
(iii) net present value.

Assumptions

- The plant and equipment will be depreciated on a straight-line basis over eight years to a nil residual value.
- ROI will be measured as average annual profit divided by average investment.
- The notional interest for a residual income calculation will be 20% of the average investment (ie interest charge pa).

(i) **ROI**

		ABE Ltd	*KIM Ltd*
		£m	£m
Total expected net cash flows	year 1	1.9	3.2
	years 2 - 8	20.3	29.4
		22.2	32.6
Less depreciation		10.0	15.0
Total expected net profit		12.2	17.6

	£m	£m
Average expected annual net profit (÷ 8)	1.525	2.2
Average investment	5.000	7.5
ROI (expected)	30.5%	29.3%

(ii) **Residual income**

	£m	£m
Average expected annual net profit	1.525	2.2
Notional interest (20% of average investment)	1.000	1.5
Expected average annual residual income	0.525	0.7

(iii) **Net present value**

			ABE Ltd		*KIM Ltd*	
Item	*Year*	*Discount factor at 20%*	*Cash-flow* £m	*Present value* £m	*Cash-flow* £m	*Present value* £m
Cost of equipment	0	1.000	(10.0)	(10.0)	(15.0)	(15.0)
Net cash flow	1	0.833	1.9	1.6	3.2	2.7
Net cash flow pa	2-8	*3.004	2.9	8.7	4.2	12.6
Net present value				0.3		0.3

(* 3.837 – 0.833)

Both investments appear worthwhile. ABE Ltd offers a ROI of 30.5%, slightly higher than the 29.3% of KIM Ltd, but both are well in excess of the cost of capital of 20%. KIM Ltd, being a larger investment, offers a higher residual income, but the expected RI of both investments is positive. The expected NPV of both projects is also positive, and approximately the same (around £300,000).

(b) The actual year 1 performance of both divisions cannot be measured by DCF, because the projects are only one year old. We can, however, measure their ROI and residual income. It is important to remember that these **year 1 performances should be worse than the average annual performance over an 8-year period,** because:

(i) year 1 cash flows will be lower than in years 2-8; and

(ii) the value of the investment declines over time, thus increasing the ROI and residual income year by year.

	ABE Ltd £m	*KIM Ltd* £m
Investment		
At start of year 1	10.00	15.000
Year 1 depreciation	1.25	1.875
At end of year 1	8.75	13.125
Average year 1 investment	9.375	14.0625

	ABE Ltd			KIM Ltd		
	Expected	*Actual*	*Expected*		*Actual*	
	£m		£m	£m		£m
Net cash flow	1.90	(× 1.05)	1.995	3.200	(× 0.95)	3.040
Depreciation	(1.25)		(1.250)	(1.875)		(1.875)
Net profit	0.65		0.745	1.325		1.165
ROI	6.9%		7.9%	9.4%		8.3%
	£m		£m	£m		£m
Net profit (as above)	0.650		0.745	1.325		1.165
Notional interest (20% of average investment)	(1.875)		(1.875)	(2.813)		(2.813)
Residual income	(1.225)		(1.130)	(1.488)		(1.648)

Combined results	*Expected*	*Actual*
ROI	$\frac{(0.65 + 1.325)}{(9.375 + 14.0625)}$ 8.4%	$\frac{(0.745 + 1.165)}{(9.375 + 14.0625)}$ 8.1%
Residual income	£(2.713)m	£(2.778)m

ABE Ltd has performed better than expected in year 1, and KIM Ltd has performed worse than expected. The improvement in Abe's performance is at the expense of KIM, and it is perhaps of some concern to the group as a whole that the **combined results of the two divisions together in year 1 were worse than expected.**

However, since the **poor results of KIM might be due to the division's purchasing policy of not buying from ABE**, it might be fair to conclude that ABE Ltd's performance should be approved by the group's management, and KIM's criticised.

25 TUTORIAL QUESTION: RESIDUAL INCOME AND ROI

(a) Residual income and ROI are commonly used as measures of performance for investment centres, such as subsidiary companies, with performance being assessed at regular intervals, such as every six months or one year. ROI usually relates historical cost profit to the book value of the investment centre's assets, to obtain a percentage return. Residual income is a profit figure after having charged notional interest to the investment centre, with interest calculated by applying a suitable percentage rate to the value of the centre's assets.

Short-term/long-term conflict

Whichever measure is used, performance of the investment centre is judged by considering the profit achieved over a short span of time and relating this in some way to asset values. As the investment centre's assets increase in value, its short term profits must increase too, otherwise ROI or residual income will fall and the investment centre management might be criticised for their poor performance.

In the long-term as well as the short-term, profits should rise if investment is increased, and so as a general principle, long term and short term interests should not conflict. However, **new investments do not usually provide a quick return, and so for long-term profit maximisation, there might have to be some short-term sacrifice of profits.**

This is the **nature of the short-term/long-term conflict.** Performance is measured in the short term, but both long term and short term considerations should influence investment and operating decisions.

The issues involved can be categorised into three broad areas:

(i) measures to boost short-term and long-term profits;
(ii) asset values;
(iii) new investment decisions.

Boosting short-term and long-term profits

Short term profits can be boosted by taking measures which could have harmful consequences for the future. For example, staff development and training might be ignored to save costs, equipment maintenance might be kept to a minimum, and if the investment has its own R&D unit, spending on R&D might be kept low.

Asset values

Asset values are important for **short-term performance measurement**, because ROI and residual income can **both be improved by keeping asset values down.**

(i) Unless current cost accounting is used, it is 'better' to have older assets than newer ones because inflation increases the comparative cost of newer assets.

(ii) If assets are valued at their net book value, it is also quite possible for an investment centre to make a good return on heavily-depreciated ageing assets, rather than to invest in new equipment which would improve output and turnover.

(iii) If an investment centre's assets are taken at their value as at the year-end, management will be reluctant to buy new assets near the end of the year, because they will have earned little or no profit, and yet still be taken into account in the calculation of ROI or RI.

New investment decisions

It is in the long-term interest of any company to make new investments. New investment decisions can be **evaluated by applying DCF** analysis to the expected cash flows of the investment over its expected operating life. Typically, profits from a new investment will be low in the early years, but will eventually rise to a high level in time (and at the same time, the net book value of the assets will be falling). With such investments, **the ROI in the early years will be low, and residual income might be negative.** This situation **might deter management from making new investments that are in the long term interests of the company.** The problem is worsened when ROI is used (rather than residual income) because any investment might be rejected if it is expected to reduce the investment centre's short term ROI below its current level. (Residual income, on the other hand, is increased provided that the extra profit from a new investment exceeds the notional interest charge on the investment's asset value).

Summary

In summary, good short-term returns are needed but longer-term considerations must not be ignored either, and a **suitable balance must be struck between short-term and long-term objectives.** For the reasons mentioned, it is unfortunately the case that by **using ROI or residual income** to measure short term performance regularly, **short-term results seem to be given too great an emphasis.**

(b) There is no obvious solution to the short-term/long-term conflict, but several **suggestions** have been made for **overcoming some of the problems.**

(i) One of the biggest problems is the measurement of asset values. Newer assets have a greater value than older ones, because of inflation and depreciation, and so it is easier to make a reasonable return by using older assets. To overcome this difficulty, **various methods can be used to compare older and new assets differently.**

(1) Assets might be valued at **gross book value** rather than net book value, and so regular asset replacement will not be discouraged. However, using gross book value has the disadvantage of ignoring an asset's loss of value over its life, and so might give unfair 'bias' in favour of early asset replacements.

(2) To overcome the problem of inflation, which makes newer assets more costly relative to older ones, a different system of accounting from the historical cost method could be used. Fixed assets could be valued on a **current cost accounting basis, a replacement cost basis,** or some sort of **CPP or price-indexed basis.**

(ii) Even so, these methods of valuing fixed assets do not resolve the problem of the effect on ROI of new investments which are not yet profitable. If long-term considerations are given proper emphasis, performance measurement ought to recognise the future earnings potential of an investment, as well as its contribution to historical profits.

It has been suggested that the future earnings potential of current investments can be incorporated into performance measurement using **DCF techniques**. This can be done by estimating the future cash flows from an investment centre's assets and converting them into a present value. This PV can then be compared with the investment centre's asset values. In my view, this suggestion is not a particularly convincing one, since estimates of future cash flows are bound to subjective, and performance measurement ought to be more objective if possible.

(iii) The performance of an investment centre manager ought to be judged to a large extent on the success of the investment decisions that he or she has made. One way of doing this is to carry out **regular post audits of investment decisions** (with the audit review done independently, perhaps by the internal audit department). Actual cash flows from an investment, if they can be measured, could be compared with estimated cash flows when the decision to undertake the project was first made. If actual cash flows match expected cash flows, the investment decisions of management can be judged to have been successful.

(iv) Another suggestion is that the performance of investment centre managers should be evaluated not only by ROI or residual income, but by other measures as well, which take longer-term issues into consideration. **Measures of staff development, staff motivation, new product initiatives, customer satisfaction or product quality** might provide a basis for assessing performance, and success in achieving targets in these areas might indicate that management is protecting the longer term prospects of the business as well as achieving good short term profits.

26 BALANCED SCORECARD

> **Pass marks**. This question should have presented few difficulties, especially if you had read the examiner's article on the balanced scorecard which appeared in the August 1998 edition of *CIMA Student* and which is reproduced at the back of the 1999 edition of the BPP Paper 16 Study Text.
>
> **Examiner's comment.** The question was generally well answered though answers to part (a) were too short or vague and common errors in part (c) included providing the case *for* using a range of measures and giving examples of non-financial measures. Too many candidates seemed to assume that non-financial means non-quantifiable.

(a) High profits or massive losses make headlines, and it is perfectly apparent from scanning the business pages of any newspaper that **profitability** remains the **principal measure by which the success or failure of a business is judged.**

There are a number of **arguments in favour of this.**

(i) The use of a **single criterion** reduces all arguments to the effect on profit.

(ii) It makes **quantitative analysis possible.** With one single, clear objective, proposals can be evaluated for their effect on profit in terms of relevant costs and revenues. This contrasts with the imprecision of cost/benefit analysis used in the pubic sector.

(iii) Profit is a **broad performance measure:** managing profit assumes ability to balance costs and revenues.

(iv) It **enables decentralisation.** 'With a clear corporate goal of profit, managers can have delegated powers to trade off costs and revenues to achieve profit. This assumes goal congruence between company and manager, and assumes that profits are additive – that everything a profit centre or divisional manager does to increase his profit will increase group profit. Questions of possible suboptimisation are not addressed' (JG Williams, 'The Balanced Scorecard', *CIMA Student*, August 1998).

(v) Profitability measures (such as ROI) can be used to **compare all profit-making operations** (although this argument ignores the difficult balance between risk and return).

(vi) Bonuses based on simple profit targets can be **highly effective motivators.**

(vii) The techniques of measuring profit are extremely **well established** and **codified** in standards of accounting practice. Even where different approaches are possible the issues are well publicised.

(viii) Profit is the **net result** of the success of marketing activities and the control of costs: as such it measures the two principal areas of concern for most commercial organisations.

(ix) It 'can be **applied to any profit-seeking activity,** whatever the nature of goods or services being produced and/or sold. It could therefore be used as a basis for comparison of apparently disparate activities' (Coates, Rickwood and Stacey, *Control and Audit in Management Accounting* (CIMA, 1993).

(x) It can be **related to aspects of output** (for example sales) or **input** (profit per machine/per employee etc), or (in the form of ROI) to **overall investment** in a business.

(xi) It is helpful for management in **deciding** which parts of a business should be **allocated resources,** and to investors in deciding **where their capital should be placed.**

(b) In spite of its widespread use as a performance measure, profitability does have a number of **limitations.**

(i) **Not all organisations have profitability as their main objective**; for example government bodies and charities. Most organisations have subsidiary objectives of varying degrees of importance, and success or failure in achieving these may not be reflected in the profit measure.

(ii) Unless supplemented by additional measures, profit **does not adequately indicate the impact of external factors** such as inflation, exchange rate movements and general economic conditions. The impact may vary widely between different types of business: a company that makes a loss in certain conditions may nevertheless have performed better than another that makes a profit, if viewed in the light of external conditions. This can affect the effectiveness of profit as a measure of managerial performance.

(iii) Even for financial reporting purposes the profit figure is **subject to a certain amount of manipulation** that may mislead the financially unsophisticated. For internal reporting purposes there is the further problem of which profit figure to use - operating profit, trading profit, profit before or after interest and tax and so forth.

(iv) A company may be **profitable and yet have severe cashflow problems**: profitability is not necessarily an indicator of continued success.

(v) The profit measure may encourage both managers and investors to take a **short-term view**. Managers may cut essential costs like training or research in order to show a profit in the short term. Investors may demand that profits are paid out as dividends when long-term interests require that the money be reinvested to fund future growth.

(vi) Focusing on a bottom line figure which is perhaps satisfactory overall may **encourage complacency**. Areas where further improvements could be made may be neglected if other areas have performed better than expected, giving a satisfactory net result.

(vii) Profit is measured by accounting rules, but **accounting conventions** on the valuation of intangibles, for example, can lead managers to make decisions which **decrease economic income.**

(viii) Profit should be **related to risk as well as capital employed.**

(ix) Profit may motivate profit centre managers but **cost centre managers may need alternative measures.**

(c) Many companies are discovering the usefulness of **non-financial indicators (NFIs)** such as quality measures, numbers of complaints, non-productive hours, system down time and so on. However there are a number of problems associated with such measures.

(i) **Too many measures could be reported**, overloading managers with information that is not truly useful (or comes to be regarded as not useful) or that sends conflicting signals.

(ii) It is **difficult to judge which** non-financial measures **are the most important**.

(iii) The ultimate goal of commercial organisations remains the **maximisation** of profit. An over-concentration on non-financial measures may lead to the **neglect of this criterion**.

(iv) Some non-financial aspects of performance are very **difficult to measure objectively**. For example a measure of customer complaints does not indicate that all customers who did not complain were entirely satisfied.

(v) Measures may **conflict with each other**: achieving measure X can be at the expense of achieving measure Y (such as productivity and quality).

(vi) If NFIs are used as the basis of **managerial performance** evaluation, the areas **not covered by the measures used may be ignored.**

(vii) With respect to the public sector, there is 'a fatal attraction for **politicians** for apparently **simple measures,** such as waiting lists and league tables, which **may not reflect key problems and strategic priorities**' (JG Williams, 'The Balanced Scorecard').

27 DESTROYING VALUE

Pass marks. The approach adopted by the analyst is based on economic value added. The topic has been covered extensively in *Management Accounting* but the examiner has stated that candidates were assumed to have no prior knowledge of it. The approach hinges on creating/destroying shareholder value and so the analyst's adjustments were intended to take account of those transactions which create/destroy value.

In part (b) you simply had to make the same adjustments to divisional results as the analyst had made to organisational results, although you did need to make a lot of assumptions (which was hinted at in the question requirements).

The subject matter of part (c) should have given you some indication that the analyst's approach was a way of overcoming short termism.

Examiner's comment. The examiner made the following comments about candidates' performance on this question.

- No prior knowledge was assumed of the specific approach taken by the analyst.
- It was clear that some candidates were surprised by the question. Answering past Paper 16 questions should have provided practice in dealing with the unexpected.
- In part (a), explanations which could be described as reasonable attempts, discussing long-term benefits from discretionary expenditure, were generously rewarded.
- Common errors in part (a) included explaining that the adjustments made were not in accordance with SSAPs and hence must be invalid, and explaining the adjustments as reflecting the items which were beyond managerial control.
- Common errors in part (b) included preparing three separate calculations on three pages for the balance sheets, and another three pages for the profit and loss accounts. Using columnar presentations ensures consistency between the divisions and saves time.
- Comments made in answer to part (b) tended to be sensible but were generally too limited for the marks available.
- The problems which arose in part (c) did not appear to be caused by lack of knowledge but by not reading the question and/or not planning the answer to focus on the question asked.

(a) REPORT

To: Chairman
From: Management accountant Date: XX.XX.XX
Subject: Destroying value in V plc

This paper considers the recent report by the analyst of X Stockbrokers on our 19X7 results. It will explain the principles of the approach taken by the analyst and will provide a commentary on the treatment of the specific adjustments made to our reported profit figure and balance sheet.

Principles of the approach taken

A management team is required by an **organisation's shareholders** to **maximise the value of their investment** in the organisation and a plethora of performance indicators is used to assess whether or not the management team is fulfilling this duty.

The majority of these **performance measures** are based on the information contained in the organisation's published accounts. Not only do these indicators often give **conflicting messages,** they can be easily **manipulated** and often provide **misleading** information. Earnings per share, for example, is reduced by capital-building investments in research and development and in marketing.

What is more, the **financial statements** themselves **do not provide a clear picture of whether or not shareholder value is being created or destroyed.** The **profit and loss account,** for example, indicates the quantity but not the quality of earnings and it does not distinguish between earnings derived from operating assets as opposed to non-operating assets. Moreover, it **ignores the cost of equity financing** and only takes into account the costs of debt financing, thereby penalising organisations such as ourselves which choose a mix of debt and equity finance. Neither does the cashflow statement provide particularly appropriate information. Cashflows can be large and positive if an organisation underspends on maintenance and undertakes little capital investment in an attempt to increase short-term profits at the expense of long-term success. On the other hand, an organisation can have large negative cashflows for several years and still be profitable.

The analyst has therefore adopted an approach known as **economic value added** to evaluate our performance. This approach hinges on the calculation of **economic profit,** which requires several **adjustments** to be made to traditionally-reported accounting profits. These adjustments are made to **avoid the immediate write-off of value-building expenditure** such as research and development or the purchase of goodwill. They are intended to produce a figure for capital employed which is a more accurate reflection of the base upon which shareholders expect their returns to accrue and to provide a profit after tax figure which is a more realistic measure of the actual cash yield generated for shareholders from recurring business activities.

Such an approach contrasts favourably with information based on traditional accounting concepts and conventions. The prudence concept, for example, requires revenue expenditure (such as maintenance expenditure on plant and machinery) to be written off to the profit and loss account in the accounting period in which it is incurred. This is to reflect the fact that such expenditure may have no long-term benefits. It is therefore not very surprising that if management are assessed using performance measures calculated using traditional accounting policies, they are unwilling to invest in or spend money on activities which immediately reduce current year's profit.

The treatment of specific items

Research and development. The analyst has added back expenditure of £2.1 million to the 19X7 profit figure on the grounds that the **expenditure is providing a base for future income growth and will create value in the future** and so is not simply an expense of 19X7. Similarly the research and development expenditure over the last seven years of £17.4 million has been added back to the capital employed figure on the basis that we are continuing to benefit from the expenditure. A depreciation charge should probably be made against this capitalised value, however, to reflect any fall in its value.

Advertising. The analyst has added back advertising expenditure of £2.3 million to the 19X7 profit figure on the assumption that the **expenditure has supported sales, raised customer awareness and/or increased brand image/loyalty,** all of which could produce significant cashflows in the future and hence are for the **long-term benefit of the organisation.** The advertising expenditure over the last five years of £10.5 million has been added back to the capital employed figure (in much the same way as the research and development expenditure) to reflect the fact that the costs will provide for future growth. Again, an amortisation charge should be made if brand values are being eroded, possibly by competition.

Interest and borrowings. Because our profits are being earned using both debt and equity finance, the **published profit figure is overstated since it takes no account of the cost of the equity finance.** The analyst has therefore added back the cost of the debt finance to the 19X7 profit figure and the borrowings figure to the capital employed. This produces a profit figure before the cost of borrowing which can be compared with a figure representing the total long-term finance in our organisation.

Goodwill. The analyst has added back goodwill amortisation of £1.3 million to the 19X7 profit figure. Goodwill is the difference between the price paid for a business acquisition and the current cost valuation of that acquisition's net assets. On the assumption that a realistic price was paid, **the goodwill purchased should provide benefits in the future,** not just in the year of purchase. And the goodwill of £40.7 million which has been written off against reserves on acquisitions in previous years has been added back to the capital employed figure so as to provide a more realistic base upon which we must earn a return. Again, the goodwill capitalised should be regularly reviewed and amortised to reflect any reductions in its value.

I hope this information has been of use. If I can be of any further assistance please do not hesitate to contact me.

Signed: Management accountant

(b) REPORT

To: Chairman
From: Management accountant — Date: XX.XX.XX
Subject: Where is value being destroyed?

An analyst working for X Stockbrokers has recently commented that 'the management of V plc is destroying value'. In an attempt to establish where value is being destroyed in our organisation, a **revised statement of divisional performance** has been prepared, **adopting an approach similar to that used by the analyst.** The statement, plus supporting explanations, is set out in Appendix 1.

The analysis shows that **value of £0.1 million was destroyed in division B, while value of £2.3 million was destroyed in division C. Division A,** on the other hand, **created value of £1 million.**

This is **in marked contrast to the performance indicated in the conventional divisional performance report** prepared for 19X7. This shows all three divisions earning a return on investment in excess of 20%, with divisions B and C, the destroyers of value, making higher returns on investment than division A, the creator of value.

The **analyst's approach** is **similar to** performance evaluation using **residual income** in that a charge is made for the capital employed within the division.

Further adjustments are also made to both profit and capital employed to provide more realistic measures for performance analysis (as explained in my earlier report and in Appendix 1). The **results of the analysis are dependent upon the following factors,** however (as is made clear in Appendix 1).

(i) Head office expenses are assumed to have been incurred in relation to divisional turnover. Any one of a number of other bases might be equally valid, however.

(ii) Tax paid is assumed to be related to divisional profit after interest and head office expenses. Deferred tax liabilities have not been incorporated into the analysis.

(iii) Each division's share of head office assets has been assumed to be in proportion to the division's share of total turnover. Other bases could be equally valid.

(iv) It has been assumed that each division has the same cost of capital. This takes no account of the individual characteristics of each division, its risk profile and its mix of financing.

Despite the limitations set out above, however, the analyst's approach provides an alternative insight into how our divisions are performing and could well prove useful in enabling us to create value for our shareholders in the future.

Signed: Management Accountant

APPENDIX 1

Statement of profitability

			Divisions		
	A	*B*	*C*	*Head office*	*Total*
	£m	£m	£m	£m	£m
19X7 PBIT	5.7	5.6	5.8	(1.9)	15.2
Add back					
Advertising	2.3	-	-	-	2.3
R&D	-	2.1	-	-	2.1
Goodwill (1)	-	0.3	1.0	-	1.3
Head office expenses (2)	(0.4)	(0.3)	(1.2)	1.9	-
Less tax paid (3)	(2.0)	(1.6)	(1.2)	-	(4.8)
Revised profit	5.6	6.1	4.4	-	16.1

Statement of capital employed

		Divisions			
	A	*B*	*C*	*Head office*	*Total*
	£m	£m	£m	£m	£m
Total assets less current liabilities	27.1	23.9	23.2	3.2	77.4
Adjustments					
Advertising	10.5	-	-	-	10.5
Goodwill	-	10.3	30.4	-	40.7
R&D	-	17.4	-	-	17.4
Head office assets (4)	0.7	0.5	2.0	(3.2)	-
Revised capital	38.3	52.1	55.6	-	146.0
Required return (5)	4.6	6.2	6.7	-	17.5
Revised profit	5.6	6.1	4.4	-	16.1
Value added/(destroyed)	1.0	(0.1)	(2.3)	-	(1.4)

Explanation of adjustments made

1 **Goodwill**

Goodwill amortised has been apportioned to divisions B and C in proportion to the value of goodwill written off to capital and reserves.

Division	*Goodwill write-off*			*Goodwill amortised*
	£m	%		£m
B	10.3	25.3	× £1.3m	0.3289
C	30.4	74.7	× £1.3m	0.9711
	40.7	100.0		1.3000

2 **Head office expenses**

No direction is provided as to the way in which head office expenses should be apportioned to the three divisions. An activity-based approach could be the most suitable but, in the absence of appropriate data, allocation based on turnover has been adopted.

3 **Tax paid**

The tax liability of £4.8 million for V plc has to be apportioned over the three trading divisions. Given that the divisions' taxable profits will be affected by the allocation of head office expenses and the interest paid, the overall tax liability has been apportioned on the basis of divisional profit after interest paid and allocated head office costs.

Division	*PBIT*		*Interest paid*		*Head office expenses*		*Apport'mnt figures*		*Charge*
	£m		£m				£m	%	£m
A	5.7	–	(0.4)	–	0.4	=	5.7	41	2.0
B	5.6	–	0.7	–	0.3	=	4.6	33	1.6
C	5.8	–	0.9	–	1.2	=	3.7	26	1.2
							14.0	100	4.8

4 **Head office assets**

Head office assets have been apportioned to the three trading divisions on the basis of divisional turnover so as to be consistent with the basis used to apportion head office expenses.

5 **Required return**

The required return is based is based on a 12% cost of capital.

(c) Despite the **limitations** of the use of **ROI** as a measure of business performance (which principally centre on the possibility for managers to manipulate short-term profits and levels of investment in order to improve the ratio), it is a **widely-used** measure of company and divisional performance for a number of reasons.

(i) It ties in directly with the financial accounting process and is identifiable from the profit and loss account and balance sheet.

(ii) If forces management to consider the level of investment in both fixed and current assets required to earn a certain return.

(iii) If a measure of the return on investment for a division or company as a single entire unit is wanted, it is the only acceptable measure of performance available (apart from residual income).

(iv) It provides a useful benchmark, facilitating comparisons both between units within the same organisation and between operating units in different organisations.

(v) Because a target ROI based on budgeted results can be established, it can form an important component of the budget monitoring process.

There are a number of ways in which **the potential problems associated with short-termism** mentioned above may be **overcome**, however.

(i) An obvious solution is to **measure ROI over a time period of more than one year**.

(ii) Many organisations are discovering the usefulness of **non-profit related performance indicators** such as quality measures, number of complaints, non-productive hours, system down-time and so on. Such measures do not require managers to concentrate on profit but to consider other aspects of performance that go towards satisfying customer needs. ROI could therefore be used in conjunction with such measures in a **balanced scorecard approach** to measuring performance.

(iii) Instead of basing the performance measurement system on short-term achievements, incentive schemes can be **focused on achieving long-term aims.**

(iv) The **pressure on managers to achieve short-term results can be reduced.** Easily-attainable short-term profit targets can be set. Managers would then feel free to concentrate on achieving long-term objectives of the organisation if they knew they had achieved the short-term goals.

(v) **Management contracts** could specify that performance would be judged on the basis of achieving certain long-term organisational objectives such as an increase in the size of customer base or an increase in quality.

(vi) Managers could be offered **bonuses relating to increases in share price** over a certain time period.

(vii) An **economic value added approach** could be adopted (as explained in parts (a) and (b)). Because the cost of long-term value-creating investments is added back to both profits and capital employed, mangers would not be motivated to avoid research and development, advertising and other expenditure which would ultimately be in the long-term interests of the organisation.

28 TUTORIAL QUESTION: INTERNAL SERVICE DEPARTMENT

In establishing a charge to departments utilising an internal service department, management should bear in mind the dual purpose of such a charge: control and motivation.

(a) **The assessment of performance of the service department**

If a **charge is determined entirely irrespective of use** then the service department is not really being treated as a profit centre, but as a cost centre where the costs are charged out to user departments. The 'revenue' for the centre is constant therefore the performance of the centre is based on an assessment of cost control. Ideally such control should use a flexible budgeting system, but if there is no measurable output then it will be difficult to determine the activity level on which to flex the budget. The method of charging out costs irrespective of use may be necessary in situations where the service department output is not easily measurable.

If the **charge is variable dependent upon use** then the unit price to be charged will depend on the activity level used to calculate the fixed cost per unit. The performance of the service department will then depend on its ability to achieve the predetermined activity level and so succeed in charging out the fixed costs. The service department will be able to improve its performance by expanding activity.

If the **charge is to be based on a combination of a fixed cost and a variable cost** then the problem of establishing a unit rate for fixed costs will be eliminated. It may be difficult to determine the basis for charging out the fixed costs and there may be problems in establishing the cost behaviour of the service centre costs. If the costs are incorrectly classified then they would not be controlled effectively because fixed costs would be charged out as variable costs, and vice versa.

If the **charge is based on actual costs** then there is no incentive for the service department to control costs. Performance assessment would be limited to a comparison of activity levels.

If the **charge is based on standard costs** then performance assessment would be greatly improved because the variances would be highlighted in the results of the service department. There would be an incentive for the service department to control costs and the variances would give an indication of their efficiency, as long as the standard costs are realistic and up to date.

If a **profit mark-up is added** to cost then there would be an incentive for the service department to increase output to earn more profit. The profit would be a measure of the wealth created by the activity of the service department.

It is important that the profit mark-up should be based on standard cost rather than on actual cost. If the service department is allowed to add a profit to actual cost then there will actually be an incentive to *overspend*, since every pound spent will be recouped with an extra profit margin on top.

If the **charge is based on estimated market rates** then performance assessment could be affected by difficulties in determining the correct price, particularly if there is no external market for a comparable service.

An additional problem would be the need to decide whether the market price should be reduced to allow for any cost savings on work done for internal customers, such as bad debts and advertising costs. If the service department is to be allowed the full benefit of these savings then its performance should be judged accordingly.

The assessment of the effectiveness of the service department would be improved if the user departments were permitted to purchase the service externally. A decision to purchase internally would suggest that the service was of at least comparable quality to the service provided by external suppliers.

(b) **The actions of user departments**

The company will **seek to establish goal congruence** whereby the user departments will automatically be achieving the company's goals and objectives by working to achieve their own departmental goals and objectives.

If a **charge is determined irrespective of use** then the user department will view the service department as an uncontrollable cost. This could have a demotivating effect if they feel that they are being held responsible for something over which they have no control. Another problem would be that the user department could view the service as having no marginal cost. There would be no incentive to control the use of the service and resources could be wasted.

If the **charge is variable dependent on use** then the opposite could occur and the user department may avoid using the resource if possible. This may have a sub-optimal effect, for example if a department defers preventive maintenance in order to avoid the resulting cost charge. A further problem could arise from the fact that the fixed costs of the service department would become apparently variable unit costs to the user department. An incorrect understanding of cost behaviour from the point of view of the company as a whole could lead to inappropriate decisions by the user departments.

If the **charge is to be based on a combination of a fixed cost and a variable cost** then the user department would have a correct understanding of cost behaviour but there may be some behavioural problems caused by disputes as to what the fixed charge should be. The charging of a fixed cost would however create an awareness in the user departments that the facilities are provided for them to use and the decision to do so should be made by them.

If the **charge is based on actual costs** then the user department would be penalised with a higher unit cost if the activity level of the service department falls. This could stop them achieving their objectives due to causes outside their control and could therefore lead to motivational problems. In addition the use of actual costs would mean that the user departments must bear the cost of the service department's inefficiencies which could lead to further motivational problems.

Basing the charge on standard costs would avoid these problems and would make it easier for the user departments to plan and control their costs.

The problem with **adding a profit mark-up** to costs arises in selecting a mark-up that the user departments feel is reasonable and which does not make them feel that they are being charged excessive amounts for the service.

The user departments should feel that they are being **charged an 'arm's length' price,** although they may believe that some discount is reasonable on internal services, as discussed earlier.

The user departments will be able to pursue their own objectives if they are given the freedom to purchase the service externally if desired. However this may lead to sub-optimal decisions from the point of view of the organisation as a whole, particularly if the service department is operating below capacity.

29 OWNERS AND MANAGERS

Examiner's comment. This question looks at performance appraisal over a period of years, rather than purely in the short term. Parts (a) and (b) seek the calculation of different project selections based on disparate criteria, and the explanation of the differences. Part of the test is that candidates should ensure that solutions to meet all the criteria (and, for part (a), are not the apparent optimal solution). Part (c) asks candidates to explain an approach to long-term performance measurement, with which they should be familiar from the recommended reading. It is not sufficient for candidates to be aware of the limitations of short-term financial measures, and to propose non-financial measures of performance; they must be aware of theoretical approaches to measuring long-term performance, and their practical limitations.

(a) The **projects' ranking based purely on NPV criteria** is as follows (W1).

Ranking	*Project*	*NPV per £ invested*
1	F	1.05
2	E	0.70
3	D	0.59
4	A	0.39
5	C	0.29
6	B	0.25

However, we are told that **cash flows must show a rising tend** over the next three years (it is assumed that this means *total* cash flows of all projects undertaken combined) and the **maximum investment is £2,500,000.**

Only three projects can be undertaken: simply on the basis of first year investment the 'smallest' projects, A, B, F and C require an investment of £2,600,000.

The combination FED is acceptable under the first criterion but not the second (W2). The combination FEA fails on the first criterion (W2). The next best choice is FDA (W2).

Projects F, D and A should therefore be selected, giving a total NPV of £1,416,000.

(*Note*. Fixed costs are ignored since these are common to all options.)

(b) Managers do not know about the owners' wish to sell the company after three years, and so will **take all four years into account**. On this basis the **ranking is as follows** (W3).

Ranking	*Project*	*Profit per £ invested*	*Investment*	*Cumulative investment*
			£'000	
1	C	1.56	900	900
2	F	1.50	600	1,500
3	E	1.20	1,000	2,500
4	D	1.10	1,000	
5	B	1.00	600	
6	A	0.60	500	

Projects C, F and E can be chosen before the funds run out.

The choice is different from the owners' choice because:

(i) four years rather than three years have been included;

(ii) the owners are interested in discounted cash flows. Managers rewards are based on accounting profits.

(*Note*. Depreciation is taken care of by netting off all the cash flows, since the investment is written off over the life of each project.)

Workings

1

Yr	*Discount factor*	*A* Cash flow	PV	*B* Cash flow	PV	*C* Cash flow	PV	*D* Cash flow	PV	*E* Cash flow	PV	*F* Cash flow	PV
		£'000	£'000	£'000	£'000	£'000	£'000	£'000	£'000	£'000	£'000	£'000	£'000
0	1.000	(500)	(500)	(600)	(600)	(900)	(900)	(1,000)	(1,000)	(1,000)	(1,000)	(600)	(600)
1	0.909	400	364	300	273			(200)	(182)	(400)	(364)	200	182
2	0.826	400	330	300	248	500	413	600	496	1,400	1,156	900	743
3	0.751			300	225	1,000	751	1,700	1,277	1,200	901	400	300
			194		146		264		591		694		626
NPV per £ invested			0.39		0.24		0.29		0.59		0.69		1.04
Ranking			4		6		5		3		2		1

2

Year	A Cash flow £'000	B Cash flow £'000	C Cash flow £'000	D Cash flow £'000	E Cash flow £'000	F Cash flow £'000	FED £'000	FEA £'000	FDA £'000
0	(500)	(600)	(900)	(1,000)	(1,000)	(600)	(2,600)	(2,100)	(2,100)
1	400	300		(200)	(400)	200	(400)	200	400
2	400	300	500	600	1,400	900	2,900	2,700	1,900
3		300	1,000	1,700	1,200	400	3,300	1,600	2,100
NPV	194	146	264	591	694	626	1,910	1,514	1,410

3

	Year	A Cash flow £'000	B Cash flow £'000	C Cash flow £'000	D Cash flow £'000	E Cash flow £'000	F Cash flow £'000
	1	400	300		(200)	(400)	200
	2	400	300	500	600	1,400	900
	3		300	1,000	1,700	1,200	400
	4		300	800			
Total inflows		800	1,200	2,300	2,100	2,200	1,500
Dep'n	0 - 4	(500)	(600)	(900)	(1,000)	(1,000)	(600)
Total profit		300	600	1,400	1,100	1,200	900
Profit per £ invested		0.60	1.00	1.56	1.10	1.20	1.50
Ranking		6	5	1	4	3	2

(c) A number of writers have suggested that many of the **problems** of 'traditional' divisional performance measurement could be **avoided** if an approach using **discounted cash flow techniques could be used instead.** In essence this would measure the difference between the NPV of forecast future cash flows at the beginning of a period and the NPV of forecast flows at the end of the period.

The advantages claimed for this approach are that it **emphasises long-termism, considers likely events in the future** (as opposed to reflecting past glories, as measures like ROI do) and that it **leads to 'optimal behaviour'** - correct investment decisions and so on.

The **problems** with the approach relate to the **difficulty of using it in practice.**

(i) Forecasts may not be accurate, either because of poor predictions, unexpected future events or manipulation of figures by managers.

(ii) It will be exceedingly difficult to determine what cost of capital to use. Again this could be subject to manipulation.

(iii) Managers tend to have a mental block when asked to accept complicated mathematical concepts. It may be difficult to demonstrate that the measure is fair.

30 MANAGERIAL MOTIVATION

Pass marks. Note that you had to comment on all three approaches in part (b). Part (b) was worth 12 marks, compared with part (a) which was worth 8 marks, you should therefore have spent more time on and wrote more for part (b).

Examiner's comment. Common errors in part (a) included discussing *how* companies could take short-term approaches and explaining why companies should *not* take short-term approaches. In part (b) many candidates produced irrelevant and obviously prepared commentaries to the first approach on ROI and RI measures, ignoring the fact that these measures depend on the calculation of accounting profit.

(a) As with all aspects of business, one can never say that there are no circumstances in which a particular approach should be adopted (unless the approach is illegal or unethical!). Although the general view is that a short-term approach is inappropriate to the general success of an organisation, there are a **number of instances** when managers may well be advised to **adopt a short-term rather than long-term view.**

(i) **In highly uncertain and changeable situations**

For organisations operating in an environment of rapid technological change or for organisations at the mercy of the quickly changing tastes of their customers, such as fashion retailers, it may be inadvisable to make long-term plans because of the uncertainty inherent in the operating environment.

(ii) **When a short-term approach is consistent with long-term goals**

There are occasions when an organisation's long-term plans can only be fulfilled by taking a number of short-term actions.

(iii) **When stakeholders also take a short-term view**

The **financial markets** are often criticised for taking a short-term view, for example by favouring those companies with high levels of current year dividends as opposed to companies looking to the long-term and investing surplus funds for future success. Other stakeholders, such as the **government**, may also influence the approach an organisation adopts. In the National Health Service, for example, funding constraints influence the strategy adopted by hospitals, even if this involves cancelling operations, closing wards and so on, in conflict with the hospital's overall mission. The views of stakeholders must be taken into account and may determine the strategy adopted by an organisation.

(iv) **When competitors do likewise**

If a competitor has adopted a short-term approach an organisation may need to follow suit in order to maintain its market share.

(v) **Under financial constraints or difficulties**

Even in the fairly short term, a profitable organisation experiencing **severe cash flow problems** may not survive. In such circumstances an organisation may therefore have to take a short-term view and take decisions which have a positive effect on cash flow, even if such decisions lead to conflict with the organisation's long-term aims. The purchase of a new asset which would enable an organisation to build up market share may have to be delayed if it would cause cash flow problems in the current period.

In more constrained and difficult circumstances, projects such as a large-scale advertising campaign which would produce benefits over a number of years would have a lower priority than the repayment of creditors and administrators.

(vi) **If the size of the organisation/decision does not warrant a long-term approach**

Long-term planning is most important for large companies and/or if major investment decisions are involved. Short-term planning may be more suited to small organisations, however, and a small investment is unlikely to have a long-term effect.

A short-term approach is therefore sometimes required and, as the examples above illustrate, this is more often than not due to the environment in which or financial constraints under which an organisation may be operating.

(b) (i) **The use of non-profit indicators**

Many organisations are discovering the usefulness of non-profit related performance indicators such as quality measures, numbers of complaints, non-productive hours, system down time and so on. There are a number of **problems** associated with such measures, however.

(1) Too many measures could be reported, **overloading** managers with information that is not truly useful (or comes to be regarded as not useful) or that sends conflicting signals.

(2) It is **difficult to judge** which indicators are the **most important**.

(3) The ultimate goal of commercial organisations is, more often than not, the **maximisation** of profit. An over concentration on other measures may lead to the **neglect of this criterion.**

(4) Some non-financial aspects of performance are very **difficult to measure** objectively. For example, a measure of customer complaints does not indicate that all customers who did not complain were entirely satisfied.

Further problems surrounding the use of non-profit indicators relate to the **importance attributed to measures of profit**. Annual reports are viewed by most of an organisation's stakeholders as the major benchmark for judging an organisation's performance over an accounting period. Profit levels will be compared to targets and levels attained in previous periods, as well as with the levels of profit achieved by competitors and other organisations operating in similar circumstances. A **concentration** by managers on **non-profit related indicators** could **affect current period profit levels and, consequently, stakeholders' views of the organisation.**

Finally, because **managers** are unlikely to want to appear to have performed poorly, they are unlikely to adopt an approach designed to encourage them to invest for the future, possibly at the expense of short-term results, if their **performance** is judged in any way on the basis of short-term results.

(ii) **Rewards for long-term performance**

The principal problem with adopting an approach which promises rewards for **long-term** profit centre performance or individual managerial performance is that the **future is uncertain**. Anticipated positive outcomes of decisions taken in the long-term interests of an organisation are less likely to occur than those of decisions taken in the short-term organisational interest: managers might therefore prefer the relative certainty of current profits than the uncertainty of future profits. Shareholders may require a **quick return** from their investment and also be unwilling to **risk** current profits for anticipated future benefits.

Moreover, because of the general perception that the assessment of a **manager's** performance and hence his or **salary** is in some way **linked to current period profit levels**, it may be extremely difficult for senior management to convince lower levels of management that current profits are not of great importance to them and that other performance indicators are of more concern. If promotion prospects are affected by current performance, managers are also unlikely to be willing to risk high levels of current performance for uncertain levels of future performance.

Schemes linking effort and reward are most effective when there is a short period of time between the effort and reward. They are less effective when they relate to longer-term achievement because the effort and reward are too distant in time from each other.

Additionally there are **administrative problems** with such an approach. It is far more difficult to set realistic targets for a number of years in the future than for the coming twelve months.

Lastly there are **problems with any approach based on profit.**

(1) No accounting measure can provide a comprehensive assessment of what a person has achieved for an organisation.

(2) An accounting system cannot fully reflect the economic aspects of performance.

(3) It is usually difficult to segregate the controllable component of performance from the uncontrollable component. This can cause 'unfairness' in performance evaluation.

(iii) **Reducing pressure on managers**

There are a number of ways in which the pressure on managers to achieve short-term results can be reduced, but there are problems associated with each option.

(1) **Easily-attainable short-term profit targets could be set.** Managers would feel free to concentrate on achieving the long-term objectives of the organisation if they knew they had achieved their short-term goals. Such an approach obviously runs the **risk of managers building too much slack into any budgetary estimates,** however.

(2) Management contracts could specify that **performance would be judged on the basis of achieving certain long-term organisational objectives** such as an increase in the size of customer base or an increase in quality. The problem of **the uncertainty surrounding anticipated future benefits** of current period decisions has to be overcome, however.

(3) Managers may be offered **bonuses relating to increases in share price over a certain time period.** The danger with this strategy is that **managers may disregard short-term performance** completely and spend too much money in the near future in anticipation of long-term growth.

Whatever option is chosen, it would require a **change to managerial priorities,** which is always a difficult task.

31 CONTROLLABILITY

Pass marks. The second part of (b) was probably the most straightforward bit of this question and the part where you were most certain of achieving good marks since it is fairly easy to put forward an argument for the inclusion or otherwise of each of the items. The first part of (b) may have caused you some problems because it is so natural for us to assume that the controllability principle *should* apply.

Examiner's comment. The examiner provided the following summary of the answers which failed to reach the required standard.

Part (a) - 'discussing only managerial motivation without mentioning other possible arguments, merely making several very similar statements regarding motivation.'

Part (b) - 'ignoring the first part of the question, asking why large firms may not adopt this principle. Proceeding to make very brief comment on each of the three specific issues, usually the same comment on each of the three, ie that the item in question is normally regarded as an appropriate charge in divisional management accounts.'

The examiner's overall impression was that many candidates were determined to display previously prepared answers regardless of the questions asked.

(a) **Responsibility accounting** attempts to associate costs, revenues, assets and liabilities with the managers most capable of controlling them. As a system of accounting, it therefore uses the principle of controllability, of **distinguishing between controllable and uncontrollable items.**

Divisional management accounts have two main **aims**.

(i) To measure the performance of the division

(ii) To measure the performance of the divisional manager

Both of these aims are more **readily achieved** if the divisional management accounts have been prepared **using the principle of controllability**.

(i) If it is possible to identify a particular manager or a particular division with the usage of particular resources or the creation of certain streams of revenue, **targets** can be set in relation to these resources or revenue streams, and actual performance measured against the targets. If performance is only assessed against such **controllable items,** managers are likely to view the performance measurement system as being just and **fair** and are therefore more likely to be **motivated** to achieve the targets, knowing that it is in their power to do so.

(ii) Making managers responsible for the items over which they have control **improves the system of delegating authority**. Divisional managers can be held responsible for a large proportion of the items associated with their division, enabling senior management to concentrate on strategic planning rather than day-to-day operational matters. An adequate control reporting system should be in place, however, with senior management aware of how actual results compare with the targets set for controllable items.

(iii) A responsibility accounting system should also assist in reducing problems associated with the **allocation of central group costs** to the various divisions because any performance report would make it quite clear that such items were uncontrollable and not to be included in the appraisal of the manager or the division.

(iv) Divisional management accounts based on the controllability principle provide the ideal basis for the **evaluation of managers' promotion prospects** and the calculation of their bonuses.

(b) **Reasons for not adopting the controllability principle**

It is generally considered to be unreasonable to assess managers' performance in relation to matters that are beyond their control. Management performance measures should therefore only include those items that are directly controllable by the manager in question.

There are a number of reasons why managers should possibly be held accountable for factors that are beyond their control, however.

(i) It has been suggested that managers should be motivated to **pay attention to** cost and revenue **factors that are relevant to their division's performance,** even if they are not controllable, such as interest expense, because such attention may result in the overall level of the cost being reduced.

(ii) Managers should be encouraged to **respond to economic and competitive conditions** such as a rival's lower prices or higher quality.

(iii) It could be argued that **central group** costs should be allocated to divisions in order to **make divisions aware of the costs of group services,** to make them reduce their demand for group services and/or to show them the need to build such costs into their pricing structures. Such allocations will often breach the controllability principle unless they are done on the basis of usage or negotiation

(iv) Even if the controllability principle is in operation it is unlikely that senior management would delegate all decisions making, especially that concerned with investing in capital and raising funds. The **impact of the decisions made by senior management** on the performance of a division **may be difficult to quantify** and might therefore be ignored, with the result that uncontrollable items are included with controllable ones in divisional management accounts.

(v) The objectives for most divisions are likely to be expressed in financial terms (such as achieve profit levels of £X or reduce costs by X%). Although actual results can be measured and compared to financially-orientated performance measures, it is far more **difficult to allocate the responsibility for any differences between planned and actual performance.**

(vi) If **divisional performance** is **measured for the purposes of group consolidation and for external reporting requirements,** controllability is unlikely to be an issue in such circumstances.

(vii) It has been argued that the **mixing of decision making by two different management levels** (divisional and senior) may lead to **sub-optimal decision making and a reduction in organisational effectiveness.**

One way in which the **problems can be resolved** is produce a **set of divisional management accounts which distinguish between controllable and non-controllable items,** so as to be able to judge the performance of the manager and the performance of the division. Head office involvement could no doubt make the split of items very judgmental, however.

The treatment of specific items

(i) **Interest**

The interest expense incurred by a group as a whole will be **depend upon the sources of finance** that the group uses and the cost of those sources of finance. Usually group financing is the **responsibility of a group treasury function,** within which divisional managers play no part (unless a multinational group allows divisions operating overseas to raise finance in the country in which they are based). A **proportion** of the overall interest charge is likely to be **included in each division's management accounts,** however. That proportion will **depend upon the division's financing requirements, which will in turn depend upon its levels of working capital and capital expenditure , over both of which the divisional manager would be likely to have control** (although the control will be subject to approval by head office of divisional plans and strategies).

(ii) **Head office expenses**

Although the level of head office expenses is unlikely to be controllable by individual divisions, it is **dependant on the demand for services made by the divisions**. Such costs should therefore be allocated on the basis of the level of services consumed by a division or possibly on the level of the benefits gained, although this is likely to be more problematic. It is important that the divisions are aware of these expenses since they must be recovered on a group-wide basis within the pricing structures adopted by the individual divisions.

It should be noted that there may be **tax advantages** for the group as a whole in **transferring** a large proportion of the head office **expenses into those overseas divisions operating in countries with high rates of local tax.**

(iii) **Changes in economic circumstances**

If major changes in economic circumstance have led to a significant change in industry volume, any comparisons made between the actual results achieved by a division and budgeted results may have become meaningless if the volumes upon which the budget was based are significantly different to the actual volumes achieved. The **budget figures** therefore need to be **flexed** to reflect the actual volume of activity achieved and, providing that the group incorporates a system of **planning and operational variances** into its budgetary control system, the variances arising because of the differences between budgeted and actual volumes would be classified as **non-controllable planning variances** for divisional performance purposes.

In practice, however, this procedure may not be quite so simple. A decision has to be made concerning the **point at which changes** in economic circumstances **convert from being controllable by the division** (so that the flexing of budget figures is not required and any adverse variances will be classified as the responsibility of the divisional manager) **to being uncontrollable by the division** (so that flexing of the budget figures is required).

32 REMUNERATION

> **Pass marks.** The answer to (a) required appreciation of the reasons for the recommendations made by the Cadbury and Greenbury reports. The kind of complex remuneration package described would be applicable only to a small number of Chief Executives. At first sight you might feel that you need specialised knowledge to deal with the scenario. Always bear in mind, however, that most questions need to be answered by applying a few general principles and common sense applied to the specific situation in the question.
>
> **Examiner's comment.** For part (b) candidates who allowed sufficient time to understand the detail, explained the effects of each element of the package in turn, and made a sensible conclusion dealing with the overall effect of the package earned good marks. There were some common errors, however.
>
> - Generally discussing motivational theories but not referring to the specific case details.
> - Implying all elements of the package were equally important.
> - Discussing possible manipulation of profits, which was not required by the question and is improbable over a longer time scale.
> - Failing to identify the separate effects of the share option scheme and the conditional allocation of shares, merely commenting that both were motivational.

(a) **The two non-executive directors constitute the remuneration committee**

The **Cadbury committee** recommended that the board should include a sufficient number of **non-executive directors** for their views to carry sufficient weight. The **minimum number** the Cadbury report recommended was **three,** as the non-executive directors would be required to staff board committees including the remuneration committee.

The **Greenbury committee** recommended that the **remuneration committee** should consist **wholly of non-executive directors**. The main purpose of the committee should be to recommend the remuneration of executive directors and having the committee staffed by non-executive directors meant that executive directors would not decide their own remuneration.

Personal financial interests

The **Cadbury report** stresses that a key role of non-executive directors is to bring an independent judgement to the board's decision-making. Hence a **majority of non-executive directors should be independent** of the company; this means that apart from their shareholdings and fees as directors, they should be independent of management.

The **Greenbury committee** reinforced the Cadbury recommendations by stating that **non-executive directors should not have cross-directorships with executive directors**. This means that executive directors of Company A should not be non-executive directors of Company B if non-executive directors of Company A are executive directors of Company B. Cross-directorships could result in agreements to set each others' remuneration at a higher level than what is considered desirable.

Chairman's service contract

This statement highlights the potential problem a remuneration committee faces when determining the length of a service contract. A **long service contract** may help retain a key member of the management team. However a long notice period means that there are **financial disincentives to remove the director**- the compensation for loss of office is likely to be high. This may in practice mean that a **fundamental shareholder right**- to remove a director under s 303 of the Companies Act 1985- is **undermined.**

The **Greenbury committee** recommends that **service contracts** should normally be for **one year,** although a period of one to two years may be acceptable in certain circumstances. Periods of longer than two years should be avoided except in exceptional circumstances. Such circumstances may have existed when the chairman was given his original contract in 1987 but would not apply long-term, and hence his service contract should now be of a shorter period.

(b) **Salary**

The basic salary of £316,000 is substantial, suggesting that the Chief Executive is one of the small number of highly-paid and highly sought-after directors able to effectively and profitably steer a large public company. Although not directly performance related, his salary can be expected to increase in line with the fortunes of the company. Its size has probably affected his decision to stay with the company.

Bonus

The size of bonus is more under the control of the Chief Executive since it is **related to the performance of the company** (which is, after all, his primary concern). The maximum bonus of 25% of salary is considerable (a possible £79,000 based on last year's salary). There are no specific criteria for its achievement, however. It is based on the Remuneration Committee's *assessment.* This may mean that the level of the bonus is **susceptible to company politics,** which **may reduce its motivational effect.**

Since it is based on annual performance it may **encourage a short-term view,** but that will depend on how the Remuneration Committee carry out their brief.

Employee profit-sharing scheme

Although this is linked to the performance of the company, the £8,000 maximum payment means that it is **insignificant** in comparison to the rest of the package. If the Chief Executive performs adequately this payment is almost certain to be made.

Other benefits, including pension contribution

As with the salary, these are **substantial** (particularly the £85,000 pension contribution). It is unlikely that these are performance related and so will have **limited motivational effect.**

Conditional allocations of shares

At an initial value of 50% of salary, these shares could represent a **significant part** of the package and thus have a **large motivational impact**. Such an incentive is **good from the shareholders' point of view** since not only is it directly related to TSR but the three-year time scale discourages short-term thinking.

An **area of concern for the Chief Executive** may be the **volatility of share values.** If the stock market falls, his shares' value may be diminished even if the company's relative performance is good. Alternatively, the group could perform well in its market sector but if the sector has not performed well in relation to the FT-SE 100, the bonus could be reduced (even to nothing).

Share options

These could also be very **lucrative** and so provide a **strong motivational force.** Their **value is dependent on the state of the stock market,** however, which is **out of the Chief Executive's control.**

From the shareholder point of view, this is a **sensible form of remuneration** for the Chief Executive as the focus is on shareholder return over three years. Whether the target of above average FT-SE 100 performance is fair depends on the company. If it is an average FT-SE company the Chief Executive will consider the target reasonable. Shareholders may consider that an above average performance is needed, however.

A **sliding scale such** as that used with the share allocations would **have a better motivational impact** than an 'all or nothing' target.

Overall effect of the total package

The motivational effect of the package is linked to how easily the Chief Executive can control the internal and external environment of the group and therefore its fortunes.

Both the share schemes are potentially very valuable to the Chief Executive and are **linked to long-term success.** They are therefore an appropriate financial motivator for the group to use since they are directly related to shareholder return.

There is a relatively large fixed element to the package (£422,000 including salary, benefits and pension contribution). Although the Chief Executive may not feel the need to increase his earnings beyond this fixed level, his personal ambitions should be considered. **People are usually motivated by success itself** as well as the financial rewards that accompany it.

33 BONUS SCHEMES

> **Pass marks.** The biggest danger in part (a) is the temptation to overrun on the time allowed for the solution, given the marks available. Bonus schemes are a recurring feature of this exam and most candidates should be able to write about them both from theoretical and personal knowledge without too much difficulty.
>
> Part (b) requires much more thought – think about the key issue of independence for NEDs. As long as the features you suggest do not compromise independence or suggest awarding too generous bonuses you will be earning marks.
>
> **Examiner's comment.** Common errors in part (a) were variants on failing to read the question carefully and plan an appropriate answer. Candidates were sensible to prepare for possible questions on bonus schemes but they must be prepared to answer the question actually asked, not the question on the topic they might have preferred.
>
> Answers to part (b) were disappointing. Most either discussed the need to motivate part-time NEDs, without mentioning the corporate governance constraints, or discussed these constraints at length, and concluded that no incentive scheme would be possible.

(a) **Limiting the range of performance within which rewards are linked to results**

Many schemes do indeed limit the range of performance within which rewards are linked to results, in particular ignoring losses and limiting maximum payments.

Unless the organisation in question was operating in an extremely stable and predictable environment, it would be **unacceptable to the vast majority of managers to be asked to participate in a remuneration system that might require them to reimburse their employer in the event of losses being incurred.** In general, managers want to receive their standard salary, they do not want the threat of some of it being taken away if their organisation reports losses. If the organisation were to **impose penalties for poor performance,** managers may well **manipulate their targets to ensure that they did not suffer financially.**

Reasons for capping maximum payments include a desire by risk averse managers to **limit the organisation's maximum liability** and the **prevention of payments which shareholders might regard as excessive.** It should be noted, however, that **unexpectedly good performance could well be the result of poor planning.** There may have been a significant rise in sales demand due to a major competitor leaving the market or costs may have fallen sharply following a world-wide drop in the price of the raw material in question, perhaps following a bumper harvest. For **managers to benefit from poor planning by receiving excessive bonuses would seem unfair.**

The effects of limiting the range of performance within which rewards are linked to results

If **losses are excluded** from the range of performance, **full participation** in the scheme is likely as no financial penalty (or negative bonus) can be imposed on a manager if levels of performance are particularly poor. Salaries will be viewed as fair payment for duties performed, with any bonus being regarded as a genuine reward for effort. Managers may **take unnecessary risks,** however, as they are under no financial risk themselves, and **poor levels of performance may be deliberately further depressed** to ensure easier future targets.

Capping maximum payments should ensure that managers **concentrate on improvements which will be sustainable year-on-year.** The financial incentive provided should be large enough to motivate without being excessive. Managers might feel **no incentive to improve performance beyond the cut-off level,** however, and they could be forced into **holding back for future periods profit-generating or cost-cutting strategies and ideas** once the maximum limit has been reached. A limit on maximum payments could also cause managers to feel **disempowered,** the message being sent out by the bonus system indicating that no matter how good their performance, the most they would receive is £X.

Linking incentive payments wholly or partly to the profits of the organisation as a whole

This is a **popular feature** in many bonus schemes for a number of **reasons.**

- Profit is widely-understood measure, and the maximisation of organisational profit is generally accepted to be congruent with the goals of shareholders.
- As profit reporting forms part of most organisation's standard reporting procedures, little additional work is required for profit to be used as the standard measure of performance (compared with more elaborate performance reward mechanisms which can generate substantial data collection costs).
- It also provides a basis for participation in bonus schemes by service centre staff such as those of internal audit and IT departments, for whom the use of other measures can be much more problematic.
- The profit reported by many profit centres will be significantly affected by head office policies on, for example, salary levels or stock valuation, and so overall organisational profit may be more objective.
- Rather than arguing over scarce resources, the use of organisational profit may persuade profit centre managers to work together to further the aims of the organisation as a whole.
- As agents of the organisation's shareholders, **managers' rewards should be closely linked to the rewards of shareholders.**

The effects of linking payments to organisational profits

A number of **beneficial** effects are likely to evolve from such a feature of bonus schemes.

- Inter-profit centre/-divisional **conflicts should be minimised,** with all parts of the organisation concentrating on group results.

- Management attention should be focused on the need to **cut unnecessary expenditure.**
- Management will **not be diverted from performing their regular duties** to agree on more elaborate performance-reward systems.

A number of **negative** effects need to be considered, however.

- If the proportion of the bonus that is linked to overall organisational performance is significant and other profit centres do not perform well, managers will get a reduced bonus payment or even no payment at all. Managers who consistently perform well and achieve their individual targets are likely to become **demotivated if they receive no bonus because of poor levels of performance in other parts of the organisation.**
- Managers could feel that their **area of responsibility is too small to have a substantial impact** on group profits and may become **demotivated**.
- Managers may **cut short-term, discretionary costs** in order to achieve current profit targets at the **expense of future profits**.

(b) **Bonus schemes for non-executive directors (NEDs)**

The design of bonus schemes for NEDs is **problematic**. If the bonus is **too small** the NEDS may **not be motivated** to do anything more than the minimum required to collect their fees. If the bonus is **too generous** they may **stop acting in the best interests of shareholders for fear of incurring the displeasure of the executive directors** and thereby jeopardizing their bonus payments.

A bonus scheme for NEDs will therefore need to include the following **features**.

- It should ensure that **high quality and motivated NEDs** are recruited, thereby ensuring that shareholders will benefit from the appointment of the NEDs.
- The bonus should be paid either **in cash or in the companies' shares**. Such methods will motivate the NED without contravening the recommendation from the Hampel report that NEDs are not granted share options.
- The bonus scheme could be **linked to the long-term performance of the company**, rather than simply to the financial performance of the current period. A **balanced range of performance measures** such as increase in market share or stock market valuation in relation to competitors over a certain period of time (depending on the NEDs' length of contract) and so on should **encourage NEDs to take a broader view of corporate governance.**
- It is important that **good corporate governance is seen to be maintained**. Shareholders' prior approval of any bonus scheme should be obtained to avoid any impression that NEDs' bonuses are being offered as a *quid pro quo* for the executive directors' remuneration.
- Any bonus scheme should be designed to provide an **incentive for the NED to achieve specific objectives or complete specific tasks outside his normal duties as a NED.**

  Bonuses are justified for tasks such as carrying out competitor reviews or designing staff remuneration schemes, which will enhance the NED's× understanding of the business without compromising his independence.
- Any **goal-oriented bonuses** should **be paid immediately following the work to which they relate**. Rolling up of bonus payments may silence any criticism from the NED as the payment date approaches.

34 TUTORIAL QUESTION: DIVISIONALISED ORGANISATION

(a) The company has entered into new product and new market areas, and is now adopting a divisionalised structure but it does not yet have an AIS for providing a management information system to reflect the radically different situation that the company is now in.

The **requirements that the company needs to focus on developing an AIS** to assist with planning and control are as follows.

(i) An AIS should be **installed fairly quickly**. Management need information for planning and control, and since divisional managers will have a greater degree of authority than before, and since the company has moved into potentially high-risk new product-market areas, it is essential that relevant information for decision making is provided soon.

(ii) The AIS can be improved over time, and **need not be 'perfect' from the outset**. Since some divisions are producing new product items, it will take time to develop a standard costing system, or to make reliable sales forecasts or cost budgets. The AIS should provide for such developments, however, as experience is gained.

(iii) The AIS should have a **common database**. The management information supplied should be consistent, and common data files would seem to be an appropriate way of achieving this consistency.

(iv) The **information** provided by the system should obviously **reflect the allocation of management responsibilities within the new organisation structure**. There should be readily-available information for budgetary control and about actual performance, relating to turnover, costs, profits, assets and liabilities for each product and/or market, identifying individual management responsibilities.

(v) Information for both planning and control should **distinguish between matters that can be decided at a divisional level, and those which are reserved for head office**. For example, the AIS must be capable of recognising the level of authority for spending decisions on capital expenditure, and of distinguishing between costs that are controllable and non-controllable at divisional level.

(vi) The information provided by the system should be **readily available**, perhaps by means of on-line file enquiry whenever this is required. The **frequency** of routine reporting should be appropriate at each level of management and items should be reported or planned at a suitable amount of **detail** at each level.

(vii) The AIS should, if possible, **allow managers** at both divisional level and at head office to **recognise the problems of co-ordination**. The manager of division A, say, should be told when his decisions might have an adverse effect on the performance of division B, and the company as a whole.

(viii) Because there will be interdependence between divisions, there will have to be a **system of transfer pricing**. A requirement of the AIS is that the transfer pricing system that is used should avoid sub-optimal decision making at divisional level. The likely effect on decision-making of different transfer prices should therefore, if possible, be monitored by the system.

(ix) When the AIS is first established, the planning information might be inaccurate, because of uncertainties about turnover and costs in the new product-market areas. To **combat the problem of uncertain planning information**, the AIS should provide for:

(1) **regular reviews of the budget**, with updated forecasts being produced at regular intervals, to reflect changes in expectations which might occur in the light of actual current results;

(2) **sensitivity analysis,** to identify key areas for control in the budget.

(x) **Control information** should be provided at all levels of management. Head office might wish to retain the authority for decisions about axing unprofitable products or markets, and will almost certainly have to make decisions about the future allocation of resources between the competing decisions. It therefore follows that the control information for head office should help senior management to make decisions about which product-market areas should get extra resources and to judge the performance of divisional managers.

(xi) Head office should remain accountable itself for its own plans and performance. The AIS might therefore **treat head office as a profit centre** in its own right, charging divisions for the services it provides.

In summary, the AIS of the company must be **suitable for the company's circumstances,** recognising the need for **prompt information in a high-risk business,** providing **information to managers at divisional level for making planning and control decisions within their sphere of authority,** and at the same time **allowing head office both to exercise a co-ordinating influence** (to prevent sub-optimal decisions at divisional level) **and also to ensure that divisional managers are using their authority and resources to operate efficiently and effectively.**

(b) Budgeted performance measures should indicate to each manager what is expected from him or her, and a comparison of actual and budgeted performance should enable managers to identify when control measures might be necessary to improve actual performance. Provided that the performance targets are clear, and that the manager has sufficient authority and control over resources to influence the achievement of those targets, the operation of a **system of control through performance measures** should **motivate managers to achieve the objectives of the company as a whole.**

The **main features** to be recognised, if such a system of performance measurement is to operate successfully, are as follows.

(i) The **individual managers** must have a **sufficient amount of authority and control over resources** to be able to influence actual results. If a manager is held accountable for performance over which he or she has relatively little control, there will be an absence of motivation to achieve the performance targets.

(ii) The **selection of performance measures** must have **regard to their possible effect on management decisions.** A major problem could be dysfunctional decision-making, with divisional managers taking measures to improve their own division's performance at the expense of another division, and regardless of their impact on the company as a whole.

(iii) There will be interdependence between the divisions, with each division providing goods or services to other divisions, and so performance (turnover, profits and so on) will depend partly on the **transfer prices** that are used. It must be recognised that it can be very difficult to establish 'optimal' transfer prices that will best promote good congruence between the divisions, and the impact of transfer prices on decision-making and performance ought to be monitored by head office.

(iv) The **performance measures** will only operate successfully if they properly **reflect the company's objectives**. There is a tendency for profitability or ROCE within the budget period to be given prime importance within a system of control, whereas other short-term objectives or constraints, and longer-term objectives are given little or no attention. For example, spending on R & D or training is often minimised, in order to boost short-term profits, even though they might be vital to a division's longer-term development and survival. The problem of striking a **balance between short-term and longer-term objectives** ought to be recognised. One way of doing this would be to establish **multiple measures of performance**. However, if multiple measures are used, a problem arises in judging performance or deciding priorities in cases where some targets can be achieved, but only at the expense of non-achievement of other targets.

(v) The **attitude of managers** can be crucial. A manager might be properly motivated to improve his or her division's performance for the benefit of the company as a whole. Alternatively, a manager might take the view that it is in his or her personal interest to achieve acceptable results, and to avoid criticisms from head office. To this end, he or she might argue for targets for performance which are relatively easy to achieve. It must therefore be recognised that control though performance measures can only be as good as the targets of performance that are established.

(vi) If divisional managers are held accountable for the achievement of certain targets, there will also be a **tendency for the managers to try to influence the figures**. This can be done in a number of different ways, such as sending out invoices early or delaying the sending out of invoices, in order to 'transfer' sales turnover from one control period to the next; another technique is to bring forward or defer spending, in order to shift costs between one control period and the next. Performance by divisional managers might therefore have to be judged over a period of time, rather than on the basis of just one set of figures.

(vii) The **costs** of a system of control can become very high, with a complex AIS for a divisionalised company. The management who set up the AIS should recognise that the costs of control should not exceed the anticipated benefits from control measures. In other words, the system should not become over-elaborate.

In summary, performance measures should be easily understood; authority, responsibility and accountability should be properly matched; performance targets should respect the corporate objectives, both long and short-term; and managers should be motivated by the system towards goal congruence, and the problems of dysfunctional decision-making should be discouraged.

35 SUBCONTRACTING SERVICES

> **Pass marks**. This question looks at different aspects of the problems of business expansion. This may be unusual to candidates accustomed in recent years to the problems of recession, but calls for the application of basic principles and well-established techniques. Part (a) requires candidates to demonstrate their knowledge of budgeting systems, and means of justifying significant changes in operations in a budgeting system. Zero base budgeting is an obvious possible solution, but by no means the only possible approach. Part (b) examines the issues involved in sub-contracting services, which has become increasingly common in both the private and public sectors, and is frequently discussed in many journals. It can be a way of reducing managerial problems in a period of expansion, as well as a possible way of reducing cost in a recession. Part (c) reviews changing internal audit requirements; the special problems of recession are well known, but there is a tendency to understate the problems of expansion.

(a)

REPORT

To: The Board
From: Finance Director — Date: XX.XX.XX
Subject: Staff expansion proposals

The company faces the following **choices** over the next few years.

(i) It can attempt to **cope with the current level** of staff.

(ii) It can yield to departmental pressure and approve requests from departmental heads for **new staff.**

(iii) It can conduct a thorough study of current and anticipated staffing needs and **reorganise** where appropriate.

Option (i) does not seem to be realistic. Option (ii) has been tried in the past and has not been satisfactory. **Option (iii)** is explored in more detail below. This is, if you like, a **'zero-based' approach,** considering staffing needs from scratch rather than merely spreading on an extra layer of staff. The aim, in outline, would be to **create a far more flexible and 'empowered' workforce, with responsibility delegated as far down the line as possible**

The only way that any action, whether expansion, reorganisation, or both, can be **justified** is if there is work that needs to be done and if the current arrangements for doing it are found to be inadequate. An **investigation** of this question may be carried out as follows.

The **first step** must be to ensure that **managers and senior managers have the same understanding of the organisation's long-term needs.** There is no point, for example, in departmental managers employing extra staff purely to deal with products that will be discontinued or replaced in a few years time. Likewise there is no point in senior managers attempting to cut down on discretionary staff costs like those of advertising or product development staff if the planned expansion is based on wide market awareness of the company and its exciting new products. (More will be said about future needs later in this report).

Departmental managers can then analyse the work that will need to be done in the future in terms of their department's expected output, the skills required, the time required, the number of supervisory and managerial staff, and the number and nature of operational roles.

The **second step** is to **identify** the **bottlenecks** that it seems are likely to be revealed, and also any **over-capacity,** whether this be within departments as a whole, within certain jobs or at certain times of the year.

The **third step** is to **compare the analyses department by department, taking account of interdependencies**: for example, do some departments' bottlenecks consist of last minute rushes caused by under capacity in, and therefore late delivery by, other departments?

Once this exercise is complete it may be possible to **deal with greater volumes of business in the following ways.**

(i) **Organising around processes rather than functions.** This helps to avoid duplication of work and improves communication and speed of response to customer needs.

(ii) **Redeploying staff from one department to another at busy times.**

(iii) Providing **training** where staff need to learn new skills in order to be able to work more flexibly.

(iv) Cutting down on (or at least not employing any extra) managerial staff, and **devolving responsibility** to those who actually do the work.

(v) Using **part-time** or **temporary staff** where possible and cost-effective.

(vi) **Contracting out** work where it is not considered essential to retain the skills or information in-house. This is the subject of a separate report.

In order to provide this justification and prepare and review new plans for incorporation in the overall budget, the following **information** will be **required.**

(i) **Forecasts of demand levels** likely to be faced in the coming years. These will be made on the basis of market research for new and existing products, and economic indicators from all available sources (national and international governments, trade bodies, market analysts, possibly competitors).

(ii) **Information about competitors' new product plans, current and anticipated market shares, recruitment policy** and so on, to the extent that such information is available.

(iii) **Analysis of workloads** where these can be measured meaningfully in terms of processing time and volumes of output. **Qualitative judgements** will also be necessary: it is difficult to quantify, say, an excellent reputation for service with customers, or an employee's infectious enthusiasm for the task at hand, but the extent to which such benefits are dependent upon certain individuals or the preservation of certain teams and relationships ought to be taken into account.

(iv) Details of any **extra facilities** that will need to be provided (equipment, accommodation and so on).

(v) Information from the **employment market** about staff costs, labour supply and so on. Are the extra staff that will be required available? What training will they need?

(vi) The **attitude of staff** to changes in working methods.

A final point to be considered is the **cost** of conducting the analysis, in terms of both money and time. It may prove to be more cost-effective to employ an independent consultant.

Signed: Finance Director

(b)

REPORT

To: The Board
From: Finance Director Date: XX.XX.XX
Subject: Sub-contracting services

One possible way of dealing with increased volumes of business without recruiting extra staff is to **contract out** some activities that are presently done in-house.

Advantages and disadvantages

The **advantages** are as follows.

(i) It would **free up time taken by existing staff** on these activities.

(ii) It would allow the company to take advantage of **specialist expertise and equipment** rather than investing in these facilities itself and underutilising them. If the contractor is judiciously chosen it is likely that the service will be performed more quickly and to a higher standard than is currently the case.

(iii) It would **free up time spent supporting these services** by staff not directly involved, for example supervisory staff, personnel staff. There would also be no need to provide facilities for the service to be performed.

(iv) It may be **cheaper**, once time savings and opportunity costs are taken into account

(v) It is particularly appropriate when an organisation is **attempting to expand in a time of uncertainty,** because it allows the use of facilities on a short-term (readily cancelled) basis which would only otherwise be available via the relatively long-term investments of a permanent employee and the training he or she requires. In other words it is a way of gaining all the benefits of extra capacity without having to find the full cost.

However there are also a number of **disadvantages.**

(i) Without monitoring there is **no guarantee that the service will be performed to the organisation's satisfaction**. There may be penalty clauses built into the contract for poor performance, but financial compensation will not necessarily undo the damage caused. However, if a contract has to be too closely monitored this weakens the argument for contracting out in the first place.

(ii) There is a good chance that contracting out will be **more expensive** than providing the service in-house.

(iii) By performing services itself the organisation retains or develops skills that **may be needed in the future and will otherwise be lost**.

(iv) Contracting out any aspect of information handling carries with it the possibility that **commercially sensitive data will get into the wrong hands.** The contractor will not be able to guarantee absolute security.

(v) There may be some **ethical reservations.** For example, contract cleaning companies are notorious for exploiting staff, offering inadequate pay and poor conditions. There may even be legal problems: a few years ago the Home Office found that it had to dispense with the services of a cleaning company because all of its employees were illegal immigrants!

(vi) There will almost certainly be **opposition from employees** and their representatives if contracting out involves redundancies.

Criteria for selection

There are three main criteria for selection of a service to be contracted out.

(i) **Whether the organisation sees the activity in question as one that is part of its 'core business'**. Most organisations do not see the ability to clean offices as one of their main objectives and this is why this service is so commonly contracted out.

(ii) **The relative costs** (staff, equipment and premises compared with the cost of the service), and **relative benefits** (in-house capabilities compared with external specialisms).

(iii) The **consequences of mistakes.**

These may be illustrated by the three areas in particular that have been suggested for comment.

(i) **Payroll services** are highly time consuming when carried out manually, though considerably less so once set up on computer. Payroll requires at least one member of staff with more detailed knowledge of the PAYE system than is required to pass professional accountancy examinations in tax. However, whilst doing the work of the DSS and Inland Revenue is not a prime objective of most organisations, it will nevertheless remain the **obligation of the employer to pay its staff's wages and salaries**, and much of the **information that is held for payroll purposes would be held in any case for labour costing and manpower planning purposes.** The extra knowledge that is required can be fairly easily acquired by an accountant, and considerable advice is available free of charge from the government bodies concerned.

The consequences of making mistakes in payroll are, at best, angry employees looking for fast rectification of errors, and at worst fines by the government. The **cost of monitoring to guard against mistakes might almost amount to doing the work in-house. Confidentiality** is another obvious drawback to contracting out: the employer has an obligation to employees in this respect, too, and may be reluctant to pass control of this to outsiders.

There is therefore **little to recommend contracting out of payroll services** in any organisation that is large enough to employ an accounts department (unless of course contracting out of *all* accounting services is envisaged.) Smaller organisations may benefit from having outside help in setting up a computerised payroll system, but thereafter may be better advised to handle it themselves.

(ii) **Legal services** such as handling patents, trademarks and brands are probably **more specialised than a typical organisation's in-house legal experts** (such as accountants, company secretaries, or even the average company solicitor) would have the time or knowledge to handle. In addition these matters often **require the setting up and maintenance of extensive databases and libraries. The benefit of having dedicated staff and facilities is likely to be far exceeded by the cost. The likelihood of mistakes through lack of expertise is high.**

The main problem with contracting out this sort of work is **confidentiality,** a particularly sensitive issue since new products will be the principal subject of the work.

(iii) **Computing services may be contracted out to advantage where an organisation generates large volumes of relatively simple processing which can most effectively be done using mainframe computers.** Only very large organisations can justify the investment in the computer equipment required. The power of **PCs and minicomputers** is now enormous, but they **still need staff to operate them** so that there *may* be an overall benefit in contracting out such work. The **disadvantages** are that the **data** may then not be available in a **form useable** by the organisation's own database, for example for marketing purposes, and once again there may be worries about **confidentiality**.

In the particular case mentioned it is unlikely that **production scheduling** could be done effectively by those not directly in touch with production management. This, surely, is a **core activity of the business.**

There may be a much **stronger case for sub-contracting ad hoc computing tasks,** such as systems development and maintenance, or training in the use of new software packages. Mistakes in such tasks can be very costly indeed.

Signed: Finance Director

(c)

REPORT

To: The Board
From: Finance Director — Date: XX.XX.XX
Subject: Role of internal audit and management audit

Although both internal and management audits may be carried out by the internal audit department, they are in fact very different kinds of audit. The CIMA *Official Terminology* describes them as follows.

> '**Internal audit**
> An independent appraisal function established within an organisation to examine and evaluate its activities as a service to the organisation. The objective of internal auditing is to assist members of the organisation in the effective discharge of their responsibilities. To this end, internal auditing furnishes them with analyses, appraisals, recommendations, counsel and information concerning the activities reviewed'.
>
> '**Management audit**
> An objective and independent appraisal of the effectiveness of managers and the corporate structure in the achievement of entity objectives and policies. Its aim is to identify existing and potential management weaknesses and to recommend ways to rectify them.'

It follows on quite logically from these definitions that **management audit will be more useful in a time of expansion than stability,** although it has an important role in contracting and stable times as well. The reverse might be said for internal audit.

It is often the case, however, that in a time of expansion, resources which are readily available are often thrown at problems, thus hiding inefficiencies and management weaknesses. Management audits are therefore **often perceived as unnecessary and are not implemented.**

The **internal** audit will be concerned with controls over systems. In a period of expansion, the main problems will involve new systems, new people and even new companies which must be incorporated into the organisation. Internal audit is a primary method of controlling systems development, although once again the involvement of internal audit is **often seen as unnecessary and time consuming in a time of expansion.**

When the **organisation is stable and contracting**, then **cost-cutting, efficiency and avoidance of loss** tend to take over as the main priorities. Both **management and internal audit are seen as important tools in this area. Management audit is used to increase the efficiency and effectiveness of management. Internal audit is used to detect fraud or loss and systems inefficiency.**

Unfortunately, these two types of audit are **frequently used only as an afterthought**. A great many savings in time and money could be made if they were used when the system is put in place during expansion, rather than when it is already up and running.

Signed: Finance Director

36 ROI AND APPROPRIATE MEASURES

Pass marks. Part (a) is an old chestnut of a question in this sort of exam and you should have had no trouble with it. You are given a reasonable amount of information about the context in which the question is being asked, so do try to use this rather than just producing an answer learnt by rote.

Prizewinners' points. Part (b) is quite hard: it is about the *process* of selecting measures, not about the measures themselves. We have answered by borrowing ideas you will have encountered in papers 11 and 14. Another valid approach would be to talk about critical success factors.

Examiner's comment. Common errors in part (a) included failing to focus on the investment, instead discussing the general problems of using a single measure to compare a variety of operations; discussing the measurement of profit which is not relevant to the question asked; and attempting to argue that the use of RI would solve the problem when it depends on the same calculation of investment. In part (b) the most common problem was a failure to recognise that the question could *not* be answered by a listing and description of the range of possible measures.

REPORT

To: The Managing Director
From: The Management Accountant Date: XX.XX.XX
Subject: Return on investment and other performance measurements

(a) **The problems of measuring investment**

Return on investment (ROI) is a simple measure to compute in theory: it is the percentage given by dividing the profit made by a business by the amount of capital invested in order to make that profit. However, both elements of the ROI fraction present problems in practice. In this report the **focus is on the 'investment' element.**

'Investment' is likely to comprise the fixed assets of a business plus its net current assets. For the business as a whole these figures may be easy to identify, but when judging the **performance of the separate operations** that make up the business it will be **hard to decide what element of assets shared by several different operations should be taken into account**. For example debtors and creditors may be managed centrally by head office, or motor vehicles used by individual shops for deliveries might be part of a pool covering several shops in a region.

Even if the assets used by separate operations can be identified there is the further **problem of ascribing a value to them.**

(i) If assets are valued at historic cost then an older asset will have a lower value than an identical one acquired more recently.

(ii) If the value is restated at current cost, this may disguise the impact of the relative inefficiency of older assets compared with newer ones (for example repair costs and lack of technological improvements).

(iii) If depreciation is taken into account, are all similar assets being depreciated according to the same accounting policy?

The ROI measure may, in any case, **not be a reliable guide to the quality of the management of the various operations.**

(i) There is a considerable difference between the return likely to be achievable by a factory on its assets compared with a shop and its, quite different, assets. **Like should be compared with like**, or allowances should be made for differences, otherwise the exercise has no validity.

(ii) If **investment decisions are made centrally** it may not be fair to measure a manager's ability to earn a return on assets that he or she might not have chosen to invest in, in the first place.

(iii) If **managers have control over the assets** in use in their operation, they may be **inclined to under-invest in new assets** in order to keep the investment figure low and their ROI high. This is **unlikely to be in the interests of the company as a whole.**

(b) **Determining which performance measurements are appropriate for particular businesses**

Overriding factors that will determine what performance measures are used in any business are the **costs of setting up information systems to provide them and the benefits of having them.**

The process is a matter of looking at **what the business is aiming to achieve (its mission) and what it actually does**. For example, one company may be aiming to be the biggest player in its market while another aims to corner the niche, luxury end of a market. Speed of delivery may be crucial to the success of one business, whereas quality of the finished product, no matter how long this takes, may be crucial to another.

The **mission of an organisation can be split into four elements and performance measures can be devised to reflect each of these.**

(i) **Purpose**, for example maximising shareholder wealth, or satisfying the needs of all stakeholders.

(ii) **Strategy**, defining the business the company is in (eg luxury cars), and the special competences it intends to use to prosper (eg hand built by craftsmen).

(iii) **Policies and standards of behaviour**, for example speed of answering telephones, courtesy in redressing complaints.

(iv) **Values**, related to the organisation's culture. For example in a role culture, or bureaucracy, measurements might be attached to the effectiveness of administrative systems and procedures.

Measures are more likely to compare performance against that of competitors.

It is less easy to generalise about **measures of what the business does**. It is necessary to have a **detailed understanding of how the business operates**, how its production systems or service delivery systems work, what channels it uses for sales, and so on. Measures such as output per machine, number of trains running on time, sales per region, or room occupancy rate can then be devised as appropriate.

Signed: Management Accountant

37 CONTROL OF R & D

Pass marks. The CIMA answer is rather longer than ours, partly because it goes into more detail (more than you could produce in the time available) and partly because it is rather repetitive. This is quite an easy question because the scenario gives you plenty to draw on.

Examiner's comment. According to the examiner, there were some surprisingly good answers to this question, especially by those candidates who followed the framework suggested in the question and dealt in turn with each of the four types of expenditure. One of the common errors made by candidates who produced poorer solutions was to go beyond the scope of the question and scenario, proposing economies in R & D expenditure or criticising all R & D expenditure as wasteful.

REPORT

To: Finance Director
From: Management Accountant Date: XX.XX.XX
Subject: Control over Research and Development

The past success of our new acquisition suggests that controls have been strong in all areas, including R & D. However discussions with one of the retiring directors confirms that **control was relatively informal**, relying upon senior management's knowledge of the business and the industry.

Our lack of experience in this area means that **formal control procedures must now be put in place**, but at the same time it is important that we **do not seriously disturb the innovative culture** of the R & D function, which is vital for the continued success of the company.

The main **problem** in controlling R & D is the **non-standard nature of much of the work**, with the consequence that the associated costs and timings are subject to a large amount of uncertainty. Top managers with no technical knowledge will find it hard to recognise what work is necessary and what is not.

(a) **Major project work** appears to be of the nature of pure research, of highly uncertain duration (though probably long-term) and with benefits that will not be immediately quantifiable.

This has previously been undertaken at the instigation the **retiring directors** using their **unique knowledge of trends**. In the long term our new managers need to acquire a similar feel for and understanding of the market. There is already an ongoing **system of review of current developments**, and this should feed into the learning process. In the short term it is almost certainly going to be necessary to **retain the services of one or more of the former directors in an advisory capacity.**

A **formal planning and authorisation system will also be needed**: plans for major projects should form part of the business's overall strategy as determined by the Board, and major expenditure (above a certain limit) should be justified to and sanctioned by the Board.

The long term nature of projects mean that **expenditure and time** spent must be **subject to regular reviews at predetermined intervals,** to keep costs under control and check on progress. Some work will not bear fruit, and the earlier such work can be identified and abandoned the better. However, technicians are likely to feel that problems could always be solved if more time and resources were given to them so the system for identifying such work needs to be based on a valid cost-benefit model that is both open and understandable and is perceived as being 'fair'.

(b) There is also **work of a more applied nature**, intended to solve specific practical problems with products. The benefits are more easily identifiable, and the duration is shorter term and easier to predict, though still uncertain.

Currently such work is undertaken either in response to customer demands or at the instigation of the marketing department. There is a potential overlap here. **Controls** need to be in place to ensure that **work is not duplicated** – perhaps by assigning specific products to specific R & D personnel, who will be the only ones that work on that product, or specific types of modification to specific specialists.

It would probably be desirable for **all ideas for modifications to be routed through the marketing department and then commissioned from R & D** by that department. This will ensure that modifications are justified in commercial terms, that as many customers as possible benefit from new ideas and that marketing managers are fully aware of customers' concerns.

Controls need to operate **within R & D** to ensure that reasonably **accurate deadlines are set, that work is completed to schedule, and that resources such as staff time are being used in the most profitable way. A transfer pricing system** may deter marketing from commissioning modifications that provide relatively little commercial benefit.

(c) **Technical support work** for internal customers in the production and engineering departments will arise on an *ad hoc* basis. If **previous years' data** can be extracted from the records it should be relatively easy to **budget** for specific levels of resources (staff time etc) that are likely to be required and to **monitor actual expenditure** on and usage of R & D services **against budget.**

Requests for support *may* need to be **authorised by senior managers** within the operational departments and R & D to ensure that work is properly **prioritised** according to its importance. Possibly this is too bureaucratic, however, and if the informal system appears to work well already it may be better to leave it in place.

Some form of recording of work done will be needed for **transfer pricing** purposes, and also to enable expenditure to be monitored and budgets to be drawn up in the future.

(d) Experience in reviewing current developments has already been mentioned as one means of controlling major project work. The **review process itself** can also be **controlled** in the sense that its success or otherwise is measurable in terms of numbers of new products introduced or technological modifications made as compared with competitors.

Control procedures, of course, need to allow for **costs to be collected and reported both project by project and work type by work type**: this level of analysis does not appear to be available at present. If formalised, the current loose matrix structure should hopefully be adequate for responsibility accounting purposes. If it is felt necessary to clarify certain responsibilities this must not be at the expense of creative input into different types of work.

Signed: Management Accountant

38 BRANCH OPERATIONS

Pass marks. In the CIMA solution there is a comment by the examiner that the underlying technique being used is Data Envelopment Analysis. We do not claim to be using this technique in our answer, but our conclusions are much the same. You may have calculated a correlation coefficient and a coefficient of determination (around 90%) (though here this does not tell you much more than you can observe simply by looking at the numbers and using common sense) or tried to draw a line of best fit. Our answer indicates that you should not be frightened of using simple techniques. The information in part (b) could be interpreted in a number of different ways. The requirement indicates that different interpretations would be accepted if valid. Our answer follows the CIMA solution's interpretation.

Examiner's comment. According to the examiner, this question produced an amazing range of answers, from the perfect or near perfect, to the completely hopeless. In part (a), the examiner was surprised both at the number of candidates who did not take the very broad hint regarding graph paper and at the amount written by some candidates without any basis in analysis of the data, and often without any cross reference to the question data.

In part (b), the examiner expected candidates to produce at the start of the answers, calculations in two columns for ease of comparison and for consistency, and that they would then continue to comment on the calculations made and the underlying assumptions. A significant number of candidates made no calculations while others did not formally set out their calculations in the answer. In the second case, if incorrect figures were quoted no marks could be allowed for logical workings. The examiner added that markers allow marks for clear and logical calculations, even if they are not correct, as long as they can be understood.

(a) It is apparent simply from inspection that, broadly speaking, the **more computerised the processing is the less staff time is taken up**. This becomes clearer if the staff hours are converted to minutes and the **data is ranked** as follows.

Branch	*Staff time (ascending order)*	*Branch*	*Computer time (descending order)*	*Branch*	*Total time (ascending order)*
	Minutes		Minutes		Minutes
09	54	**05**	40	**09**	91.5
05	60	**09**	37.5	**05**	100
06	90	**06**	35	**06**	125
01	120	**01**	30	**04**	140
04	120	**02**	20	**01**	150
02	180	**04**	20	**02**	200
03	240	**03**	10	**03**	250
08	270	**07**	10	**08**	280
07	300	**08**	10	**07**	310

Similar results are obtained if the computer time is expressed as a proportion of staff time and then the proportions are ranked.

Branch	*Staff time*	*Computer time*	*Computer time/ Staff time*	*Branch*	*Computer time/ Staff time*
	Minutes	Minutes			
01	120	30	0.250	**09**	0.694
02	180	20	0.111	**05**	0.667
03	240	10	0.042	**06**	0.389
04	120	20	0.167	**01**	0.250
05	60	40	0.667	**04**	0.167
06	90	35	0.389	**02**	0.111
07	300	10	0.033	**03**	0.042
08	270	10	0.037	**08**	0.037
09	54	37.5	0.694	**07**	0.033

The **data may also be graphed** as shown below.

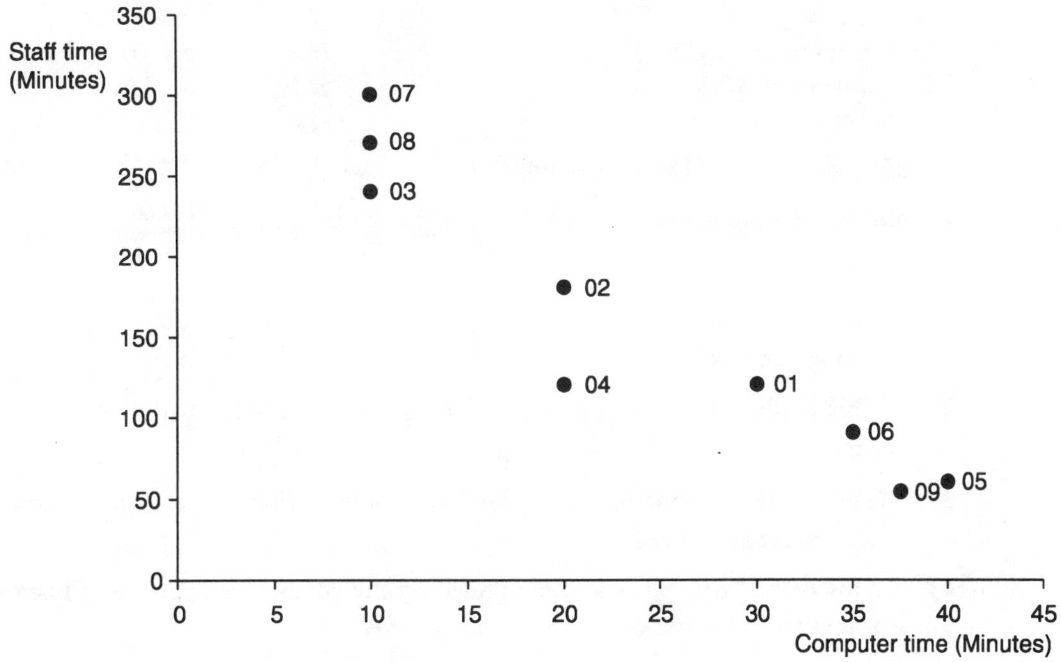

Collectively the analyses may be **interpreted** as follows.

(i) Branch 09 is the most efficient and branch 07 the least.

(ii) The branches fall into sub-groups: those that take around 10 minutes on the computer (where branch 03 is more efficient than branches 08 and 07, those that take 20 minutes (where branch 04 is more efficient than branch 02) and those that take between 30 and 40 minutes (where branch 09 is more efficient than the remaining branches).

By 'efficient' here we mean taking the least staff time to process an application.

Presumably ten minutes is the minimum time it takes to input standard data that is required to be collected and recorded. It is likely that where computer time exceeds 30 minutes it is being used as a decision support tool.

(iii) In terms of total time spent the observations in (ii) still hold true, but it may be added that branch 04 is also more efficient than branch 01.

The main reservation about the above observations is that it **may not be valid to make comparisons between the branches because they do not use standard packages and grades of staff. The definition of 'efficiency' is also open to question**. We need to know the **opportunity costs** of the inputs (staff time and computer time), and the nature of the output: it may be simply a processed application, or else it could be an *accurately* processed application, or a secure lending decision, or a profitable loan, and so on.

(b) The **data may be analysed** as follows. **Assumptions** are indicated by the workings.

	£	£
Profit (W1)	574.66	818.04
Bad debt (W2)	(62.32)	(66.28)
Repayment processing (W3)	(78.72)	(104.15)
Cost of approval (W4)	(152.54)	(214.29)
Profit per loan	281.07	433.33
Profit as percentage of loan outstanding (W5)	8.57%	9.15%
Profit per application (W6)	165.83	182.00

Workings

1 This is the amount of the average loan outstanding × the margin × the average duration.

2 This is the amount of the average loan outstanding × the bad debt provision percentage.

3 This is the amount of the average loan outstanding × the loan repayment processing percentage.

4 This is the loan approval cost divided by the percentage approved. (The cost is incurred whether or not the loan is approved.)

5 This self-explanatory.

6 This is the profit × the percentage of loans approved.

Commentary

General comments that may be made are that **branch 04** tends to **loan larger amounts over slightly longer periods and at a lower rate,** it **approves fewer applications,** and has a **lower incidence of bad debts.**

This would appear to be a more prudent policy (though the differences are relatively small) and this is borne out by the further analysis above, which shows that branch 04 loans **give a slightly better return per loan**. The lower level of approvals in branch 04 may mean that branch 03 is more profitable overall because of higher volume.

The more **prudent approach** may be due to the greater **use of the computer** in branch 04, perhaps leading to less risk-taking than a human processor might be prepared to tolerate.

The **comparisons are only valid if the figures given are reliable and if all else is equal.** This is highly **unlikely**: the figures, for example, are averages and may not be representative. The costs may contain arbitrary allocations; the percentages may be estimates (the bad debts provision *must* be). **Other factors** that need to be taken into account include the following.

(i) The **nature and purpose of the loans,** for example are they business loans or personal loans.

(ii) The **socio-economic backgrounds of borrowers.**

(iii) The **quality of the decision making process in the different branches**: do both use a standard system of credit scoring with no flexibility or are there elements of human judgement involved? If the latter, how experienced and knowledgeable are the humans in question?

(iv) **It may not be valid to look at loans in isolation,** because banks often use lending as an opportunity for cross-selling of other bank services such as insurance.

It is worth quoting an observation by John Smullen (*Management Accounting*, November 1995) in this context: 'The retail banking industry has produced a plethora of branch profitability systems, but in general institutions have not been satisfied with their results and they have been scrapped or ignored. ... Profitability measures do not easily reflect the ways in which the branches create value for the business', and a comprehensive set of targets and measures is what is really required.

(c) Internal audit will **review** the provision for doubtful debts for **two reasons**:

(i) to ensure that the **provision** for the current year is **fairly stated**; and

(ii) to judge whether the company's **credit control policies** are being **followed,** and whether these are **adequate** in controlling bad debts.

The **main procedures** will be as follows.

(i) Compare the bad debt provision to the previous year in relation to the level of debtors, ie perform **analytical procedures**. Consider the criteria used to identify bad debts and whether these were applied correctly and with clear judgement.

(ii) Extend these analytical procedures to the **ageing of the debtors balance**. Compare to previous years and consider whether further provisions should be made for old debts. A total bad debt provision based on aged debtors or on some alternative criteria could be compared with the provision as it stands.

(iii) IA should consider **correspondence** with all debtors, but predominantly those with older outstanding balances, to determine whether there is a serious intention to pay back the balance, or whether settlement could or should be made for a proportion of the balance.

(iv) Recoverability of debtors might also be considered by examining **post year end receipts,** but IA is likely to be involved very soon (or even before) the period end, so this may not be feasible.

The act of **lending money** is a **primary transaction for a bank**; for a **manufacturing company**, however, it is **incidental** to the main purpose of selling goods at a profit. For the manufacturing company, 'lending money' by allowing credit to customers is part of the cost of selling their goods. Banks must ensure that the return they get (in interest and charges) is higher than the cost of lending (interest paid and bad debts). These differences mean that an IA review of bad debts will be different in emphasis, although some of the same procedures might be followed. In the case of a **bank**, the following procedures may be relevant in an **IA review of the bad debt provision**.

(i) IA should consider whether the **bank's lending formula is being applied correctly**. If it is, then its adequacy should be judged by the frequency of its failure to detect clients who have received loans but subsequently become bankrupt. Alternative formulae may be used, particularly for business customers, eg Altman's Z scores etc.

(ii) The **loan portfolio** as it stands should be **examined**, together with an analysis of overdue amounts, exceeded credit limits and related correspondence.

(iii) IA should **compare the bad debt provision to the previous year,** taking the relative levels of lending into account. The judgement and reasoning used to reach an overall bad debt figure should be examined and considered for prudence and objectivity.

(iv) The **accuracy of the underlying records must be assured** by IA, by systems and transactions checking.

Banks have a much wider range of debtors than companies (who only tend to 'lend' to other companies). Although this **creates higher risk, banks have greater control over the repayment of debt,** because clients will pass many transactions through their account (giving the bank power of information); and also banks usually demand and receive security for the loan, say, in the form of a charge over a house. Manufacturing companies have far less information available in order to make decisions about offering credit; banks, however, will take a day-to-day interest in the state of their clients' finances.

39 OUTSOURCING

Pass marks. The important distinction in (a) is between what should be controlled if the service is provided internally (ie segregation of duties, cash security, etc), and externally (where the key judgement is made at the tendering stage). Outsourcing does mean certain information will be more difficult to obtain than if a service was provided in-house; hence in (b) VFM work is likely to concentrate on quality of products or services being provided.

Examiner's comment. According to the examiner, although this question was popular it was generally poorly answered because candidates did not focus on the exact question asked.

Answers to part (a) were very weak and they tended to discuss a wide range of irrelevant issues. Answers to part (b) were generally very thin, common errors including the following.

- Providing a definition of the three E's as an answer.
- Assuming that a comparison with an internally-produced service was readily available.
- Making vague reference to approaches such as cost benefit analysis, and data development analysis, without any indication of how they could be applied.

Answers to part (c) were very mixed. Common errors included emphasising budgetary control and monthly reporting against the budget (which is *not* relevant with long-term contracts) and discussing service quality at great length (the opportunity to discuss quality issues being in part (b)!).

(a) **Internal services**

A major concern of internal audit will be **segregation of duties**; internal audit needs to ensure that procedures laid down are reasonable and are being followed. In addition internal audit will be concerned with authorisation controls, which should complement segregation of duties.

A further concern will be **safeguarding of assets**. This particularly applies for any internal services (for example a staff shop) where significant amounts of cash are handled. Sample testing of cash receipts and payments is likely to be required; internal audit may well regard this an area of high risk and hence carry out significant testing.

Outsourced services

Internal audit will not generally be concerned with segregation of duties at the external supplier - this will be the responsibility of the external supplier's auditor. As regards authorisation, internal audit should consider procedures when the supplier is chosen, and authorisation of payments to the supplier.

With outsourced services, the **choosing of the supplier becomes important**. Hence internal audit will need to check that the tendering process has been fair, and that there has been consideration of a range of options. Internal audit will need to consider whether the supplier appears to be a reasonable choice, and that the terms are not unusual.

Once the supplier has been chosen, **authorisation of payments** will need to be checked in the same way that other payments would be checked. Payments to external suppliers would generally be considered a low risk transaction, since the terms would have been authorised when the supplier was chosen. Internal audit would, however, check that any material changes in the terms of the contract have been properly authorised.

It should be added that internal audit will have to **consider in detail controls exercised by the external suppliers if data processing is outsourced**, for example to a computer bureau. The internal auditors would be concerned with controls over security as indeed they would be if the service was provided in-house. They would also need to check the controls over the transfer of data.

(b) Use of VFM procedures will require further judgements during the tendering process. The balance will be considering different levels of cost both internally and externally, weighed against quality of service.

Once the service has been chosen, traditional **value for money techniques** will still be relevant. **Economy** will have been considered at the tendering stage, and this should be kept under review. **Efficiency** may be difficult to gauge, since outsourcing is likely to mean it is difficult to measure inputs. Hence VFM techniques are likely to be used particularly for checking the quality of outputs, checking the quality of goods or services provided. This can be done through setting certain performance criteria, for example a canteen providing a certain number of choices each day. Alternatively outputs can be measured by obtaining reaction from the people who use the services, for example, review forms at the end of training courses.

Alternative techniques to traditional value for money approaches will include **regular competitive tendering,** so that comparisons can be made with other possible sources of supply including the possibility of having the services supplied internally. Other means include **ascertaining the services supplied elsewhere**, for example by other similar businesses.

A further question is whether the **resources freed by outsourcing are being used more effectively internally as a result**. For example, outsourcing training may free up the time of operational managers, who previously were responsible for training courses, for revenue-earning work.

(c) (i) **Exercising control over the cost of outsourced services**

The **most significant controls** will need to be **implemented at the planning stage of the process of outsourcing a service.**

(1) The organisation should **document details** of the level and quality of the service it requires from the external organisation.

(2) External organisations should then be invited to **tender** for providing the service. A documented policy as to the tendering process is required and should cover factors such as the number of bids required, whether the bids should be sealed and so on.

(3) The organisation must confirm a **price** for the service with the successful bidder.

(4) **On-going control** involves ensuring that the service delivered is actually of the contracted level and quality.

(5) The organisation must also give consideration to drawing up **policies** to deal with problems which could arise in the following areas.

- Judging the quality of service provided
- Approving any costs in excess of those agreed
- Including a get-out clause in the contract (to be used if the contractor becomes complacent following a desire by the organisation to build up a long-term relationship)
- Including a price increase clause in the contract
- Reducing prices if the level of service is lower than anticipated

(ii) **Budgetary control within organisations using outsourcing**

The basic budgetary control procedure will involve **comparing actual costs with the budgeted cost based on the contracted price.**

If the actual level of service provided differs from the budgeted level and if the contracted price varies according to the level of service provided rather than being fixed, the budgeted cost will need to be **flexed** to the actual level of service. If the price is fixed rather than variable, budgetary control will simply highlight differences between actual and contracted costs.

The comparison of actual and budgeted costs provides no information as to the **quality of the service** provided, however. For example, if external organisations agreed prices at which they could never deliver the service as contracted, they may reduce the actual quality of the service provided, a situation which would not be highlighted by simple budgetary control.

There is therefore some value in operating a system of budgetary control over outsourced services but the main thrust of any control procedures should be at the stage of actually planning to outsource services.

40 DIVISION X

Pass marks. The division calculates ROI using asset base at the beginning of the year. This is not stated until the last line of the question and highlights the need to read all of the question carefully before starting. Since time is short, one sample calculation for RI, ROI and bonuses is sufficient.

Examiner's comment. The examiner noted that there were a number of critical prerequisites for success. Adequate time had to be allowed for a careful reading of the scenario. For both (a) and (b), there was a considerable advantage to be gained from careful thought about the layout of the answer, which could have led very successfully to a good commentary on the two bonus schemes. As is normal at Stage 4, calculations were not sufficient without commentary. The commentary required in both (a) and (b) should have summarised the effects of the bonus scheme in encouraging a particular project choice, and compared this with the choice that would have been made based on NPV criteria, explaining the main cause of the differences.

In part (d) answers were generally too short and weak. Substantial discussion was needed for ten marks. Furthermore, many candidates did little but agree with the statement. A requirement to discuss implies that at least two viewpoints are possible, and some effort should have been made to think of the advantages of ROI and RI.

(a) (i) ROI is calculated as $\frac{\text{Profit before interest and tax}}{\text{Asset base at beginning of year}} \times 100\%$

Special purpose machine

The ROI for Division X if the special machine is purchased

Year 1	*Year 2*	*Year 3*	
$\frac{3.0}{24.0} \times 100\%$	$\frac{2.7}{25.0+0.5} \times 100\%$	$\frac{2.4+2.0}{26.0+0.5+0.5} \times 100\%$	
12.5%	10.6%	16.3%	

					Total
		£	£	£	£
Bonus achieved with special machine	=	15,625 (W1)	13,250	20,375	49,250
Draft bonus		15,625	13,500	-	29,125
Extra/(reduced) bonus		-	(250)	20,375	20,125

(ii) **R&D Project**

The ROI for Division X if the R&D project is undertaken

Year 1	*Year 2*	*Year 3*
$\frac{3-1.6}{24.0} \times 100\%$	$\frac{(2.7-1)}{25.0} \times 100\%$	$\frac{2.4+4}{26.0} \times 100\%$
8.3%	6.8%	24.6%

				Total
	£	£	£	£
Bonus with R & D project	-	-	25,000 (W2)	25,000
Draft bonus	15,625	13,500	-	29,125
Extra/(reduced) bonus	(15,625)	(13,500)	25,000	(4,125)

(iii) **Advertising**

The ROI for Division X if the advertising campaign is run in years 1 and 2

Year 1	*Year 2*	*Year 3*
$\frac{3-0.6}{24.0} \times 100\%$	$\frac{2.7+0.5}{25.0} \times 100\%$	$\frac{2.4+1.1}{26.0} \times 100\%$
10%	12.8%	13.5%

				Total
	£	£	£	£
Bonus achieved with advertising campaign	12,500	16,000	16,875	45,375
Draft bonus	15,625	13,500	-	29,125
Extra/(reduced) bonus	(3,125)	2,500	16,875	16,250

Workings

1 Sample working: £50,000 (25% + (2.5% × (12.5 – 10)))

2 Bonus = £50,000 (25% + (2.5% × (ROI – 10)))

Upper limit is 50% of salary (ie £25,000) reached when ROI = 20%

Effect of bonus system on manager's choice of project

We assume that the manager's **choice of project will be influenced by the size of his bonus.** The **length of time he thinks he will stay in his current position** will determine how long-term a view he takes. It may not be his sole criteria, however, as good investment decisions for the company may improve his promotion prospects.

Whether he considers a **one-year or a three-year time scale, his bonus will be maximised by choosing the special-purpose machine.** Over three years it would increase his bonus compared to the draft plan by £20,125 (although for year 1 his bonus would be unchanged).

Advertising would be his second choice, improving his bonus by £16,250 over three years (although for year 1 his bonus would be reduced by £3,125).

Using a 10% cost of capital, the **R&D project is the most worthwhile for division X,** having the highest NPV. This would be **rejected by the manager,** however, as it decreases his three-year bonus by £4,125 and his one-year bonus by £15,625 from the current draft. The manager's choice of the special machine would yield the lowest NPV for the division.

The **conflict** arises partly because the **manager** is only considering a **three-year timescale** whereas **project** investment decisions ought to be evaluated over the **life of the project,** which could be longer. Although the year 3 bonus for the R&D project is restricted, the **manager would still make the same decision if the restriction were lifted** as the bonus would only increase by £5,750.

(b) (i) **First draft of plan**

	Year 1	*Year 2*	*Year 3*	*Total*
	£	£	£	£
RI (W3)	0.6 m	0.2m	(0.2m)	
Bonus	12,000 (W4)	4,000	nil	16,000

R&D project

	Year 1	*Year 2*	*Year 3*	*Total*
	£	£	£	£
RI (W5)	(0.4m)	(0.8m)	(3.8m)	
Bonus	nil	nil	25,000 *	25,000

(*Note this is restricted to the maximum 50% of salary)

Advertising

	Year 1	*Year 2*	*Year 3*	*Total*
	£	£	£	£
RI (W5)	nil	0.7m	0.9m	
Bonus	nil	14,000	18,000	32,000

Special purpose machine

	Total
	£
Bonus	40,000

Workings

3 *Sample calculation of residual income*

PBIT – 10% (asset base at beginning of year)

= 3m – (10% × 24m) = £0.6m

4 *Sample calculation of bonus*

RI × 2% = 0.6m × 2% = £12,000

5 The PBIT for the R&D project and Advertising = PBIT for first draft of plan + cash flow associated with project.

(ii) Using **RI** to calculate the bonuses still gives the **manager the largest three-year bonus from the special-purpose machine** (although there is no change over the draft proposal for year 1).

This **conflicts with the decision based on NPV** as in (a). If the decision is made on the basis of three years of bonuses, the R&D project is unattractive because the third year bonus is restricted. In the short term it is unattractive compared either to the status quo or the special-purpose machine because it provides no bonus until year 3.

If the year 3 R&D bonus were unrestricted it would be £76,000 (£3.8m RI × 2%). This would make it the **most favourable project but only if the manager were willing to wait three years for a bonus** (and if he considered he would still be around to receive it).

(c) As explained in parts (a) and (b), the **manager** is likely to **choose the special-purpose machine under both the current and proposed bonus schemes**. This project provides the least increase in NPV for the division and therefore the company, however. So although the project would increase the company's NPV, and is therefore beneficial in that sense, it is **not the optimal choice for the company**.

An **ideal bonus system would ensure goal congruence** for the manager, division and company (that is the best decision for the company would lead to the highest bonus for the manager). The following points should be considered.

(i) **ROI and RI are based on accounting flows.** A **bonus system** based on **cash flows,** for instance one based on NPV, would be more likely to result in **goal congruence.**

(ii) **Projects usually need to be assessed over the long term.** Annual bonuses focus attention on the short term, particularly since future profits are only predictions and therefore uncertain. An ideal **bonus system** would reflect **cash flows over the whole life of a project** (one using NPV would do this), perhaps with **bonus payments on account.**

(iii) The **upper bonus limit** in any one year either needs to be **removed or,** as suggested above, the **bonus should be calculated for the whole life of the project spread over the years.**

In addition any change in bonus system should **consider the absolute amount as well as the relative amount of bonus paid.** For example, the bonus system based on RI generally resulted in lower bonuses overall than those using the ROI-based system. Although this would save the company money, it is likely to lead to demotivation or even the departure of the current manager.

(d) **The use of ROI, RI and other managerial performance measures**

The statement states that the **Board of Directors** rather than managers **make investment decisions,** implying that managers have control over profits and not investments. A tenet of good performance appraisal is that people should only be assessed on what they can control. As ROI and RI are calculated using profit *and* investment base, the statement suggests that **managers should be assessed on controllable profit.**

In practice, the **degree to which managers control the investment base varies widely between organisations.** In some cases broad policy decisions are made at corporate level, with detailed implementation left to divisional managers. Some divisions and managers are given a completely free hand provided performance is good. In most cases, even if decisions are made by head office, a considerable part of the input and information for the decisions comes from managers.

If managers clearly have a major influence over investment decisions, ROI and RI considered in the long term may be reasonable. For managers who implement board-level investment decisions, controllable profit may seem fairer (particularly where their bonuses may depend on it). In practice, however, there may be no clear distinction between what is controlled centrally and what is controlled by the division. Pay scales, suppliers, product ranges and overhead allocation may all be at least partially decided at a corporate level. **Controllable profit** may therefore be **difficult to define.**

Even if controllable profit can be defined and agreed, it can be argued that a **measure that relates profit to level of investment** is better, even for the manager of a profit centre. Divisions are usually assessed using divisional profit including apportioned head office costs. This is to highlight the idea that divisions need to ensure head office as well as their own survival, to stress their interdependence. In the same way managers should ensure that they are **making adequate returns on the investment** made by head office and measures such as ROI and RI draw attention to this.

The goal of any performance appraisal system is to encourage decisions which benefit the company as a whole. The problems with the use of ROI and RI, which are short-term measures and rely on accounting conventions, were highlighted in parts (a), (b) and (c). These problems apply equally to the use of profit. Usually the **long-term ability to generate cash is what is desired** and this needs to be monitored by **considering a range of factors such as comparison with competitors, status of research and development and changing markets**. The best approach is to use a **'balanced scorecard'** of performance measures for the short and long term.

41 BENCHMARKING

Pass marks. Part (a) was fairly straightforward. Your application skills were tested in part (b), however. All too often it is assumed that the introduction of AMT and new manufacturing management systems bring nothing but benefits to the organisation concerned. Here you were asked to think about why standard costs might *increase* as a result of their introduction, however. Don't forget that the management team may have forgotten to take certain factors into account. Never assume that the mangers in the question scenarios are above making mistakes.

Examiner's comment. Part (a) was generally well answered but answers to part (b) were poor. Problems were caused by allowing too little time, failing to read the question or not focusing the answer on the question asked. Recommendations of appropriate benchmarking measures often deteriorated into listings of possible measures with minimal explanation of their purpose or calculation. Listings and short notes are not likely to earn good marks, if any.

(a) **Benchmarking**

The CIMA *Official Terminology* describes benchmarking and its aims as 'The establishment, through data gathering, of **targets** and comparators, through whose use relative levels of performance (and particularly areas of underperformance) can be identified. By the adoption of identified best practices it is hoped that performance will improve'. Smith's clearer description is 'the formalisation of the basic notion of comparing practices. It is a **systematic analysis of one's own performance against that of another organisation** ... the overall objective of benchmarking is to improve performance by learning from the experience of others'. Benchmarking therefore aims to **achieve competitive advantage** by **learning from others' experiences and mistakes,** finding **best practice** and translating this best practice into **use in the organisation.**

Types of benchmarking

There are a number of different types of benchmarking. **External benchmarking** involves comparing the performance of an organisation with that of a **direct competitor** - ideally one that is acknowledged to be the 'best in class' (**competitive benchmarking**) or comparing the performance of an internal function with those of the best **external practitioners of those functions,** regardless of the industry within which they operate (**functional benchmarking**). Given that the benchmark is the 'best' in a particular field, it provides a meaningful target towards which the organisation should aim.

Internal benchmarking, on the other hand, involves comparing the performance of **one part of a business with that of a different part of the same business** with the aim of establishing best practice throughout an organisation. Some external benchmarking is still required, however, in order to establish best practice.

Operation of benchmarking

The basic approach to both internal and external benchmarking is very similar. The **chosen activity needs to be broken down into specific processes or outputs that are capable of measurement**. External benchmarking might look at the percentage of rejects from a particular manufacturing process; internal benchmarking might consider the success of several bank branches' lending operations. At an early stage, consideration needs to be given to the way in which the data collected will be analysed since this will impact on the type of data required and the way in which it is collected.

Internal measurement then needs to be carried out and, on the basis of the data collected, the **activity needs to be analysed** to see whether it is delivering what the (internal or external) customer wants. It is at the next stage that the two approaches to benchmarking differ, however.

For **external benchmarking**, 'best in class' organisations need to be identified and performance data collected. Data from non-competitors might be fairly easy to obtain; **companies engaged in different industries might agree to collaborate** and exchange data on, for example, debt collection as this would not involve sharing potentially-damaging confidential information but would facilitate an assessment of internal processes that are essentially the same. Obtaining data from competitors for the purposes of **competitive benchmarking** might be more **difficult**, however. Customer and supplier interviews and any publicly available data (such as promotional material and advertising, inter-firm comparison reports and information from credit rating agencies) can be used. Benchmarking clubs exist, run by firms of management consultants, several trade associations and professional bodies.

The collection of data for **internal benchmarking** is obviously far more **straightforward**.

Once the data has been collected, it needs to be **analysed**. Any **changes** suggested by the exercise should be **implemented** and their **success monitored**. The whole process should be monitored periodically to ensure that the benchmarking is still being carried out against the 'best in class'.

Limitations

Both approaches to benchmarking suffer from a number of limitations. Those particularly associated with **external benchmarking** include the following.

(i) Deciding which activities to benchmark

(ii) Identifying which organisation is the 'best in class' at an activity

(iii) **Persuading that organisation to share information**

  (1) If it is a direct competitor, there is little incentive for it to give away its secrets or reveal its weaknesses. Worse, it may provide information that is not authentic.

  (2) Even if it is not a direct competitor, a rapport needs to be built up between the organisations and this will take time.

(iv) There is little point in comparing performance with an organisation that is not 'best in class' since it will only lead to complacency.

(v) Practices that get good results in one organisation may not transfer successfully to another organisation: they may depend on the talents or knowledge of particular individuals or on a particular culture.

The principal limitation of **internal benchmarking** centres on the **relevance of the other part of the business.**

(i) The amount of resources devoted to the units may differ.

(ii) There may be local differences (use of different computer hardware or software packages).

(iii) Inputs and outputs may be difficult to define.

(iv) Comparisons will only be valid if the figures reported are utterly reliable, but this is highly unlikely in practice.

(v) The possibility of the manipulation of figures must be considered.

Despite these limitations, however, many benefits have been reported from the use of benchmarking, both internal and external.

(b) **Possible reasons for similar standard costs in plants with differing technology**

There are a number of possible reasons why standard costs may not have fallen as a result of investment in new technology and introduction of new systems.

Long-term benefits such as increased customer satisfaction **as opposed to immediate cost savings** may well have been the aim of introducing the new technology and systems. If cost savings could not be made in the short term, standard costs would be unlikely to fall immediately.

The standard costs may have **incorporated one-off costs** associated with AMT, JIT and TQM. For example, additional technicians may have had to be employed to oversee the introduction of new machinery.

The introduction of new technology is likely to involve some sort of **learning curve effect**. In the period immediately following investment and the introduction of new systems, the labour force will be learning how to work with the new machines, systems and processes, but as they become more familiar with them, they will become more efficient and work more quickly. Standards may have been set to take account of this learning curve effect and hence would be higher than those ultimately envisaged once the learning process has stopped.

The standard costs may have revised to **incorporate actual costs associated with unexpected problems** surrounding the implementation of the new technology and systems. For example, stricter quality control standards introduced as part of the TQM exercise may have led to the number of raw materials consignments rejected being higher than anticipated. This may have led to a shortage of materials and hence the labour force were idle for significant lengths of time, thereby reducing their planned efficiency level.

The introduction of AMT may have succeeded in reducing the size of the labour force required and hence the standard labour cost, but other costs, especially **fixed costs** (depreciation and so on), may have **increased.**

The introduction of AMT, JIT, TQM and so on is likely to lead to a **change in the fixed overhead cost structure** and hence require a change in the approach used to apportion overheads to products, which may not have been taken into account when the standards were set. For example, activity based costing may be more appropriate than absorption costing. Once an alternative approach is adopted, the standard cost may change.

New manufacturing strategies such as JIT and TQM do involve additional costs. In a JIT environment, the responsibility for the quality of goods lies with the supplier. It is his responsibility to inspect the parts before delivery and to guarantee their quality. This may involve paying a premium for such supplies. Although TQM programmes seek to reduce the costs of producing poor quality products, there are a multitude of costs associated with the implementation of a TQM programme. Training in quality control needs to be provided, inspection procedures need to be set up and so on. Such costs need to be incorporated into the standard cost.

It is thus imperative that management take into account such factors before deciding on the success or otherwise of the new technology and systems.

Appropriate benchmarking measures

Because of the different levels of technology used in the various plants, it could be **dangerous to benchmark product costs** (and the labour, material and overhead components of those costs), whether standard or actual.

Investment in new technology and new manufacturing systems should lead to reliable, quality products, a flexible approach to customer requirements, increased customer satisfaction, lower levels of stocks and shorter lead times. Of more relevance, therefore, are **benchmarks which assess how well the plants are satisfying customers, whether they be external or internal customers.**

Quality benchmarks to assess the effectiveness of TQM might include the proportion of items rejected, the costs of a customer service section as a proportion of turnover, losses from faults/defects in items sold as a proportion of turnover and the number of customer complaints as a proportion of items sold.

Other customer satisfaction-orientated benchmarks might include the **proportion of orders completed on time** and the **proportion of turnover attributable to recurring business.**

Benchmarks covering **stock levels** as a proportion of cost of sales (raw materials) or turnover (finished goods) could be used to assess the effectiveness of JIT systems.

Benchmarking could also cover **labour productivity levels, machine productivity levels, material wastage rates and lead times** (from placing of an order to delivery to the customer and from the start to finish of production).

Overall, the measures should be **relevant to the objectives of the organisation** and should allow the group to **gain competitive advantage.**

42 THREE DIVISIONS

Pass marks. The question asked you to examine four different issues and so you should endeavour to cover each of these issues for each division. Research has shown that this sort of action by management actually occurs and so your comments must be founded in reality.

Examiner's comment. The examiner listed the following common faults made by candidates.

- A complete lack of obvious answer structure, often linked with a complete lack of answer planning
- Because of a lack of answer planning, omission of part of the required answer (usually a reference to group management action)
- Muddled understanding of the financial accounting treatment of the three transactions
- Quoting the CIMA Ethical Guidelines without applying them to the situations
- An assumption that there had to be something wrong
- A belief that all the divisional managers should, at the very least, be dismissed
- A willingness to write about topics which were actually relevant but without referring them to the transactions

Division A

Financial accounting issues. There are **no financial accounting issues** associated with Division A's proposed action. This is discretionary expenditure for divisional management and, because no commitment to spend or actual expenditure has taken place, no accruals would be necessary within the financial accounts. Because group profits would be lower than they might have been, it could be argued that the group published accounts would be slightly misleading. But although the amounts in question would be significant in terms of achieving Division A's budgeted results, they are **unlikely to be significant in terms of the group as a whole.**

Ethical issues. The **ethicality** of any action by divisional management for the sole purpose of affecting the payment of their annual bonus **must be questioned.** A **decision to postpone repainting** is likely to be one which is **delegated to divisional management** and so would **not be deemed unethical** if carried out. A **cut-back in training could affect the viability of the division,** however, unless the training, and hence the associated expenditure, occurred early in the next period.

Motivational issues. The current **management accounting control system** operating in Division A appears to have the propensity to **motivate the management team** to act in such a way (to manipulate actual results) that would ensure that they received their bonus but **the overall objectives** of the organisation suffered. **Goal incongruence** would occur.

Budgeting issues. The **value of the budget** in division A must be called into question. There appears to be little point in carrying out any sort of planning exercise if management can act in their own best interests rather than in accordance with components of the division's management accounting control system.

Division B

Financial accounting issues. At the end of the financial year, **accruals** should be made for expenditure relating to the work already carried out, but not yet invoiced. If the management of Division B were to make such an accrual for the cost of the consultancy services, actual profit would be reduced and the payment of their bonus would be affected. Failure to make such a provision, however, would be in **breach of accounting**

practice and would presumably **contradict the group's accounting policies.** If the auditors were to discover that the payment schedule had been renegotiated in this way, it may result in audit comment.

Ethical issues. If the divisional management do not include a provision against the costs of the consultancy services, a number of ethical issues need consideration. It is surely **unethical** to contemplate deliberately **preparing accounts that do not offer a true and fair view** of the division's state of affairs, even if the managers are not bound by professional ethical guidelines. For the **finance director** in particular, the dilemma is compounded by the fact that he is very likely to be bounded by **society's views on ethical behaviour *and* professional ethical guidelines.**

Motivational issues. It again appears apparent that the **management accounting control system** could **motivate division B's management to manipulate the results** to the detriment of the group as a whole in order to ensure that they receive their bonus.

Budgeting issues. If the provision is not made, **next year's budgeted expenses** will have to be increased to take account of the total cost of the work, and hence budgeted profit will be reduced accordingly.

Division C

Financial accounting issues. There are **no financial accounting implications** associated with this action. It would be perfectly acceptable to register the sale and hence take the profit in the current year because the goods would have been delivered before the year end. The published accounts would be accurate and so no external audit comment would be necessary. The accounts would, however, be **misleading** because **next year's profit would probably be lower** than it would have been because profit would have been brought forward into the current year.

Ethical issues. Although there are no financial accounting implications of the action, the manipulation of profit is very **unethical** and it gives a misleading view of the division's activities. Moreover, it would be **inappropriate to involve customers** in such behaviour and it would raise the real possibility that those involved might take their custom elsewhere.

An added problem with this course of action is that it would leave **stocks at a very low level.** There is the possibility that the division would be unable to satisfy customers' orders in the first few weeks of the following year unless stocks could be replenished very quickly. The loss of sales revenue and the loss of customer goodwill should be seriously considered by the management concerned.

Motivational issues. Yet again it seems that the **management accounting control system can induce** the management of division C to act in a way which is at odds with both the overall objectives of the organisation and sound management practice.

Budgeting issues. Next year's **sales budget and opening stock budget** would need to be reduced to take account of the proposed action. Next year's budgeted profit would likewise need to be reduced.

Group management action

There is **nothing illegal** in any of the divisions' proposed actions. Division B's proposed method would not comply with generally-accepted accounting practice, however, and it is debatable whether 'income-smoothing' or 'window dressing' should be used simply to allow management to earn bonuses.

Group management typically adopt a **'hands-off' approach** when dealing with divisional organisations, subject to certain parameters such as the achievement of budget targets. That being the case, it could be argued that group management should **take no action** given that divisional management are simply trying to achieve budget targets. Moreover, it is fairly **common practice** for managers to '**income-smooth**' results, especially as stock markets rate stocks with a more stable earnings record higher than those with a fluctuating record.

Group management would **not be acting in the best interests of their shareholders** (despite the stock market rating) is they allowed such action by divisional managers. All of the divisional actions are **short termist**. The bonuses in all three divisions would be paid at the expense of next year's profits since all three actions would lead to lower profits next year. Shareholders are likely to want to reward genuine operational performance, not profit manipulation.

Group management will need to **tread carefully,** however. Divisional management teams may **resent head office interference,** particularly if they have a significant amount of delegated authority.

Finally, it could well be the case that the bonuses of the group management team depend on the profit reported by the divisions. Moreover, all of the transactions increase group profits and are therefore to the benefit of the group. **Group management might therefore behave unethically and take no action, as both they and the group will benefit.**

43 UNIVERSITIES

Pass marks. In part (a) there is little guidance on how to choose the selection criteria. You should have chosen neither too many nor too few. It is easy to spend too long agonising. After ten minutes rough analysis, take the plunge even if you are not absolutely sure you are on the right track. Marks can only be awarded for comments made. Latitude in marking is given for reasoned argument even if it doesn't agree with the model answer. The question is demanding in that it requires a decision that is not clear cut. It is a good idea to write or at least make notes for part (c) while completing (a) and (b), as the limitations of the data will occur to you as you make your analysis.

Prizewinners' points. Good answers to part (a) would have included discussion of capacity issues (which university could best cope with additional students) and would have pointed out that the staff:student ratio could be seen as both a measure of efficiency and a measure of quality.

Other points. A number of approaches to part (a) were possible.

- Using the framework of the 3 Es
- Using an input-output framework
- Using ranking tables
- Devising new ratios to relate the existing ratios

Part (c) could have used Fitzgerald's service framework.

Examiner's comment. Markers are instructed that the conclusion to questions such as part (a) is not important but that marks are to be awarded for the quality of the candidate's argument. Good marks were available for well-argued recommendations for any of the four universities. Answers which failed to make a recommendation received far fewer marks. Among the common errors made in part (a) were failure to structure answers in any noticeable way, repeating the data with very little comment or explanation and repeating the question data inaccurately and then providing confused comments. A common error in part (b) was failure to make any feasible suggestions, while in part (c) it was failure to deal with both parts of the question.

(a) **Data comparison**

The central authority wants the best value for money when providing a grant for additional places, which probably means that the **maximum number of places must be made available for a fixed grant, provided quality of output is high**. Cost efficiency measurements must therefore be compared, as well as measures of achievements of students and research staff.

Many performance indicators can be used but the table below has been restricted to the most important. It has been split between measures for the Business & Management Department and measures for the university.

	Ranking			
Business and Management Department	*North*	*South*	*East*	*West*
Cost efficiency measures				
Cost per undergraduate	3	4	2	1
Total cost per academic staff member (W1)	3	4	2	1
SSR	1	4	2	3
Revenue generation				
Research income	2	1	3	4
Graduate quality measures				
% 1st and 2.1 degrees *	2	1	4	3
% graduates employed	2	4	1	3
% completing course in normal time *	3	1	2	4
University data				
Financial surplus/deficit	1	3	2	4
% of funds from other sources (W2) *	4	1	2	2

Notes to table

The numbers in the table represent the relative rankings. For example, East has the worst proportion of 1st and 2.1 degrees and so is ranked 4.

* indicates that there is little absolute difference in the figures.

Workings

1 This is the cost of each academic staff member plus support staff costs.

North	*South*	*East*	*West*
£69,990	£84,800	£46,100	£42,100

2 This is the total percentage of revenue from funds other than grants and fees.

North	*South*	*East*	*West*
33%	39%	37%	37%

Analysis and recommendation

It is important to bear in mind that the aims of quality and low cost tend to conflict. The ideal is a reasonable balance between the two. This means that the **recommendation is bound to be subjective.** In addition the performance measures are open to differing interpretations.

The main points are summarised below.

(i) **South University**

South University clearly has the most active research department indicated by the high level of research income and the relative number of postgraduate students. This probably accounts for the high cost of academic staff and support staff ; it has the **worst cost efficiency measures.**

Success with undergraduates is mixed. **Teaching** must be of a **high quality** judging by the percentage of upper class degrees awarded a and the percentage of students completing the courses in normal time. The **unemployment** levels for graduates is the **worst,** however.

Despite its clear strengths in quality, the **cost per student,** at twice that of other universities, means only half the number of students could be taught for the same grant and for this reason South **cannot be recommended.**

(ii) **Cost per student**

The **remaining universities** have **fairly similar** undergraduate costs and could therefore teach roughly the same number of students for a fixed grant. Other factors must therefore be considered in order to choose between them.

(iii) **Other cost, efficiency and quality measures**

The **SSR** can be seen as **both a measure of efficiency and a measure of quality. North** has a **high SSR** but also **high academic staff costs.** This may reflect the fact that, since there are fewer teaching staff, they have to be highly qualified and efficient and therefore better paid. North has **reasonably good quality measures.**

East has **reasonable cost efficiency** and is best in terms of **popularity** with employers.

West comes out **worst on graduate quality measures** and since the cost per undergraduate is only marginally lower than those of the other two, it **cannot be considered the best value for money.**

Conclusion

On balance **East** is **recommended** for the grant since its student costs are reasonable and the employability of its graduates is very good.

(b) In order to draw general conclusions about West University it is assumed that the Business and Management department is representative of the University as a whole.

Relative performance of West University

In addition to the information in part (a), West is ranked fourth for A level points on entry and has the second highest proportion of postgraduate students after South.

Problem areas

The university has the worst **deficit,** despite having the lowest average undergraduate and staff costs. Despite cost cutting, the university is obviously having financial trouble.

The low A level points on entry and the relatively high graduate unemployment level suggests that the university has a **poor image** with students and employers. The **absence of research revenue** may be due to lack of resources but equally well may arise from lack of contacts in the commercial sector.

Recommended changes

Low quality staff and facilities may have resulted in a poor reputation which has made it hard for the university to raise revenues, and so expenditure levels may have been, by necessity, low.

The university does not have spare money to make major investments in staff or facilities but other changes could begin to steer it in the right direction.

(i) The SSR is not particularly high compared to North or East and both have better graduate quality measures. The **SSR could be raised** and the staff savings used to improve staff quality and facilities.

(ii) The University could find out **what potential employers are looking for and ensure courses meet such requirements.** Opportunities for work experience in the holidays could be found for students. Forging closer links with industry would also help in finding commercial research projects. If the university profile is raised in this way it should also help attract better quality students.

There should also be a general focus on ways to **promote the image** of the University. There are bound to be some strengths which can be exploited.

(c) **Limitations of the data for assessing quality**

Measurement of quality is determined by how quality is perceived.

(i) The government may be concerned with the quality of students as measured by the **class of degree earned** and the **employability of students**. Both of these measures may be **affected by the quality of students admitted,** however. In addition, it may be **difficult to check that the standard of university examinations is uniform**. A higher proportion of 1st and 2.1 class degrees may reflect lower standards or it may be that marks are moderated so that roughly the same number of each class of degree are awarded each year. And short-term employment figures may be distorted by graduates taking 'time out'.

(ii) **Students may be more concerned with the quality of their job prospects,** having **fun,** developing skills while undertaking the course and **personal development**. These are more **difficult to quantify.**

(iii) Other **data may be open to different interpretation**. Low costs per student and high SSR may improve cost efficiency but may also compromise quality. High teaching staff costs may reflect high quality teaching, not merely an inability to controls costs.

(iv) **Cost per student is likely to contain an element of arbitrary allocation**. If different universities use different bases for allocation the figures may not be comparable.

Other ways of measuring quality

(i) **Research** can be seen as a means to generate funds but it may also be important for maintaining high teaching standards, impressing prospective employers and attracting overseas (and therefore high-fee-paying) students and postgraduates. As well as measuring **research income, research quality** and effect could be assessed by **auditing staff qualification levels** and the **number of research articles published.**

(ii) As mentioned above, **quality of graduates** may be affected by a quality of intake. Relative performance could be assessed by collecting and **comparing data on A level entry points with the degree class awarded.**

(iii) A number of pieces of data would need further analysis to determine their **effect on quality.**

(1) **Student numbers**. A high number of students may indicate that a course is popular or that teaching is impersonal and conditions overcrowded.

(2) **Unemployment levels.** An analysis of unemployed graduates could determine if a lack of skills, the status of the university or both is the cause of their unemployment.

(3) The reasons for lack of **research income.**

(iv) In much the same way as schools are inspected, an **inspection** of the university by a team could provide a qualitative report on morale, teaching practices and use of facilities. The report would then not only support decisions on grant allocations but, if available to the public, would provide information for potential students and employers. The universities themselves could also learn from one another.

44 MUSIC SOCIETIES

Pass marks. It is vital in part (b) that you take account of the fact that X Music is just a small organisation, with few staff and limited resources. There is little point in recommending modern cost management techniques.

Examiner's comment. According to the examiner, unsuccessful attempts at part (a) were distinguished by a number of fairly obvious common faults.

- Providing nothing but figures
- Providing nothing but words
- Making no comparisons
- Restating the question without adding any significant analysis
- Misinterpretation of the data
- Careless calculations

Answers to part (b) were generally weak and notably short. There was little sympathy for listings of all possible new cost management techniques with no indication of their purpose and usefulness in the circumstances.

(a)

REPORT

To: The Chairman
From: Management Accountant Date: XX.XX.XX
Subject: Comparison of the performances of X Music and Y Music

This report provides a comparison of the key features of the business and financial performance of X Music and Y Music.

Overview

X Music's results for **19X7** show a **marked deterioration** in financial performance. The society reported a **deficit** of £88,000 in 19X7 (compared with surpluses of £27,000 and £34,000 in 19X2 and 19W7 respectively) and a worrying **cumulative deficit** of £686,000 (compared with surpluses of £80,000 in 19X2 and £141,000 in 19W7).

Y Music, on the other hand, was **more successful** and reported a **surplus** of £182,000 and a cumulative surplus of £311,000 in 19X7. A deficit of £15,000 in 19X2 and a surplus of £12,000 in 19W7, and a cumulative deficit in 19X2 (£26,000) and a cumulative surplus in 19W7 (£62,000) point to the possibility that the society's **results have been fluctuating widely** over the last decade, however.

An analysis of business and financial data for the two societies highlights a number of factors which may well have played their part in these results.

Number of performances

Since 19W7, the **number of performance** given by **X Music** has **dropped** by 17% (from 181 to 150), while the number given by **Y Music** has **dropped** by 15% (from 152 to 129). The similarity in these figures tends to suggest that both societies have been **affected to a similar degree by competition from foreign orchestras**. Despite this fall, however, Y Music has reported both a surplus and a cumulative surplus in 19X7.

The **number of performances of all types of concert** given by **X Music in 19X7** have **dropped** from those in 19W7 and 19X2. The number of concerts in other areas of the country (not the home city) in particular has dropped by over 28% to 63 from the 88 reported in 19X2. The number of performances in the home city has remained fairly constant (75 in 19W7 and 74 in 19X7).

Y Music has seen a significant **fall in the number of concerts played elsewhere in the home country** (a drop of 50% from 52 in 19W7 to 26 in 19X7). From playing no concerts abroad in 19X2, Y Music played 8 in 19X7 (as did X Music), and made 11 TV/radio/recording appearances in 19X7, compared with only five in 19X2.

In 19X7, **Y Music** gave 84 **concerts in its home city,** 10 **more than** the number of performances by **X Music** in its home city. This is **surprising** given that Y Music is based in a smaller city with, one assumes, a smaller concert-going population. **Overall,** however, **X Music** gave 150 performances in 19X7, 21 **more than Y Music,** principally because it made 63 performances in other areas of the country. X Music's disappointing results cannot therefore be attributed to the number of concerts it performed.

Income

Both societies have reported a **significant increase** in total earned income over the ten-year period. X Music's earned income was 137% higher in 19X7 (£2,829,000) compared with that in 19W7 (£1,193,000). Y Music's was 205% higher (£3,088,000) compared with £1,014,000). It is, however, the **income per concert** that has **led to X Music's poor financial performance,** as illustrated by the following figures for 19X7.

	19X7	
	X Music	*Y Music*
Income per concert in home city	£9,432	£12,417
Income per concert in home country	£14,540	£29,308
Income per overseas concert	£35,250	£41,625
Income per TV/radio/recording event	£14,000	£19,091

X Music achieves a significantly lower income per performance for all types of performance than that achieved by Y Music. The difference is most marked when comparing **concerts in the home country,** with **Y Music's income per performance is over double that of X Music's.** This could be because audience sizes are smaller at X Music's performances or ticket prices may be lower, but on the basis of the data provided it is not possible to state definite causes. If you were able to provide me with attendance figures and information about ticket prices I could provide you with a more detailed analysis.

X Music's other earned income of £466,000 in 19X7 (16% of total earned income) is significantly **higher than that of Y Music** (£133,000, representing 4% of total earned income) and hence its catering and merchandising activities are probably considerably more effective than those of Y Music. X Music's figure also compares well with the £56,000 earned ten years previously.

On the other hand, **business sponsorship** appears to have been extremely **lucrative for Y Music** in 19X7, bringing in £607,000, almost the same income as that earned for concerts in other parts of the country. X Music's business sponsorship at £397,000 was only 65% of Y Music's, although both societies have shown significant increases from the levels in 19W7 (X Music £56,000; Y Music £44,000) and 19X2 (X Music £141,000; Y Music £135,000).

The **grants** from both central government and the local authority **awarded to Y Music** in 19W7, 19X2 and 19X7 were **higher than those awarded to X Music.** In 19X7, grants represented 44% of Y Music's total income, compared with 41% of X Music's, with Y Music receiving £2,450,000 in grants compared with £1,955,000 by X Music. **Y Music's committee** appear to be **far more effective** in **applying for**

grants and X Music's committee should be encouraged to actively pursue this source of income.

Costs

Despite the fact that X Music put on more performances than Y Music in 19W7, 19X2 and 19X7, **X Music's costs have always been lower**. In 19X7, X Music's costs per performance were £32,480 (£4,872,000/150) whereas Y Music's were £41,519 (£5,356,000/129). Given that one would expect overseas concerts to be the most expensive to put on, and both societies gave eight overseas concerts, this cost difference **may highlight particular cost control skills at X Music** (or alternatively, of course, particularly poor cost control at Y Music). On the other hand, because 75% of the costs are related to the orchestra, it **could point to lower quality performances by X Music** (which might explain X Music's lower income per performance) **or to different forms of performance** by the two societies, the two forms requiring different numbers of musicians.

Given that **X Music's total costs were not covered by total income** in 19X7, and that there is no guaranteed level of grant income, **X Music should carry out a detailed review of expenditure.**

I hope this information has proved useful. If I can be of any further assistance, please do not hesitate to contact me.

Signed: Management Accountant

(b) It is clear from the analysis in (a) above that X Music should pay close attention to the level of costs being incurred. **Seventy five percent of costs are orchestra related** and given the low levels of remuneration, especially for musicians, cost cutting will be difficult. The society therefore needs to consider ways of managing its costs more effectively. There are a number of cost management techniques which might prove particularly useful to an organisation such as X Music, with a small number of accounting staff and limited available data.

All of these techniques would involve setting up a more **detailed cost recording system** than exists at the moment. Until costs can be traced to and identified with performances, they cannot be managed.

Budgeting

Even the smallest of organisations needs to operate some form of **budgeting system**. It is vital that X Music undertakes a simple **planning exercise** to ensure that it is able to **finance its activities** during the next accounting period. The planning exercise needs to start with an **estimate of the number of performances** that are likely to be given in the home city, the home country and overseas and the TV/radio/recording work likely to be available. On the basis of these estimates, monthly **budgets for the various costs** (musicians, administration, concert hall and so on) can be set. Although these costs are largely fixed, they may behave in a step fashion and so could vary to a certain extent with the number of performances given. Each month, **costs can be compared against budgeted costs** and **control action** initiated if budgeted cost levels are being exceeded.

Using the estimates of the number of performances, budgets for the various forms of **income** can be drawn up. If grant income is not known with certainty, estimates will need to be made. **Contingency plans** (such as other sources of income or cost reduction measures) will need to be made, however, to ensure that the society is able to continue operating should the grant income be significantly less than anticipated. Once budgets for monthly income have been set, **cash budgets** can be drawn up to ensure that the society has sufficient funds to finance its activities during the coming accounting period.

Cost benefit analysis

On the basis of the information available, it does not appear that X Music is aware of whether particular activities make a profit or a loss. It is possible to determine average income per concert in home city, concert in home country and so on, but it does not appear that the **actual income per performance** is available from the current recording system. Such data needs to be available. What's more, there is currently no analysis of costs into those associated with, for example, concerts in the home city. A basic cost recording system therefore needs to be established so that **costs** can be **traced to specific types of concert**.

Although the majority of costs are fixed, it is still possible to **apportion** staff costs, for example, on the basis of how many members were in the orchestra during a particular performance. **Profitability** per home city concert, overseas concert and so on could be ascertained and it will then be possible to ascertain which are the profitable forms of performance, which type of performance result in a loss and the committee will be able to determine the **range of concerts that should be provided**.

Contribution analysis

Rather than look at the profitability of each type of concert, the society could look at the **contribution** earned by each type of performance or each individual performance. If a revised cost recording system were set up, fixed costs associated with each type of performance could be ascertained, the contribution compared with the fixed costs, and the **breakeven** number of concerts and breakeven revenue determined. The society would then have more of an idea of the type of performance it should be putting on.

Activity based costing

Given that the majority of costs are fixed, some sort of activity based costing analysis might be appropriate. The identification of the **drivers of the various costs** would enable the society's committee to control those drivers and hence manage the costs. For example, concert hall costs might be driven by the length of the concert and so the committee might try to avoid putting on particularly long concerts.

Summary

Whatever cost management technique is adopted it should be simple and enable the society to control finances more effectively.

(c) **Pass mark**. The points emphasised in (c) are the main risks and how the existence of different types of control will impact on the rest of the internal audit.

An internal audit should consider all the different types of sales made in the concert hall. The **major risks** internal auditors will be concerned with are threats to the **society's assets** and **loss of customer goodwill.** Although cash sales do represent a significant problem because of the lack of documentation, credit sales must also be considered, as they represent over 80% of tickets sold.

Factors such as analytical evidence and previous experience will influence the extent of work done, and the amount of detailed checking of controls will also be determined by the auditors' assessment of general controls, particularly those affecting staff.

Staffing controls

Because of the opportunities for dishonesty, a vital staffing control will be obtaining **references** for everyone who receives or holds cash. There should also be controls in place to ensure that staff and volunteers have the **necessary knowledge** to be able to deal with different types of sales, and customer complaints and queries. Internal auditors should plan to review these controls early in their audit; if the controls are not working as well as they originally assumed, they can then modify their original planned work on other controls.

Controls over cash and other assets

Internal auditors should confirm early in their audit the extent of **segregation of duties**, since appropriate segregation will be a major control strength. If possible separate staff should be responsible for receiving cash, holding and paying it into the bank, and recording it.

Segregation of duties is linked to another important control, **reconciliations,** since staff who are carrying out the reconciliations should not be responsible for the assets concerned. Internal auditors should re-perform a sample of reconciliations. In particular internal auditors should review the following:

(i) reconciliations of ticket receipts to numbers and value of tickets sold;

(ii) reconciliations of the results of stock counts to movements in stock apparently shown by sales and purchases.

Hall staff should also check subsequent clearance through the society's bank account of payments made by cheque or credit card.

Certain controls will need to be checked by internal auditors actually **observing the operation of controls on concert nights.** These include **separate accounting** for, and **appropriate controls** over, **different types of receipts.** Internal auditors should attend both on nights of major concerts (where risks may be significantly greater because say of the use of inexperienced staff), and on a random basis on 'ordinary' nights.

Controls over seats

As well controls over monies received for seats, appropriate controls must be exercised over records of who has booked what seat, as double booking will lead to loss of customer goodwill. If bookings are made on computer, there should be programmed procedures to prevent double booking. Internal audit work should include checks on records of seats sold for forthcoming concerts, and also **comparisons** of records of **seats occupied** with **total tickets sold** for concerts that have already taken place.

Inadequate controls

If the controls mentioned are not working satisfactorily, the impact on internal audit planning will be significant, because major **investigation work** (including analytical analysis and detailed record checking) will be required to ascertain whether there has been a significant defalcation or other loss of cash and other assets. In addition, once internal auditors has made recommendations about improvements, they will need to check that the changes recommended have been implemented. Significant internal audit time will be needed to carry out the necessary checks, and this will impact significantly on longer-term audit planning.

45 MULTINATIONALS

> **Pass marks**. One of the problems with this question is that it has a broad scope, bringing in many aspects of the MCS syllabus, contained within a relatively loose scenario. A useful starting point is to make some assumptions about the business – the degree of inter-dependence between individual country units and so on. This gives you some structure upon which you can deal with the required issues.
>
> **Examiner's comment.** Good answers gained marks for using Goold and Campbell's strategies and styles framework in addition to merely stating it.

With a **smaller** business and a more **dynamic** environment, **radical changes** will be required to the existing and apparently cumbersome control system.

Whilst these changes will **downsize the control systems** in place, **the same control objectives exist** – that the geographically-dispersed business units are aware of what they need to achieve and head office management can monitor their progress.

Minimum central control system

The fast-changing business in which X plc is involved requires that local management are able to respond to events and problems that occur within their area. The **current requirement for head office approval** for a wide range of actions **slows down the speed of decision making; authority needs to be delegated.** The control system should therefore be based on a system that treats **the overseas businesses as profit centres or investment centres.**

At a **minimum**, a **'strategic control' style of management (as opposed to the current 'financial control' style)** should be applied, allowing profit/investment centres to act with far more **autonomy**. Plans will be made and budgets will be set locally, although head office could review them as part of a formal planning process. Head office is unlikely to advocate strategies or interfere with major decisions but will maintain control through financial targets and strategic objectives. |

For **core parts of X plc's operations** more control may be necessary, however. A **'strategic planning' style of management** could be appropriate. Head office will participate in and influence the strategies of the core businesses, will establish a planning process for them and contribute to strategic thinking. Performance targets will be set flexibly and reviewed within the context of long-term progress.

Decisions to be retained by head office

The decisions taken by head office will **depend on whether or not the area of business concerned is central or core to X plc's operations**. In general, however, decisions on the following areas are likely to be made at head office level.

IT strategy. To allow for smooth flows of information between all business units, head office must ensure that common IT standards are being followed. With a wide geographical spread, there will be local differences which should be minimised as far as possible. The policies adopted need to ensure that individual units can communicate both with head office (for reporting purposes and so on) and with each other (for transfers of spare parts, production scheduling and the like).

Manufacturing strategy. There is the chance that different factories will engage in dysfunctional decisions over the manufacture of products with common parts. Head office must be involved in ensuring production scheduling is optimal for the group.

Research and development. To maintain and improve the group's position in the specialist electronic market, head office must be actively involved in ensuring adequate resources are devoted to R&D. If R&D is taking place at separate manufacturing sites, the group must have systems which ensure that cross-sharing of information takes place and unnecessary overlaps are prevented.

Foreign exchange. Rather than duplicate activities, the management of foreign exchange should be conducted centrally. Not only will this minimise costs, it will allow for easier control of the group's risk exposure.

Transfer pricing. Individual units could easily become embroiled in arguments over recharges for goods, services and/or spare parts. Head office must be responsible for maintaining a fair transfer pricing system.

Long-term financing. Decisions regarding, for example, the raising of equity finance, should be made by head office.

Capital investment. Decisions involving expenditure over a certain level should be referred to head office.

Social and environmental concerns. Head office may determine minimum standards for wages, age of employees, health and safety and so on.

Minimum reporting system for control

The minimum reporting system is one that will **allow head office management to ensure that the group's overall objectives will be met.**

Given their material **impact** on group results, **the larger manufacturing plants** should provide **detailed monthly reports**. The group's financial position after the forced restructuring will determine the basis of preparation for these reports. They should be cash based if the company has liquidity problems. If not, the accounts should be prepared on the normal accruals basis.

An **aged stock report** should be included within the reporting package, as there is a high risk of stocks becoming **obsolete**.

The **smaller operations** should not be required to produce monthly accounts. **Quarterly accounts** would be reasonable given their potential impact on overall results. With as few as ten staff the effort of monthly accounting seems disproportionate to the benefits obtained.

All units should be required to produce monthly information based on their **critical success factors**. For larger units these are likely to include productivity and quality levels. The reports of smaller units, which are focused on sales and service, should concentrate on new sales for the month and the number of service contracts renewed (an excellent indicator of quality of service). They are also likely to include **non-financial measures**, for instance the number of service calls answered within the unit's standard response period. These non-financial measures should focus local managers' attention on managing critical aspects of the business and give head office managers a low-cost early warning of any potential problems.

Quarterly forecasts should also be provided by each unit in order to highlight any potential problems in relation to annual budget targets. A system of **rolling budgets** could be employed as an alternative to quarterly forecasts, a twelve-month period being constantly monitored.

Criteria for performance evaluation purposes

The criteria used should **ensure** that the objectives of the group as a whole are met and that management are appropriately motivated, that there is **goal congruence.**

Before the restructure, it is likely that individual units were evaluated by a **monthly comparison of actual results to a budget prepared by head office**, a method which is **no longer appropriate** to the environment in which the group is operating.

Given the **specialist nature of the electronic equipment** and the likely **variations in market conditions** between the various countries in which the group has a presence, the **management of each unit should be heavily involved in preparing the unit's budget**, using their local specialist knowledge. The basis of preparation will incorporate the requirements of the reporting system mentioned above (cash based if necessary, use of CSFs and so on). Given the fast-changing nature of the business, these budgets should be **revised on a quarterly basis** to ensure that units are reacting appropriately to changes in market conditions. Actual results should then be evaluated against these more accurate and up-to-date budgets.

The criteria for **management performance** evaluation should ensure that consideration is given to issues such as the **relative strength of the local economy**. In addition, managers should only be **evaluated on issues that are within their control**. For example costs which are essentially centrally-imposed transfer prices should not form part of the range of factors upon which management are evaluated. And **benchmarks** against which the performance of managers is measured should be chosen to ensure goal congruence.

Problems in performance evaluation

A number of problems could arise in evaluating the performance of individual country operations and those of their managers. To a large degree, however, these **problems will be affected by the level of autonomy given to individual units and their managers**. It is far easier to assess equitably the performance of a manager who operates fairly autonomously than the performance of one to whom very little is delegated.

A principal problem is the effect of the **different nature of the overseas operations**. With some units employing fewer than ten and others employing in excess of 200, a relative performance measure such as return on investment may have to be used. Such a measure will need to be designed very carefully because of the different levels of investment required for service-only and manufacturing operations.

The issue **of foreign exchange** must also be dealt with. **Individual managers** should probably **be evaluated in reports prepared in the local currency**, as the strength of local currencies against X plc's currency could be difficult to plan for. **Individual units** should **be evaluated in terms of X plc's currency**, however, as world-wide profits will be consolidated for group financial reporting purposes. If there are substantial exchange rate movements during a period, a revised budget should be prepared on the basis of what should have been achievable given these new rates.

Local managers may try to explain all differences from budget as being due to local market conditions. Head office must should obtain other sources of local market information in order to verify the validity of such claims.

46 QUALITY COSTS

Pass marks. You would not be expected to reproduce CIMA *Official Terminology* definitions in the exam; any concise explanation in your own words would be more than sufficient. The tricky bit of part (a) would have been providing measures appropriate to the management accounting section. It is far easier to think of measures for manufacturing environments. Use your own experience, however, if you work in such an environment.

Examiner's comment. The examiner reported that many candidates were determined to provide a general essay on TQM (the question they thought he should have asked) and ignored the question actually asked. In part (a), errors included the provision of poor examples and imaginative but inaccurate examples. Part (b) was very badly answered by weaker candidates, who did not recognise management accounting as an internal service.

(a) The 1996 edition of the CIMA *Official Terminology* defines the **cost of quality** as 'The difference between the actual cost of producing, selling and supporting products or services and the equivalent costs if there were no failures during production or usage'. In other words it is the costs incurred by an organisation because the quality of its products or services is not perfect.

The *Official Terminology* goes on to split the cost of quality into the **cost of conformance** and the **cost of non-conformance**. The cost of conformance is 'The cost of achieving specified quality standards' whereas the cost of non-conformance is 'The cost of failure to deliver the required standard of quality'.

The cost of conformance is further analysed into the **cost of prevention** and the **cost of appraisal** while the cost of non-conformance is analysed into the **cost of internal failure** and the cost of **external failure**.

These four categories of quality cost are defined in the *Official Terminology* as follows.

(i) **Prevention cost** is 'The costs incurred prior to or during production in order to prevent substandard or defective products or services from being produced'.

(ii) **Appraisal cost** is 'The costs incurred in order to ensure that outputs produced meet required quality standards'.

(iii) **Internal failure cost** is 'The costs arising from inadequate quality which are identified before the transfer of ownership from supplier to purchaser'.

(iv) **External failure** cost is 'The cost arising from inadequate quality discovered after the transfer of ownership from supplier to purchaser'.

Examples of each category appropriate to a manufacturing environment

(i) Examples of **prevention cost** include the following.

(1) Cost of training personnel in quality control

(2) Cost of designing, developing and maintaining quality control and inspection equipment

(ii) Examples of **appraisal cost** include the following.

(1) Cost of the inspection of finished products or services and other checking procedures and supplier vetting

(2) Cost of the inspection of goods inwards

(iii) Examples of **internal failure** cost include the following.

(1) Cost of material scrapped due to inefficiencies in goods receiving procedures and stores control

(2) Cost of material lost or wasted during production

(3) Cost of units rejected during inspection processes

(4) Losses due to lower selling prices for sub-quality goods

(5) Cost of reviewing product specifications after failures

(iv) Examples of **external failure cost** include the following.

(1) Cost of product liability claims from customers

(2) Cost of repairing products returned from customers

(3) Cost of providing replacement items due to sub-standard products

(4) Cost of delivering returned units

(5) Cost of administration of customer services section

(6) Cost of customer services section

Examples of each category appropriate to management accounting

(i) Examples of **prevention cost** include the following.

(1) Cost of staff training programmes

(2) Cost of introducing computers to perform tasks previously performed manually

(ii) Examples of **appraisal cost** include the following

(1) Cost of batch input controls to check the validity of processed data

(2) Cost of performing computer audits to confirm the reliability of computer software

(iii) Examples of **internal failure cost** include the following.

(1) Cost of reprocessing data input to the system incorrectly

(2) Cost of reproducing incorrect reports

(iv) Examples of **external failure cost** include the following.

(1) Cost to other functions in the organisation of incorrect decisions made on the basis of inaccurate or untimely information provided by the management accounting function (such as quoting uneconomical prices for jobs on the basis of incorrect information about labour, material and overhead)

(2) Cost of dealing with external audit queries

(b) **How the categorisation of quality costs can help to develop management accounting performance measures**

Given the increasing importance of quality as a tool for competitive advantage, quality-based performance measures are extremely useful.

The **categorisation** of the total cost into the four categories detailed in (a) above provides a **useful data collection framework** which has a number of advantages.

(i) The categorisations facilitate a **clearer understanding of the important factors** in the objectives of the management accounting function.

(ii) They provide management with an opportunity to **concentrate on the more important and more expensive quality issues.**

(1) It may be evident, once the measures have been established, that the cost of dealing with external audit queries is excessively high compared with the cost of reproducing reports for user departments, highlighting the

need for management to concentrate on reducing external failure cost. Without the analysis of quality cost into its various components, concentration on such problem areas may be difficult.

(2) If one or more quality cost areas are more critical than others, such as the provision of information for quotations, the categorisation will enable management to concentrate on these particular areas.

(iii) They may provide a **basis for benchmarking** the management accounting function against that of comparable organisations.

The categorisation of quality costs can therefore be usefully employed in developing measures within management accounting in a number of ways.

Performance measures suitable for assessing the management accounting service

Before performance measures to assess the management accounting service can be drawn up, it is important to **recognise that the users or customers of the management accounting service are other functions and departments within the organisation.** It is therefore from the perspective of such users that the performance measures must be established since their opinions of the quality of the service provided are of overriding concern considering the increasing popularity of outsourcing functions such as accounting and finance.

Once the users of the service have been established, the **objectives of the management accounting function must be defined,** which may involve discussions with the function's customers. The overall objective is the provision of a quality service but it will be possible to break down this objective into a number of sub-objectives.

(i) **The provision of good information.** This requires supplying information that is **relevant** to the needs of the users (which involves identifying the user, getting the purpose right and getting the volume right), that is **accurate** within their needs (in the sense of correct, although an approximate or average figure is often suitable), that **inspires their confidence** (so it should not be out-of-date, badly presented or taken from an unreliable source), that is **timely** (it must be in the right place by the right time) and that is **appropriately communicated** (since it will lose its value if it is not clearly communicated to the user in a suitable format and through a suitable medium).

(ii) **The provision of a value-for-money service.** User departments are likely to be charged in some way for the management accounting service and are therefore likely to require that the charge incurred is reflected in the level of service and the quality of information provided.

(iii) **The availability of informed personnel.** Users will require management accounting staff to be available to answer queries and resolve problems as and when required.

(iv) **Flexibility.** The management accounting function should be flexible in its response to user requests for information and reports.

Once the objectives have been defined, the **activities** that the function should carry out to achieve its objectives must be ascertained. The function must be sufficiently organised and staffed, for example, to ensure that reports are received on time and that queries can be answered promptly.

Appropriate measures can then be established on the basis of the objectives and activities identified. There should not be too many measures or too few, but just enough to provide relevant indicators, on a timely basis and in a readily understood form. The 'pyramid' approach should be considered, whereby successively more detailed information is provided for successively junior levels of staff.

Suitable specific performance measures might be as follows.

(i) **Relating to the provision of good information**

(1) Number of complaints from users about accuracy/timeliness and so on of reports and information

(2) Number of computer downtime hours in a period (which affects timeliness of report and information provision)

(ii) **Relating to value for money**

(1) Cost of similar service provide by specialist contractor

(2) Cost of service provide by function in similar organisation (via benchmarking)

(iii) **Relating to the availability of informed persons**

(1) Levels of overtime (excessive amounts indicate that the current demand for the service is too great for the function to cope with in the long term without obtaining extra human resources)

(2) Proportion of the time the staff mix and numbers are within required limits

(3) Proportion of telephone calls answered within, say, eight rings

(iv) **Relating to flexibility**

(1) Proportion of reports issued on time

(2) Number of ad-hoc reports/requests for information issued within pre-set time limit

(v) Given the continuing importance of the views of the function's customers, any ratings provided from user satisfaction surveys would provide extremely useful measures of performance.

47 TUTORIAL QUESTION: INTERNAL AUDIT AND INTERNAL CONTROLS

(a) The other means of obtaining internal control are as follows.

(i) **Segregation of duties**

This refers to the need to ensure that duties are divided so that no single person records and processes a complete transaction. Segregation of duties provides a method of **checking** for **errors** as well as **reducing** the **risk** of **fraud.**

(ii) **Physical**

These internal controls provide for the **custody** of **assets,** ensuring that procedures exist so that only **authorised personnel** have **access** to assets.

(iii) **Authorisation and approval**

All transactions should be **authorised** and **approved** by a designated responsible person with **specified authorisation limits.** For example a departmental head may be responsible for authorising revenue expenditure up to, say, £500 but any higher amounts of expenditure must be approved by a director. These controls ensure that no expenditure is incurred without approval and that responsibility for all expenditure can be traced.

(iv) **Supervision**

The completion and recording of all transactions must be carried out under the supervision of a responsible official. This ensures that all individuals are aware that their work will or may be **checked,** thus **reducing** the risk of **deliberate falsification.**

(v) **Organisation**

All organisations should have a structure of **defined responsibilities** and authorities with **delegated responsibility** and authority and lines of reporting clearly specified. This ensures that the established controls have a structured framework within which they can operate effectively.

(vi) **Arithmetical and accounting**

These internal controls provide the check that transactions have been **recorded** and **processed correctly**. These controls include checking the arithmetical accuracy of the records, the maintenance and checking of totals, reconciliations, control accounts and trial balances, and accounting for documents.'

(vii) **Personnel**

An organisation must have established procedures to ensure the provision of personnel, who are suitable in terms of qualifications, experience and temperament to be able to carry out their responsibilities competently and with integrity. Important controls include **training** and **recruitment**. Even the most effectively designed internal controls will fail if they are not operated by the right personnel.

(b) **Planning internal audits**

An internal audit department must plan its work carefully if it is to achieve the audit objectives efficiently and effectively. There are three main aims in audit planning:

(i) to **decide priorities** for audit work;

(ii) to **establish objectives** and **determine control measures** to ensure that audit objectives are achieved; and

(iii) to **ensure** that **audit resources** are **used efficiently, effectively** and **cost-effectively**.

Generally speaking the planning of an audit can be divided into three parts: strategic, tactical and operational.

(i) **Strategic planning of internal audits**. The strategic plan sets out audit objectives in broad terms, including the **areas** to be covered, the **frequency** of **coverage** and an estimate of **resource requirements.**

(ii) **Tactical planning** follows on from strategic planning. The tactical plan will include a **programme** of internal audits to be carried out, a detailed **definition** of the **objectives** of each audit and a detailed allocation of audit resources. The plan must include a **contingency allowance** for factors such as staff movements and unexpected requests from management for special investigations.

(iii) **Operational planning**. An operational audit plan should be drawn up for each individual audit, within the framework set by the strategic and tactical plans. It should show the **detailed audit objectives**, the **extent of coverage** and **procedures** to be used, the **target dates** for individual stages of the audit and the **names** of auditors responsible for the completion of the audit.

Recording audits

All internal audit work should be recorded on working papers which allow the **chief internal auditor** to **check** and confirm that the audit work has been properly performed. Preparing working papers encourages the auditor to adopt a **methodical approach** to the work undertaken and enables one auditor to take over from another if necessary.

Properly prepared working papers should be kept for reference purposes and should provide evidence of the **work done**, the **problems encountered** and the **conclusions** that have been drawn.

Quality control

An old **Auditing Practices Committee** guideline sets out further guidance on how audit work can be planned, controlled and recorded to a sufficient standard of quality. The guideline includes the following points.

(i) **Standardised procedures** should exist and should be applied for all audit work. They should be laid out in up to date **audit manuals** issued to all relevant staff.

(ii) **Ethical standards** of independence, objectivity, integrity and confidentiality should be adhered to through established procedures.

(iii) **Procedures for consultation** between audit staff must exist, including a **structured approach** to the **review** of audit files and working papers.

(iv) **Quality control measures should be monitored** to ensure their effectiveness and application. If any weaknesses are discovered then improvements should be made so that quality control is an ongoing matter.

Staffing

The internal audit department should possess or have access to all the necessary skills for performing its function.

Internal audit staff should be given **suitable training**, and all staff must be kept up to date with changes. Technical updating should be provided through courses, internal circulars and so on.

As mentioned in (a) all individuals must be **adequately supervised**. As well as monitoring the quality of work, effective supervision can be a way of providing on the job training for all personnel.

48 IA EFFECTIVENESS

Pass marks. Questions on internal audit will generally concentrate on the strategic and managerial implications of the function, and you must approach the question accordingly.

In part (a) you need to state that internal audit's independence must not suffer as a result of the function being audited. One way of ensuring this is the involvement of the audit committee; the corporate governance reports demonstrate that the audit committee and internal audit should be complementary functions.

In (b) a key element of the process is setting objectives.

The hints given in the question should have meant your answer to (c) was a discussion of the information needed to assess internal audit's performance on a VFM basis.

Examiner's comment. A good answer should have brought in knowledge of the use of VFM audit to assess services in the private sector; the way the *Cadbury Report* has increased the importance of internal audit; and the guidance given in the question in (a) to (c), particularly the emphasis on *effectiveness*.

REPORT

To: Chairman
From: Finance Director Date: XX.XX.XX
Subject: Effectiveness of the Internal Audit Department (IAD)

Internal audit is an **independent appraisal function** established by the management of an organisation for the **review** of the **internal control system** as a service to the organisation. It objectively examines, evaluates and reports on the adequacy of internal control as a contribution to the **proper, economic, efficient** and **effective use of resources.**

It is an internal control therefore and, like all internal controls, it should be assessed for effectiveness. This appears to be a suitable time for such an investigation.

(a) **Who should carry out the assessment?**

The IAD must **maintain** its **independence** from those parts of the organisation which it audits (ie most of the operations of the business). This independence must be maintained when the IAD is itself the subject of the audit for the sake of future IAD audits, and to obtain an objective result in this case. This criteria would exclude me as Finance Director. Other members of the board might be appropriate investigators, but the prime candidate would be a member of the **Audit Committee** (AC) as the IAD acts as almost an executive arm of the committee. A member of the AC with appropriate knowledge and experience would be required.

Alternatives to the AC which we might consider include the **IAD** of **another company,** which might be approached through contacts of our executive directors. Confidentiality might be an issue here; we would need to make sure that the other company was not a competitor etc.

Another option would be to use our own **external auditors**. If they were happy with our IAD, then future co-operation between the two sets of auditors might produce a saving in the external audit fee. However, if they were unhappy with the work of our IAD then the external auditors may decide that they need to perform extra audit work in future, and **fees might** then **rise**.

I do not feel it is appropriate for me to decide who should carry out the investigation of IAD: this is a decision which should be made by the board.

(b) **Detailed work**

Like any other audit, a management audit involves deciding the **audit objectives** (which managers to audit, what aspects of their work and so on), carrying out an investigation, gathering evidence and reporting the results.

The objectives are very important: they must be positive, to encourage co-operation in the IAD staff. The objectives will determine exactly what information is required, but at the least IAD files and reports will be accessed. This will require **explanation** and **comment** from members of the IAD. Samples will be taken of the IAD's work as it will not be possible to examine all of it.

Information, both written and oral, will also be **collected** from those **outside** the IAD, including the external auditors, the board members of the AC and the operational staff audited by the IAD. In the case of the latter, given the nature of the work, the weight of their evidence will have to be judged according to the level of criticism raised against them by the IAD in the past.

In all cases the information collected should be **properly recorded,** and the documents collected and created should be controlled. This is a sensitive audit, so working papers should remain confidential and kept secure at all times.

(c) **Information required**

The audit will seek to determine whether the IAD operates:

(i) **economically,** producing the appropriate quantity and quality of work at lowest cost;

(ii) **efficiently,** using minimum resources for the quality and quantity of service provided; and

(iii) **effectively,** achieving its set objectives.

Comparatives are important for VFM audits. However, it may be difficult to obtain any **industry averages.** Two possible sources are non-executive directors who can gain information on IADs in other companies; and bodies regulating auditing, for example the Institute of Internal Auditors. In addition, **information over time** needs to be collected, again for comparative purposes. Such data should be both quantitative and non-quantitative.

The detailed information to be collected should cover the following main areas.

(i) **General set up of the IAD**

This will involve investigating the **structure** of the IAD; what **work** the IAD has been asked to carry out (routine vs specials); **who requests** work to be done; **who receives IA reports.**

(ii) **Resources used by IAD**

The resources used by the IAD should be quantified: **staff, equipment** (computers etc), **training.** It should be relatively easy to compare such costs with industry data.

(iii) **Utilisation**

How well is the IAD **utilising** these **resources**? Is training undertaken in slack periods? Are IA staff sitting around the office too much?

(iv) **IA procedures**

The methods and procedures used by IAD to carry out investigations should be examined. Does the IAD use **standardised procedures** and **documentation**? Are **files up to date** and **well maintained**? Is **staff time recorded accurately** and **compared to budgets**? Are **audits completed in time and to budget**? Are **review procedures appropriate** and **effective**?

(v) **Report effectiveness**

The efforts of the IAD must be in vain if the reports do **not reach the appropriate decision-makers**. They in turn must **take action** based on the IAD reports. Assessment is also needed whether, as a result of IAD investigations, **costs** have been **reduced** (including external audit costs).

I hope that this report has provided a good starting point for an assessment of the IAD function and I suggest that you pass it to the Audit Committee with your comments.

Signed: Finance Director

49 OBJECTIVES OF INTERNAL AUDIT

> **Pass marks**. Although this question is located in the quality assurance section of the Kit, it requires consideration of issues raised in other areas of the syllabus, in particular performance measurement. Your answer needed to be structured clearly structured, relating aims to objectives and providing sufficient examples of performance measurement. You should have included a wide range of objectives, not just those relating to financial controls.
>
> **Examiner's comment**. The examiner emphasised that justification of the existence of internal audit was an important topic in this paper. Answers tended to be stronger on aims than objectives and performance measurement, and a number of answers focused too heavily on a single objective. Many answers also bore little relation to the question, and instead contained a general discussion of topics such as the balanced scorecard and the dimensions framework.

Aims and purposes of internal audit

The responsibilities of internal audit will be determined by management, ideally by an **audit committee** of non-executive directors, which will keep the function under regular review.

One aspect of internal audit's work is certainly to **review** and **report** on the **adequacy and effectiveness of an organisation's internal controls** The review of controls should cover accounting controls and non-financial controls, controls that ensure compliance with external laws and regulations and internal policies.

Internal audit's role should also **contribute** to **overall organisational effectiveness,** by, as the Institute Of Internal Auditors have commented, 'assisting members of the organisation in the effective discharge of their responsibilities...(and furnishing) them with analyses, appraisals, recommendations, counsel and information'. This aspect of internal audit's work will cover recommendations for improvements in the organisation's information systems or its utilisation of resources.

Objectives and performance measurement of internal audit

Accounting controls

The main objectives are to obtain evidence of whether the business has **appropriate controls** in place that are operating effectively, and to **recommend improvements in control** that may be required. Internal audit's work would cover reviewing the design of internal controls systems, detailed testing of controls and recommendation of improvements.

Specific performance measures would depend on the reports made by internal audit. A satisfactory report in a particular area could be measured against the **problems** that arise in that area. Thus for example a satisfactory report on controls over the security of stock could be measured against the level of stock loss.

If internal audit recommend improvements in an area, evaluating these recommendations is more difficult. Internal audit's recommendations may make no apparent difference to the problems occurring in a particular accounting area. However their work may act to **prevent more serious problems,** in which case an appropriate measure of success would be the **non-occurrence of fraud**. In addition internal audit's recommendations may not be implemented. This may be due to other failings in the organisation's system or **shortcomings** in the **reports** given by internal audit, something considered below.

Non-financial controls

Again the objectives will be checking whether **appropriate controls** are in place that are **operating effectively,** in areas such as responses to customers. However what is appropriate is likely to be determined by management. The audit committee may require that internal audit **concentrate** on **certain important controls** within an area rather than reviewing the whole range of controls. In particular auditors will wish to see that control systems have changed in accordance with **changes in important variables,** for example changes in the requirements of customers.

It is also likely that internal audit's role will be **more proactive** than for accounting controls; recommendations will be expected that mean that improvements are made in the matters reviewed.

Compliance with laws and regulations

The objectives here are similar to those on work on accounting controls except that internal audit is seeking to **prevent non-compliance** with relevant laws and regulations. These laws and regulations may also demand that certain **specific controls** must be **operating** effectively, and so internal audit must check those controls are working.

The performance would be whether **breaches** that were not identified by internal audit have **occurred,** and the consequences of those breaches; payments of fines or penalties or time spent dealing with communications with regulatory authorities.

Internal practices

The areas of internal practices that internal audit may seek to consider include policies for **compliance with codes of best practice** such as the corporate governance reports, but they also include **general business practices** such as planning, internal communication and staff problems.

Performance of internal audits will be judged by the activity being reviewed. Compliance with codes of best practice may be **reported** on by **external auditors** or **commented** on by **shareholders** or the **media,** and avoidance of adverse comments from these sources will be a measure of success. The results of review of staff policies can be measured by the rate of **staff turnover** or the number of staff grievances. Internal audit's comments on **planning** could be judged by the quality of plans produced, and improvements in adherence to those plans.

Improvements in information systems

Internal audit's recommendations in this area relate very strongly to the general aims described above, of making sure that management are furnished with the **information necessary** to do their job effectively.

Important measures are **management reaction** to recommendations made and whether the improvements **change management behaviour** (for example management modify plans because the information system identifies the probability of an overspend on budget). Recommendations for improvements in information systems should also lead to **improvements** in the **quality and timing of external reporting.**

Utilisation of resources

A major part of internal audit's activities may well be a review of **value for money,** the economic, efficient and effective use of resources.

Performance measures should focus on **recommendations** on **each of the elements** of value for money, whether costs have been reduced, better use made of available resources and the desired results achieved. Excessive emphasis by internal audit on cost control for example may mean that costs fall, but sales fall as well because of reduced levels of customer service.

Internal audit reports

The quality of internal audit reports has obvious relevance to all the other objectives, since it will influence the response to recommendations. Criteria that would be used to judge reports include the **speed of issue,** whether **presentation** is clear, whether **sufficient prominence** is given to the **most important points** in the report, and whether **recommendations** are **specific** and **practical.**

In addition internal audit's role will assume enhanced importance if, as well as issuing reports, internal audit is allowed to follow up its reports by **seeking and obtaining action** by operational departments on recommendations included in the reports. Over time there should be a **reduction** in the **number of reports,** as improvements are implemented and weaknesses are corrected.

50 INDEPENDENCE

> **Pass marks**. The practical aspects of *independence* are discussed here, and you should be able to describe the meaning of the term in that context. A good way to approach (a) is to think of the ways in which operational departments can have contact with or influence internal audit. (b) brings out the important links between internal audit and the audit committee.

(a) An internal auditor cannot have the same amount of independence as an external auditor. However, internal audit can be given various **powers and access** to senior managers which allow independent comment, in a free and professional manner, about the internal control of the business (or any matter under investigation).

In particular, the following points will ensure a satisfactory level of independence within the organisation.

(i) Internal auditors should **not act** in any **operational capacity,** particularly at managerial level. They should be concerned *only* with the functioning and management of the internal audit department.

(ii) The internal audit department should **not** be **controlled** by any **operational managers.** It should be **controlled directly** by the **board** of directors or **audit committee.**

(iii) **No area** of records, personnel or assets should be **closed** to the internal auditor. Any such restrictions would invalidate internal audit's full power of investigation.

(iv) **Recruitment, training** and other personnel matters within the internal audit department should be **dealt** with only by the **Chief Internal Auditor,** not by outside managers or the board.

(b) There are two structures in which the internal audit department may operate.

(i) **Reporting to the board**. Even though not a voting board member, the internal auditor will report directly to the full board. This is far superior to reporting directly to line management or to the finance director or managing director, as it does not allow an individual manager or director to suppress or neglect an internal audit report.

(ii) **Reporting to the Audit Committee**. This is the method recommended by the **Cadbury report** on corporate governance. The audit committee will consist mainly or entirely of non-executive directors, and thus internal audit will maintain the independence of his or her report.

This method is advantageous as it brings together people with great expertise in such control matters who have the **time** to **discuss** them without bias and outside any operating considerations. The committee will also be able to **advise internal audit** on procedures and further action and, because of its seniority, be able to persuade the board to **take action** on any matters raised by internal audit.

A further advantage of an audit committee is that it can act as a **forum** for **communication** between the various parties involved in financial control. The Cadbury report recommended that audit committees should be attended by the finance director, the head of internal audit and a representative of the external auditors.

(c) In external auditing it is considered to be a **compromise** of **independence** to accept presents, discounts, bonuses or commissions from audit clients. In many ways this will also apply to the chief internal auditor, as an 'officer' of the board.

Conversely, the chief internal auditor is an employee of the company, which pays a salary to him or her already. As part of the internal control function, helping to **keep down costs** and **increase profitability**, surely the chief internal auditor should have a reward for adding to the profit of the business.

The problem remains that, if the chief internal auditor receives a bonus based on results, he or she may be tempted to allow certain actions, practices or transactions which should be stopped, but which are increasing the profit of the business, and therefore the bonus.

51 CONTROLS IN NEW COMPANY

Pass marks. The report in (a) starts by stating the main transactions that the system will have to process. It then discusses the key areas of information required, assignment of responsibility and reporting mechanisms. However your answer to (a) should only briefly mention reporting mechanisms as these are dealt with in more detail in part (b).

Part (b) covers a very important theme for this part of the syllabus, how the board acts as an overall supervisory control on the rest of the business. This involves taking the decisions that follow from the board's responsibility for strategy (such as fixed asset purchases), and also reviewing the operations of the business using internal and external data.

Prizewinners' points. An answer focused on the points above would have been sufficient to pass. Extra credit would be given for discussion of the uncertainties involved in gathering information in (a), and the need for the system to develop as the company's activities develop in (b).

Examiner's comment. According to the examiner, this was the last question for many of the candidates who attempted it and they did not allow themselves sufficient time. Many did not exploit the scenario to make obvious points on the requirements. A common error in part (a) was failure to point out the need for the reporting of costs and revenues to be more frequent than quarterly. In (b) some candidates failed to answer one or other part of the question. Although knowledge of Cadbury recommendations helped in answering part (b), it would be inappropriate to apply all the Cadbury recommendations to a small new company.

REPORT

To: Potential investors
From: Management Consultant Date: XX.XX.XX
Subject: Controls in the new computer services company

(a) **Form and level of detail of budgetary control**

A useful starting point is to consider the likely revenues and costs that will have to be considered when designing the budgetary control system.

(i) **Revenues**

Income will be derived from two main sources: **existing** local government **work** and **new work** from neighbouring authorities or commercial customers.

The local government work could be **subdivided further,** either according to the nature of the work (one-off data processing tasks, long-term systems development etc) and/or according to the particular local government department (education, housing, etc).

The other work may also be subdivided according to its nature and/or type of customer. This will aid **analysis** of **profitability**.

(ii) **Costs**

Operational costs are likely fall into the broad categories listed below. More detailed sub-categories will be desirable in practice. Most costs will be fixed costs, although there will be sundry equipment, administrative and marketing expenses that are variable.

(1) Technical staff costs
(2) Equipment costs (depreciation, maintenance, etc)
(3) Administrative costs (mainly financial management)
(4) Marketing costs

(Development costs are considered later in this report, as is capital budgeting.)

The main areas of concern are as follows.

(i) **Forecasting** the **level of income** to be derived from **new work** (the level of existing local government should be easy to predict). Assessment of likely new work will include the likely duration of contracts to be carried out, and how new contracts will be priced and billed.

(ii) **Allocating** and **monitoring expenditure** for the **areas** that are **new** to the company, particularly financial administration, working capital management and marketing. Particularly close attention should be paid to the 'set-up' costs of new systems in these areas.

In the light of the above a system for budgetary control along the following lines may be proposed.

(i) A recording system capable of **analysing costs** and **revenues** in the various ways suggested above. (This may seem self-evident but it has not been the norm in public sector bodies in the past.)

(ii) Clear **assignment** of **responsibility** for **controllable costs** and **revenues** to **individual managers,** using a **cost** or **profit centre system**. Again this may seem self-evident, but detailed apportionment of what have previously been regarded as lump-sum allocations has been a serious problem for public sector and former public sector bodies.

(iii) **Operational reports** at least **weekly** in the initial stages to catch bugs in the system and spot areas for improvement. Reports may be less regular once the system is up and running, especially for work that the company is already used to doing. Some of the information collected can be of a non-financial nature, for example staff and computer time for frequently performed tasks.

(iv) **Monthly reports** for **submission** to **senior management**, summarising the operational data. This area is addressed in more detail in the second part of this report.

(b) **Structure and formal controls at Board level**

Personnel

The Board is likely to consist of a Managing Director (the current Director of Computing), a Technical Director, a Finance Director and a Marketing Director. **Non-executive directors** should also be appointed. One should represent the interests of investors and may be appointed by the venture capital company involved; a second could bring in commercial sector experience and a third might have local government knowledge.

Scrutiny of budget reports

One of the key controls operated at board level will be the **monthly budget report**. Particular attention will need to be paid to the areas that are new to the proposed company's experience, most especially **control of finance** and **cash flow**. Given the Board's lack of commercial experience an **internal auditor** should be appointed to report directly to the board and provide reassurance that unfamiliar areas are being properly managed from day to day. Our firm would be pleased to undertake this role.

External monitoring

Presumably in the medium term the company will wish to reduce its reliance on existing local government work, although it will wish to retain its original main customer. **External monitoring** of **potential markets, competitors**' **activities** and of the **political environment** will therefore be crucial. This can be in the form of SWOT analysis or similar.

Analytical measures

Likewise **measurement** of **current performance** in terms of **market share,** new **business won** and so on will help to guide the overall strategy. In any case, local authorities are likely to set their own performance criteria. Board level checks therefore need to be in place to ensure that the required standards are being maintained.

Focus of board

The Board's responsibility is the **strategy** of the company rather than its day-to-day management and this will include the long-term investment strategy. The Board should focus on **recognising future needs** and ensuring that they can be met at the appropriate time.

The Board's focus on strategy should also mean that certain matters are **reserved** for **decision** by the **full Board.** Although the company is not a listed company, they could usefully follow the Cadbury recommendations, and reserve the following decisions for full approval.

(i) Acquisition and disposal of major assets.

(ii) Investments, capital projects, authority levels, treasury policies and risk management policies.

Future developments

If the company is likely to be taking on new work such as systems development, there should be **formal controls** in this area, since this type of work tends to be long-term. It is also difficult to judge, and so control, what progress has been made and how much progress should have been made. **Separate reports** in addition to the main monthly package may be called for, here.

Signed: Management Accountant

52 PURCHASING AND ENTERTAINMENT

Pass marks. The key point in part (a) was a recognition of the risk of collusion between purchasing staff and suppliers. The answer should have concentrated on controls which minimised this risk, particularly authorisation and monitoring.

In part (b), we have looked at the ways in which the code can be seen as acceptable and the ways in which it can be seen as unacceptable and have then suggested ways in which it could be improved.

Other points. You may have simply concentrated on the factors within the code that required amendment and have redrafted it, or alternatively you may have defined and justified the code as it stands. Any reasonable approach will be rewarded.

Examiner's comment. Many candidates spent too much time on part (a) and little if any time on part (b), which was worth the same number of marks. The examiner noted that part (b) was significantly harder than part (a). Common errors included repeating the code in the question without adding any substantial commentary and commenting that it was a contentious subject, without either agreeing with the existing approach or proposing an alternative.

(a) The following features of the system should help minimise the risk of fraud.

(i) **Risk assessment**

Examples of purchase fraud include **rigged tendering, goods being supplied** for **private purposes** and **fraudulent transactions** with **connected**

companies. In setting up a control system therefore, management should be aware of what kinds of fraud the business may be at risk of experiencing.

One possible danger is **collusion** between the person authorising purchases and suppliers. Once purchases have been authorised, there may be nothing further that can be done to prevent fraud. The important controls therefore are normally those which are aimed at identifying unusual suppliers or circumstances.

(ii) **Monitoring of suppliers**

The risk of collusion between suppliers and employees can be minimised in a number of ways.

(1) The person using the goods should only be able to choose suppliers from an **approved list.**

(2) The use of new suppliers should be **authorised** by **someone other** than the person using the goods. The person authorising new suppliers should be particularly wary of any of the following:

- abnormal terms;
- suppliers providing goods which they would not normally supply;
- suppliers which appear small compared with the proposed volume of purchases.

(3) In addition these should be **regular monitoring** by management of arrangements with suppliers. Warning signs should be investigated, such as suppliers handled directly by senior staff, or suppliers handled outside the normal control systems.

(iii) **Controls in the payment cycle**

(1) **Segregation of duties**

Segregation of duties can reduce certain risks. **Segregating** the **cheque-signing role** from the **payment authorisation** role can reduce the risk that payments are made out to certain types of bogus supplier, for example those with abbreviated names. Part of the process of reviewing suppliers can be carried out at the payment stage, by checking that **individual** or **total payments** do **not appear excessive**.

(2) **Documentation**

Requirements for **full documentation** should be linked to segregation of duties. Full documentation would include **purchase requisitions, purchase orders** and **purchase invoices**. These can help prevent purchases for private use.

Documentation of returns is also important; **credit notes** should always be obtained from suppliers when goods are returned in order to prevent stock losses through bogus returns.

(iv) **Contract management**

There are a number of different types of contract fraud including fixing the contract tendering process and undue payments in advance. Ways of preventing contract fraud include the following.

(1) An open **competitive tendering** process.

(2) Interim payments being made on **certification** from **independent valuers.**

(3) Any **changes to terms** being **authorised independently** of the person who deals with the contractors on a day to day basis.

(v) **Organisation and staff controls**

(1) **Personnel**

References should be obtained for all new staff, and details retained of previous employers so that possible collusion can be checked.

(2) **Ethics**

A **business code of ethics** can remind staff of what constitutes unreasonable inducements.

(vi) **Internal audit**

Internal audit can play a role in a number of the above checks, particularly the following.

(1) **Detailed checks** of documentation.
(2) **Scrutiny** of suppliers and payments for suspicious circumstances.

(b) As with many codes of conduct adopted in practice, there are both acceptable and unacceptable aspects to the code in question.

Aspects of the code which are acceptable

(i) The organisation has adopted a code of conduct which attempts to **conform** with **customary business practices**. It wishes to behave in a manner consistent with that of others in the market.

(ii) The code appears to imply that employees can take **slight risks** and go beyond behaviour that might be construed as strictly correct in order to secure sales. It would be logical and reasonable to do this in order to gain a sales advantage.

(iii) The conduct of the members of the staff working in the **purchasing function** is **controllable** by the organisation and so the organisation can determine the code of conduct which should apply. The code of conduct covering the **selling operation** has to meet the **expectations** of the **market** and **customers,** however. The organisation has **no control** over its **potential customers,** who can decide whether or not they should accept any gifts, favours or entertainment offered. That part of the code of conduct relating to the purchasing activity is therefore necessarily stricter and more stringent than the part relating to the sales activity.

(iv) Any **gifts,** favours and entertainment **provided** by a **supplier benefits** an **employee** whereas those provided for **customers benefit** the **customer** rather than the employee (unless the entertainment is lavish). There are therefore stricter controls over purchasing staff than sales staff.

Aspects of the code which are unacceptable

(i) The code **fails to provide sufficient guidance**. For example, it does not specify the nature of customary business practices, common courtesies and so on. Employees have no idea about whether they can offer a potential customer a glass of wine, a bottle of wine or a case of wine.

(ii) The code gives **no information** about the **repercussions** for employees for contravening the code. There is therefore no indication of the seriousness with which the organisation views breaches of the code.

(iii) The penultimate sentence about 'favours or entertainment, appropriate in our sales programmes' implies a **double standard** and may encourage sales personnel to adopt a position which could damage the good name of the organisation.

(iv) The unclear nature of the code relating to sales means that, because **behaviour is not actually illegal**, it may be **adopted** because it increases the organisation's short-term profits (despite the fact that it might have longer-term repercussions).

(v) If **performance measures** are based on **short-term profit, employees** may feel **pressurised** into adopting unethical or even illegal behaviour.

Suggested amendments to the code of conduct

Given the above comments there are various amendments which could be made to the code of conduct to increase its acceptability.

(i) **Ambiguous terms** should be **clarified**.

(ii) **Penalties** for contravening the code could be **included**.

(iii) It could be drastically **simplified** and the entire section on business courtesies deleted since the information provided in the remaining section provides an adequate and concise code of conduct.

(iv) The **code relating** to the conduct of employees working in the **sales** function could be **rewritten** with the intention of making it as **strict** and **clear** as that covering the purchasing function employees (no entertainment, no gifts and so on). There are commercial problems associated with such an approach, however; the market and customers may expect a more liberal attitude.

Such changes would produce an **unambiguous, clear** and **concise code of conduct** which will **protect** the **integrity** of the organisation and allow **employees** to be **confident** that their efforts for the organisation will remain within acceptable limits.

53 SEGREGATION OF DUTIES

Pass marks. A temptation that must be resisted is to write too much on part (a) at the expense of the other parts. In (a) you must understand why segregation of duties is an important organisational control. Parts (b) and (c) require discussion of alternative means of achieving control when management autonomy means a lack of segregation of duties. Review of performance indicators (outputs) is particularly important in both cases; other important controls are organisation controls and internal audit.

Examiner's comment. Part (a) required a statement of why segregation of duties was important and the consequences of lack of segregation. A common error in part (b) was to suggest the imposition of very tight controls from head office; branch managers must have some autonomy if they are to manage properly. Various approaches were possible to part (c); good answers concentrated on the balancing of empowerment and control. The reduction in bureaucracy should have meant that the remaining controls were essential, not merely desirable.

(a) **Definition**

The Auditing Practice Committee's guideline on internal controls defined segregation of duties as 'the separation of those responsibilities or duties which would, if combined, enable one individual to **process a complete transaction**'.

Importance

The main purposes of segregation of duties are as follows.

(i) It allows **independent checking** of one person by another, thus reducing the risk of intentional discrepancies and unintentional errors.

(ii) By increasing the number of people in the transaction process, it **reduces** the **risk of collusion**.

(iii) Effective segregation means that **responsibilities are established clearly**.

Role of internal audit

Internal audit can ensure segregation is operating properly by means of the following checks.

(i) **System reviews**. These should ensure in particular that the **functions** of authorisation, execution and recording of transactions, and safeguarding of assets are **kept separate**.

(ii) **Detailed checks**. Internal audit should ensure segregation is operating as laid down, and in particular **authorisation controls** are adequate and are fully operational.

(iii) **Follow-up of other weaknesses**. Certain other failings in internal controls may imply lack of segregation of duties. Examples include **lack of documentation** of transactions or decisions and **poor controls** over the **custody** of cash and cheques.

(b) Head office can compensate for the lack of segregation of duties by use of the following controls.

(i) The branch manager should, when recruited, have been subject to a **full reference check**.

(ii) Head office should ensure that the branch manager exercises appropriate control over **day-to-day transactions**. He should for example sign all cheques for significant amounts.

(iii) **Certain decisions**, for example fixed asset or other large purchases, should be **authorised** by **head office** as well as by the branch manager.

(iv) Head office should receive **regular returns** from the branch manager and should **investigate unusual sales patterns**, and **shortages** of cash or stock. The branch's performance should be compared with the performance of other branches.

(v) **Internal audit** should visit the branch regularly. **Surprise visits** can serve as a **check on stock or cash levels**.

(vi) **Expected visits** should be used as a check that the **authorisation procedures** laid down by the company are being followed. In addition internal audit may substantively test certain transactions, particularly large or unusual payments.

(c) The company's commitment to a flatter, less bureaucratic structure means that certain controls will no longer be operating. Responsibilities will not be laid down in detail, and junior managers will not be subject to detailed supervision from the company's head office.

What the company must do to maintain control is as follows:

(i) concentrate on effectively **implementing controls** that can work in a more **informal structure**;

(ii) ensure **goal congruence** so that junior managers have a personal interest in achieving the company's objectives.

Organisation controls

(i) Although the company can no longer rely on a hierarchical structure, it can still issue a **mission statement** setting out objectives and business ethics.

(ii) There will still be **some limits** to managers' authority, for example annual budget limits.

Personnel controls

(i) Personnel controls will be of increased importance. These should include controls not just at the **recruitment** stage but also at the **key promotion stages.**

(ii) **Training** will be important as a means of developing management skills and another means of communicating the aims of the company.

Management controls

(i) Review of management performance should be achieved by **financial and non-financial indicators.**

(ii) **Management audits** either by other managers or internal audit will be a useful quality control check.

(iii) Certain traditional internal audit checks, such as checks on **custody of assets** and that **separate authorisation** is obtained on the (rare) occasions it is required, will still be used.

Reward

As well as controls, the reward system should encourage the **achievement of objectives** in accordance with the aims of the organisation. A range of measures may be required, including financial targets and total quality management.

54 MANAGEMENT CONTROL FRAMEWORK

Pass marks. Corporate governance is of relevance to (a), but the answer also requires an appreciation of how the board should operate. In (b) our answer was based on a long-term supply contract.

Other points. An answer based around the treasury function should have concentrated on setting limits on investments and establishing segregation of duties. There should also be a proper system of risk management in place with particular emphasis given to management of exchange exposure. The board should also review the operation of the function on a regular basis.

An answer dealing with long-term purchase contracts should have dealt with the procedures for entering into contracts and limiting risks should the supplier default. Service contracts should also be monitored on a regular basis and a summary of the monitoring process given to the board.

Examiner's comment. A number of candidates in (a) failed to follow the rubric of the question which required answers to follow the control cycle model described, discuss board level action and comment on internal control. A number of candidates merely wrote a "standard" essay. Others failed to relate the framework to anything specific. Answers to (b) often explained the problems in great detail but failed to provide solutions. The examiner emphasised that reading the financial press could have been of great assistance when answering part (b).

(a) (i) **Defining the objectives**

The directors are responsible for setting the **overall objectives** of the business. These include the **organisation's commitment** to **internal controls** and related matters such as **business ethics**. The board also should be aware that other decisions they take will have a significant impact on controls. If for example one of the objectives is to give greater autonomy to remote operating units, this will mean that central controls will decrease but **overall supervision controls** such as review of budgets and variances will become more important.

The **board** should **review** the **objectives** of the control system on a regular basis to see if they still accord with the other business objectives, and also other developments within the business for example greater computerisation.

The directors should also ensure that the **control objectives** and procedures are **communicated clearly** to **employees**. The directors should also consider **enforcement mechanisms**, for example discipline mechanisms and appraisals.

(ii) **Planning activity**

The board should consider what **organisational structure** will achieve the defined objectives. This means **consideration** of the **appropriate levels** of **delegation** and also **segregation of duties**, which is a key accounting control. The board should consider how **responsibility** is to be **exercised**. This will mean **defining responsibilities** for **setting budgets** and **reporting performance** against budgets. The board should also consider how to **balance accountability** with **autonomy**, that is how much scope to allow staff to take risks that are considered acceptable.

(iii) **Organising resources and directing performance**

The directors should consider not just the **direct costs** of internal control (in terms of staff resources required) but also whether **controls** may **inhibit enterprise** necessary for the business's expansion.

In order to make this assessment, the board will have to consider the **business risks** the organisation faces. This will involve identification of the **resources** that may be **vulnerable** and the potential for liabilities. There should be assessment not just of existing risks but of **potential risks** including the likelihood of these risks crystallising. **High risk** to **important resources** for example cash will have to mean significant controls in that area. **Appropriate controls** must always be maintained over **areas** that are **fundamental** to the **organisation's ability to continue**, for example compliance with a statutory licence.

However the **directors** will also need to decide which **risks** can be **tolerated**, and whether **resources** would be **best used** in for example obtaining insurance rather than implementing a system of low-level controls.

(iv) **Monitoring results**

In order for monitoring to be effective, comparisons must be made of actual performance against targets. Such comparisons should not only be made by the board but by **management** at all levels of the organisation. The board must determine the appropriate level of **management review** at each level.

For the board, this is likely to mean taking an **overview** of the most **important areas** of the business. Some of the comparisons will be **financial**; a review of the **results** and **assets** held of the organisation as a whole and of its most significant operating units. It also means monitoring **major expenditure** and **investment projects**.

Certain **non-financial criteria** should also be reviewed by the board on a regular basis. What is reviewed will depend on the company, but possible areas might include extent of **staff training** or progress towards **environmental objectives.**

(v) **Regulation and review**

An **audit committee** is important in regulation and review. The audit committee should be responsible for **liaison** with **external auditors** and for discussing serious problems that the external auditors have found. The committee should also be responsible for setting out the scope of the **internal audit function** and monitoring its work. The committee should also have an **ongoing** role in **monitoring** internal control systems.

(b) Application of the management control framework to long-term supply contracts

(i) **Defining the objectives**

Long-term supply contracts can guarantee significant income. However they are likely to demand **considerable resources** and the organisation may be subject to **significant penalties** should it fail to provide a service. Hence the board needs to consider whether it will have **sufficient resources** at all times to provide the service required. The board should assess the **risks** to the resources it proposes to devote to the contract, would, for example, the departure of a handful of key staff undermine the organisation's ability to complete the contract.

The board should also analyse the **wider strategic implications** of dependence upon a few contracts. The consequences of the customer defaulting on payment could be significant. The **impact** on **existing customers** should be considered; would **performance** on **short-term contracts suffer** as a result of priority being given to large long-term contracts.

(ii) **Planning activity**

The board should consider how **tendering** for long-term contracts is to be **co-ordinated.** Partly this will be a question of ensuring know-how and resources are pooled in order to maximise chances of obtaining contracts. There is also the issue of **resource control,** whether if the business wins all the contracts sought, it will have sufficient resources to fulfil them.

Board approval should be obtained for tendering for **significant contracts**. These will be contracts above a certain level of fee, contracts with onerous terms, or where there are doubts about the financial stability of the customer. (the board should ensure there are procedures in place for investigation of financial stability).

(iii) **Organising resources and directing performance**

The board should ensure that a proper system of planning is implemented so that the **performance targets specified** in the contract can be met, and **resource usage** is **planned** a long time in advance. This should enable management below the board to identify the possibility of bottlenecks or shortage of resources. These should be reported to the board so that the board can authorise appropriate action, for example recruitment of sub-contractors.

(iv) **Monitoring results**

The board should ensure that staff carrying out the contract have **clear channels** of **communication** with management so that management remain informed and can be contacted to discuss problems. The **board** should also be

informed if there is evidence of **serious customer dissatisfaction** which may jeopardise the contract or mean that the organisation may incur penalties.

The **board** should also be **informed** if the customer is jeopardising the contract by **failing to make prescribed payments** or by failing to fulfil other conditions in the contract.

(v) **Regulation and review**

There should be a system of **regular internal reviews** during the course of the contract of the quality of work on the contract and a summary of results should be given to the board.

The board should also implement a **system** for **ascertaining customer opinion** of performance. This should certainly happen at the end of every contract. The board should be informed of adverse findings, particularly on contracts which might have been, but have not been renewed. A system of obtaining customer reaction during the course of the contract would also be advantageous.

55 NEW SUBSIDIARY

Pass marks. Our answer to (a) focuses on the specific risks and is used as the basis for the initial audit in part (b). You should remember in part (b) that an initial audit should focus on the most serious potential problems. The results can be used as a basis for directing audit work in future years.

Other points. You could have approached (a) by explaining audit planning and risk analysis; you could assess the risks and show how they could be avoided, decreased or bore.

Examiner's comment. Common faults in (a) were lack of depth and failing to make obvious points. In (b) many answers were too vague and showed a lack of understanding of the aims of the initial audit which should have been to concentrate on systems. Many candidates failed to realise the limits of an initial audit.

Generally many answers were disappointing, some answers displaying little more than rote learning. The question demanded case analysis skills and practical recommendations, as well as knowledge of the objectives of internal audit. 'Considerably more work is required on this part of the syllabus by most candidates, since it cannot be assumed that audit questions will only appear in the optional part of the paper.'

(a) The potential audit problems can be identified by using a **risk-based approach** which concentrates on certain features that the subsidiary has.

(i) The **features** of the **market** the subsidiary operates in must be identified since it differs from the retail market in which the rest of the group operates. Although the subsidiary appears to be doing well, the **volatility** of the market should be assessed (would the subsidiary be seriously damaged by a recession in certain sections of the building trade for example?).

(ii) An assessment of the **effectiveness** of **management** will be required. Key issues in this assessment are likely to be:

(1) **The effectiveness of the subsidiary's senior management team.** The fact that management team's remuneration will depend on results may mean there are **pressures** to **overstate profit**. The lack of detailed controls at head office means the importance of management supervision is enhanced.

(2) **Regional warehouse management.** The most significant issues will be whether monitoring of regional managers appears to mean **potential**

signs of fraud can be **identified** quickly, and whether the controls exercised by regional management over their staff are likely to be effective.

(iii) Which **balance sheet areas** are likely to be particularly **prone** to a risk of **material error** should be ascertained by a combination of **analytical review** and use of **knowledge** about the business already possessed. Areas that are likely to be material and important for most or all of the business are as follows.

(1) **Stock.** Details of **stock security** and **recording** procedures will be needed, and also **valuation** since the specialist nature of stock may mean it is difficult to value.

(2) **Credit control.** The generous terms may mean it is not easy to identify bad debts, and hence **credit limit approval** and **payment procedures** (including follow-up) of overdue payments should be checked. In particular the consequences of the **largest customers defaulting** should be carefully considered.

(3) **Purchases. Procedures for choosing** suppliers should be confirmed, since although the terms the warehouses are obtaining appear to be good, the prices paid may not be the best available and there is certainly the possibility of collusion between the warehouse managers and suppliers. The warehouses operating abroad may mean there is an element of **exchange risk.**

(iv) The new subsidiary may pose problems of **audit management** and I would need to identify these. The **independence** of the **regional warehouses** plus the doubts mentioned above about the subsidiary's management may mean it is desirable to **visit a significant proportion** of the warehouses fairly soon after the subsidiary is acquired. However the resources available to internal audit may mean this is difficult to arrange.

Audit programmes will also have to be **re-designed** to reflect the fact that the subsidiary is not selling to retail customers, and also to reflect major differences in the control environment and control procedures between the subsidiary and the rest of the group.

(b) **Aims of initial audit**

These will be :

(i) to **assess** the strength of the subsidiary's **control environment;**

(ii) to **assess** the **functioning** of **internal controls** and in particular whether assets are properly safeguarded.

Both of these will obviously be influenced by the factors identified in (a).

Assessment of control environment

The most important elements of this assessment will be as follows.

(i) **Assessment of head office management.** Assessment would be needed of how head office management **set** the **tone** of the subsidiary as regards performance standards and commitment to ethical behaviour.

(ii) **Monitoring of warehouses.** Because the subsidiary does not exercise detailed controls at head office level, the procedures for **monitoring** the **performance** of warehouses would need to be examined. This will involve an assessment of the **management information systems** including how **detailed** the information provided is, how **regularly** it is provided, and what **action** is **taken if unusual items** are found.

(iii) **Monitoring of warehouse managers**. This will obviously be connected to monitoring of warehouses, but the effectiveness of certain specific controls should be checked because of the considerable autonomy warehouse managers possess. These include **recruitment** and **training procedures**, how the **performance** of warehouse managers is **assessed** (in particular the use of budgets) and procedures for appraising warehouse managers.

(iv) **Effectiveness of organisational structure**. Although on first glance the organisational structure appears to be uncomplicated (most authority devolved), **certain minimum checks** should be built into the system. These should include clear instructions about the **information** to be **communicated** to head office and which **decisions are reserved** for head office management (for example major fixed asset expenditure). The **communication** of these controls should be checked. Consideration will also be needed of whether **too many responsibilities** are **devolved** upon regional warehouse managers with the result that certain controls which they should be operating fall into abeyance.

Testing of controls

The initial audit should concentrate on the most significant controls which are likely to be as follows.

(i) **Segregation of duties**. This will be a very significant control as regards **safeguarding of assets**, because proper segregation **reduces** the risk of **collusion**. It will also be an important accounting control **reducing** the risk of **unintentional error** since more staff will be involved in recording the transaction. Segregation of duties is particularly important in the areas of stock, debtors and sales, purchasing, and between all these functions and accounting.

(ii) **Authorisation**. As considerable authority is given to the regional/warehouse managers, the initial audit should check that **transactions** are being **authorised** and that the managers' overall responsibilities are being exercised effectively.

(iii) **Asset protection**. The most important areas as indicated in (a) will most likely be controls over the **custody** of **stock**, the **authorisation** of **credit terms** and pursuit of **overdue debts**, and **purchasing policies**.

(iv) **Accounting systems**. Internal audit will have to record and assess whether the accounting systems **record** transactions **completely** and **accurately**.

A final aim of the initial audit will be to use the findings as the basis for **strategic audit planning** of the subsidiary in **future years**. Regional warehouses may continue to enjoy the degree of autonomy that they do (the subsidiary after all does appear profitable). However this may mean that internal audit itself is an important control, and this will clearly impact on the extent of future audits.

56 CODES OF CONDUCT

Pass marks. The *Cadbury Report* has emphasised the importance of both internal audit and the audit committee. As important is the relationship between the two: IA acts almost as an 'executive arm' of the audit committee. In (b) the problems with auditing compliance with the code mean that the board must consider other steps.

(a) An audit committee normally consists of the **non-executive directors** of the company, though there is no reason why other senior personnel should not also be involved.

The **advantages** of setting up an audit committee are as follows.

(i) The existence of an audit committee should make **executive directors** more **aware** of their **responsibilities**.

(ii) The audit committee should normally consist of **non-executive directors,** drawn from outside the company. They can apply their **experience** of other companies in recommending how problems such as failures of communication can be overcome.

(iii) The audit committee can act as a **deterrent** to the commission of **illegal acts** by **executive directors,** and may discourage directors from behaving in ways which could be **prejudicial** to **shareholders' interests.**

(iv) The audit committee can act as a forum for **liaison** with the **external** and **internal auditors.** The auditors will have an opportunity to express any concerns or problems they might have, such as inability to obtain information or lack of confidence in executive management.

(v) The audit committee can act as a convenient forum for **reviewing financial documents** such as the year-end accounts or interim statements.

(vi) The audit committee can use their collective experience to **review objectively** the **operation** of **internal control** from a perspective outside any operating considerations.

There are however a number of **disadvantages** to the establishment of an audit committee.

(i) Since the findings of audit committees are rarely made public, it is not always clear **what they do or how effective** they have been in doing it.

(ii) The audit committee's approach may prove somewhat **pedestrian**, resolving little of consequence but acting as a **drag** on the drive and entrepreneurial flair of the company's senior executives.

(iii) Unless the requirement for such a body were made compulsory, as in the US, most likely those **firms** most in **need of** an audit committee would nevertheless **choose not** to have one. (Note that the Cadbury report now requires listed companies to have an audit committee.)

In this case, the audit committee could help in the following ways.

(i) **Prevention** and **detection** are the two major functions of both the internal audit function and the audit committee. The committee would consist of people who are senior enough to appreciate the delicacy of the position of defence companies in both security and political terms and therefore would have foreseen problems such as this.

Prevention could have been achieved by a **positive review** of the company's operations. **Detection** could have been achieved by providing a **confidential listening post** for suppliers, customers and members of the public, but most particularly for employees. These roles would be carried out in tandem with the internal audit function.

(ii) After discovery of this kind of problem the committee has a role as **'independent' investigator**. The resources at the audit committee's disposal will be both internal and external audit. The investigation will try to discover **how** such **sales** came to be **made,** on what was obviously a fairly regular basis, **who knew** about it and whether anyone on the board knew. The committee can also investigate how the **internal control** and **reporting function failed** to alert the board to the problem.

(iii) The audit committee should also be in a position to help the company decide **what to do** about the situation. The sensitive nature of this area means that the company's public image may be badly affected and contracts, particularly with the government, may be threatened. In such a politically sensitive arena, the committee's expertise should be invaluable.

(b) **Involvement of internal audit**

Whether the internal audit department is directly involved in ensuring compliance with the code depends to a great extent on the department's **terms of reference**. Normally, the central function of internal audit is to test the system of internal control. Ideally, the department should have been involved in **designing** the code and then **monitoring compliance** with the code. This seems unlikely to have happened here.

It is more likely that internal audit will **react** to **reported breaches** of the code, or breaches uncovered by normal internal audit work on the control system. At worst, internal audit may have no reference to the code, although it is possible that the department is involved in occasional studies.

The ideal type of involvement of internal audit may be developed in future, but there are problems, particularly where the code is a very vague 'be good' document. **Internal audit** will need more **specific rules** in the code so that compliance can be judged more objectively.

Internal audit may also need to **abandon** the **usual standards** of **documentation** and **proof** as breaches of the code are unlikely to be very public or documented at all.

The department is being asked to behave like a private detective, rather than an internal audit department.

Other steps

Given the difficulty of implementing an ethical culture, a good code of conduct and of monitoring the situation, the following should be carried out.

(i) **Review** the **existing code** and develop it as necessary to be as specific and comprehensive as possible.

(ii) **Check** that the **code** is **disseminated** throughout the whole company, from board level downwards.

(iii) **Implement** a **confidential reporting system** for staff, using the audit committee, internal audit department and possibly other more informal routes.

(iv) **Ensure staff** are **trained** in ethical matters and that ethics are included as a component in all managerial decision-making, including budgeting and reporting.

(v) **Introduce** a **formal punishment and reward structure**. Staff should know that they will be punished for ethical breaches, but also that there is a positive reward for being ethical and reporting any breaches of the code.

The most important aspects are the attitudes of the main board and the audit committee and how these are communicated to the rest of the company. The code must have the full authority of the board and the committee behind it.

57 FRAUD DETECTION

Pass marks. Relevance to the scenario is a must. This is a hotel company – which has its own implications for inherent risk – which actually has been defrauded. Address this and begin to suggest actions that will prevent a recurrence of this fraud and you are off to a good start. Mention of the Turnbull report and the requirement for directors to review the company's risk management systems would have been helpful.

Examiner's comment. In (a) candidates should have mentioned the internal controls necessary to prevent fraud, but they should also have discussed how risk analysis would affect the internal controls set up and the work of internal audit. There should have been some discussion of cost-benefit issues, weighing the costs of fraud, against the costs of additional controls. Sadly many candidates discussed issues that were not relevant to the question such as rote-leant lists of internal controls, and whether an organisation should always prosecute in cases of suspected fraud.

In (b) answers should have stated that the problem needed to be addressed, but that it should be handled sensitively bearing in mind the past situation. Answers tended to lack a discussion of how practices could be changed; dismissal of all offenders was the panacea some candidates suggested for all problems.

(a) REPORT

To: Chairman
From: Chief Internal Auditor Date: XX.XX.XX
Subject: Fraud Detection and Internal Audit

This report is written in response to concerns expressed about the failure of the Internal Audit Department (IAD), amongst others, to detect the fraud recently perpetrated by one of our hotel managers.

Actions to detect fraud

An immediate first step must be to undertake a full investigation of the recently uncovered fraud. The nature of the fraud should be determined and from that the **weaknesses** in the **internal control system** that permitted this fraud to be perpetrated, and continue undetected, must be **identified.**

Having identified and corrected weaknesses in internal control, the next stage will be to identify whether further controls should be introduced and the work done by internal audit should change. We need to undertake a **risk analysis** as the costs of extra controls could outweigh the benefits in areas where the risk of fraud is low, or any frauds could only be for minimal amounts. The risk analysis is likely to focus on areas such as assets that are liable to pilfering, for example bar stocks, kitchen stocks, room televisions, also cash of course.

Having undertaken the risk analysis, **appropriate internal controls** must be **designed** and **implemented** to prevent a recurrence of this fraud at this hotel and any other serious frauds. **IAD's role** in fraud detection is likely to have three aspects.

(i) **Visiting hotels regularly** and **checking on areas** that are particularly **susceptible to fraud.** IAD must maintain a high presence at hotels. The threat of discovery arising from IAD performing regular stock checks, fixed asset inspections, till roll and banking verifications will create an environment where fraud will be much less likely. It is recommended that each hotel is visited at least twice a year, without prior warning, and these key checks performed.

(ii) **All aspects** of every hotel's operations should be **tested in detail** every two to three years.

(iii) A detailed **analytical review** of each hotel must be conducted regularly to see whether profit margins, bar sales, occupancy levels and other high-risk areas are in line with expectations or whether there is an indication of unusual activity. At the first sign of such activity IAD staff should be sent to that hotel for an investigation to be conducted.

Desirability of emphasising fraud detection.

There are clear reasons for IAD emphasising fraud detection. Not least is the discovery of this recent fraud, which highlights the fact that **controls** have, in the past, not **worked adequately**, and similar frauds may have occurred. **Shareholders** will be concerned to know what steps we have taken to prevent future frauds. One could argue that there would be even greater damage to senior management's credibility should subsequent frauds be uncovered.

Because of these concerns we need to emphasise to all levels of management their responsibilities for **proper stewardship** of the organisation's assets. However this needs to be promoted sensitively. Manager co-operation is more likely to occur if an amnesty is granted for previous practices that are questionable, but not clearly fraudulent.

Whilst internal audit has an important role to play in fighting against fraud, **other** aspects of its role need to be emphasised. There is a danger that staff co-operation with IAD may be jeopardised if its sole purpose is perceived to be to uncover fraud and to 'catch staff out'.

Appropriate future policy

A climate that encourages honesty should be fostered. Measures that can be taken include the following.

(i) A **clear code of conduct** should be introduced, emphasising what is, and is not acceptable.

(ii) '**Whistleblowing**' **systems** (possibly offering rewards) to encourage staff to report any irregular activity should be set up.

(iii) A **bonus scheme** based on profit participation for staff could be a means of discouraging fraud.

(iv) **Fraud prevention** should be made a **performance objective** for all managers.

As mentioned above, a **strong, visible IAD** must be maintained, with hotels being visited by IAD staff regularly. Fraud detection should not though be the only emphasis of IAD. IAD can contribute to the group's profitability in other ways, such as **establishing effective control procedures, advising hotel managers** on **staffing levels** and visiting hotels to **review quality standards** and **ensure adequate quality controls** are in place.

The board and audit committee have an important role to play in the prevention and detection of fraud. The company should adopt the recommendations of the Turnbull committee.

(i) The board should consider **risk identification and management,** and the **effectiveness of internal controls** on a regular basis. Directors should be asked to make regular reports on the steps they have taken to combat fraud.

(ii) The board should conduct an **annual review,** covering how the most important risks that the organisation faces have changed and the quality of the regular review process.

(b)

MEMORANDUM

To: Operations Director
From: Chief Internal Auditor Date: XX.XX.XX
Subject: Internal Audit and the impact on staff morale

Whilst we accept that there may be relatively informal practices within hotels, there is a need for establishing a **boundary** for these 'customs and practices'. You might accept, for instance, that staff working over standard mealtimes are entitled to hotel food, but would limit this to, say, a sandwich.

If a boundary is not established there is the risk of creating an environment where 'anything goes' and ultimately this could be seen as **condoning fraud**. Even if the taking of unofficial income does not qualify as fraudulent, we could have a situation where staff believed that they operated in a climate where they could '**pay' themselves** what they believed they were worth. I would also point out that the company has a duty to account to the Inland Revenue for **tax and national insurance** on all employee remuneration and benefits and that there is a need to have systems in place to allow us to do this. This need not have any implications on employees' take-home pay.

I would also point out that IAD has a duty to review the rewards for staff to **confirm** their **acceptability,** even though the payments may be perfectly acceptable and encourage staff to work harder. I would emphasise that our audit staff are **commercially experienced** and I believe they will already be aware of, and able to judge, reasonable practices. I am sure that you too would want to ensure that payments and benefits remain within the limit of what you considered acceptable.

If you are concerned that IAD might interfere with 'reasonable' customs and practices then I would suggest that we collaborate in drawing up **guidelines** of what are considered acceptable practices and I will ensure that IAD staff are aware of what is acceptable. I would suggest that you distribute the guidelines to hotel managers to ensure they too are aware of what is considered acceptable.

I appreciate that the introduction of a Code of Conduct, together with other changes that are being proposed to reduce the likelihood of fraud may cause difficulties, particularly if there is a reduction in the ability of managers and staff to obtain additional rewards. I would emphasise that **previously accepted practices** are **not** being **investigated**. In addition I accept that we need to consider **compensating managers and staff** for loss of perquisite income by increasing their remuneration in other ways. One way of doing this would be to introduce **bonuses linked with financial results,** particularly financial results that could be affected by fraudulent practice, such as bar takings.

To conclude, it is not our intention, nor is it in our interests, to interfere adversely with the operations of hotels. We do have a duty to advise you on any legal implications of your policies and to use our knowledge of the hotel business to make suggestions that contribute to their suitability. Thereafter we hope to ensure that the policies you believe to be appropriate are being implemented on the ground.

We are both working towards the same end – **increasing the value** of Y plc.

If you do have any specific concerns or would like to discuss this further, please do not hesitate to contact me.

58 PERFORMANCE REVIEW

Pass marks. Try to use the information you have been given. It is easy to overlook data, such as the 19X7 historical figures or the information that pre-inflation sales growth is expected to be no more than 3%. The best way to avoid this type of omission is to re-read the data provided after you have made your preliminary calculations. If there is any unused information at that point, think about why you were given that information and where you might be able to use it in your answer.

Avoid the temptation to look to the environment for explanations of differences in performance. For instance the variations in wage costs cannot be put down to having to pay different rates according to each store's location as we are told that the three stores are in the same region.

In part (b) (ii) you are going to have to give another answer based on the ratios calculated for part (a). The obvious danger to avoid is repetition of what you have already said – no matter how good it is, you'll only get marks for saying something once. Using the scenario and putting yourself into the position of the internal auditor should give you enough of a change of mindset to achieve this, becoming more concerned that the figures upon which you have based your calculations may be wrong.

In the exam hall if you are faced with a case study like this you might consider completing another question between answering parts (a) and (b) to give yourself time to come up with a fresh perspective.

Other points. You may well have included different ratios in part (a). Any of the following, for example, would have been equally valid.

Labour costs as a % of sales
Other costs as a % of sales
Creditor days
Fixed asset turnover
Employee turnover

Examiner's comment. The situation and information given in the question should have been well within candidates' experience. A major aim of the question was to provide a comparison between the management accounting approach to reviewing data (part (a)) and the internal audit approach (part (b)).

Answers to part (a) were generally good with reasonable ratios being selected and sensible comments being made. Some answers were, however, undermined by a failure to explain the reasons why the selected ratios had been chosen. A number of candidates failed to provide examples of ratios to be used for operational control. Other mistakes included failure to take into account relative store size, failure to compare store performance with group performance, calculating the return on (negative) capital employed rather than fixed or gross assets, and failure to realise creditors would be dealt with at the centre.

Many answers to (b) (i) demonstrated a lack of knowledge of what analytical review was. A general essay on internal audit was not required. Answers should have focused on how analytical review can give assurance that the figures 'make sense' and highlight unexpected figures that warrant further investigation. Some candidates confined their discussion of methods to ratio analysis, and failed to consider trend analysis or model procedures.

Answers to (b) (ii) should have concentrated on matters that were mostly controlled by stores such as labour costs, stock, gross profit and waste. Fixed costs, purchase prices and terms of payment were head office matters, of less importance in this context. A large number of candidates repeated answers to part (a). Other answers discussed planning in general rather than focusing on the specific matters affecting the audit of stores.

(a) Set out below is a commentary on the performance of stores A, B and C. Key ratios are shown in appendix A.

Store A

Store A seems to be **suffering** more than stores B and C from the highly competitive environment in which the group operates, with **turnover down** 7.7% from the previous year and profits having fallen dramatically from £317,000 to £50,000.

Compared with an above average net profit margin of 3.8% in 19X7, the **current year's profit margin** of 0.7% is particularly **disappointing.** A significant contributor to this is the **cost of wastage** – at 2.3% of sales this is almost 28% higher than the average for the group. Combined with an **above average cost base** in terms of both labour and other costs, store A has succeeded in achieving only disappointing levels of profitability.

Although **turnover per square metre** for all three stores is significantly higher than the group average, store A's figure of £6,400 is surprisingly low given that all three stores are in the same region.

There were some **positive aspects** to store A's performance. **Stock turnover,** at 18.46 times, was comfortably above the group average of 17.57 and **fixed asset turnover** (10.67 times) was well above the group average of 7.02.

Given that all three stores are in the same region and given that store A has the greatest floor space and the lowest level of fixed assets (£720,000 compared to £1,122,000 in store C, which is 100 square metres smaller), it is likely that the store **A is operating with older fixtures and fittings.** This may be worth investigating: a refit of the store may halt the decline in sales and newer, more efficient refrigeration and racking systems may improve performance in wastage and other costs such as power.

The low fixed asset base is a major contributory factor to store A having **net current liabilities** of £197,000. Although this is hardly a problem given the group's net assets of £96,000,000, the store's management may wish to reflect on the fact that their **creditors** wait an average of only 75.72 days for payment compared with the 77.87 days which store B's creditors wait.

Store B

Store B has managed a 3.4% **increase in year-on-year sales,** which is creditable given that sales growth is 'at best 3%, excluding inflation'. This excellent sales growth has led to **higher than average gross profit margins both before and after waste.**

The **net profit margin,** at 2.6%, matches the average earned by the group. This is disappointing given the higher than average gross margin. The main **factor holding back the net profit margin is labour related.** Although **turnover per square metre** is the **highest** of the three stores, **turnover per employee,** at £102,857, is almost 5% **lower** than the average for the group. As well as this apparent inefficiency, **labour costs** (at 12.6% of turnover) are well above the group average of 11.3% and it would be sensible for management to carry out an investigation into this level of labour costs.

The store's **working capital management** figures are in line with group average figures. **Additional stock days appear to be financed by additional creditor days,** while the fixed asset turnover at 7.66 times is 9% higher than the figure for the average store.

Were management to exercise some control over labour costs and efficiency levels, store B's excellent turnover per square metre and strong gross margins would generate a much more creditable return.

Store C

Like store B, store C has **managed to reverse the group's declining profit** and post an increase in **net profits for the year.** Profits are up from £152,000 to £160,000, an increase of 5.3% and there has been an excellent **increase in turnover** of 4.7%.

Turnover per square metre is comfortably above the group average and **staff efficiency is good,** the 67 employees generating an average of £110,000 each compared to a group average of £107,815.

Like both other stores in the region, **staff costs** (at 12%) are above the group average of 11.3%. Store C also needs to **improve controls over other costs,** as at 9.4% of sales these are substantially in excess of the group average of 8.5% and this is a major contributing factor to the store's disappointing profit margin of 2.2%.

The net assets of store C are much higher than those of the other two stores and the group average. Consequently the stock days and fixed asset turnover figures are particularly poor.

Key ratios

For operational control and performance evaluation purposes of existing stores, the following key ratios could be used.

- **Gross profit margin (before wastage)**. Given both the narrow margins within which S plc operates and what is likely to be limited opportunity for cost control in other areas, this is a key determinant of success. It provides a measure of the effectiveness of the purchasing function and the ability of the store management to pass onto customers increases in purchase prices.
- **Wastage.** This is one of the major areas over which store managers should have direct control and which has a direct and substantial impact on S plc's tight profit margins.
- **Sales growth**. Given the highly competitive nature of the supermarket business and the speed of new store openings, this is a key measure of S plc's on-going competitive success.
- **Turnover per square metre.** This is another key determinant of success for the retail trade and measures the effectiveness of the way in which space is utilised within the store. It is worth noting that store B has both the highest profit margin and turnover per square metre.
- **Turnover per employee**. Hourly pay rates can be set as a matter of group policy and so it is the efficiency of labour which managers can and must control.
- **Net profit margin**. Whilst there is little discretion for cost control on the part of managers, this measure of a store's overall profitability should be included as part of performance evaluation to ensure that managers do still pay some attention to the control of costs
- **Stock in days.** This measure must be carefully monitored as it indicates how well a store is balancing customer needs with effective warehousing.
- **Growth in turnover and net profit.** This measure assesses store management's ability to meet customer needs.
- **Price of key products compared to competitors**. The prices of staple products (milk, bread, butter and so on) should be compared to those of S plc's rivals to ensure that local and national price wars have been responded to sufficiently and adequately.
- **Supplier deliveries on time as a proportion of total deliveries.** Stores must maintain low levels of stock but stockouts must be avoided to ensure high levels of customer satisfaction.

- **Actual customers as a proportion of total customers.** A measure of market share enjoyed by a store is a vital indicator of the effectiveness of a store's policies.

Operational control will be most helped by **a range of financial and non-financial indicators,** possibly based on the **balanced scorecard approach** and hence covering its four perspectives. Those ratios which can be **controlled by store management** are of particular relevance.

The key ratios below (in appendix A) could be **compared over time within each store and with the group average,** as well as **benchmarking** them against best practices in other stores.

Particular attention should be paid to the medium- to long-term movement in sales growth and net profit margin, other ratios being useful indicators of areas of operations that could affect the long-term profitability of a store.

Appendix A

	Store A		*Store B*		*Store C*		*Group*
	19X8	19X7	19X8	19X7	1X98	19X7	19X8
Gross profit % (before waste)	24.4%		25.6%		25.5%		24.2%
Gross profit % (after waste)	22.1%	23.4%	24.2%	24.3%	23.6%	23.5%	22.4%
Net profit %	0.7%	3.8%	2.6%	3.3%	2.2%	2.2%	2.6%
Turnover increase/(decrease)	(7.7%)		3.4%		4.7%		2.9%
Net profit increase/(decrease)	(84.2%)		(18.1%)		5.3%		(12.3%)
Turnover per sq metre	£6,400		£7,200		£6,700		£6,110
Turnover per employee	£106,667		£102,857		£110,000		£107,815
Labour costs as % of sales	11.9%		12.6%		12.0%		11.3%
Other costs as % of sales	9.5%		9.0%		9.4%		8.5%
Stock turnover	18.46		16.58		16.42		17.57
Fixed asset turnover	10.67		7.66		6.57		7.02
Creditor days	75.72		77.87		77.19		76.01
Stock days	19.77		22.00		22.23		20.77

(b) (i) **Purposes**

The purpose of analytical review is contained within its definition in CIMA's Official Terminology: 'The examination of ratios, trends and changes from one period to the next to obtain a **broad understanding** of the financial position and results of operations'. For internal audit purposes, analytical review provides assurance about the **reasonableness** and **consistency** of management information. For both external and internal audit, analytical review also highlights areas where **unexpected variations** have occurred that warrant **further investigation.**

Methods

(1) **Comparisons to predictions.** From previous years' results, the results of other stores and information regarding that specific store, the internal auditor could create a spreadsheet model of what he believed would be a reasonable set of results for that operation. This model would be

compared against the actual results and explanations for any differences obtained.

(2) **Ratio analysis.** Key ratios could be calculated and then compared to other financial data or to items of non-financial data. Suitable financial data would include those ratios in other similar stores, for the chain as a whole or against industry averages. Non-financial comparisons might include checks such as total labour costs compared to the number of employees or stock quantities compared to purchases.

(3) **Trend analysis.** This is where the figures would be broken down period by period to see whether items such as gross profit margin or wastage had a consistent pattern throughout the period or whether there were particular months where performance was substantially different from others. For example, if a store has a wastage cost of 1.5% through the year but in one particular period this rose to 4.5%, useful information has been obtained both about sustainable targets for future years (1.5%) and the causes of poorer performance.

Limitations

The **assumptions and figures** used may be **misleading.** The trends and ratios that are used for comparison will be drawn from previous periods' financial results. These may be no more accurate or reliable than the results to which they are being compared.

The **assumptions** made may also be of **limited relevance** if there are changes in the conditions affecting stores, for example the opening of local rivals. Models based on current and expected activity may themselves be based on the wrong assumptions such as the controllability of costs. Hence the discussion of differences may become diverted into a discussion on whether the internal auditor's predictions are flawed or whether reasonable comparatives have been chosen.

Analytical review will be more reliable the greater **the level of detail** that is available. Figures for the business as a whole may conceal **wide local variations** which need to be investigated. Similarly annual figures would need to be supplemented by monthly data if there are wide seasonal variations.

Inevitably auditors will have to allow **certain variations** from what is predicted due to the imprecision of the techniques used. However these small differences may be due to fraud rather the techniques employed. Hence analytical review is much more likely to **highlight** problems that can be identified by **large variations** from what is expected, or that have built up over a number of years, rather than small variations in a single year.

Once differences have been identified there is in any event a tendency to try to **explain away the differences** – the assumption made is that the current accounts are correct and that differences between stores or periods are the cause of the difference. It may be that the expected performance was correct and that the accounts contain errors which cause the difference. These errors may not be investigated if the given explanations are plausible.

(ii) When using analytical review to assess the risk for each store, auditors will focus on areas where there are likely to be **problems** *and* the **areas** that are **controllable** by each store. For example the level of wages paid to stores staff will be influenced by the wage rate (which is likely to be decided centrally) and also the hours worked (which will be decided and recorded locally).

Hence internal audit will focus on the reliability of the time recording at stores and the authorisation of overtime.

The major factors affecting each store are as follows.

Store A

(1) **Gross profit percentage** (after waste). At 22%, this is significantly lower than for Stores B and C, and also lower than for the group as a whole. An explanation will be needed, focusing on sales and wastage.

(2) **Sales.** The level of sales has decreased by 7.7%, whereas for stores B and C in the same area the level of sales has risen. The level of sales per square metre is also lower than for stores B and C, although it is higher than the group average. Internal audit will need to investigate the pattern of sales of major product lines, and also factors affecting Store A by itself, for example an increase in local competition.

(3) **Wastage.** At 2.3% wastage in this store is very high both compared to the stores in the area and the group average. Of particular concern would be the store's procedures for quality inspection of goods received. That the high wastage may be due to failure to identify deliveries in poor condition is suggested both by the high wastage margin, and the relatively prompt creditor settlement period compared to other stores, indicating that the store raises fewer quality disputes with its suppliers.

(4) **Fixed asset valuation.** With the largest floor area, store A's having the lowest fixed asset value is odd. Other costs should be reviewed to ensure this does not include expenditure which ought to have been capitalised. The store's asset replacement policy and the physical condition of assets should be reviewed, to ensure they are in line with group policy.

Store B

(1) **Labour costs.** Store B's performance is generally good. The biggest single issue relates to labour costs, running at 12.6% of sales compared with an average of 11.3% for the group. Sales per employee of £102,857 are the lowest of three stores and well below the group average of £107,815. The manager should be asked to explain his staff planning system and justify the number of staff he feels he requires per shift. A survey of customers should also be conducted to see whether these high staff levels are contributing to the store's high turnover per square foot, and comparison should be made between this store and the store with the highest sales per employee. If there is direct evidence of higher staff levels contributing to higher turnover, a cost benefit analysis should be conducted to see if this practice should be introduced in other stores.

(2) **Net profits.** Net profits have decreased by 18.1% despite the increase in turnover and gross profit. The reasons for this should be ascertained, focusing on labour costs (discussed above) and other costs (discussed below).

Store C

(1) **Stock turnover.** At 16.42 times, compared to 17.57 as an average for the group, stock turnover in this store is low. A review of stock turnover by product line should be undertaken to see if there are any particularly slow areas. A review of that store's stocktaking procedures should be carried out. The low turnover could be due to that store conducting

insufficient stocktakes resulting in a failure to identify stock losses through theft or food going beyond its sell-by date.

(2) **Sales.** The group expects sales growth to be at least 3% pre-inflation. With 19X8 having been a year of low food price inflation, the 4.7% sales growth in this store is exceptional. Cut-off checks should be performed to ensure that all of the sales do correctly belong to this period. Product mixes and competitive pressures in the area should be reviewed to identify from where the strong growth came and whether further increases are possible.

(3) **Labour costs.** At 12% these are higher than the average for the group, so the sorts of procedures that are applied to store B should also be applied here. Comparisons between the two stores are likely to be helpful.

All stores

(1) **Other costs.** Each of the three stores has a much higher proportion of other costs compared to sales, varying between 9% and 9.5% of sales compared with 8.5% for the group as a whole. The nature of this additional expenditure must be identified and reviewed to determine if it is valid and controllable expenditure for this region. If it can be controlled to bring it more in line with the group average, there will be a direct benefit to bottom line profits.

(2) **Other stores.** The performance of these stores should be compared with any other similar stores in the same region.

59 ANALYTICAL REVIEW AND SAMPLING

Pass marks. Our answer to (a) is focused on the level of detail required and the need to concentrate analytical review on the most significant areas. (b) requires application of different methods of sampling. Note the mention of quality control; this paper has on occasion required discussion of the use of different methods of sampling, such as acceptance and discovery sampling, to obtain evidence of the operation of quality control procedures (see question 60).

Examiner's comment. The difference between sampling methods and methods of choosing samples (such as stratified, interval) must be known.

REPORT

To: The Board
From: Internal auditor Date: XX.XX.XX
Subject: Internal audit

(a) **Analytical review**

Analytical review procedures are an efficient and effective way to spot problem areas in an organisation. The form of analytical review here would be detailed **ratio analysis** on a **branch by branch basis** comparing **actual results** with **historical and budgeted results. Inter-branch comparisons** would also be possible, where, say, cost ratios are expected to be the same nationwide. This type of comparison would obviously have to take local and geographical factors into account. This assumes that detailed management accounts are available at branch level.

Analytical review could be **concentrated** on those **areas** where the company is considered to be most **vulnerable**: to pilfering, fraud or poor controls. Examples of suspicious results would be branches with high stock write-offs or with low gross margins. These may indicate pilfering or fraud, or they may show problems with ordering and cost controls.

Detailed internal audit testing should **concentrate** on these areas if **analytical review produces unsatisfactory results,** since these are the areas where the company could lose most revenue.

(b) **Sampling**

In a large business, examination of every transaction becomes an impossibility. Even in smaller organisations, looking at every item will not be cost effective. Sampling therefore makes audit work quicker and cheaper. While it does not guarantee 100% accuracy in the population, it gives a **comfort level,** by which we can be sure that a high enough level of accuracy has been achieved. Of course, if a sample reveals errors, then the sample size can be increased to the size of the whole population if necessary.

Methods of sampling

There are various sampling methods and descriptions of four are given here.

(i) **Estimation sampling**: enables the auditor to **estimate** the **maximum possible error rate** in the population. This can then be compared with the auditor's maximum acceptable error rate. Obviously the maximum acceptable error rate will depend on the characteristic being tested. If for example an error is taken as being the lack of authorisation then the auditor would be less concerned with errors in the approval of overtime working than with those in the authorisation of major capital expenditure.

(ii) **Discovery sampling**: this type of plan is designed so that if the **actual error rate** in the population exceeds the auditor's **maximum acceptable** error rate, he will be **certain** to **find at least one error** in the sample he tests. If no errors are found, the auditor infers that with a known confidence the error rate in the population is within acceptable limits. The maximum acceptable error rates are often set so that the discovery of one or more errors in the sample indicates a major breakdown in internal control. The discovery of an error will involve the auditor in further tests, possibly starting with the use of estimation sampling to find the maximum possible error rate.

(iii) **Acceptance sampling**: more widely used in quality control than in auditing, the plan is structured to enable the auditor to '**accept**' or '**reject**' the population on the basis of the **number of errors found**. For example, the auditor might use the following plan. If, from a population of 1,000, a sample of 150 items is drawn and three or fewer errors are found, then he would have the desired assurance that the population error rate did not exceed (say) 4%, where the figure of 4% represents the maximum acceptable error rate.

(iv) **Judgemental sampling**: this is where the auditor chooses a sample as he or she sees fit. This method is generally unacceptable as it **incorporates** the **bias** and **subjectivity** of the auditor.

Signed: Internal Auditor

60 DIVISION X

> **Pass marks**. This question demands an appreciation of the judgements made when carrying out sampling, and the objectives of sampling. Even using statistical sampling, certain judgements will be necessary (for example tolerable error rate). In part (d) your answer should have considered whether testing a limited quantity of (representative) items will always achieve the desired objective, in both internal audit and quality control.
>
> In (a)(ii) the answer considers the various ways of obtaining evidence about the extent of the problem.
>
> **Examiner's comment**. Sampling is emphasised in the Syllabus Guidance Notes, and hence a question on it should not have surprised candidates the way it did. Some answers to (a)(i) did not use the figures provided. Answers to (a)(ii) were often too general.
>
> In (c) many candidates failed to treat common costs consistently and recognise fixed overheads were irrelevant. Many answers lacked workings.
>
> In (d) answers were generally better on the practical use of sampling in internal audit than on its use in quality control.

(a) (i) The difference between the sample sizes is due to the difference in tolerable error rates.

With **discovery sampling**, the aim is to gain confidence that **errors** are **not occurring**; it is used in circumstances where a single error may indicate a significant failure. In the circumstances described, the tolerable error rate will be 50/8,296 ie 0.6%.

With **attribute sampling**, the auditors will be willing to accept the population as 'correct' if the **error rate** is at or **below** a **certain level** ie their expectation is that a few errors will not be materially significant. Hence a 5% error rate is tolerated in the question.

(ii) **Testing of sales administrator**

There should be further detailed testing of the work of the sales administrator who did not carry out credit checks. Tests should include the following.

(1) The **files of customers authorised** by the sales administrator should be **reviewed** to see whether credit checks were carried out on other occasions.

(2) The **files** of **customers** where **credit checks were not carried out** should be **reviewed** to determine whether there are any signs (for example unusual addresses) which may indicate a connection with the sales administrator or that they are dummy customers entered to boost the administrator's commission.

(3) The **payment records** of customers who did not receive credit checks should be **examined**. The failure of internal control may be less serious if all the customers concerned are paying promptly.

Other error

The **reasons** for the other error should be **checked**. Further testing may be required if the other error was not due to an isolated lapse. As this is a new system auditors may not be able to prove the error was isolated.

General tests

General tests are also important particularly as the proportion of debtors that are overdue exceeds the proportion of failures to carry out credit checks. General tests should include **examining** the **files** of **customers** who are

overdue to ascertain why, and also examining **procedures** for the **pursuit** of overdue debts. **Training procedures** also need to be considered to ascertain whether administrators have been properly trained.

(b) **Advantages of judgmental sampling**

(i) The auditor can **use judgement** about sample sizes, based on previous experience and knowledge of problem areas. In (a) it may be desirable in future years to reduce sample sizes if the reasons for the errors in the first year no longer apply.

(ii) **Sample sizes** can be **determined simply** and **quickly**, without the need for complex calculations.

(iii) The **sample sizes** chosen may be **less** than those chosen by statistical methods, but may nevertheless be felt to give sufficient coverage of the population.

Limitations of judgmental sampling

(i) Determination of the **sample size** may be **biased** by considerations such as available time.

(ii) Test **results cannot** be **evaluated** in **quantitative** terms.

(iii) Sample sizes **chosen** may **not** necessarily **depend** on the **risk** or the **materiality** of the area being tested. Hence excess testing may be carried out in less significant areas, and not enough testing in material, high risk areas.

(iv) If **too small** a **sample** is chosen, it may **not** be **representative** of the whole population.

(c) (i) **Marginal costs of BCY**

	(1)	(2)	(3)
	£	£	£
Cost of 100 units (£5.70 × 100)	570.00	570.00	570.00
Cost of additional CY's (W1)	56.37	51.30	-
Stripping down and other variable costs (W2)	98.90	90.00	-
Inspection costs (W3)	-	16.48	183.15
	725.27	727.78	753.15

Workings

1 **Cost of additional CY's**

For option (1), with a 9% error rate 100/0.91 CY's will need to be purchased in order to obtain 100 good ones.

$$\therefore \text{ Costs of additional CY's} = 5.70 \times \left(\frac{100}{0.91} - 100\right)$$

$$= 5.70 \times 9.89$$

$$= \underline{\underline{£56.37}}$$

For option (2), for every 100 CY's purchased, 9 will be defective, therefore a further 9 will need to be purchased. Because these 9 are pre-inspected, there will be no further expenditure, since credit will be obtained if any are found to be defective.

$$\therefore \text{Costs of additional CY's} = 5.70 \times 9$$

$$= \underline{\underline{£51.30}}$$

2 **Stripping down costs**

As above, for option (1) these will have to be 9.89 stripping downs, and for option 2, 9 stripping downs. As well as labour, variable overheads will also be incurred.

∴For option 1

Stripping down costs $= (8 + 12) \times 0.5 \times 9.89$

$= \underline{\underline{£98.90}}$

∴ For option 2

Stripping down costs $= (8 + 12) \times 0.5 \times 9$

$= \underline{\underline{£90.00}}$

3 **Inspection costs**

For option 2, because of the 9% error rate, 9.89 CY's will have to be inspected to obtain 9 good components. For option 3, 109.89 components will need to be inspected. Variable overheads will be incurred as well as labour costs.

∴For option 2

Inspection costs $= (8 + 12) \times \frac{5}{60} \times 9.89$

$= \underline{\underline{£16.48}}$

∴ For option 3

Inspection costs $= (8 + 12) \times \frac{5}{60} \times 109.89$

$= \underline{\underline{£183.15}}$

(ii) Option 1 is most cost-effective.

∴Maximum price from alternative supplier $= \frac{725.27}{100}$

$= \underline{\underline{£7.25}}$ per CY component

(d) **Objectives of sampling**

The objectives of sampling in internal audit are to obtain **sufficient appropriate evidence** about some aspect of a population by means of testing less than 100% of items within that population. If testing **controls**, the objectives will be to test whether the **internal control system** is achieving the aims of **safeguarding assets** and **providing reliable information** for internal and external reporting purposes.

Limitations of sampling

Sampling in internal audit has the following limitations.

(i) **Sampling tests** can be **time-consuming** to set up and carry out. The internal auditor has to ensure the completeness of the sample and also carry out any stratification of the sample that may be appropriate.

(ii) As discussed above, **bias can occur** in sampling. Even statistical sampling involves using judgement to determine the level of risk and tolerable error rates.

(iii) Sampling is testing of a random selection of individual items, and this may **not** be the **best way** of testing a population. A better way might be to identify the items within the population that are most likely to be in error (for example transactions processed by someone who is new to a job), and concentrate testing on these items.

Quality control

The objectives of sampling in quality control are:

(i) to ensure **inputs** of **appropriate quality** are **used**, and hence **production costs minimised**;

(ii) to **maximise customer satisfaction** by ensuring that **products or services** sold are **fault-free.**

The major limitations when using sampling for quality control purposes are as follows.

(i) Auditors may have trouble **determining** what **constitutes** an **acceptable error rate**. For example, faulty products sold to an important customer may seriously affect the business's profitability if the customer is lost as a result. This, however, implies a discovery sampling approach which, as demonstrated above, can lead to uneconomic sample sizes.

(ii) **Certain objectives,** for example gauging customer satisfaction, may **not** be **best achieved** by sampling. For example, at the end of a training course, it may well be better to give a review form to everyone on the course rather than just a sample. The extra time taken in looking at review forms from everyone may be a better use of resources than time spent setting up a sample, ensuring the students polled are representative of the whole class etc.

(iii) The **timing** of sampling may be **important.** In (c) by carrying out inspection early on it was possible to gain credit from suppliers for faulty components. Once the components had been used, however, they could not be returned to suppliers; hence the components identified as faulty by the later testing were worthless.

61 CORPORATE GOVERNANCE

Pass marks. Part (a) requires an understanding of what management controls can do; obviously it is impractical for the board to review the detailed operations of internal control themselves. Part (b) requires an understanding of what information remuneration committees need to fulfil the Greenbury recommendations. You will need knowledge of the Hampel report for future questions on corporate governance that are similar to part (c).

Examiner's comment. A question on corporate governance should have been anticipated, given its topicality. A good approach to part (a) was to define what reporting and monitoring procedures needed to be set up. Answers should have covered a range of controls, not just internal audit. Many candidates failed to appreciate in part (b) that the remuneration committee should consist of non-executive directors, so that executive directors did not fix their own pay. Good answers to (c) concentrated on the importance of non-executive directors, and the problems of reporting on internal controls. A number of answers lacked detail on the aims, as opposed to the recommendations, of Cadbury and Greenbury.

(a) The board's principal concern is with controls that can be classified as organisation or management.

Organisation controls are designed to ensure **everyone** is **aware** of their **responsibilities,** and **provide** a **framework** within which lower level controls can operate. **Management controls** are designed to **ensure** that the **business** can be **effectively monitored.**

(i) **Organisation**

Key organisation controls include the following.

(1) **Setting up** an **appropriate structure** for the organisation and **delegating** appropriate levels of authority to different grades.

(2) **Setting up** an **appropriate internal accounting system**. The board should ensure that the system is providing accurate and relevant information on a regular basis. Good quality information will enable the board to assess whether targets are being met or losses are possible.

(3) **Communication** of organisation **policies** and values through manuals and other guidance.

(ii) **Management**

Key management controls include the following.

(1) **Monitoring** of **business risks** on a regular basis. This should include assessment of the potential financial impact of contingencies.

(2) **Monitoring** of **financial information**. Management should also be alert for significant variations in results between branches or divisions or significant changes in results.

(3) **Use** of the **audit committee**. The committee should actively **liaise** with the external and internal auditors, and **report** on any **weaknesses** discovered. The committee should also regularly **review** the **overall structure** of internal control, and investigate any serious weaknesses found.

(4) **Use of internal audit**. Internal audit should be used as an independent check on the **operation** of **detailed controls** in the operating departments. Internal audit's work can be biased as appropriate towards areas of the business where there is a risk of significant loss should controls fail.

(iii) **Other controls**

The Cadbury report recommended other controls should on certain occasions be exercised by the board. Examples include **authorisation** for material **acquisitions** and **disposals of assets**, and **supervision** of **investments** and capital projects.

(b) **Purpose of remuneration committee**

The purpose of the remuneration committee is to provide a **mechanism** for **determining** the **remuneration packages** of executive directors. The recent Greenbury report makes clear that the scope of the review should include not only salaries and bonuses, but also share options, pension rights and compensation for loss of office.

The committee's remit may also include issues such as director appointments and succession planning, as these are connected with remuneration levels.

Constitution of remuneration committee

The Greenbury code recommends that the remuneration committee should consist entirely of **non-executive directors** 'with no personal financial interest other than as shareholders in the matters to be decided'. In addition there should be no conflict of interests arising from remuneration committee members and executive directors holding directorships in common in other companies.

Functioning of remuneration committee

The Greenbury report states that remuneration should be set having regard to market forces, and the packages required to '**attract, motivate and retain**' the **desired calibre** of **director**. The committee should pay particular attention to the setting of performance-related elements of remuneration.

In addition a **report** from the committee should form part of the annual accounts. The report should set out **company policy** on remuneration and give details of the **packages** for **individual directors**. The **chairman** of the committee should be **available to answer questions** at the annual general meeting, and the committee should consider whether **shareholder approval** is required of the company's remuneration policy.

Information requirements

In order to assess executive directors' pay on a reasonable basis, the following information will be required.

(i) Remuneration **packages** given by **similar organisations**.

(ii) **Market levels** of remuneration. This will particularly apply for certain industries, and certain knowledge and skills. More generally the committee will need an awareness of what is considered a minimum competitive salary.

(iii) **Individual performance**. The committee's knowledge and experience of the company, which Greenbury stresses as being important, will be useful here.

(iv) **Organisation performance**. This may include information about the performance of the sector which the director controls, or more general company performance information such as earnings per share or share price.

(c) The Cadbury committee was set up to address concerns about the system of **financial reporting** and the **safeguards** provided by **auditors**. Other concerns that the committee addressed included unexpected failures of major companies and lack of accountability of directors. With these concerns in mind, the committee's suggested reforms had the following major aims.

(i) **Better board governance**

The committee did not recommend formal two-tier boards with a supervisory board overseeing compliance with laws and regulations. Instead the report placed significant emphasis on the role of **independent non-executive directors**. However there are a number of examples of companies' failing with a significant non-executive presence on board. The impact of the committee's suggestions may thus be limited, for the following principal reasons.

(1) The role of non-executive directors is essentially a **part-time, limited** involvement.

(2) Whilst the report recommends that certain tasks should fall specifically within the remit of non-executive directors (membership of the audit and remuneration committees) their impact on the main board depends on the **constitution** of the board and the **division of power** amongst executive directors

(ii) **Improvement of disclosure in financial accounts**

Certain recommendations of Cadbury in the area of financial reporting have been further developed. Listed companies now should produce an **operating and financial review**, and the board should comment on the operation of internal controls and the entity's future as a **going concern**. There should be **improved disclosure** of **directors' remuneration**.

Undoubtedly therefore there is more information but its added value remains uncertain. In particular the guidance on internal controls does not lay down the form of report, and does **not require** directors to make any statement on **effectiveness**. In addition there is **little guidance** on **design** and **implementation** of controls; industry-specific guidance may be helpful in this area.

(iii) **Strengthening the role of the auditor**

Undoubtedly the committee has demonstrated how auditor concerns can be raised at the audit committee. However whether the reforms have increased the value of audits to shareholders is doubtful for the following reasons.

(1) The audit committee's ability to express concerns will depend on its **members' position** on the **main board**.

(2) The report lays some stress on the role of the audit committee in selecting and if necessary recommending **changes** in **auditor appointments**. However it is doubtful whether in most instances changing the auditor will mean the scope of the audit will increase significantly. Few of the biggest listed companies are now audited by accounting firms other than the 'Big Five', and 'Big Five' spokesmen have indicated that their fears about increased exposure to liability mean that they are unwilling to take on extra reporting responsibilities.

(iv) **Protection of stakeholders**

The above measures are designed to increase shareholder protection by increased control and availability of extra information. The committee rejected calls for shareholder committees, and stressed instead how **shareholders** could take advantage of their rights to **speak** at Annual General Meetings. However the committee also acknowledged the influence of **institutional shareholders**. Although the report stressed how institutional shareholders could be a force for good within companies, it did **not address** the question of whether the **interests** of different types of shareholders would **differ**, and, if so, how each type could be protected.

Likewise the concern over corporate collapses, which influenced the setting up of the committee, included concern for the position of stakeholders other than shareholders, notably creditors and employees. The report again does **not discuss** the **interests** of **different stakeholders**.

62 AUDIT COMMITTEES

Pass marks. Although the examiner did not want a discussion of the provisions of the corporate governance codes, (a) focused on two areas identified as important by the codes. An understanding of these areas must include an understanding of the limitations involved. Reading of the press about the problems of former statutory monopolies would have helped your answer in (b).

Prizewinners' points. The last part of our answer to (b) discusses how the *operation* of internal audit may have to change as a result of expansion of its responsibilities. It may be valuable for the audit committee to be given extra responsibilities, but the audit committee should, under the corporate governance codes, be staffed by non-executive directors with limited time.

Examiner's comment. The examiner stated that the answer to (a) should have focused on the general issues of control in an organisation rather than being a discussion of the corporate governance codes. In (b) only the better answers tended to discuss focusing on the needs of customers, and obtaining feedback from customers. Candidates also needed to discuss how the audit committee could be involved, by reviewing the reliability of measuring customer feedback, and in their role as directors advising on strategic issues.

(a) (i) The effectiveness of non-executive directors may be limited by the following factors.

Having the same perspective as executive directors

The corporate governance reports stress the importance of non-executive directors possessing independent judgement and being appointed by a nomination committee. However the nomination committee may restrict its search to **directors** who will **'fit in'** with the rest of the board, and may be **unwilling to recruit** from a **diversity of backgrounds,** for example +stakeholders such as employees. In addition many non-executive directors will only agree to serve on the boards of companies if they admire the company's chairman or its way of operating.

Limited time

The most knowledgeable and effective non-executive directors are likely to have other significant demands on their time. As directors they have to fulfil **certain legal requirements.** Apart from their contributions to the main board, they will also probably spend time at **meetings of board committees** such as the audit and remuneration committees. The limited involvement resulting from the lack of time may limit their ability to contribute to board meetings since they are **unable to obtain a broad enough picture** of what is happening throughout the organisation.

Information available

Non-executive directors' contribution will also depend on the information that is readily available to them as directors. This will be influenced by the quality of the **organisation's information systems,** and also the **willingness** of **executive directors** to supply information about their activities.

Role of board

The corporate governance reports stress the importance of non-executive directors being involved in **strategic decisions.** If non-executive directors are involved in formulating strategy, they can fulfil what Sir John Harvey-Jones sees as their key role, of **warning of potential problems** and hence **preventing trouble.** However board meetings may focus almost entirely on **current operational matters** and **short-term operational results.** In addition a focus at board meetings on short-term results may mean that non-executive directors **assess** the **performance** of the organisation using short-term indicators and its management, and do not focus on **longer-term issues** such as changes in product mix or re-engineering of the organisation's processes.

Inability to resist pressures

Non-executive directors have limited options when faced with a **united group** of **executive directors** who are determined to push through a policy with which the non-executive directors disagree. Their ultimate weapon is **resignation,** but if all or a number of non-executive directors resign, they may precipitate a **crisis of confidence** in the company. Alternatively they can **remain in office,** but then if serious problems arise, the executive directors may have to depart from the board, leaving the non-executive directors with the responsibility for '**picking up the pieces**'.

(ii) The effectiveness of audit committees could be improved in the following ways.

Appointment requirements

Appointments could be **recommended** by the **annual general meeting**. Alternatively certain stakeholders, for example employees could have the right to appoint a member. These measures might improve the independence of committee members.

The **term of office** of committee members could be **limited** to ensure the committee retained a fresh perspective.

When nominating potential members, the selection process could be biased towards **recruiting members** with **financial accounting experience** or **experience of large control systems**. Members who have accountancy experience will be able to question the judgements management make when preparing accountancy information.

Expansion of responsibilities

There are various ways in which the committee's remit might be expanded. They could have responsibility for **reviewing compliance** with **laws and regulations** such as environmental legislation or ethical codes. Certain **transactions** could also be **referred automatically** to them for review.

Internal audit

As a major function of many audit committees is to oversee the role of internal audit, it follows that a **more effective internal audit function** will lead to more effective operation of the audit committee by improving the quality of information that the audit committee review.

Statutory backing

Audit committees may become more effective if their establishment by certain organisations is made **compulsory.** The recommendations of internal audit will also be **reinforced by stricter accounting and auditing standards.**

Improvement in operations

Changes that might improve the way audit committees operate include the following.

(1) Having **clear terms of reference** agreed by the board

(2) Establishment of an **annual plan** giving details of the areas on which the committee will focus

(3) Establishment of **standards** for the **frequency** of; and **form of reporting** to, the main board

(4) Regular **review** of the **effectiveness** of the audit committee including whether its recent work has been correctly focused.

(b) **Improvements in control systems**

One aspect of control systems improvement will be **dealing with complaints** from customers. The existence of regulators or ombudsmen will mean that customers can enlist powerful weapons on their behalf if dissatisfied. However the control systems cannot just concentrate on dealing with complaints as even resolved complaints may lead to regulatory action, and poor experiences may influence the subsequent purchasing decisions of customers.

Controls must also be implemented to obtain **customer feedback** on an ongoing basis. These may enable management to obtain a more representative view of customer reaction; those who complain may not be typical, and the regulatory body may take into account overall customer reaction. A variety of methods will be necessary as individual means may be unrepresentative (because for example only a small minority return customer service questionnaires).

The results of complaints and surveys must influence the controls that **prevent problems.** An enhanced regulatory regime means that this type of control is likely to be more important. A **customer charter** should be introduced. Other prevention controls may have to be better directed than they have previously; **training** may have to be focused more on staff in direct contact with the customer, and address specifically the issues that can cause problems with customers.

Change in audit committee role

Audit committees may have to spend more time on **reviewing compliance** with the **regulations** set down by the regulatory bodies, and also on compliance with the organisation's own charter. In their role as supervisors of internal audit, the committee should **check** that **internal audit** adequately **consider** the **procedures** designed to **prevent problems** and to **obtain evidence** of **customer views.**

Because audit committees are reviewing these matters, they may be able to **anticipate future developments** such as increased regulation or changes in customer demands. This intelligence will affect the discussions on strategy of the main board.

If audit committees responsibilities are to increase in this way, there will be certain implications for the way they operate. Their **membership** is likely to be **expanded,** with the addition of members with the necessary knowledge of customer requirements and industry regulations. Audit committees may no longer be able to consider all matters as one body, and may split into **sub-committees** with one concentrating on financial controls and another on responses to industry pressure.

63 VFM AND PERFORMANCE INDICATORS

Pass marks. Our answer to (a) discusses inputs, outputs and impacts/outcomes. In part (b) note that a balanced view of performance indicators is required; the answer explains why they are necessary, but also demands a realisation of the problems of measuring quality of service.

Other points. For part (a) there are several possible sets of methods you could choose. You could continue with the theme of the three E's. You could write about detailed investigations of selective parts of an organisation, more broad-based investigations of the organisation as a whole, and reviews of the organisation's standard operations.

Methods of analysis

(a) Three methods of VFM analysis which may be employed in value for money audits are as follows.

(i) A study of **economy, efficiency and effectiveness** (the '3 Es') with reference to **inputs.** Inputs mean the money or **resources** - ie cost - that has gone into a programme. For example, the provision of a health visitors' service could be investigated from the point of view of the cost of labour and materials etc that go into providing the service.

(ii) A study of the '3 Es' with reference to **outputs**. Outputs mean the **results** of a programme, measured either by the **type** and **quantity** of the **service** provided, or by **quality**. In the example of a home visitors' service, an audit could look at the type of services provided, the numbers of people served, and the quality of the service.

(iii) A study of the **impacts**. Impacts mean the effect that the outputs of a programme have had on the **achievement** of **policy objectives**. Again, using the example of a home visitors' service, an audit could assess to what extent the services provided, the number of people served and the quality of service are consistent with the original aim of setting up the service in the first place.

In the public sector, inputs, outputs, and impacts are all difficult to quantify in practice.

(b) **Performance indicators**

A central theme of many of the government's pronouncements on the public sector throughout the 1980s and early 1990s has been the need to improve performance. However basic control theory tells us that in order to improve we first need to know where we are going wrong and *how far* we are going wrong.

With **public sector services**, there has generally been **no market competition** and **no profit motive**. In the private sector, these two factors help to guide the process of fixing proper prices and managing resources economically, efficiently and effectively.

Since public sector organisations cannot be judged by their success against **competition** nor by **profitability**, some other methods of assessing performance have to be used. In the public sector, however, performance measures are difficult to define. Measures of output **quantity** and output **quality**, by themselves, provide **insufficient evidence** of how well the community is served by a programme.

Performance can be measured by:

(i) **progress** towards **appropriate objectives**, for example success in cutting hospital waiting lists to a specified maximum;

(ii) **progress** in **improving efficiency**, for example increasing the number of dustbins emptied in comparison to the resources (labour and vehicles) used. Measuring efficiency in the public sector is difficult. Activities can be defined in words and inputs are often clearly measurable but expressing outputs and efficiency in numerical terms is often only possible in a crude way;

(iii) **control** over **spending**, for example keeping energy costs per square metre of public buildings to a minimum.

Problems with performance indicators

Those who have an interest in the performance of public organisations (taxpayers, community charge payers, customers, the government and Parliament), seek a few

simple and **understandable indicators** which show the trend in efficiency over time and compared with other similar organisations, both in the UK and overseas.

These groups are entitled to performance indicators and explanations of performance and results. There are however difficulties which must be appreciated by them.

(i) There are real problems of **measurement** of **output** and the **accumulation** or **attachment** of **costs** to them, without going into misleading and meaningless allocations of 'overheads'.

(ii) It is often difficult to establish a relationship between cause and effect, especially where:

  (1) **several activities interact** but contribute to achieving a desired (or sometimes undesired/unanticipated) result; or

  (2) where **one activity contributes** to **more than one objective**. For example, to what extent does expenditure on street lighting contribute to road safety as opposed to the reduction of street crime?

(iii) **Performance indicators,** if simple, may be **misleading.**

(iv) Members of the **public** who receive measures of performance by a public sector department may **not fully understand** the nature of the organisation and its environment and may be unable to put into proper context any information or explanation they receive. The government would argue that this is precisely the case with the widely criticised publication of league tables for schools.

In spite of the difficulties there are benefits to be gained if performance indicators can be successfully developed.

Advantages of performance indicators

(i) They **increase the accountability** of those running the organisation to those using it and paying for it.

(ii) They give the managers of the organisation **targets** to aim at.

(iii) They need **not be absolute** (unlike financial indicators). For example different parts of an organisation can be set different targets that make allowances for local conditions. Their success in achieving those targets can be expressed in percentage terms. Different London Underground lines have been set different standards for percentage of timetabled trains run.

64 VFM AND PAYROLL

> **Pass marks.** In (a) you needed to consider not just cost control, but also the quality of the service provided. The information given in the question should have influenced significantly your discussion of the desirability of an internal audit of the payroll of XY Ltd. In (b) your answer should cover a range of controls, but you needed to discuss the controls over engineers working from home in some detail. Because of the emphasis placed on fraud detection in the question, you needed to cover management review of accounting information as well as controls over authorisation of payments.
>
> **Examiner's comment.** Answers to (a) often failed to apply candidates' good knowledge of VFM to the circumstances given in the question. A number of answers placed too much emphasis on economy and did not discuss the other elements of VFM. However, the most important weakness in (a) was the failure to discuss whether a VFM audit was worthwhile at all.
>
> Various approaches could have been adopted in (b). Whilst answers were often detailed, many lacked structure and focused too heavily on less important points. Some candidates failed to realise that the fact that engineers worked from home would render certain controls ineffective, and the principal concern was checking hours of entitlements of homeworking engineers. Some answers failed to specify actions needed to deal with the possibility of non-existent employees.

(a) REPORT

To: Cost Reduction Team Leader
From: Internal Auditor   Date: XX.XX.XX
Subject: VFM audit of payroll

Value for money will be concerned within **minimising** the **inputs** (the costs of processing payroll information) whilst **achieving required results**. Some of the results are fixed; employees must be paid at the right rate and on the right day, and taxation and other deductions must be made correctly. The internal management information the bureau provides may be changed and should be considered in the light of problems over contract costs; is more information required if costs exceed certain limits, is sufficient detail given about individual contracts and so on.

Inputs

The payroll of XY Ltd first went out to tender a number of years ago. A system of **regular re-tendering** should be **introduced** if it is not already in place. Internal audit might review the tendering process every time the work is re-tendered, and should consider the following.

(i) Whether the company's laid down **tendering policies** have been **followed.**

(ii) Whether a **range of options** has been **considered.** One way of doing this would be to invite other external suppliers used by the group to tender. Internal audit should also see whether fair consideration is given to bringing the function back in-house, since the costs of employing the bureaux and checking its work might exceed the costs of XY carrying out the work itself. The tendering process should take into consideration the degree of payroll work that is already done in-house by the personnel department.

(iii) The **nature** of the **arrangements** with the successful contractor. The contract should cover not just payroll arrangements but also arrangements for changing the price, the ways in which service delivery will be measured and whether there are any get-out clauses should service requirements not be met.

(iv) How the **results** of the **tendering process** are **communicated** to other group companies to help them make decisions on provision of payroll services.

Internal audit can also review the **ongoing controls** over the **costs** of the payroll arrangements. The main element here is considering whether comparisons of actual costs are being made with budgeted costs, and whether the costs of the payroll function in XY are being compared with the costs of payroll administration in the rest of the group.

Results

Evidence of **incorrect** or **late payments** to **wage-earners** or the **tax authorities** should not be difficult to find. The **company's personnel department** should have been **notified** of any queries. The **quality** of **information provided** to management may be less easy to assess and the **opinions** of **management** should be **actively sought.** In particular internal audit should ascertain whether a sufficient level of detail is being provided; do managers know how much time has been spent on work for each customer and on each contract.

Internal audit

We need to decide whether the **internal audit resources used** are likely to be **justified** by **improved value for money.**

Given the fixed nature of much of the services provided, and the relatively settled nature of the costs, a separate value for money exercise purely on payroll is unlikely to be worthwhile, unless there have been significant problems. Instead aspects of the value for money of payroll could be included as part of **larger exercises covering** the **whole group,** for example group-wide tendering procedures or the quality of information supplied throughout the group. Value for money recommendations may also be an incidental part of internal audit investigation of the operation of controls and the company's compliance with statutory requirements.

(b) The payroll system should have certain **general controls** in place, but the control system should reflect the different arrangements under which the staff are employed. A **distinction** should be **drawn** between salaried employees, engineers who work in workshops and engineers who work from home. Internal audit should check controls over each category, but concentrate on engineers who work from home, since they constitute the majority of employees, and opportunities for fraud may be greater.

General controls

Internal audit should check the following.

(i) The **procedures** for **adding** and **removing staff** from the **payroll**. Internal audit should **check** that **all changes** are **authorised,** and check payroll records to see that **monies paid** are **consistent** with **dates of employment** as shown in personnel records.

(ii) The **procedures** for **changing pay rates.** Internal audit should obtain details of changes during the year, **check** that the **changes** were **authorised** by senior management and **check payroll records** to see that wages and salaries paid have **changed** on the **right date.**

(iii) The **existence** of **employees** on the payroll. Internal audit should **check** a sample of **employees** as shown on the payroll to personnel records to see whether those employees actually **exist**. The personnel records should also contain details of current remuneration, and internal audit should **confirm** that **current remuneration** is **consistent** with **payroll records.**

Internal audit should also check that the **calculations** of **tax** and **national insurance** deductions and other voluntary deductions (e.g. pension contributions) are **correct.**

Controls over salaried employees

The general checks outlined above should give most of the assurance required for this category of employee. Internal audit should check that **overtime** has been properly **authorised.**

Controls over engineers located in regional workshops

These engineers will be paid according to time clocked on. Internal audit should **observe clocking on** and **clocking off procedures** to see if they are being operated correctly. They should **agree payroll records** with **records** of **hours worked,** and **check** that **records** of **hours worked** have been **authorised. Overtime** should be specifically **authorised.**

Controls over engineers working from home

Internal audit should carry out the following checks.

(i) **Check** that **timesheets** are being **completed promptly** by engineers and have been authorised by management.

(ii) **Compare customer details** per **timesheets** with **maintenance contracts** to ensure that work is only being carried out for customers who have a valid maintenance contract.

(iii) **Consider** whether **items** on **timesheets appear reasonable,** that **time spent** on **individual jobs accords** with laid down rates and that any **travelling time claimed accords** with **rates allowed.**

(iv) **Examine feedback** from customers, and **check** that **adverse reports** from customers have been **investigated** by management.

(v) **Consider** the **pattern** of **maintenance** on **individual contracts,** and **check** that **management** has **investigated reasons** for unusually **high amounts** of **maintenance** on individual items of equipment or for certain customers.

Analytical review

Internal audit should check that **management** are **reviewing** the **information** supplied by the bureau and should themselves review that information. There should be a system of standard times in place for jobs of individual types, and management should be **reviewing significant variances.** Additionally because the **data** will be **analysed in different ways** from the payroll, it may show **unusual patterns** relating to certain jobs, customers or employees that warrant further investigation by internal audit.

Signed: Internal auditor

65 TUTORIAL QUESTION: SECURITY FACTORS

(a) Security in this context must be taken to mean the **prevention of system breakdown, loss** or **corruption of data, theft of information.** There are a variety of factors which affect the security of an organisation's computer systems.

(i) **Physical threats**

There are threats of physical damage to the system and the information it produces. These include obvious dangers like fire, floods and so forth, which can have a devastating effect both on system hardware, and on computer files and stored programs. The use of **networks** might have the effect of **dividing** the **risk**: if only one machine malfunctions this need not necessarily affect the working of the entire system. In a system dependent on a single mainframe, the whole system fails if something goes wrong with the computer.

Similarly, there are **threats** to data held on **magnetic storage devices**. For example, data held on a floppy disk can suffer during the minor accidents of office life (eg tea spillage or being dropped on the floor).

(ii) **Human errors or intervention**

Other threats can be caused by human error or intervention.

At the systems design stage these can occur in **faulty programming**. Some bugs in a system do not emerge until after the system has been up and running for a while. Faulty programming may be the result of poor initial design. Bugs or other problems are just as likely to be an unforeseen consequence of alterations to the system.

The scope for **operational error** is also quite large. A simple error is the incorrect keying-in of an item of data. These problems are likely to become more prevalent with the rise of end-user computing, when applications are designed and operated by users rather than data processing professionals. Data validation programs, check digits etc are used to pick up any errors before they are input.

Unauthorised intervention or tampering is also a problem. **Hacking** is made possible by the increasing use of telecommunications links and network technology. **Viruses,** which are programs that attach themselves to other programs and can destroy both data and programs, are also a growing problem. Other computer-based problems are fraud, and **physical damage**.

(b) **Investigation**

In order to manage the risk, a coherent strategy must be adopted rather than a series of *ad hoc* knee-jerk responses. A team of managers and/or consultants and/or staff may be appointed to investigate the matter.

(i) The team should assess how **vulnerable** it is in principle to any of these **problems** drawing on past experience. It may help to do an estimate of the likely costs of any particular threat identified. It is obviously easier to identify the costs of replacing hardware than the costs caused, for example, by a virus infection.

(ii) The team will then assess how far **current security measures** are **sufficient** to cope with the vulnerabilities discovered. This study might be quite a lengthy process, covering detailed technical issues (for example how easy might a hacker find it to enter the network? Is there a proper lock on the computer room door? Fireproof cabinets? etc).

(iii) Some analysis will be made of the extent to which the **security procedures** theoretically in force are in fact being **followed** in practice (for example users might share passwords which they are supposed to keep confidential).

(iv) Once some assessment of the risk, both qualitative and quantitative has been made, **additional security measures** may be suggested. These too, will have to be costed, as far as possible, so that the costs of security do not outweigh the anticipated costs of the threats identified.

Prevention of problems

The measures recommended can be divided into measures designed to prevent problems, and measures which are designed to minimise the consequences should problems occur. Prevention measures include the following.

(i) **Physical security** of both hardware and site (entry cards, guards)

(ii) **Organisation controls** (staff training and references)

(iii) **Operational controls** and procedures (a password system stock controls)

(iv) **Fire safety procedures** (fire doors, smoke detectors, sprinklers, fire safety training)

(v) **Environmental controls** (air conditioning, dust-free environment, clean power supplies, location of computers in areas not vulnerable to flooding)

(vi) **System development controls** (proper updating procedures, documentation of program changes)

Dealing with problems

Steps which can minimise the consequences of any problems include the following.

(i) **Back up of files** or **systems**. This includes copies of files being kept in a separate (remote) location and systems regularly being 'backed up' daily.

(ii) **Stand-by hardware facilities** whenever a hardware item breaks down. These may include vendor supply agreements and contingency facilities.

(iii) **Insurance** to **mitigate** the **financial effect** of major problems.

66 COMPUTER PROBLEMS

> **Pass marks**. This is a good meaty practical problem, one which occurs all too frequently in real life. You would do well to use common sense and any relevant practical experience when forming your answer. Note that solution of the personnel problems forms a significant part of the answer to (a), but it is important to discuss back-up facilities and the wider issue of systems development strategy. A number of systems development controls are mentioned in part (b), but our answer also considers the failure of other general controls, and *why* internal audit has failed to report on the lack of controls.
>
> **Examiner's comment**. Common errors in part (a) included wasting time repeating the question, failing to distinguish between actions and discussions, and failure to distinguish between short-term and long-term actions. In part (b) some candidates failed to address the scenario set and some thought that IA could act to correct problems, rather than just reporting them.

CONFIDENTIAL MEMORANDUM

To: Managing Director
From: Financial Controller Date: XX.XX.XX
Subject: Computer system and departure of the computer services manager (CSM)

(a) **Urgent action**

I have been unhappy to learn that the Computer Services Manager (CSM) has just given a month's notice in order to take up another post. This is unfortunate, but I feel it gives us an opportunity to undertake a wide-ranging review of the **computer system,** covering its operation, control and security. There are some long-term plans which should be made, but of more immediate concern is how the situation should be dealt with before the CSM leaves, ie within the next month. I would therefore like to propose the following.

(i) **Replacement CSM**

It is obviously vital that a suitable candidate should be found. To this end a **job specification** should be prepared for the position. As this is, potentially at least, a strategic role within the group, I feel a wide range of views should be heard on this matter. A committee formed for the purpose (me, Chief IA, FD, MD?) could report in, say, one month.

(ii) **Temporary CSM**

In view of (i), we should consider appointing a temporary CSM, either externally (from a computer consultancy) or internally (possibly the shift supervisor who was helping the CSM. He may then take the position of assistant to the new CSM. A temporary CSM would aid the transition between the departing CSM and any new recruit and it would also free the current CSM to perform various tasks before he leaves, which I consider to be vital (see below). Also, the **current** CSM can be **relieved** of **day-to-day contact** with the system, to avoid any new problems being created and as a general security measure.

(iii) **Current CSM's duties**

Before he leaves, the CSM must put his handwritten system amendment notes into a **logical order** and have them typed up so he can check them. We need a **permanent copy** of amendments made to the system. In addition, any problems or errors which become manifest under the new (temporary) CSM can be cleared up by the old CSM during his final month.

(iv) **External consultancy**

An external consultant could be used to **aid** the **departing CSM** to put his amendment notes in order. The external consultant may also act as the **temporary CSM** as discussed above. In the longer term an external consultancy may be required in order to **address** the **IT problems** of the division (see below).

(v) **Back-up facilities**

Alternative back-up facilities must be found immediately. The division's computer operations are extremely **vulnerable** to any **major** (or even minor) **disruption** due to, say, fire, flood or hardware breakdown. A search should commence for some comparable facilities to our own. We need to negotiate for use of such facilities, although we may be required to offer reciprocal arrangements.

(vi) **Systems development**

The system we have is now five years old and there have been problems with it since installation. In view of this, and the departure of the CSM, an information **systems development strategy** needs to be **formulated** at divisional board level. This can be commenced at the next board meeting. In fact, the new CSM (or some other title) may be appointed at board level, in order to be involved directly with the control of systems development.

(b) **Internal audit (IA) involvement**

It is disappointing to note that the IA department has not been able or willing to help the computer services department to avoid the crisis situation in which it now finds itself. Obviously I was not present at the time, but it seems that there were some obvious areas to which both the internal and external auditors could have made a direct contribution in terms of **reporting difficulties** and **problems** encountered and thus aiding their prevention.

(i) **Systems amendments**

These amendments should require **formal authorisation** and then proper documentation, but in fact they have been carried out on an *ad hoc*, informal basis for five years. This is a serious breakdown in control over the computer system and its development. The IA department should have reported on this.

(ii) **Operating manual**

The **lack** of an **operating manual** which is up to date and complete is also a **serious breakdown** in control. It also implies that, as the internal auditors have not reported on it, they are in fact **ignoring** the **computer system** by auditing 'round' ot rather than 'through' it.

(iii) **Segregation of duties/personnel**

The **operators** of the system should *not* be able to **implement changes** to the system, as has been the case with the shift supervisor helping the CSM. As well as being a grave breach of a key control, this is also a symptom of a **breakdown** in **personnel policy**. For example, why is there no successor in line to the CSM? Why was such a senior member of staff of the CSM on only one month's notice?

(iv) **Back-up system**

Given that a back-up system was thought necessary in the past, the IA department should have commented when the division lost such facilities. The **lack** of a **disaster recovery plan** should have been commented on by both the internal and external auditors.

Summary and conclusions

The situation in the CSD is critical and should be of paramount importance to the board. Any disruption or breakdown in the computer service would disrupt the division's entire operations, affecting as it does sales, production and stock. I would appreciate a rapid response to my proposals, particularly as I am due to meet key staff tomorrow who will have a direct input into the situation.

Signed: Financial Controller

67 INFORMATION PROCESSING

Pass marks. Most of the general framework outlined in (a) can be widely applied. In (b) you needed to discuss a range of controls, but you should have emphasised the importance of specific controls over the database and access controls, since other controls would not operate very well in the system described or would be undermined by lack of segregation of duties.

Examiner's comment. In (a) candidates often failed to apply their chosen internal control framework to the circumstances given in the question. Answers to (b) were generally weaker. Candidates showed limited knowledge, producing answers that were shorter than answers to (a) despite the fact that (b) carried 50% more marks. A number of candidates failed to read the question, discussing systems other than real-time and the changeover from manual to computerised systems, topics which were not relevant to the question set.

(a) Important general controls are as follows.

Organisational structure

Clear systems of **authorisation** of transactions and **delegation** of responsibilities should be important elements in any organisational structure.

A further significant element is **segregation of duties**. Segregation allows miscreants limited opportunities to cover their tracks and also acts to detect unintentional mistakes by allowing cross-checking of work done by a different person. Since there are a significant number of functions involved in data processing, it may be difficult to segregate all the duties. In any event, however, those responsible for maintaining and developing the system should not be responsible for the actual data processing.

Supervision controls

Management should be responsible for setting of **budgets** and **operational targets,** and reviewing performance against standards set. Management should oversee the overall development of the system. In particular they should be concerned with whether the information produced has resulted in **improved service** for grant recipients and **better information** for management.

As well as senior management exercising supervision, certain staff should be exercising full–time supervision over the system, particularly if there is a lack of segregation of duties. Key tasks of the system supervisor include ensuring **authorisation procedures** are **appropriate** and properly carried out, checking that the **necessary information** is **available** should problems occur, and **investigating problems.**

Operating manual

Guidance from management covering the system should include the following elements:

(i) Clear statements of **targets,** such as length of turnaround period for all documentation

(ii) **Organisational structure**

(iii) **Job descriptions** containing responsibilities and duties of management and staff

(iv) Controls, in particular **documentation standards, security** and **integrity controls,** and **back-up** procedures

(v) A commitment to **information security** and details of legal **data protection** requirements

Staffing controls

Recruitment and **training** will be key controls. References should be requested for new recruits; this is particularly important because some of the information processed may be quite sensitive. Staff should receive sufficient training in both the technical knowledge required to carry out their work and also internal procedures.

Development controls

The system should be able to develop as the **needs of users change.** Development should however take place in accordance with defined guidelines covering **design standards,** requirements for **adequate documentation, testing procedures** and **training.** Each stage of development should be approved by both the management of the processing function and representatives of users of the information. **Internal audit** should also be involved in checking development standards have been met.

However internal audit should not be involved with actually implementing developments since this would destroy its function as an independent check.

Internal audit

Internal audit's role in checking development has been mentioned above, and it should also be responsible for carrying out regular review. It should consider whether current **controls** are **operating effectively** and are **adequate** in the light of any changes in processing. Internal audit should also carry out **substantive testing** on a selection of **payments** of grants.

(b) Real-time systems permit immediate updating of computer systems by a variety of users. An important feature is likely to be a lack of segregation of duties; the same person being responsible for originating and inputting data.

The most important controls are as follows.

Access controls

There should be **physical controls** over the computers, with access obtained only by an entry code, and the premises being kept shut outside operating hours.

A system of **passwords** should be in operation. This should be hierarchical with one level of password being required for access to information, another for the user to be able to process information. There may also be restrictions of certain users to certain files, for example restrictions on the amendment of standing or permanent data

The **effectiveness** of a **password** system will be improved by appropriate guidance and features built into the system. For example passwords should be changed regularly and no-one should use a password that could easily be guessed because of its simplicity or because of personal connection with the user. Terminals should automatically log off if no entry is made within a certain time or a wrong password is entered say three times in succession, and all attempted violations should be logged.

Input controls

Access controls should ensure **input** is only made by **authorised** staff. Various **accuracy** controls are likely to be required. Examples include check digit verification (a check on the validity of the coding of input), checks that input is within the permitted range, existence checks that recipients of grants have valid accounts within the system, and checks that all the necessary information is present.

Processing controls

Operating instructions should be clearly laid down, and updated whenever significant changes occur such as changes in the data dictionary. Controls should ensure that all input data is processed and the processing of each transaction is accurate.

The department should have **backup** and **emergency procedures** in place to ensure data processed is not lost through computer malfunction, and that processing can continue if a disaster occurs. Procedures include daily backup of processing and **storage** of what has been processed in a **remote location. Virus protection controls** should be embedded within the system. There should be **protection** of equipment against **fire** and other hazards, and arrangements to use **back-up facilities** if processing on the main site has to be suspended.

Output controls

Output controls may include an **audit trail,** the ability to trace output back to originating documentation. This may be difficult if only summary control totals are produced at the end of daily processing. A further problem with some output controls e.g. one-for-one checking with input is that they may be carried out in the real-time system by the person who input the information, and the lack of segregation of duties will mean that the control's reliability is undermined.

Hence other controls will be significant. **Exception reports,** highlighting rejected transactions should be printed out on a regular basis and reviewed by management. Management should also **review reports** of **changes** to **specified files,** particularly standing data files Internal audit can use computer assisted audit techniques to review output, in particular **SCARF,** which automatically writes transactions of certain types or certain amounts to a separate file for later review by the auditors.

The **distribution** of **output** should also be controlled carefully.

Controls over programs

These controls are particularly important because errors in programs may impact upon the processing of all transactions. **Password protection** is particularly important; no-one except computer support staff should be able to access live programs. An important review control would be periodic **comparison** of **live production programs** to **control copies** and supporting documentation. **Back-up copies** of programs should be stored away from the main site.

Controls over database

The database system will also need controls to **maintain** the **integrity** of the database. Again restriction of access is vital; **access** to the **data dictionary** should again be **restricted** to computer support staff, because the dictionary contains what is integral to the running of the system, standard descriptions including definitions, characteristics and inter-relationship of data. There should be segregation of duties between the data processing and database administration functions.

68 INTEGRATED COMPUTER SYSTEM DEVELOPMENT

Pass marks. Part (a) deals with wider considerations than pure audit questions. You should note in part (b) the emphasis on *user* needs both as regards the operation of the system and training in it. The answer to (b) also matches the principal accounting and audit problems with their solutions, rather than going into detail about the whole of the systems development process.

Examiner's comment. A common failing on even good scripts was to write more on part (a) than part (b), which had more than twice as many marks. Other weaknesses in part (a) were writing generally about systems, failing to discuss the role and operations of a committee and proposing that the project start all over again. In (b) many answers failed to discuss how the problems related to the introduction of the new system and standardisation, and the solution of the problems. A number of answers failed to focus on the requirements of the question but were general essays on internal control guidance and computer auditing.

The examiner stated that although the project mentioned in the scenario was the development of a computer system, the question raised a number of points that were applicable generally to project management scenarios.

(a) **Planning the project**

If progress and problems are to be communicated effectively, projects must be properly planned. The choice of the new computer system should have been based on a **feasibility study** with alternative solutions assessed. This study should have highlighted **possible problems** with the implementation of the new system, for example the need to have it fully operational before the next year-end.

Once the system had been decided on, the following should have been approved by management.

(i) **Overall project targets** for costs, timescale or resource usage should have been **established.**

(ii) The **project** should have been **divided** into **activities,** time and cost budgets set and resources allocated for each activity.

(iii) A **framework** should have been set for **monitoring** the project.

The monitoring process

In order for management to monitor the project effectively, the following must be established.

Measurement mechanisms. Time taken can be measured by reference to network analysis or Gantt charts. **Resources** used can be measured by available resources and percentage utilisation. **Costs** can be measured by reference to budgets.

Lines of reporting. It is necessary to establish to **whom progress** should be **reported** and to **whom problems** should be **reported.** As well as reporting to senior management user departments should be contacted if **time and budget constraints** mean that **features** they have **requested cannot be implemented.**

Reporting to management. Reporting to management of progress and expenditure should take place **every so often** as a matter of course and also at the **completion of every major stage** of the project. Additionally **time** or **budget overruns** or **excess resource usage** should be reported **as soon as they appear likely** to occur.

(b) The new system may pose the following audit and accounting problems.

Capacity of new system

Assurance is required that the new system will be able to **cope** with the **volume of processing.**

Local requirements

The new system is replacing a number of systems, and it is possible that **local needs** will be **ignored.** This may mean the **information available** under the new system is **less** than before, and it may mean the **system cannot cope** with all the **necessary accounting requirements,** for example valuation of stock.

Master files

New master files which contain the appropriate information must be set up but this may be difficult given the **variety** of **local requirements.**

Transfer of data

There is a risk of **data** being **lost** or **corrupted** when being transferred.

Staff problems

Lack of training of staff and **lack of documentation** of the new system may increase the risk of errors when the system does become operational.

Disaster recovery

Because the group will now be dependent on a single system, the consequences of a **system breakdown** could be **catastrophic.**

Audit problems

Amongst the audit problems the new system could pose are the following.

Loss of controls. Controls which the auditors will be particularly concerned with are **lack of segregation of duties**; in a single system only a small number of people will be involved. The Finance Director's concerns also indicate that **supervision** by management may be **more difficult**.

Loss of audit trail. Auditors may not be able to trace transactions through the system.

The following actions should enable the risks to be reduced.

Capacity of new system

The **operation** of the whole of the new system should be **tested** prior to implementation using the kind of data volumes from different users that it will have to cope with when operational. In addition the **new system** should be **run** in **parallel** with the old systems initially, to minimise disruption should the new system be unable to cope with the volume of data.

Local requirements

All **users** should be **consulted** about their needs prior to the system being designed. They should also be involved in testing the system to ensure it meets their requirements.

Master files

Design of an **appropriate system** of master files and coding system should be a **priority** in the development process. Consultation with users is particularly important here.

Transfer of data

Data files from the old system should be **copied** before conversion in the case of failure or corruption. **Master file** data should be **input in stages**, with the data input being copied at each stage. Once the data has been input, it should be printed out and compared with an independent source.

Staff problems

These can be overcome by **proper documentation** and **training**. Documentation of the system should include:

(i) **listings** of program instructions, flowcharts, file layouts, input and output documentation, and the **procedures** which each program module covers;

(ii) details of **procedures** to be followed if a **systems crash** occurs;

(iii) an **operating manual**, containing instructions on setting up and operating the system, and details of error messages and what action to take if they occur.

Training sessions should also help staff. These should include **posting** of **test data**. Attendance records should be kept so that management can ensure that all potential users of the system are trained.

Disaster recovery

There should be **formal plans** for disaster recovery. These should include ongoing controls such as **backup of systems** and **storage of files** in a remote location. There should also be arrangements for **alternative facilities** to be provided should a catastrophe occur. The plan should cover different types and levels of disruption and should be properly tested.

Audit problems

Audit problems can be reduced by having **internal audit specify** their **requirements** at the start of the design process. These may include for example having a Systems Control and Review File (SCARF) built into the system so that certain general ledger accounts are designated as SCARF accounts. Transactions within those accounts which are above a certain monetary value should be posted to a separate SCARF file. Auditors should also consider whether certain key controls will be in operation, for example segregation of duties, access to data and provision of information to management.

69 TUTORIAL QUESTION: COMPUTER SYSTEM AUDIT

(a) (i) A **preliminary analysis** describes the stages in development leading up to and including the feasibility study. The function of a preliminary analysis is to **assess requirements** and **alternatives** before committing large quantities of resources to system development.

These stages could be listed as follows.

(1) Having identified the need for a new system, **specifying** the **objectives** of the system and the requirements/functions that it must fulfil.

(2) **Defining** the **environment** within which the system must operate, which might impose various constraints on the system design.

(3) **Carrying out** a **feasibility study**, which will include the identification and evaluation of alternative systems, and outline design proposals for the preferred new system. A feasibility study should help to ensure that the proposed system will do everything that will be required of it, and that there is no better alternative system.

The costs of a preliminary analysis should be justified by the avoidance of inefficiency or wasteful expenditure that might be incurred if the new system were designed without a clear understanding of objectives, needs and alternatives.

(ii) Studies would be carried out to record the existing system and its weaknesses. This would involve investigations into:

(1) what **information** is **currently produced**, and why it might be inadequate;

(2) the **purpose** of the **information** that is **currently provided,** and whether there are other ways in which accounting information could be used which the current system fails to cater for;

(3) **who uses** the available information (and who *ought* to use it);

(4) **when** the information is **used;**

(5) what **future information requirements** might be;

(6) the **volume of data processed** by the system and the **quantity** of information **produced;**

(7) the **availability** of, or requirement for, **information** from **external** sources;

(8) the **personnel** who will **input** data and the sources of data;

(9) the **personnel** and other resources **available** to **develop** a new system;

(10) the **personnel** and other resources **available** to **operate** the new system;

(11) the various types of **hardware** and **software systems available**;

(12) **cost/benefit studies** of alternative systems.

(b) A computer systems efficiency audit will set out to check both the **effectiveness** and the **efficiency** of a system, and so could be described as a value for money audit of a computer system.

Efficiency is measured by relating the outputs of a system (and their value) to its inputs (and their cost). **Outputs** from a computer system consist of **information** and **processed transactions. Inputs** consist of **equipment costs, labour costs, materials consumed** and so on.

(i) One approach to an audit is to establish what the **valuable outputs** of the system are, and what the **cheapest alternative system** for providing these outputs would be. The costs of the cheapest alternative should then be compared with the actual costs of the system in use. This comparison might help the auditor to identify inefficiencies or unnecessary costs within the current system.

(ii) An alternative audit approach would be to **study the system** and **identify** any **weaknesses** in it.

The various aspects of the computer department which the auditor will look at are as follows.

(1) **General environment of the department**. A visit to the computer department itself will be made in order to look at:

- the **layout** of the department, to check whether it is conducive to good work flow, and easy access to equipment for maintenance engineers and so on;
- the **stock room**, to check that it is well organised and that stores items are not being wasted;
- the **physical working conditions** for staff, such as lighting, seating, table heights;
- the **relationship** of **various rooms** in the department, to check on ease of access and security (non-access by unauthorised personnel) and the security of the files;
- the **security of files** (are they kept locked up?);

(2) **Security**. Security measures should be checked, including:

- **physical access** to the **computer**, and access via remote terminals (for example all data links should be disconnected whenever the computer room is left unattended, and all attempts to 'log on' should be printed out as soon as the attempt is made);
- the use of **passwords** and the methods used to change passwords regularly;
- **emergency procedures** in the event of fire or flood; use of back-up files.

(3) **Housekeeping**. These matters relate to the simple routines of the department, such as regular cleaning and maintenance of equipment.

(4) **Organisation of the department**. The organisation of the computer department should be checked, and matters to look into include:

- **shift work** in the department (hand over and communication procedures between shifts);
- the **organisation** and **timing** of **computer runs** (actual run times should be checked against planned times, and significant differences queried;
- checking the '**complaints file**' (complaints from user departments of bad service from the DP department);
- whether the computer's work load involves **peak loads** at certain times, and whether work loading could be smoothed out more evenly;
- **staffing levels**: are they excessive or inadequate;
- the **control of expenditure** by DP staff (are expenditure budgets prepared, and are budgetary control measures enforced?)

(5) **Standards**. The procedures used in the department should be checked, and in particular:

- the **DP Standards** in use;
- the **quality** of the **documentation** in use;
- whether **all operating** and **programming documentation is properly maintained** and **up-to-date**;
- whether **amendment procedures are suitable** and **properly enforced**?

(6) **Controls**. The auditor should check the controls that would also be carried out in the course of a statutory audit by the external auditors, such as checks on:

- controls over **data entry**;
- **control totals**;
- **audit trails**;
- **password** security and user identification checks;
- the **accuracy** of **programs**: are programs written in a modular fashion, for ease of correction and amendment?
- the adequacy of procedures for **checking programs** before they go operational;
- the adequacy of **procedures** for **approving** new jobs for development and loading on to the computer.

(7) **PC links**. Where the mainframe has links with remote PCs, the auditor's terms of reference might include a requirement to check:

- the **cost-effectiveness** of the current use of the **network** of department should be checked, and matters to look at include:
- the **compatibility** between the mainframe and the satellite PCs.

Weaknesses might be apparent from:

(1) **long waiting times**/response times;

(2) **low capacity usage** of some items of equipment;

(3) **high error rates**, for example a high volume of validation errors;

(4) **poor security,** for example passwords that can be fairly easily discovered by unauthorised hackers.

(iii) Another approach would be to **compare** what the **system actually does** to the **system requirements** that are set out in the original system specification. Weaknesses in the system could be identified by divergence between system requirements and actual performance.

(iv) A computer system that processes financial data needs to process data accurately and completely. One of the tasks of the external auditor (and internal auditor) will be to check that **transactions records** are **fully** and **accurately processed,** by means of selected control tests and substantive tests. Satisfactory testing would provide some indication of system efficiency.

70 NEW SYSTEM

Pass marks. The important point in part (a) is that because of limited time a full balance sheet audit is not possible. Hence the instructions have to demonstrate the extent of work required. The main part of the answer to (b) concentrates on investigating why the discrepancies might have arisen.

Prizewinners' points. The answer to (b) also considers disaster recovery procedures and changes to standing data, since the new system may have rendered previous arrangements inadequate.

Examiner's comment. The better answers to (a) justified the level of review to be undertaken, and specified what should be done. Important points in (b) were the ability of the group system to cope with the division's needs, instruction of staff, and problems of systems implementation.

(a) MEMORANDUM

To: Finance Staff
From: Finance Director Date: XX.XX.XX
Subject: Financial Accounts Investigation

Risk areas

We need to obtain assurance that **assets and liabilities** are **not misstated** in the interim accounts, as any misstatements may also have a significant impact on interim profits. Because of the timescale available, we need to concentrate on the areas where there is highest risk of material misstatement. These are likely to be the following.

(i) **Stock**. Misstatement of stock will have a significant impact on divisional profits. Initial investigations have indicated potential stock control problems, and this may mean that **significant movements** of stock have **not** been **recorded. Valuation** of stock may well be problematic given the amount of work in progress within stock.

(ii) **Debtors and sales.** One explanation for poor results could be **understatement of sales.** This could be caused by failing to invoice sales made, or omission of invoices or receipts from accounting records.

(iii) **Creditors and purchases.** We need to check why **purchases** may have **increased.** It may be due to poor ordering policies or be linked to lack of control over stock.

(iv) **Expenses.** We need to check **major changes** in **significant expenses,** in particular whether major capital expenditure has been misclassified as revenue expenditure.

The work we will do will consist of analytical review and verification work on major areas.

Analytical review

The problems with the new financial accounting package mean we can only place limited reliance on analytical review using the financial accounting data. However analytical review may help highlight discrepancies in the following areas.

(i) **Sales.** We should try and identify **lines** where **sales** are significantly **below** sales in **previous years,** what was **budgeted** or what was **shown** in the **management accounts** prepared by the division.

(ii) **Stock.** If possible, we should try and **reconcile opening stock balances** and stock **movements** during the year with **current stock balances** for the major stock lines. We should also check whether **stock held differs** significantly from **previous years.**

(iii) **Debtors.** We need to identify **major debtors** where **balances** have **significantly increased.**

(iv) **Expenditure.** Review should highlight **regular expenditure,** such as rent or insurance, which is **significantly different** from what is usual and **large items of discretionary expenditure** (expenditure which does not follow a predictable pattern.)

Substantive testing

The extent of substantive testing we do and the items we test will depend on the results of our analytical review. Testing is however likely to be concentrated in the following areas.

(i) **Stocks.** We should carry out a **stocktake** of major lines comparing physical stock counted with stock records. The stocktake should concentrate on **lines** where there have been **unexpectedly large movements** or **little movement** at all, and sites where a significant amount of stock has been held in previous years.

We should also check the **valuation** of stock, concentrating again on major lines. This will involve consideration of whether stock has been **costed** correctly, and whether a **provision** is **required** against slow-moving stock.

(ii) **Debtors.** We need to **confirm balances** held with **major debtors** by **circularisation** of those debtors.

(iii) **Creditors.** We should **obtain suppliers' statements** for major suppliers and **attempt** to **reconcile balances shown** with **balances** recorded in the **purchase ledger.**

(iv) **Expenditure.** We need to **confirm expenditure** highlighted, by **analytical review** as large or unusual to authorised invoices, orders and other relevant evidence.

(b) To: Internal Auditor
From: Chief Internal Auditor   Date: XX.XX.XX
Subject: Review Of Computerised Financial Accounting System

The main purposes of your review will be to ascertain whether problems have arisen as a result of the system failing to meet the needs of the department or whether problems have occurred in systems implementation.

Systems design

You will need to discuss with the Divisional Managing Director and other senior management how they believe that the **system fails to fulfil** their **requirements** and if they have any idea **why** the **financial accounting figures differed** significantly from their own **management accounting** information. The division may for example have unusual features which were not taken into account when the system was designed, for example costing of stock.

You should also **compare** the **system specification** against **details** of the **flow of documentation** within the division; this may highlight needs which the computer system does not address.

Systems implementation

The Divisional MD has commented that the new system has caused problems because of the inexperience of the staff. You need therefore to assess whether the **training** of staff and the **documentation** of the new system were **adequate** for the staff's needs, in particular how far their instruction has reflected what they have been trying to do in practice.

You also need to check **how** the **new system** was **implemented**. You need to find out whether there was **parallel running** of the new system and the old system, and if so, how discrepancies found were followed up. Even if there was no parallel running, there should have been reviews of the initial operation of the system.

How the **new system** has **changed operations** will need to be examined. You should ascertain whether new input and amendments to existing data that were previously checked and authorised are now not being checked. The new system may have meant a lessening of segregation of duties.

You need to consider **why** the **differences** between the financial and management accounts have **surprised** the accounting staff. This may be due to shortcomings in the new system for example an **absence** of **reasonableness checks**. It may also be due to a **failure** to **review** the **output** of the system for accuracy and completeness, and this may indicate a lack of supervision by management.

Other areas

As well as considering why problems may have arisen, you need to consider **how future problems** may be **prevented**. You should consider the adequacy of **computer maintenance arrangements** in the division, and also **emergency** and **disaster recovery procedures**.

You should also examine **controls** over **amendments** to **master files** and **standing data** since problems with these may seriously affect the results given by the package.

Reporting

Once your review has been completed, you should report the results with appropriate recommendations. These should highlight what **action** needs to taken at the **divisional level** and what action is required to **amend** the **financial accounting package**. You should also highlight **when recommendations** should be **implemented** and in particular what **actions** must be taken **prior to** the preparation of the **final accounts**.

71 REAL TIME TRANSACTION PROCESSING

Pass marks. Real-time transaction processing, as the question states, is becoming quite common and this is likely to be a continuing trend. Consequently, the examiner may feel that this is the area which he should concentrate on when asking questions about computer auditing. Do not get sidetracked into discussing computer controls and computer auditing in general terms; the answer to (b) concentrates on access controls, programmed procedures, maintenance of an audit trail using hard copy and back up controls.

Examiner's comment. Too much time was spent on part (a) on many occasions. A number of scripts contained a general discussion of computer audit, rather than concentrating on the specific difficulties of real-time systems. Parts (b) and (c) were less well answered; many answers to part (c) contained little discussion on the problems of using CAAT's.

(a) **Problems with real-time transaction processing**

The main problems arise because of the way previous information and transactions are constantly being overwritten by new transactions. In these situations, **operators** at **remote terminals** (of which there may be a substantial number) can **input** data and **update data files** directly. On-line systems which do *not* operate in real time will collect transactions for batch processing and subsequent update of files.

As with all computer systems, controls over **security of files** and **completeness** and **accuracy** of **input**, **processing** and **output**, are fundamental. Real-time systems, however, offer the internal auditor additional problems.

(i) **Segregation of duties**. When remote terminals are located at the point at which data is originated, the same person may be responsible for producing and processing the same information. To compensate for the reduction in internal check, **supervisory controls** should be strengthened.

(ii) **Data file and program security**. The ability of a person using a remote terminal to gain access to the computer at will results in the need for special **controls** to ensure that **files are neither read** nor **written** to (nor destroyed), either accidentally or deliberately, **without proper authority**.

(iii) **Audit trail**. The **usual 'vouching'** method of auditing a system may **not** be **possible** if there is no initiating document or voucher, eg an order form.

(iv) **Completeness** and **accuracy** of **processing cannot** be **assured** because there are no batch controls, as there are in a batch processing system.

(v) **File reconstructions**. **Dumping**, the method of allowing for the reconstructing of direct access files in batch processing systems, is of **limited use** in on-line systems as the contents of the file are being continually changed. Although the complete file will be dumped periodically, it is also necessary to maintain a **file giving details** of all **transactions processed since the last dump**.

(b) **Internal audit procedures**

To solve the problems listed above, the internal auditor should undertake the following procedures.

(i) Ensure **access** is **restricted** to the system by the use of both **physical access controls** (terminal restrictions) and **operating system controls**, such as strict passwords.

(ii) Ensure there are **controls** over the **validity** of **input**, by checks on the parameters in different fields, input reject reports, etc.

(iii) Check that there are **restrictions** imposed, by the operating system, of **certain terminals** to **certain files**. For example, the terminal in the wages department may only be given access to the wages file. Some terminals might be 'read only' or 'write only'.

(iv) **All transactions** should be **recorded** as **hard copy output**, identifying the operator who input the data, time and date of transaction etc. The internal auditors should check that this is the case.

(v) The internal auditors could introduce the concept of a **standard source document**, where no source document currently exists. This document should have a unique reference for the transaction which can be traced to hard copy output.

(vi) All **attempted violations** of the above controls should be **logged**, possibly accompanied by the automatic shut down of the terminal used. Obviously all violations should be speedily and thoroughly investigated. The internal auditors should check that all violations are investigated and follow through some of the investigations to their conclusion.

(vii) The internal auditors should check that **data files** are **dumped** on a regular basis, **at least daily** and that **transaction files** are **retained**, so that an audit trail can be traced in support of current transactions.

(c) **Use of computer-assisted audit techniques**

CAATs can be used to great effect on real-time systems, where testing of controls (compliance testing) will be of much greater importance and value than substantive procedures. However, the usual 'test data' type of CAATs used on batch processing systems will not be of use on real-time processing system files and programs because **audit data introduced** into the system (to compare with manually calculated expected results) may **corrupt data files** which are being continuously updated.

Embedded audit facilities would be the most useful type of CAAT to use on a real-time system.

(i) **Integrated test facilities (ITF)** could be used to **process dummy audit data** using a fictitious entity; dummy audit data would be processed alongside real data, but without corrupting it. This is a useful test of the computer processing controls.

(ii) **Systems controls and review files (SCARF)** can be used to **record transactions** of a type flagged by the auditors, eg all sales over a certain value, or all postings to a certain customer's account. Again, this will test processing controls.

(iii) **Program comparisons** can be made, where the auditors check their 'authorised' version of a program with that which is being used. This will allow the auditors to discover unauthorised amendments to programs.

Stage 4 — **MOCK EXAM**

Paper 16 — November 1999

Management Accounting Control Systems

MCS

INSTRUCTIONS TO CANDIDATES

You are allowed three hours to answer this question paper.
Answer the TWO questions in section A. *Answer TWO questions ONLY from section B.*

DO NOT OPEN THIS PAPER UNTIL YOU ARE READY TO START UNDER EXAMINATION CONDITIONS

SECTION A - 60 MARKS

ANSWER ***BOTH*** QUESTIONS

1. **(a)** The apportionment of costs to separate operational units within an organisation is often criticised for its apparently arbitrary nature and because the costs may not be controllable by the operational unit manager.

REQUIREMENT:

Explain the following.

(i) The arguments for apportioning central costs to the divisions in a decentralised organisation

(ii) The criteria which you would use in assessing the suitability of a system of cost apportionment **14 Marks**

(b) A small hotel group, comprising five hotels, has installed a central reservation system with the long-term strategic aim of increasing profitability by improving marketing and management information.

In the first year of operation, the annual costs incurred in respect of the central reservation system were as follows.

	£'000
Fixed (leasing equipment, computer costs)	430
Fixed (marketing)	250
Variable (enquiry staff)	180
Total	860

It is considered that these costs should be apportioned to each hotel. The new system has not saved significant costs at each hotel, but has provided better management information locally, and for central marketing. Additional sales of accommodation (room nights) have been achieved by central marketing, using the information now available.

The finance director has proposed apportioning all the costs of the central reservation system on the same basis, that of the total room revenue for each hotel.

The hotel managers' total remuneration includes a significant bonus element related to their hotel's profit performance. The managers of hotels A and D have protested strongly about this proposal, which they consider could have an adverse effect upon their total remuneration.

Summary data for the hotels for the first year of operation of the central reservation system is as follows.

	Hotel A	*Hotel B*	*Hotel C*	*Hotel D*	*Hotel E*	*Total group*
Number of rooms	180	104	96	88	70	538
Room revenue for year (£'000)	6,833	2,050	2,264	3,003	864	15,014
% occupancy *	80	60	68	85	52	71
Reservation system enquiries	7,000	3,375	5,140	3,800	2,340	21,655
Room nights sold by central marketing	4,900	6,200	7,300	1,700	5,500	25,600

* This is the room nights sold compared with the total number of room nights available per year.

REQUIREMENTS:

(i) Explain, with supporting calculations, why the managers of hotels A and D dislike the finance director's proposal to apportion the costs of the central reservation system on the basis of total room revenues for each hotel.

Evaluate whether they are justified in claiming that it could have an adverse effect on their remuneration.

(ii) The managers of hotels A and D have expressed the view that they would prefer a system under which the costs of the central reservation system are apportioned on the basis of room nights sold by central marketing, a flat rate charge per room night sold.

Explain and discuss the arguments, other than the financial advantage to the managers of hotels A and D, that could be advanced to justify this approach.

(iii) As group management accountant, recommend with reasons, using the data available, how the costs of the central reservation system should be related to individual hotel operations. Compare the results per hotel with the finance director's system, and with the system described in (ii) above preferred by the managers of hotels A and D.

(iv) Explain briefly the management issues arising from the question of relating central reservation system costs to individual hotel operations.

26 Marks

Total Marks = 40

---

2. A public sector body has been providing free professional advice to the public for a considerable time. The administrative procedures and management structure have not changed significantly for many years. Funding has been provided by central government, but administration has been entirely local with little detailed central guidance. It has been assumed that professional qualification provides sufficient proof of competence.

In recent years, the service has come under pressure as funds have been restricted and the service has been less able to cope with the increasing volume of public demand.

Waiting lists of members of the public waiting to see professionally-qualified staff are kept locally by the service. The numbers on these lists have increased considerably, and the time that members of the public have to wait appears to have increased significantly.

Public dissatisfaction with lengthening waiting lists has been considerable. There has been much disquiet regarding the fairness of the administration of waiting lists, and with some professional staff providing the same service on a private basis for a fee in their own time in the evenings and at weekends.

Disquiet has been caused by 'whistleblowing' employees. These employees have been reported extensively in the popular press complaining (often anonymously) of senior professional staff using public facilities for private practice and favouring their friends in determining waiting list priorities.

Policy decisions have now been taken by central government that the service must be improved and waiting lists reduced.

REQUIREMENTS:

(a) Explain what new central control systems are required immediately and how they will contribute to the improvement of the service, and/or reduce the waiting lists.

(b) Discuss what control problems are likely to remain, and explain briefly what further control and information systems may be required. Include in your discussion comment on the following.

- The reliability of waiting list statistics, and the importance of such information for resource allocation
- The monitoring of quality standards
- Whether professional staff should be allowed to practise privately in the manner described in the scenario

20 Marks

SECTION B - 40 MARKS

ANSWER ***TWO*** QUESTIONS ONLY - 20 MARKS EACH

3. **(a)** Explain what substantive tests would normally be undertaken on debtors in the audit of sales to corporate customers. **8 Marks**

J plc sells by mail order from catalogues issued several times a year. These are aimed at lower income customers who are attracted by the credit terms offered. A wide range of products can be obtained immediately even by customers who would find it difficult to obtain credit elsewhere.

Easily-available credit is the most important part of J plc's business. Credit control in this business does not compare with other kinds of business where sales are to business organisations, ie corporate customers.

J plc is reviewing its sales policies and is considering further relaxation of its checking of the creditworthiness of potential customers. The directors are well aware that problems with lower income customers will involve administrative costs and significant losses from default, but they consider that the additional volume and profit earned will compensate for this.

REQUIREMENTS:

(b) Explain how tests on debtors may differ if sales are to a large number of individual customers each purchasing small amounts on extended credit. **6 Marks**

(c) Explain how the customer databases in J plc can be interrogated to provide a better assessment of the risks than would be possible by the examination of sample individual accounts. **6 Marks**

Total Marks = 20

---

4. **(a)** Internal control and audit have always involved the assessment of risk. Many approaches to this have been developed: a formula which has been much used is

$$AR = IR \times CR \times DR$$

where AR is audit risk, IR is inherent risk, CR is control risk and DR is detection risk.

REQUIREMENT:

Explain this formula and its use in internal audit. **8 Marks**

(b) Recommendations on corporate governance have stressed the need for directors to consider control procedures within the organisation in the context of a review of the range of relevant control objectives for the organisation.

These recommendations regard business risk assessment and response to this assessment as key internal control objectives.

REQUIREMENT:

Explain what is meant by **business risk assessment and response** and the importance of this in the evaluation of internal control. Explain and discuss the case for the publication of a statement of business risk as part of the disclosures in the annual report. **12 Marks**

Total Marks = 20

5. B plc is a very large bank/financial services organisation. It takes deposits, and sells a wide range of financial services and products to individual customers, for example, current account services, medium- and short-term loans, insurance products. B plc differs from a number of other banks in that it does not lend significantly to businesses. It regards itself as more innovative than its competitors in promoting new products.

Whilst it operates some postal accounts, and is experimenting with telephone banking, B plc's main customer contact is through a network of several hundred branches in shopping centres.

Products for sale are all designed and publicised centrally. Customer care procedures, ensuring that customers understand what they are buying and that the product is suitable for their needs, are centrally determined, in response to industry regulation. Staffing of branches is authorised by head office which determines the required number and grade of staff.

Senior management wish to review and possibly change the system of branch control, because it does not appear to offer sufficient scope for managerial freedom at branch level.

REQUIREMENTS:

(a) Discuss the benefits and problems of systems of central authorisation of branch staffing levels as a means of controlling costs, performance and quality. **6 Marks**

(b) Discuss the consequences of a change in the control systems away from systems of detailed head office control to devolved branch budgets. **6 Marks**

(c) There is some opposition within senior management to the proposed changes. This comes primarily from those who are responsible for product design and marketing who regard product sales and profitability as all-important and the branch network as merely a cost of selling a mixture of products.

Explain the arguments for central management concentrating on the control of product profitability. Discuss whether central management should regard product profitability as their main concern, or whether they should be more concerned with branch profitability.

8 Marks

Total Marks = 20

---

6. Manufacturing company PQ has adopted just in time (JIT) techniques, and has simplified its manufacturing accounting and standard costing system.

Under the simplified system, the following occur.

- Material receipts are recorded as before, and a purchase price variance calculated.
- Works orders are no longer used. The flow of raw materials and components from stores through work in progress to finished goods is on demand (a Kanban system).
- On product completion, the standard material cost is charged to the profit and loss account and credited to the combined raw material and work in progress account (the RIP - raw and in-progress account).
- The monthly operating statement shows the standard material cost and variances, and actual labour and overhead costs for the period. For financial reporting purposes, adjustments are required for the labour and overhead content of work in progress and finished goods.

Despite this simplification, the number of transactions has increased significantly, mainly because of more frequent deliveries from suppliers, but also from calculations for smaller production quantities. Bar coding has been introduced to cope with the increased volume of transactions.

A more ambitious simplification of the manufacturing accounting system has been proposed which would eliminate recording the receipt of materials. All transactions would be triggered by the receipt into finished goods of a successfully completed item, which would lead to recognition of the material purchase and lead to payment by electronic funds transfer.

You, as internal auditor, have been asked to comment on this proposal.

REQUIREMENT:

Recommend, with reasons, whether the proposal should be implemented. Your answer should include the following.

- An explanation and discussion of whether there are any conditions which have to exist for this proposal to be successful
- Comment on the practical problems for the supplier, the management accountant and the internal auditor

20 Marks

ANSWERS

DO NOT TURN THIS PAGE UNTIL YOU HAVE COMPLETED THE TEST PAPER

The examiner for Management Accounting Control Systems offers the following background and guidance on the questions included in this examination paper.

Section A - compulsory

Question 1, which is in syllabus section (c), requires the evaluation of a range of approaches to a cost apportionment problem. Cost apportionment can have a significant effect on the motivation and earnings of managers of separately managed profit centres. Making and justifying an appropriate apportionment is not easy. While many managers hold firm, if unclear views on the need for equity, there are the competing criteria of benefit and ability to pay. This is made more complex by the frequent justification for central services in providing benefit to the centre as well as to the operational units, and possibly changing the balance of responsibility between the centre and the separate units.

Question 2 is on change management in a monopoly service. The scenario could apply to a public sector service or to a privatised utility. It essentially deals with change management. The problems are devising control systems, and measurement systems; control will be ineffective without reliable and appropriate information. A particular problem is that of employees using their professional skills privately. There is scope for debate on whether this should be allowed, but some consideration is needed of whether it can be controlled. The question is in syllabus sections (a) and (d).

Section B - two questions from four

Question 3, on computer audit, requires the explanation and comparison of audit testing of corporate customers and a large number of small individual customers. It further requires the explanation of the scope for a database system to provide the information for a better assessment of the overall risk than the normal audit procedure of working from samples. The question is in syllabus section (d). It should be noted that the question does not require a discussion of the commercial decision to accept poorer customers, and possibly more bad debts, to achieve greater volume and contribution.

Question 4, which is in syllabus sections (a) and (d), initially requires a quite straightforward explanation of audit risk. This sets the scene for the more substantial question of business risk and the explanation of this in the annual report. There have been a number of proposals for this as part of better corporate governance, notably in Hampel. The question does not require knowledge of the precise current requirements of the Turnbull Report, but requires understanding of the case for risk disclosure.

Question 5, on devolved budgets, deals with the problem of branch autonomy. Retaining and motivating good branch managers depends on systems, such as devolved budgets, to provide local authority and discretion and scope of action. Without these, good managers will not be retained. The issue is whether central controls are desirable as well as feasible. The more difficult part of the question deals with alternative views of responsibility for profit. The question is in syllabus section (b).

Question 6, which is in syllabus sections (b) and (d), deals with the consequences of pressures for greater integration of manufacturing systems with supplier systems to speed the progress through the supply chain to the ultimate customer. The case for such changes is based on the need to achieve speed as well as to save costs. Candidates are required to recognise the problems, and recommend whether the proposed changes are made.

1

> **Pass marks**. Time management and answer planning in this question are crucial. The overlap between parts (a) and (b) is substantial. In answering part (a) it would be easy to begin relating your answer to the hotel industry given in the scenario. It would therefore be better to write about organisations in general, thereby leaving yourself something to write about in part (b).
>
> Similarly in part (b) there is a high risk that you could include information relating to the latter sections of the question in your answer to the earlier sections.
>
> In identifying an alternative recharge method in (b)(iii), the most important issue to identify is that the cost base contained both fixed and variable elements.

(a) (i) There are a number of **arguments for apportioning costs** met centrally (for example accounting, advertising and marketing, treasury and legal) to the divisions that are receiving the benefit of the costs incurred through the provision of a service.

- The system is **fair**. If the divisions were separate entities they would have to meet the costs directly.
- Apportioning central costs can be a useful method of **evaluating the performance of individual divisions**. Not only can the true profit of each division be evaluated for inter-divisional performance comparison purposes, useful information may be revealed when comparing the divisions to smaller companies.
- The apportionment of costs may also lead the managers of decentralised units to complain if they consider they do not **receive value for money in the services they are paying for**. Senior management may therefore take control action to ensure that the cost-generating departments improve the services, either in terms of quality of service or by reducing recharged costs or both.
- Similarly if the managers responsible for the central costs know that they will have to justify their costs to divisional managers, they may become **more cost conscious** and actively try to provide a value-for-money service.
- If central costs are apportioned on a volume basis, divisions may need **to become more efficient** and **reduce their demand** for group services to keep recharged costs as low as possible.
- The apportionment of central costs to divisions should make the **divisions aware of the costs of group services** and will allow them to build such costs into their **pricing** structures.
- Cost apportionment may be necessary from a **regulatory** point of view (to avoid the accusation of profit manipulation in foreign divisions - the transfer pricing issue) or may be useful if there is a **legal** requirement for absorption costing stock valuations in published accounts (as only one costing system will be required).

(ii) The following criteria would be useful in assessing the suitability of a system of cost apportionment.

- **Value for money.** The system must be relatively cheap to administer as it is not directly providing any value added.

- **Fairness**. The results of the apportionment should be justifiable. An activity-based approach, with costs being apportioned to those divisions generating the expenditure, is one possible method.
- **Reliable.** Costs should be traced accurately to cost objects, otherwise divisional managers will have little faith in the value of the system.
- **Autonomy**. As far as possible, the apportioned costs should relate to activities in which managers have agreed to participate or over which they have some control of the level of incidence.
- **Goal congruence**. The apportionment should result in behaviour which is generally beneficial to the group as a whole. It should not permit manipulation by divisional managers for their own benefit and should encourage divisional managers to make maximum use of central services, while at the same time ensuring that managers of cost-generating departments keep costs under control.
- **Simplicity.** The system needs to be easy to understand and manage. Complicated systems could be treated with scepticism by divisional managers, who might see them as a way of accountants blinding them with numbers.
- **Acceptance.** The system and its results should be acceptable to the divisional managers concerned.
- **Decision making.** The resulting information should be useful for decision making (such as pricing and resource allocation decisions) and therefore it may be more appropriate to apportion costs on a standard cost basis to avoid cost inefficiencies being passed on to user divisions.
- **Performance evaluation.** The system should allow for evaluation of the cost effectiveness of the central services provided.

(b) (i) **Hotels A and D** reported the **highest room revenues** for the year (£6,833,000 and £3,003,000 respectively). Given that the Finance Director's (FD's) proposal is to recharge the costs of the reservation system on the basis of room revenue, hotels A and D would **suffer the highest recharges**, as shown below.

			Hotels			
	A	*B*	*C*	*D*	*E*	*Total*
Room revenue (£'000)	6,833	2,050	2,264	3,003	864	15,014
Room revenue (%)	45.5%	13.7%	15.1%	20.0%	5.7%	100%
Apportioned costs	£391,300	£117,820	£129,860	£172,000	£49,020	£860,000

They could therefore **claim** that they are **being penalised for managing the most successful hotels** within the group (in terms of revenue), rather than being rewarded for their efforts. And the success or otherwise of the central reservation system **(CRS) is not the only influence on revenue**. Even if all the hotels were the same size and enjoyed the same occupancy rates, revenue would still be affected by the room rate charged.

As the figures below show, the **percentage of room nights available that were actually sold by central marketing were lowest for hotels A and D** and the **conversion rates of enquiries to bookings were unimpressive**.

	Hotels					
	A	*B*	*C*	*D*	*E*	*Total*
Room nights available (no of rooms × 365)	65,700	37,960	35,040	32,120	25,550	196,370
% of room nights available sold by central marketing	7.5%	16.3%	20.8%	5.3%	21.5%	13.0%
Room nights sold by central marketing in relation to the number of enquiries	70%	184%	142%	45%	235%	118%

As the hotel managers' total remuneration includes a significant **bonus element related to their hotel's profit performance**, the managers of hotels A and D would therefore be **justified in asking for a review of the system** of apportionment given that the recharge will have some effect on the level of profit reported for the hotel.

Whether they would be justified in claiming that the FD's proposal could have an adverse effect on their remuneration would depend on whether the **contribution earned on the sales generated by the CRS offset the apportioned costs**. The figures below show that the revenue generated should provide an adequate level of contribution to cover the allocated central costs in the case of hotel A, but the case is not so clear cut in respect of hotel D.

	Hotels					
	A	*B*	*C*	*D*	*E*	*Total*
Number of rooms occupied (room nights available × occupancy rate)	52,560	22,776	23,827	27,302	13,286	139,751
Rate per room per night (annual revenue ÷ no of rooms occupied)	£130	£90	£95	£110	£65	£107.43

- Revenue generated by central marketing for hotel A = £130 × 4,900 = £637,000
- Revenue generated by central marketing for hotel D = £110 × 1,700 = £187,000

It may be possible to amend the bonus scheme to take into account this proposed new recharging policy, however. For example, the bonuses could be calculated on profits before recharges and associated revenue or the profit target after which bonuses are earned could be reduced.

(ii) Using the **basis of room nights sold** by central marketing, the costs of the CRS would be apportioned as follows.

	Hotels					
	A	*B*	*C*	*D*	*E*	*Total*
Room nights sold by central marketing (CM)	4,900	6,200	7,300	1,700	5,500	25,600
Room nights sold by CM as % of total sold by CM	19.1%	24.2%	28.5%	6.7%	21.5%	100%
Apportioned costs	£164,260	£208,120	£245,100	£57,620	£184,900	£860,000

There is some **justification** for allocating the costs of the CRS on the **basis of room nights sold** rather than using the basis suggested by the FD.

- A room nights sold by central marketing basis for the cost apportionment would provide a **link between the costs charged to the hotels and the benefit they receive** from the CRS (the additional revenues). For example, nearly 30% of the room nights sold by central marketing were in hotel C and so it would seem fair than hotel C should be charged with nearly 30% of the costs of the CRS.

- The **FD's proposal** to recharge costs based on total room revenue **may not be equitable.** If **hotel managers** carry out their own marketing and **make efforts themselves to increase room sales,** thereby increasing hotel revenue without the assistance of the CRS, it would be unfair (and arguably unwise) to penalise them for doing this by recharging CRS costs against revenues which were not generated by the CRS.
- Allocating costs on a **rooms sold basis does not penalise hotel managers for the favourable impact they may have on the room rates at which accommodation in their hotel can be sold**. Improvements in service, menus offered and so on are actions under the control of the hotel manager which will increase the total revenue of their hotel and thereby attract a higher recharge using the FD's proposed approach.

(iii) The **system** used to recharge the costs of the CRS should be **fair** and should provide the management team of the hotel group with appropriate **information on each hotel's profitability.**

The most appropriate method might be to **separate the costs to be recharged into those that are fixed and those that are variable** and use an appropriate apportionment basis for each component.

Fixed costs. Presumably in setting up the CRS system an estimate was made of the capacity that it would have to handle, that capacity being largely based on the total number of room nights that would have to be sold. The fixed costs of running the system would be closely aligned to that anticipated capacity. The fixed costs of the CRS should therefore **be apportioned in line with hotel capacity** (the number of room nights available). If the managers of the hotels were recharged at the start of each period with a share of the fixed costs of the system, they would have an incentive to use the service rather than incur additional costs by duplicating reservation systems.

Variable costs. The variable costs should be apportioned on the basis of the activities that generated those costs. Given that the variable costs are incurred in line with the number of enquiry staff that are required, it might seem reasonable to recharge costs based on the number of enquiries generated per hotel. Such an approach should improve the level of performance of the enquiry staff as hotel managers may well complain to group management if they feel that too low a proportion of enquiries are turned into firm bookings (so that hotels cannot offset the charge for the CRS against increased revenue). Hotel management could argue that such an approach is not linked to the results of central marketing, however, and so a more appropriate basis might be **room nights sold by central marketing.**

Such an approach would result in the following cost apportionment figures.

	Hotels					
	A	*B*	*C*	*D*	*E*	*Total*
Room nights available as %						
of total for group	33.4%	19.3%	17.9%	16.4%	13.0%	100%
Fixed costs apportioned	£227,120	£131,240	£121,720	£111,520	£88,400	£680,000
Room nights sold by CM as %	19.1%	24.2%	28.5%	6.7%	21.5%	100%
of total sold by CM	£34,380	£43,560	£51,300	£12,060	£38,700	£180,000
Variable costs apportioned						
Total apportionment	£261,500	£174,800	£173,020	£123,580	£127,100	£860,000

The results of this approach can then be compared with the results of the approach suggested by the FD and those of the approach suggested by the managers of hotels A and D.

	Hotels					
	A	*B*	*C*	*D*	*E*	*Total*
Grp man accountant's method	£261,500	£174,800	£173,020	£123,580	£127,100	£860,000
FD's method	£391,300	£117,820	£129,860	£172,000	£49,020	£860,000
Managers of hotels A and D's method	£164,260	£208,120	£245,100	£57,620	£184,900	£860,000

These figures highlight the significant differences in the costs apportioned to the hotels, and the different impacts on their reported profits, under the three methods. **Compared with the FD's scheme, hotels A and D are not charged nearly as much of the system cost using either of the other two methods, thereby reflecting more accurately the benefit they receive from the CRS.**

The costs apportioned under the **group management accountant's approach** are **significantly higher for hotels A and D** than those under the scheme proposed by the hotel managers, however. This seems **reasonable** given that they account for more than 50% of the capacity of the rooms to be sold by central marketing.

(iv) A number of **management issues** arise from the question of relating CRS costs to individual hotel operations.

- A **significant proportion of the costs (79%) are fixed** and management need to **ensure that the system is used to capacity**.
- The recharge must be seen to be **fair** because it will have some impact on the bonuses of hotel managers. A fair system will increase the likelihood that all managers will act in a manner which will improve the profits of their hotel as well as the profits of the group as a whole, and will avoid the de-motivating effects of an unfair system.
- The apportionment should **encourage feedback**, and given that the managers of hotels A and D have already taken issue with the FD's proposed recharge method, it is likely that the CRS manager will become more cost-conscious than might have been the case without the recharge.
- As hotel profitability is now determined by the efforts of both the hotel manager and central marketing, the **performance of the hotel manager must be assessed separately from that of the hotel.**
- A **cost-benefit analysis** of the central reservation system should be carried out regularly to ensure that the contribution earned on additional room sales more than covers the high fixed costs of the system.

2

> **Pass marks.** The scenario provides a lot of information in addition to the main problem of increasing waiting lists - under-funding, whistleblowing and a lack of control over staff are mentioned, albeit only briefly. Plan what you are going to write and then check that your plan has dealt with these issues. If it has you are likely to have generated an answer that would score well in the exam.

(a) The **overriding objective** of the control systems introduced should be that the public sector body provides a **cost-effective and value-for-money service** (given that it is funded by the tax payer) that **satisfies consumers.**

To ensure that consumers' expectations are met, a **'citizens' charter'** should be established which would set out clearly and simply the **objectives** of the professional service and would clarify the **standards of service** that should be provided for consumers. This 'charter' would provide **benchmarks** which the organisation should constantly be striving to attain.

A **formal internal complaints process** should be established for the use of the organisation's staff. It would need to be set up by an individual (or team) with substantial credibility: staff would need to be assured of **anonymity** if they were to use the system; they would also need to be convinced that they were being provided with a **genuine** complaints procedure which would result in appropriate action and which offered a **better solution than going to the press,** thereby avoiding further damage to the body's reputation. Giving the 'whistleblowers' the opportunity to air their grievances should mean that **more precise information could be gathered about their grievances,** a fuller investigation carried out and action required to improve the service implemented more quickly.

Given that **resources** within the public sector body are **scarce,** an **analysis of demand** for the service in each area should be carried out on a regular basis so that **resources can be targeted more appropriately and overall resource requirements determined.** Service provision and quality at the local level should therefore improve and waiting lists should fall.

The introduction of a **centralised booking system** would bring two immediate benefits. **Professional staff** would have to state when they were available to see clients so that appointments could be made, thereby providing a **check** on whether or not they were available during their contracted hours. This may result in a **reduction in waiting lists** if professional staff are currently failing to meet their obligations, may **improve public confidence** in the waiting list system and should improve service as members of the public could be directed to the centre in their immediate area with the earliest available appointment.

A range of **non-financial indicators** should be established for performance measurement purposes. **Targets for consumer throughput rates** would be extremely useful, for example, as they should help to reduce waiting lists. The number of **complaints** received could also be monitored to ensure that any improvements made to the service were maintained.

Financial targets should also be established, such as the unit cost of dealing with a consumer requiring a particular piece of advice. Any cost saving made could then be used to improve the quality of the service offered.

(b) Despite the introduction of these new central control systems, a number of **control problems** are likely to remain.

It is not clear the extent of the **computer systems** currently in place, but given the level of funding and the fact that the management systems do not seem to have been updated regularly, it can be assumed that these are low. As soon as funding becomes available, a wide area network of PCs should be installed to allow for better inter-office communication and to manage effectively the central booking system.

Waiting list statistics

The **centralised booking system** will do much to improve the reliability of the waiting list statistics. Given that central government policy decisions are that waiting lists must be reduced, however, there is a risk that staff will begin to behave **dysfunctionally**, cutting sessions short to increase throughput and reduce waiting lists but in so doing failing to provide the required level of service.

Waiting list statistics are a fairly **crude indicator** of service quality, however. They can of course be reduced by moving consumers more quickly through the system, thereby failing to provide them with the appropriate level of service. Such statistics also infer that the needs of consumers are identical, but differences may be caused by the age of the consumer, the area in which they live and so on.

Despite this, waiting list statistics are a **vital control measure** to determine whether professional staff are providing an appropriate level of service and whether the level of funding is sufficient to provide adequate levels of resources to enable the desired level of service to be offered. The waiting list statistics currently available may be **insufficient**, however. Waiting times could be long for many reasons, underfunding and improper practices by professional staff being the two most likely. Calculating **average session times** and making available data about the **number of new appointments requested** may provide a better basis for allocating resources. The use of **additional measures** of service quality and efficiency would ensure that too much reliance was not placed on waiting list statistics.

Quality standards

The fact that it has been assumed that professional qualification has provided sufficient proof of competence suggests that there are few, if any, quality control mechanisms in place. The following controls should therefore be implemented as a matter of urgency.

- **Recruitment.** In addition to proof of qualification, references should be taken. Depending on the nature of the service, the interview process could involve some simulation of typical client contact sessions to determine competence. A probationary service should be introduced and employees assessed at the end of it to determine whether they are suitable for the position.
- **Client reviews.** Clients should be asked to provide feedback on all aspects of the service, both administrative and professional.
- **Peer reviews.** Professional staff could be asked to listen in on colleagues' sessions and/or read case notes as a means of sharing knowledge and monitoring the abilities of professional staff.
- **Technical updates.** A central support function should be provided to ensure, by whatever means suitable for this service, that practices remain up-to-date.

Private work by professional staff

The **system currently in place is flawed** in that it opens up the public sector body to allegations of malpractice. The professional staff appear to be giving the message that if a member of the public wants their advice within a reasonable period of time, they must pay for it. There is a risk that the public sector body then effectively becomes a **marketing service for the professional staff's private practice** (the public sector service is publicised, members of the public get in contact but are then given the details of private practices rather than the free service).

In principle there is nothing wrong with professional staff using their skills outside the service, provided that they work their contracted hours for the public sector body and provide an adequate level of service. Indeed, one could argue that this **private work is to the public sector body's advantage as those who can afford to pay are removed from the waiting list**, giving those who cannot the benefit of a free public service.

If professional staff are to be allowed to perform work privately, controls need to be in place which **restrict the referrals** that they make from the public sector body to private practice and which ensure that they fulfil their contractual obligations to the public sector body.

3

Pass marks. In part (a) of the question you must take care to stick to the requirement of giving substantive tests on debtors. Your answer to (b) should demonstrate clearly how the auditors' approach would differ as compared with (a). In (b) both control and substantive tests would be relevant to include in an answer. They key issue is to design tests for the environment provided in the scenario, one where a high risk of default has been accepted on commercial grounds. It would have very difficult to answer parts (a) and (b) without making any reference to the matters discussed in (c), but you should nevertheless have tried to keep overlap to a minimum.

(a) The normal substantive tests to apply to a list of corporate debtors would be as follows.

(i) Obtain a copy of the **list of sales ledger balances** at the report date and **reconcile the list** to the **sales ledger control account** and the **debtors figure** in the financial statements.

(ii) **Select** a **sample** of debtors, stratifying balances selected with a bias towards larger debts, or using a statistical sampling technique such as Monetary Unit Sampling (MUS).

(iii) **Debtors' circularisation.** For that sample of debtors, **print out statements** of account at the report date. **Send** the **statements** to the **customers** with a covering letter, asking them to reply to the auditor. If they do not agree with the balance they should be asked to state what the **discrepancies** are. These discrepancies should be followed up.

(iv) Where debtors **agree** with the balance, the debt can be considered as existing. The circularisation will also provide evidence that the **sales ledger** has been **maintained correctly.** However work on after-date payments (see below) will be required to make sure the debt is realisable.

(v) **Follow up debtors** who **fail to reply to the circularisation** with further letters and phone calls. If there is still no response, review the cash received after the year-end, and the supporting documentation, as described below.

(vi) Where debtors **dispute** the **balance, investigate** the **underlying transactions.** An audit trail showing the customer order, and acknowledged dispatch note and a corresponding invoice should substantiate the existence of the transaction.

(vii) **Review** the **cash received** from debtors after the **report date** to see what proportion of the debts have been collected in the post balance sheet period.

(viii) **Analyse** the list of **debtors by age.** If old balances do exist, **review** the **correspondence** between the **credit control department** and the **customer** along with any provisions against them to ensure the overall debtor figure is not overstated.

(ix) **Review other balances** with **unusual features** such as credit balances, balances with employees, unusual settlement or discount terms. These might be circularised 100%.

(x) **Review** the **sales day book** and the **sales ledger** for the next accounting period for large, unexplained **credits** which may indicate that the debtors figure included false transactions.

(xi) **Review** the **sales figure** for **reasonableness** in light of the sales figure for previous periods.

If all of the above are reasonable then the auditor can have confidence that the debtors figure is not materially overstated.

(b) The problem with relying solely on substantive tests in this situation will be that a very large sample size would be required in order to substantiate an adequate proportion of the debts. Therefore the auditors should concentrate first on testing controls to ensure the required controls were operating.

The tests of control would depend on the specific controls that the organisation had in place. They would normally include the following.

(i) Use of **test data** to check that the system **rejected transactions** that took **customer accounts** over **credit limits,** or which were for customers who had definitely **defaulted** on payments.

(ii) Use of **test data** to check that the **system raised queries** on transactions that took total debts over a certain amount or a specified percentage of customers' credit limit.

(iii) **Regular review** and investigation of sales ledger accounts where the risk of default appeared high, using the criteria set out in (c) below. There should be **procedures** for **chasing slow payers,** including correspondence by the credit control department, and legal action.

Some substantive testing should still be carried out. Even if the auditors carry out extensive tests of control, and find there are no problems, there will still be an element of control risk. The **debtors' circularisation** would be based on the concept of **negative circularisation** rather than the positive approach mentioned above. Here statements would be sent to customers, who would be asked to reply to the auditor only if they **disagreed** with the balance shown. MUS or random selection may be used to select the sample, but stratification is unlikely to be used because the amounts owed will vary much less than for the corporate customers in (a).

As well as considering **provision** against **specific bad debts,** the auditors will need to consider whether a **general provision** will be required, because of the much greater degree of uncertainty surrounding these debtors as compared with the debtors discussed in (a). Factors to be considered when assessing the adequacy of a general provision will include the company's previous record with bad debts, and factors influencing future payments including general economic factors such as interest rates.

(c) J plc's customer database could be interrogated in a number of ways. These would include:

(i) **Searching** for **customers** who had **long outstanding payments,** had been paying **round sum amounts,** who had **paid** for **later invoices before earlier** invoices had been **settled,** or who were **continually paying late.** All of these would be considered as indicating a risk of future default.

(ii) **Searching** for **customers** with **addresses** or **telephone numbers** that were the **same** as those of customers who had previously **defaulted.** This might indicate successful attempts to get around the company's credit rating system.

(iii) **Producing** a **report** showing **customers** who **owed more** than a certain **amount,** say, £1,500 and who might therefore begin to have problems keeping up with repayments.

(iv) **Identifying** whether **previous defaulters** fell into **any sort of pattern,** for instance customers who had bought a specific type of product or a product from a particular supplier. If so, the payment profiles of other customers with the same pattern should be reviewed to see whether this problem persists.

(v) **Using** the information given in **customers' applications** for credit to identify types of debtor, for example by age, employment or credit rating.

Each of these would mean that the auditors' attention was focused on high-risk accounts. The results of the interrogations (iii) to (v) would indicate trends. Interrogations (i) and (ii) would gather together high risk customers into a single report for easy follow up and investigation.

4

> **Pass marks.** The concept and relevance of audit risk is a fundamental part of the way auditing is examined in this paper. Knowledge of the Turnbull report would help produce a good answer for part (b) although a strong answer could have been derived from considering the basic principles of business risk.

(a) The formula **AR = IR × CR × DR** is often used in internal audit to ensure that the audit process reaches an appropriate balance between obtaining sufficient audit evidence and minimisng costs.

The terms can be defined as follows.

(i) **Audit risk** (AR) is the overall risk that the final audit report contains errors or that the auditors fail to pick up errors in internal control systems.

(ii) **Inherent risk** (IR) is the risk associated with the type of enterprise or account balance being audited. For example stock which is prone to theft would have a high inherent risk.

(iii) **Control risk** (CR) is the risk that the entity's internal control mechanisms fail to prevent or detect errors. For example lack of central review of the activities of outlying branches would probably mean that control risk was high.

(iv) **Detection risk** (DR) is the risk that audit tests fail to detect errors.

In practice the formula is used in the following way.

(i) The organisation will, as a matter of policy, **set** a rate of **audit risk,** often around 5%. The lower the risk the more confident the organisation can be in the accuracy of the audit process and the final audit report. The higher the level of audit risk, the smaller sample sizes will be and so the cheaper the audit function will become. With this, however, comes the greater chance of the audit opinion being incorrect.

(ii) Before the audit begins the internal auditors will **assess** the **inherent risk** of the business entity by considering how **susceptible** items in the accounts are to **misstatement**. For example if the business entity carries stocks of high-technology items this would carry a high level of inherent risk due to the possibility of those stocks becoming **obsolete** and so being currently overvalued.

(iii) During the early stages of the audit an assessment should be made of how **strong** the business entity's internal **controls** are. Signs of possible weakness would include significant changes in the staff who operate the internal controls.

(iv) These assessments of inherent and control risk will be **expressed** as a **percentage** and then used in the formula $AR = IR \times CR \times DR$ to derive a figure for detection risk. (AR given as a matter of policy, IR and CR being calculated as above). This figure defining **detection risk** will be **used** in **calculating sample sizes** to be used in the tests to be performed during the audit itself. Where the auditors believe that IR and CR are low, DR can be reasonably high and so sample sizes will be smaller. Conversely if IR and CR are high, DR becomes low (the auditors do not want to accept the risk that their tests fail to detect errors which they now believe may well exist) and so sample sizes will increase.

(b) **Guidance on business risk assessment**

Business risk can be **defined** as the threat that an event or action will adversely affect an organisation's ability to **achieve** its **business objectives** and **execute** its **strategies effectively**. The issues of business risk assessment and response are dealt with in the Turnbull Report and the Combined Code on Corporate Governance. These now require companies to:

(i) **undertake a review** to **identify** and **evaluate** the **significant business risks** to which they are exposed;

(ii) **assess** the **effectiveness** of the **internal control mechanisms** in protecting the company against these risks. In doing this directors should **maintain** and **review controls** relating to all relevant control objectives, and not merely financial controls.

Effects on evaluation of internal control

Raising **business risk assessment** to an issue that must be reviewed at board level should mean that boards become much more thorough in **considering** all possible **losses** to which the organisation may be exposed, and how the risk of losses may be minimised. This assessment can be enhanced by the broader experience that non-executive directors can bring to this assessment.

The response to this assessment, coming from board level, should **improve** companies' **internal control systems** by ensuring that they do address the key risks in a cost-effective manner. In addition the requirements as to what constitutes **effective internal control** have been clarified. The Turnbull report states that a company's internal control system should:

(i) be **embedded** in its **operations** and not treated as a separate exercise;

(ii) be able to **respond** to **changing risks** within and outside the company;

(iii) enable each company to apply it in an **appropriate manner** related to its key risks.

Statement in accounts

The Turnbull code also requires directors to include a statement of **business risk assessment** and their response in the company's annual report. These reporting requirements, focusing primarily on the previous accounting period, allow the users of the financial statements to **form an opinion** on how well the company has been governed. The inclusion of a statement on internal controls should give the users of these financial statements confidence of good governance into the future.

Advantages of including the report are as follows:

(i) it will **increase** the **level** of **awareness** that shareholders and other stakeholders have about the key issues facing the business and how the risks are being managed. Hence it enables readers of accounts to make a better assessment of the board's **stewardship** of the business;

(ii) it will **increase** the **awareness** of **board members** to the issue of risk assessment and response;

(iii) it will **increase** the **pressure** on **executive management** to manage risks effectively through an effective internal control system;

(iv) that the **pressure** for **increasing shareholder wealth** will **not** be substantially **diminished** by the requirement to report on how decreases in shareholder wealth are being guarded against.

There have been arguments against the inclusion of such reports. These have included:

(i) **increasing directors' responsibility** for risk assessment may make them **more risk averse** and in the long-run **reduce returns** for shareholders;

(ii) publication of risk assessment information may be **commercially sensitive**;

(iii) to avoid releasing commercially sensitive information, **statements** by directors will be so **bland** as to be meaningless.

5

> **Pass marks.** This question on the popular topic of centralisation versus decentralisation has a very specific scenario. The key to getting more than half marks is therefore to resist the temptation to go for 'volume' and to write fewer points, ensuring that they are related to the scenario provided.
>
> The scenario describes an organisation in which a high degree of control is almost certainly going to be required. All three parts of the question have a 'discuss' requirement, however, which means that you need to give points both for and against each issue.

(a) Staff costs are likely to represent a **significant proportion of B plc's total costs** and hence a suitable system of control over branch staffing levels is of vital importance to B plc's profitability.

Branch staffing levels are currently controlled by a **system of central authorisation**. This has a number of **benefits**.

- **As a means of controlling costs.** There will be no duplication of functions or facilities. It could be wasteful for an individual in each branch to be in charge of staffing levels. Head office management can take a wider view of problems and consequences and a more strategic perspective can be put on the staffing level decisions taken, for example reducing the risk of branches being over-staffed, causing unnecessary expenditure.

- **As a means of controlling quality.** Staffing level decisions can be made that are in the interests of the organisation as a whole. For example, a decision might be taken to over-staff to ensure that queues can be kept short, even at the busiest times, in an effort to provide a high quality service. And crisis decisions, such as the need to recruit to replace staff who are absent due to sudden long-term illness, can be taken more quickly by head office, without the need for the branch to refer back and get authority. Again, this will ensure that customers are not inconvenienced.

  Centralised control will also bring with it standardised recruitment and training procedures. Customers should therefore receive a consistent level of service at all branches, an important consideration in a highly regulated industry such as banking/financial services.

- **As a means of controlling performance.** Decisions are made at one point and so control and co-ordination are easier. Head office management can keep a proper balance between different branches by deciding on the staff resources to allocate to each. And policies, procedures and documentation can be standardised across the whole organisation, thereby ensuring that all branches are operating to the same level of performance.

Systems of central authorisation of branch staffing levels can be **problematic**, however.

- **As a means of controlling costs.** There is a danger that any staffing budget given to branches will be fully utilised, regardless of branch staffing needs, in the fear that cost savings will result in budget cuts in the future.

- **As a means of controlling quality.** A system of central authorisation assumes that each of the branches is operating in a similar environment. This may not necessarily be true. The annual holidays of local factories are likely to have a significant effect on the volume of business in the branch, for example, increasing it before the holiday and reducing it during the holiday period. A centralised system may not be able to identify all such local variations whereas a system devolved to branch level would be likely to take them into consideration. Failure to react to these local variations will result in the quality of the service offered to customers suffering if there are too few staff and costs increasing if there are too many.

  Branch level authorisation also allows for greater response to changing events (such as unexpected staff absence), since there is no need to refer decisions upwards. This is valued by customers, who appreciate adequate staffing levels of appropriately skilled staff, and is particularly important in rapidly changing environments such as the one in which B plc finds itself.

- **As a means of controlling performance.** Branch level authorisation is likely to be more successful in the control of performance. The staff grades used by head office for planning purposes might not reflect the abilities of staff and there is little chance that a centralised system would be able to track abilities. Devolving responsibility for staffing levels to branches enables branch managers to utilise their knowledge of individuals and the shifts that suit them to choose staff who provide the best performance for particular shifts.

  In addition, branch managers' performance is likely to improve if they are given responsibility for staffing levels, given that the additional participation in running the branch can lead to increased motivation.

(b) There are likely to be a number of consequences of a change in the control systems away from systems of detailed head office control to devolved branch budgets.

- **Branch managers** may find that they adopt a more **entrepreneurial** approach to the performance of their duties and, if branches can be treated as profit centres, they can take responsibility for branch financial performance.
- The devolution of control would require a **change in the style of budgeting** used within the organisation. **Head office responsibilities and powers would need to be clarified. New products** are likely to come under the jurisdiction of head office given the regulations within the industry. But **will head office set budgets** and leave branches to achieve targets using whatever methods they deem appropriate? If **resources** are finite, how will they be **allocated** to branches?
- Depending on the amount of responsibility to be devolved, **additional branch managers** may need to be recruited. Certainly the **training** for existing managers would need to be revised to ensure that they were technically competent and entirely familiar with financial services industry regulations. This would be vital to ensure that customer care procedures were maintained at an appropriate level.
- **Reporting mechanisms** may need to be adapted to ensure that branch management reports are sufficiently frequent and detailed for branch management purposes. An **internal audit process** should be created to ensure the accuracy of these management reports and the integrity and competence of branch management generally.
- A **range of branch management performance measures** may need to be introduced to cover the managers' wider area of responsibility. These may need to focus on service quality, competitive performance, resource utilisation and so on.
- **Communication channels** would need to be established **between branches and the central product design and marketing functions.** Where these central functions are involved in promotions likely to increase the volume of business, branches would need to be notified in time for managers to make the necessary staff changes.
- The devolution of power to branch level would produce a significant change in the **culture** of the organisation and hence changes in personnel controls would be required. Regular **staff reviews** between branch managers and senior management would be needed (a number of area managers may need to be employed) and a **bonus system** rewarding branch managers for achieving budget targets could be introduced.

(c) **Arguments for central management controlling product profitability**

Branch costs (rent, rates, heat, light and so on) are likely to be relatively **fixed** and generated by the presence of the branch. Although B plc is experimenting with telephone banking, it will be some time before they can dispense with branches completely, and so these fixed costs must be covered and carried, almost as if they were **sunk costs**. Those members of the senior management team responsible for product design and marketing could therefore argue that it is far more important for central management to concentrate on product profitability, **leaving branch managers the task of keeping branch costs within budget limits**.

In addition, given the highly-regulated nature of the financial services industry, it is vital that new products are submitted to an in-depth appraisal and that existing products are reviewed on a regular basis, both to ensure that they are profitable and that they offer the customer value for money. Central management control of product profitability would allow for **the establishment of a specialised team**

charged with this appraisal and review process which would take into account competitors' products, market research, customer requirements and industry regulations.

Central management's prime concern - product or branch profitability?

Of central importance to this question is the issue of the **source of profit**. Do the products create profit for the organisation or is profitability generated by the branches? Given that products are publicised centrally but sold through the branches, the **overall profit of the organisation is dependent on effective branch management**. Profitability can only be improved if branch managers improve the sales mix of the products sold, while at the same time improving levels of customer satisfaction using a lower level of costs. Central management might therefore be advised to **concentrate on branch profitability rather than the profit generated by products.**

Moreover, the **calculation of product profitability may be problematic**. Many costs associated with designing and publicising products will tend to be fixed (such as the costs of running product development teams) and so, although some costs such as the costs of market research for a particular product can be allocated to individual products, most will be difficult to allocate.

It should be borne in mind, however, that **telephone banking** (and Internet banking if B plc were to move into this area) are effectively '**branchless**' and so this issue will need to be **reconsidered in the future**, when these new areas of operations are more established.

6

> **Pass marks.** You should have recognised the proposed system as a variant of backflush accounting, a topic covered in Paper 10.

A number of **changes** to the manufacturing accounting system have been proposed.

- **Receipts of materials are no longer recorded.**
- **Material purchases are only recognised when a successfully completed item is received into finished goods.**
- **Recognition of the material purchase results in payment to the supplier by electronic funds transfer.**

A number of **conditions** must exist for these proposals to be successful.

- **Materials delivered from suppliers must not sit in stock** but must be used almost immediately as the valuation of stocks of raw materials will not be possible under the proposed system.
- **Stocks of work in progress should be negligible** as valuation will not be possible under the proposed system.
- **Adequate production controls** must exist so that cost control during the production process is maintained.
- There must be **predictable levels of efficiency and fixed price and quality of materials** (or costs must be promptly revised) so that costs can be applied to products at the trigger point (receipt into finished goods of successfully completed item). Each unit of output will contain the standard inputs for each element and so suppliers will only be paid according to finished product specifications.

- Payment is only made for materials included in successfully completed items; any material incorporated in scrap or used in reworkings will not be paid for. The company's **manufacturing process must therefore be 100% effective and efficient** to ensure that all units achieve finished goods quality.
- Only one supplier can be used for each type and quality of raw material (because the production of finished goods will trigger a supplier payment) and so the organisation must be confident that the **suppliers used are reliable in terms of delivery and quality of material.**
- The **information system** required to supported the proposed changes to the manufacturing accounting system must be **reliable, cost effective and compatible with that of the organisation's suppliers**. The back-up and disaster recovery features need to be regularly tested to ensure data recovery is possible, given the paperless nature of the system.

Practical problems for the supplier

The supplier will face a number of practical problems if the proposed changes to the system are implemented.

- As mentioned above, the supplier will not be paid for raw material or work in progress losses, spillages, faulty workmanship and so on, but he has **no control over PQ's raw materials handling and production processing systems responsible for such events.**
- The supplier needs to ensure that **prices agreed with PQ are those used in the finished product specification.**
- Suppliers will receive a large number of smaller payments, the payment being identified as necessary when an item passes into finished goods stock rather than when there is a receipt of raw materials into stock. This may cause some **confusion when reconciling what has and has not been paid for.**
- Although in a JIT environment raw materials should not be ordered until they are required for manufacturing, **any changes to production scheduling that do occur will delay supplier payment**.
- There may also be practical problems associated with the **system interface** between the supplier and the supplier's bank and between the supplier and PQ. Suppliers may be reluctant to embark on costly system amendments if amendments were required for the current manufacturing accounting and standard costing system and are proving to be worthless.

Practical problems for the management accountant

The management accountant will also have to deal with a number of problems.

- **Identifying the value of stocks and work-in-progress** for working capital management and profit reporting purposes will be more difficult. Stocks should be minimal in a JIT environment but a suitable system may need to be established.
- Any **changes to manufacturing processes or product specifications** that affect the raw material content of a product need to be **reflected immediately in the finished product specification** used as the basis for paying suppliers (otherwise payments will be incorrect).
- In the event of a regular supplier failing to deliver or delivering faulty raw materials, an **alternative supplier** will need to be found (given that stocks of raw materials will be negligible in the organisation's JIT environment). The **finished**

product specification will need to be revised (with a new supplier coding) to ensure that the alternative supplier is paid rather than the regular supplier.

- Given that there should be insignificant cost variances, **daily reports detailing production and rework problems** might be more appropriate than monthly standard costing management reports. Indeed **standard costing may become entirely unsuitable.**
- **Existing software is likely to require modification or replacement.**

Practical problems for the internal auditor

The new system selected will need to have a proven record of **reliability** and to have been thoroughly **tested** during implementation given the potential inaccuracy and financial loss arising from the automated payment system.

Internal audit will have a number of concerns about the movement of stock.

(a) No checks may be made on the **receipt** of materials. There is therefore a risk that deliveries will be taken of **sub-standard goods** or of **goods** that have **not** been **ordered.**

(b) Internal audit will have problems tracking stock through the various stages of production. This has various implications.

  (i) There may be problems over the **custody** of stock; the lack of records may make stock more **prone** to **theft,** and decrease the likelihood that thefts will be noticed quickly. **Security controls** may need to be strengthened.

  (ii) The auditors may not be able to track how **stock** is **held** and **used.** The use of the Kanban system may minimise inefficiencies in stockholding; however auditors will have difficulty assessing the **efficiency** of **usage** of material.

  (iii) It may be difficult to ensure that stock received and used around the year-end is recorded in the right financial year (**cut-off** problems).

  (iv) Failure to record goods purchased until final stock is received may mean that the company is not keeping **proper accounting records,** as required by the Companies Act.

Purchasing procedures should be **reviewed.** The delay in recording means that significant reliance is being placed on suppliers of materials. There should therefore be strict controls over **choice of suppliers,** with regular **review** of **supplier reliability,** the **terms offered** and the **need for changes** if the design of products change. If suppliers other than normal suppliers have to be used, **authorisation** of payments to them should be required.

Internal audit should also look at **systems development** issues. It does appear that PQ's **project management** could be made **more efficient,** given that the recently introduced system is already under strain. Internal audit should consider whether a **post completion audit** should be carried out both for the recent changes and for this proposal.

Recommendation

Despite the problems detailed above, the **proposed changes** have a number of **attractions.** For example, **the number of transactions recorded will be significantly reduced** (the high level of transactions being a problem under the current system). And in the **longer term,** the **improved level of quality of production** implied in the proposals should produce **significant cost savings.**

The proposal should therefore be implemented, although perhaps not immediately. The new JIT system has been expensive and is not yet operating as efficiently as it could. Before spending any more money, it might be advisable to allow a period of, say, three months in which no further adaptive maintenance or development is carried out. This would allow the system time to settle down and solutions to some of the initial teething problems may become apparent. A better understanding of the system will be possible and a full review of its success can be carried out, after which the proposals could be implemented.

See overleaf for information on other BPP products and how to order

CIMA Order

To BPP Publishing Ltd, Aldine Place, London W12 8AA

Tel: 020 8740 2211. Fax: 020 8740 1184

Mr/Mrs/Ms (Full name) ____________________

Daytime delivery address ____________________

Postcode ____________________

Daytime Tel ____________________ Date of exam (month/year) ____________________

	7/99 Texts	1/2000 Kits	1/2000 Psscrds	1999 Tapes	1999 Videos	1999 CDs
STAGE 1						
1 Financial Accounting Fundamentals	£18.95 ☐	£9.95 ☐	£5.95 ☐	£12.95 ☐	£25.00 ☐	£34.95 ☐
2 Cost Accounting and Quantitative Methods	£18.95 ☐	£9.95 ☐	£5.95 ☐	£12.95 ☐	£25.00 ☐	£34.95 ☐
3 Economic Environment	£18.95 ☐	£9.95 ☐	£5.95 ☐	£12.95 ☐	£25.00 ☐	£34.95 ☐
4 Business Environment & Information Technology	£18.95 ☐	£9.95 ☐	£5.95 ☐	£12.95 ☐	£25.00 ☐	£34.95 ☐
STAGE 2						
5 Financial Accounting	£18.95 ☐	£9.95 ☐	£5.95 ☐	£12.95 ☐	£25.00 ☐	£34.95 ☐
6 Operational Cost Accounting	£18.95 ☐	£9.95 ☐	£5.95 ☐	£12.95 ☐	£25.00 ☐	£34.95 ☐
7 Management Science Applications	£18.95 ☐	£9.95 ☐	£5.95 ☐	£12.95 ☐	£25.00 ☐	£34.95 ☐
8 Business and Company Law	£18.95 ☐	£9.95 ☐	£5.95 ☐	£12.95 ☐	£25.00 ☐	£34.95 ☐
STAGE 3						
9 Financial Reporting	£19.95 ☐	£10.95 ☐	£5.95 ☐	£12.95 ☐	£25.00 ☐	£34.95 ☐
10 Management Accounting Applications	£19.95 ☐	£10.95 ☐	£5.95 ☐	£12.95 ☐	£25.00 ☐	
11 Organisational Management & Development	£19.95 ☐	£10.95 ☐	£5.95 ☐	£12.95 ☐	£25.00 ☐	
12 Business Taxation (FA 99)	£19.95 ☐	£10.95 ☐	£5.95 ☐	£12.95 ☐	£25.00 ☐	
STAGE 4						
13 Strategic Financial Management	£20.95 ☐	£10.95 ☐	£5.95 ☐	£12.95 ☐	£25.00 ☐	
14 Strategic Management Accountancy & Mktg	£20.95 ☐	£10.95 ☐	£5.95 ☐	£12.95 ☐	£25.00 ☐	
15 Information Management	£20.95 ☐	£10.95 ☐	£5.95 ☐	£12.95 ☐	£25.00 ☐	
16 Management Accounting Control Systems	£20.95 ☐	£10.95 ☐	£5.95 ☐	£12.95 ☐	£25.00 ☐	
					£	

POSTAGE & PACKING

Study Texts

	First	Each extra	
UK	£3.00	£2.00	£
Europe*	£5.00	£4.00	£
Rest of world	£20.00	£10.00	£

Kits/Passcards/Success Tapes

	First	Each extra	
UK	£2.00	£1.00	£
Europe*	£2.50	£1.00	£
Rest of world	£15.00	£8.00	£

Master CDs/Breakthrough Videos

	First	Each extra	
UK	£2.00	£2.00	£
Europe*	£2.00	£2.00	£
Rest of world	£20.00	£10.00	£

Grand Total (Cheques to *BPP Publishing*) I enclose a cheque for (incl. Postage) £

Or charge to Access/Visa/Switch

Card Number

Expiry date ____________ Start Date ____________

Issue Number (Switch Only) ____________

Signature ____________

We aim to deliver to all UK addresses inside 5 working days. Orders to all EU addresses should be delivered within 6 working days. All other orders to overseas addresses should be delivered within 8 working days.

* Europe includes the Republic of Ireland and the Channel Islands.

REVIEW FORM & FREE PRIZE DRAW

All original review forms from the entire BPP range, completed with genuine comments, will be entered into one of two draws on 31 July 1999 and 31 January 2000. The names on the first four forms picked out on each occasion will be sent a cheque for £50.

Name: ______________________ **Address:** ______________________

____

____

How have you used this Kit?
(Tick one box only)

☐ Home study (book only)

☐ On a course: college ____________

☐ With 'correspondence' package

☐ Other ____________

Why did you decide to purchase this Kit?
(Tick one box only)

☐ Have used complementary Study Text

☐ Have used BPP Kits in the past

☐ Recommendation by friend/colleague

☐ Recommendation by a lecturer at college

☐ Saw advertising

☐ Other ____________

During the past six months do you recall seeing/receiving any of the following?
(Tick as many boxes as are relevant)

☐ Our advertisement in *CIMA Student*

☐ Our advertisement in *Management Accounting*

☐ Our advertisement in *Pass*

☐ Our brochure with a letter through the post

Which (if any) aspects of our advertising do you find useful?
(Tick as many boxes as are relevant)

☐ Prices and publication dates of new editions

☐ Information on Kit content

☐ Facility to order books off-the-page

☐ None of the above

Have you used the companion Study Text for this subject? ☐ Yes ☐ No

Your ratings, comments and suggestions would be appreciated on the following areas

	Very useful	*Useful*	*Not useful*
Introductory section (Advice on revision, question practice and exam technique, question and answer checklist, etc)	☐	☐	☐
'Do you know?/Did you know? checklists	☐	☐	☐
Tutorial questions	☐	☐	☐
Examination-standard questions	☐	☐	☐
Pass marks	☐	☐	☐
Content of answers	☐	☐	☐
Mock exam	☐	☐	☐
Structure and presentation	☐	☐	☐

	Excellent	*Good*	*Adequate*	*Poor*
Overall opinion of this Kit	☐	☐	☐	☐

Do you intend to continue using BPP Study Texts/Kits? ☐ Yes ☐ No

Please note any further comments and suggestions/errors on the reverse of this page.

Please return to: Alison McHugh, BPP Publishing Ltd, FREEPOST, London, W12 8BR

REVIEW FORM & FREE PRIZE DRAW (continued)

Please note any further comments and suggestions/errors below

FREE PRIZE DRAW RULES

1 Closing date for 31 July 1999 draw is 30 June 1999. Closing date for 31 January 2000 draw is 31 December 1999.

2 Restricted to entries with UK and Eire addresses only. BPP employees, their families and business associates are excluded.

3 No purchase necessary. Entry forms are available upon request from BPP Publishing. No more than one entry per title, per person. Draw restricted to persons aged 16 and over.

4 Winners will be notified by post and receive their cheques not later than 6 weeks after the relevant draw date. Lists of winners will be published in BPP's *focus* newsletter following the relevant draw.

5 The decision of the promoter in all matters is final and binding. No correspondence will be entered into.